Ableton Live™ 7 Power!: The Comprehensive Guide

Jon Margulies

Course Technology PTR
A part of Cengage Learning

COURSE TECHNOLOGY
CENGAGE Learning™

Australia • Brazil • Japan • Korea • Mexico • Singapore • Spain • United Kingdom • United States

COURSE TECHNOLOGY
CENGAGE Learning

Ableton Live™ 7 Power!:
The Comprehensive Guide
Jon Margulies

Publisher and General Manager, Course Technology PTR: Stacy L. Hiquet

Associate Director of Marketing: Sarah Panella

Manager of Editorial Services: Heather Talbot

Marketing Manager: Mark Hughes

Executive Editor: Mark Garvey

Project and Copy Editor: Marta Justak

Technical Reviewer: Brian Jackson

PTR Editorial Services Coordinator: Erin Johnson

Interior Layout Tech: ICC Macmillan Inc.

Cover Designer: Mike Tanamachi

Indexer: Sharon Shock

Proofreader: Gene Redding

For product information and technology assistance, contact us at
Cengage Learning Customer & Sales Support, 1-800-354-9706

For permission to use material from this text or product, submit all requests online at **cengage.com/permissions**
Further permissions questions can be emailed to
permissionrequest@cengage.com

Ableton, Ableton Live, Operator and Sampler are trademarks of Ableton AG. Mac, the Mac logo, Mac OS, Macintosh, and QuickTime are trademarks of Apple Computer, Inc., registered in the U.S. and other countries. The Audio Units logo is a trademark of Apple Computer, Inc. Windows, Windows 2000, Windows XP, and DirectX are registered trademarks of Microsoft Corporation in the United States and other countries. Intel is a registered trademark of Intel Corporation or its subsidiaries in the United States and other countries. SONiVOX is the brandname trademark of Sonic Network, Inc. VST is a trademark of Steinberg Media Technologies GmbH. ASIO is a trademark and software of Steinberg Media Technologies GmbH. ReWire and REX2 are trademarks of Propellerhead Software. Mackie Control is a trademark of LOUD Technologies, Inc. All other product and company names are trademarks or registered trademarks of their respective holders.

Library of Congress Control Number: 2008921612

ISBN-13: 978-1-59863-522-5

ISBN-10: 1-59863-522-0

Course Technology
25 Thomson Place
Boston, MA 02210
USA

Cengage Learning is a leading provider of customized learning solutions with office locations around the globe, including Singapore, the United Kingdom, Australia, Mexico, Brazil, and Japan. Locate your local office at:
international.cengage.com/region

Cengage Learning products are represented in Canada by Nelson Education, Ltd.

For your lifelong learning solutions, visit **courseptr.com**

Visit our corporate website at **cengage.com**

Printed in the United States of America
1 2 3 4 5 6 7 11 10 09 08

This book is dedicated to the music makers and the dreamers of dreams. You know who you are.

Acknowledgments

I would first like to acknowledge the authors who worked on the earlier editions of this book: Dave Hill, Jr., Chad Carrier, and John Von Seggern. I'm honored to be keeping such good company, and hope to be living up to the high standards that all of you set.

I would like to thank Paul Halley and Fred Renz for giving me a world-class musical education very early in life—before my voice changed and I started playing guitar. In recent years, I have learned more from friends and colleagues than I could possibly account for, but I send big thanks to Pete Drungle, Christian Rutlege, and everyone from Hippocampus for expanding my world and presenting me with highly significant learning experiences. Thanks also to my partners at Tribeca Recording, Brian Bender and David Gervai.

I offer my sincere gratitude to everyone I have worked with on making this book a reality: Marta Justak for editing me and making sure I make sense, Brian Jackson for his outstanding technical editing, and Mark Garvey for giving me the chance to do this book and overseeing the project.

Finally, my deepest thanks and love to Susanna. Without you, I would not be where I am or who I am today.

About the Author

Jon Margulies is a New York-based producer, guitarist, composer, and DJ. He has been performing professionally since he was 11 years old, and has worked with some of the best musicians around in a dizzying array of styles. After many years of performance and study as a jazz guitarist, he purchased his first sampler in 1998 and has been passionate about discovering and using music technology ever since. You can always catch up with Jon's latest gigs and projects at heatercore.net.

Contents

Chapter 3
Live Interface Basics   45

Chapter 4
Making Music in Live
83

Chapter 5
The Audio Clip   139

Chapter 6
The MIDI Clip   175

Chapter 7
Using Effects and Instruments   193

Chapter 8
Live's Instruments   223

Chapter 9
Live's Audio Effects   **277**

Chapter 10
Live's MIDI Effects   329

Chapter 11
ReWire   343

Chapter 12
Playing Live...Live   353

Chapter 13
Live 7 Power   377

Introduction

Ableton Live 7 Power!: *The Comprehensive Guide* is the all-inclusive guide to making music with Ableton's revolutionary live performance and studio software, Live 7. Written for all Live users, from digital audio beginners to seasoned pros, this book explores each fundamental feature in Live. The book provides power-user tips and insider tricks for integrating Live into your home or professional studio in order to provide a more comprehensive overview of this powerful software. But Live's in-studio capabilities are just the beginning. Every last feature, button, fader, instrument, and effect in Live 7 was also designed with the live performer in mind. *Ableton Live 7 Power!*: *The Comprehensive Guide* is a book written for musicians by a musician who uses and discusses the software on a daily basis. Whether you use Live for producing, composing, DJing, or film and television, *Ableton Live 7 Power!* will help you put the fun back into making music with computers, while taking your music to the next level.

What You'll Find in This Book

You'll get in-depth coverage on the following topics:

- Installing, running, and updating Live 7 on your computer
- Creating and arranging music with Live
- Editing and recording audio and MIDI clips
- Utilizing Live instruments, including Sampler, Operator, Impulse, and Simpler, in your projects
- Performing with Live in front of an audience
- Much more!

1 Live 7

Every so often, a new piece of technology or software application makes an indelible mark on the way things are done. Ableton's Live has instigated a revolution in the audio software world by transforming computers into playable musical instruments, real-time remix stations, and the world's most dexterous audio environment. Live is the culmination of years of studio software development and the infusion of DJ and electronic music-making instincts. Live is also a labor of love born out of the desire of a few software-savvy musicians to take their elaborate computer-based recording studio on the road.

With its flexible recording and MIDI functionality, Live is a full-blown music production environment suitable for any artistic style. You'll find all the features you'd expect from other digital audio workstations, such as multitrack audio and MIDI recording, nonlinear editing, quantization, pitch shifting, freezing, delay compensation, and more. Live's advantage is that all these common features are implemented within its unique sequencing interface.

Live is also a digital DJ performance tool and has begun to replace MP3-based DJ units, CD spinners, and turntables. It is also becoming increasingly common to see laptop performing artists utilizing computers as their primary sound source or record collection. This makes perfect sense when you stop to think that—for the last couple of years—synthesizers, samplers, and their sounds have been purchased en masse via Web download or e-mail, instead of as a separate hardware component or sound module. In the next couple of years, more and more musicians, bands, and solo artists will be using Live's technology to realize their artistic vision from the comfort of their own laptop.

What Is Live?

In January 2000, Berlin-based Ableton knocked the audio software world on its ear by releasing Live 1.0. Since its inception, Live has evolved into a real-time music production system allowing users to integrate samples, MIDI, effects, and live audio data quickly and musically enough for a live performance.

Similar to modern software MIDI sequencers or production suites, Live (Figure 1.1) allows you to create and modify musical elements, such as guitar riffs, bass lines, and piano parts, which can be arranged and played from a large, customizable grid. The grid can be thought of as both a

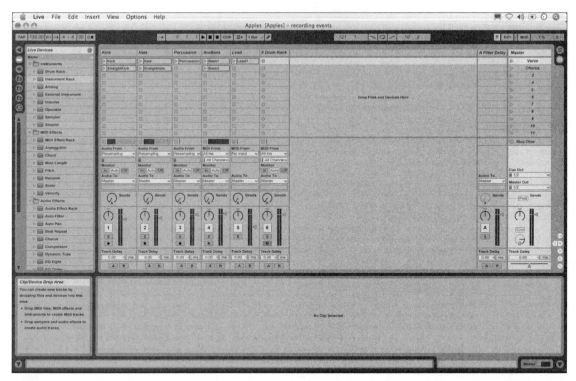

Figure 1.1 Here is a quick peek at the Session View grid in Live 7. The rows make up musical sections called scenes, and the columns function as virtual mixer channels.

music organizer and sonic palette. Once elements have been placed into a cell on the grid, you may designate MIDI or computer keyboard triggering options for these pieces, alter their playback parameters, add effects, and more. After enough cells for the song are filled, it is time for "the take" or live performance.

This grid/sonic palette makes up the improvisational sequencer component of Live and can be used to trigger groups of musical elements, like sections of a song. For instance, during a live performance, you might want to progress from the verse to the chorus and back to the verse—something you'd never done in practice. You can do so by triggering a specified row (scene) in Live's grid matrix that, in turn, directs Live to play the second group of elements (the chorus) and ceases play of verse parts. To go back, you would merely click on the preceding row. The song arrangement is under full real-time control. This makes it easy to jump around through various subsections of the song, break down important song sections, and come up with new possibilities. In addition, any individual piece contained within a slot can be played independently, in similar fashion to an "old school" phrase sampler (like Roland's Dr. Sample). It is quite possible to make new parts and original ideas by playing these parts as one-shot samples or to overdub a previously made arrangement. Keep in mind that these pieces can be tweaked to oblivion, much like the sounds in a hardware sampler or synthesizer, only more flexibly with Live.

The true power housed within Live is the software's ability to play, or play with, sound. Live can be played in a "jam" situation or simply used as a creative tool for building a song in layers. Live specializes in stretching audio alongside MIDI to any desired tempo or pitch. What's more, Live can bend audio within itself so that a sound may start at one tempo or pitch and end up in an entirely different place (all within the same performance). The editing possibilities are nearly infinite. Ableton has made recording and editing the performance a main function of Live, so that a single software application turns your laptop (or desktop) PC or Mac into a live performance system, a multitrack audio and MIDI recording studio, a powerful loop and song editor, and a full-blown remix factory. Live enables you to map the cells of your grid-palette (full of musical parts) to a MIDI controller or computer keyboard. In essence, you can record a live improvisation or band performance for later editing, further arranging, overdubs, and added automation. If the final mix isn't to your liking, you can always take another pass. To get an idea of what we're talking about, look at Figure 1.2, which features a screenshot of Live's Arrangement View.

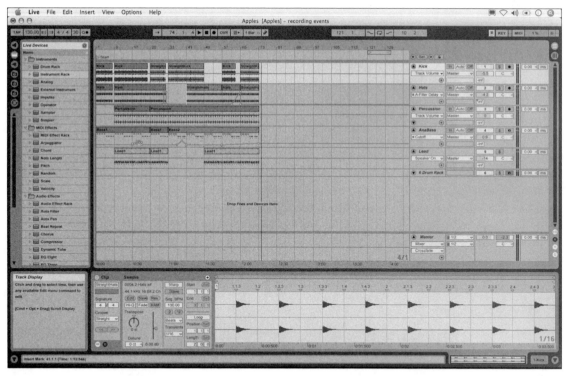

Figure 1.2 If you are familiar with desktop audio, Live's Arrangement View may remind you of many different programs. However, Live's feature set is sure to raise a few standards for many years to come.

Musically speaking, Live is a one-two punch whose focus is spread equally between live performance and recording/editing, all in one application. As you learn how to play (jam) in Live, you will also be gradually setting up your song's arrangement and learning new tactics to apply to your live performance. In other words, Live is quite unlike any other software application currently on the market, and it fills a certain void that has been overlooked by the majority of developers—the needs of the performing and recording musician.

Why Was Live Developed?

One of the greatest advantages for musicians employing Live is that it is a program written for musicians by musicians—they actually use the very software they create. Initially, Robert Henke and Gerhard Behles (paired in the Berlin-based electronica group Monolake) were looking for a better way to create their own music through the use of a computer. Both were experienced sound designers and had spent time working for Native Instruments, one of the industry's chief authorities on virtual or "soft" synthesizers and sound design software. At the time, the industry lacked a user-friendly software application conducive to creating music as a musician would: both intuitively and spontaneously. There were plenty of "loop-friendly" applications and more than a couple live jamming programs, but most audio software was built for studio use and lacked the interface necessary to create music the way a musician does: *live.*

Since the drawing board days of development, Behles, Henke, and the Ableton team have honed Live's interface and functionality with the performing artist in mind. While complex, build-your-own software suites such as Native Instruments' Reaktor and Cycling '74's Max/MSP are powerful sound generators, they often prove too complex for the performing musician who may be contending with any number of distractions—including lighting, sound system woes, fog, and so on. Live, on the other hand, was developed (and has been continually improved) to be the best possible live recording and performance system available on a computer. It contains professional-grade audio tools and software compliance, such as VST and Audio Units effect plug-ins and instruments, plus ReWire software-studio synchronization. These tools will be discussed in greater detail as we progress. For now, recognize Ableton's commitment to the performing artist and to the end user. Don't just take my word for it; jump on out to Ableton's closely monitored user forum at www.ableton.com, where you can anonymously enter your own wish list of ideas for future development of Live. Don't be too surprised if Ableton CEO Gerhard Behles, conceptualist Robert Henke, or any of the other Ableton developers chime in to discuss how your idea might better the world of Live.

The World of Live

Over the past several years, the idea of music creation and live performance on a PC or Mac has become increasingly attractive. With the increase in processing power and audio storage capacities, even relatively inexpensive computers have become powerful audio editing and recording studios. Producers using audio software have enjoyed exponential improvements in performance and the number and types of tasks that computers can perform. Also, the customization and potential for add-on software and hardware as new technology emerges have made jumping into the fray less intimidating. For less than $2,000 (U.S.), you can acquire a decent laptop, a soundcard, and Live, the most powerful and flexible music creation and performance software on the planet. For just a bit more, it is quite possible that your bedroom studio could compete with the pros, not to mention the fact that an investment in an Ableton Live performance rig is cheaper and easier to maintain than a stack of hardware samplers, rack-mounted sound modules, outboard mixers, and, well, you get the point.

How Does It Work?

Live allows you to sort your music into easy-to-define sections, called *scenes,* while maintaining all the flexible effects and routing options made possible only via PC- or Mac-based software. These scenes, which are spread horizontally across the screen, look like the rows of a spreadsheet or graph. The columns that are formed correspond with mixer channels. Within each column, only one sound—be it a MIDI sequence or an audio sample—can play at a time. So to play through your song, you can literally run down the rows, letting each row represent a musical section. Live also enables you to trigger sequences, loops, and samples; tweak effects; and change mix settings from a MIDI controller, MIDI keyboard, or computer keyboard. You can preview any audio loop in real time at any tempo from within your project. You can even record new pieces into your song without ever stopping playback. Enhancements in Live empower users to handle different kinds of musical parts according to their content. For example, a drumbeat can be handled differently than a synthesizer or vocal take. A drum loop typically contains several short sounds, such as hi-hat, snare, and kick drum hits, while a synthesizer or vocal part will most often sustain or consist of longer sounds. Since Live analyzes the audio's contents, it is necessary for Live to "look" at each loop in a different way to achieve the best results.

You may also turn off Live's time-correcting Warp feature to make your loops behave more like standard multitrack recording software. Live also encourages plenty of manipulation in terms of feel, tempo, and pitch, but how Live really works is up to you. Never before has software been so dependent upon its owner's proficiency, and never before has software been so intuitive and musical after a few basic principles are understood. Live works with your audio loops, MIDI sequences, hardware synthesizers, recorded material, and other software applications to make music. You can create new music from scratch or build a "remix" from previously recorded material. When it comes to making music in Live, the creative possibilities are limitless.

What Sets Live Apart?

If you are an audio software enthusiast, you've certainly heard of powerful digital multitrack studio applications such as Digidesign's Pro Tools, Apple's Logic, MOTU's Digital Performer, Cakewalk's Sonar, and Steinberg's Cubase (and Nuendo). These programs, and their hardware counterparts, are often referred to as *digital audio workstations,* or *DAWs.* Their main task is to ensure that music is recorded and played back properly in a studio situation. Other, more loop-oriented, products such as Propellerhead's Reason, Arturia's Storm, Sonic Foundry's Acid Pro, Cakewalk's Project5, or Sonic Syndicate's Orion Pro are also touted in the media for their originality and have become popular along with the self-contained studio paradigm. Each of these programs allows for use of the computer as a stand-alone music composition center and loop factory. Like the aforementioned products, Live can operate by itself, record multiple audio and

MIDI sources, integrate loops, and handle other basic studio functions. But Live also introduces the idea of performing with software and editing your improvisation afterwards, and automation has never had a better platform.

To fully understand why Live is such an innovative program, it helps to take a look at Live 7's feature set.

- First, Live works on both Mac (OS X 10.3.9 or later) and PC (Windows XP or Vista) platforms and takes advantage of all current industry standards, such as ASIO drivers, VST and Audio Units effect plug-ins and instruments, and ReWire synchronization technology.

- Ableton was one of the original innovators in the area of real-time time stretching and pitch shifting, and Live remains at the forefront of this area, with a powerful feature set enabling you to easily stretch your clips in time and sync them together.

- In addition to generating MIDI Time Code and MIDI Beat Clock, Live can also be synced to another program's MIDI clock.

- As mentioned previously, MIDI note information can be used to trigger sounds or MIDI controller info for knobs and sliders. Even your laptop computer keyboard can trigger parts. Better still, all MIDI controller and keyboard triggering information can be assigned while Live is in playback mode, so the music doesn't have to stop.

- In terms of routing, Live is constrained only by the limitations of your soundcard and MIDI interfaces. And ReWire-compatible software applications (such as Reason, Max/MSP, FL Studio, and ReBirth) can be directed through Live's mixer in a variety of ways. Live's output may also be ReWired to another program's inputs. You can record audio from an outside source straight into Live or render (record) Live's own output to a fresh track (for later use) while you play.

- Another distinguishing feature of Live is the customizable DJ-style crossfader built right into the performance mixer. Just like the DJ mixer pictured in Figure 1.3, you can assign mixer channels to A, B, or both channels and mix between the two. This subtle tool can be configured for anything from gradual song transitions to DJ-style fader-flipping tricks.

- And while all of these elements make Live sound attractive, Ableton's not-so-secret weapon, the Warp Engine, is the feature that has caused many a jaw to drop. Aside from being able to quickly quantize an audio loop's start and end points at the current project tempo, Live uses what's called *elastic audio* to time-stretch or compress your audio files so they can be played back at any tempo.

- Confused? Here is an example: Live can speed up a 25-second sample so that it will play in 5 seconds or vice versa (slowing down the 5-second sample to take up more time). Taking it a step further, you could resize select portions of the sound, causing the first half of the sample to play faster than the last, for instance. Amazingly enough, Live can do this with just

Figure 1.3 Live can be set up to function as a DJ system that will blow the doors off what a standard mixer can do, as you'll see in Chapter 13.

a couple of mouse clicks, while you monitor the results. More common examples include matching up bass and drum loops, correcting sloppy takes, fixing near-perfect ones, humanizing a drum machine part, and the list goes on. For more on the power of elastic audio, see the section on Clip View in Chapter 4, "Making Music in Live." You can also truncate the loop's end points, move the loop reference (starting point) anywhere you like, and fine-tune the pitch in either half-step or cent increments.

- To give us even more flexibility and elasticity, the Slice to New MIDI Track command can cut a loop into multiple samples and generate a MIDI file to play them back in order, much in the way Propellerhead's ReCycle would. And speaking of ReCycle, Live natively supports REX files as well!

- The elastic audio concept has been expanded in Live to the "elastic song." Global groove allows us to apply subtle shuffle feels to all MIDI and audio parts in a project—all in real time. Have you ever wondered what Kraftwerk's "Trans Europe Express" would sound like swinging? You can now find out within seconds. This will be extremely helpful for DJs who want to mix from a track with a straight feel to one with a triplet swing feel. The straight song can be gradually swung until it matches the second track without ever stopping the beat!

- Thanks to the crafty implementation of Racks, Live lets you build customized groupings of effects and virtual instruments to your heart's content. With powerful routing options and programmable key zones, you can create layers, splits, and complex effects like never before. Drum Racks take this concept to a whole new level, allowing you to build drum machines with combinations of synthesized and sampled sounds along with built-in effect returns and choke groups, while workflow enhancements make putting everything together a breeze.

Because Live has been engineered for live performance, Ableton has also created a powerful studio ally, almost by accident. After all, if Live makes it so easy to handle music in front of a stadium audience, it will be able to keep pace easily with the creative flow in a studio session. While most applications are focused on a specific task, such as sound design or the recording process, Ableton has zeroed in on the concept of making music, from the first iota of inspiration to the perfected performance, while still catering to the studio all the way.

Possible Applications

As a Live user, you will be joining an incredibly diverse crowd of composers, DJs, instrumentalists, and producers. Each uses the program in a slightly (or dramatically) different way. Part of the fun of Live is discovering how it can work for your musical process, as either a production tool, an instrument to perform with, or both.

Super New York session drummer Shawn Pelton (The Saturday Night Live Band, House of Diablo), whose setup is pictured in Figure 1.4, has taken to using Live onstage for creating music in ways he had only dreamed of previously. DJ superstar Sasha is a Live user as well, for production and performance—he's even gone so far as to make a custom MIDI controller for Live!

Figure 1.4 Shawn Pelton incorporates a laptop running Ableton Live by triggering additional loops with foot pedals and a controller. This is but one imaginative way to use Live.

Here are some other possible Live scenarios:

- **Stage:** Live thrives as a live looping device for recording loops on the fly. It's also the perfect tool for filling out your band's sound with prerecorded loops or backing tracks.

- **Studio:** I have already mentioned why Ableton Live is a perfect addition to any studio. It can function as a high-powered drum machine, a flexible loop remixer, or a versatile musical sketchpad. While some may use Live as their only studio application, bigger Pro Tools studios may simply enjoy Live for its ability to take bits of a project and let artists, producers, and engineers hear some different arrangements quickly and easily.

- **Bedroom:** With a nice audio interface and a decent computer running Live, platinum hits can be fashioned while you're still in your shorts. If professional studios can benefit from the power of Live, a solo musician can reap the rewards 10 times over. Recording a simple guitar and vocal demo or producing a full-blown masterpiece is all within the scope of Live's capabilities.

- **Club:** The laptop DJ trend has been building steam for several years now. The benefits include less wear and tear on your vinyl, lightweight transport, and the many possible software tricks for enhancing the sound. To be fair, there are a few compromises to recognize, such as the time it takes to digitize vinyl and the look and feel of the performance. While paradigm shifts are always tricky, one thing is for sure: Vinyl weighs a ton (and that's one paradigm that doesn't seem to be shifting!).

Goals of This Book

Like Live, *Ableton Live 7 Power!* has been written by musicians, but don't let that scare you. We've spent plenty of time performing with Live and have been recording and remixing in Live for years. Live is built to be musical, and this book will aspire to be the same. It is my hope that you have many long hours of enjoyment using Live while creating some interesting new music. Although this book is designed to be a "power user" book, don't be deterred if you are new to Live, new to music, or new to computer-based production. This book will serve as a basic guide to interfacing with Live and an advanced tips and tricks collection for taking advantage of Ableton's industry-rocking technology.

Some sections in this book are not specific to Live but are included as a reference for novice and intermediate digital audio studio owners. General audio computing tips, such as configuring your PC for audio, will help you make the most of any audio application you currently use and will only bolster your basic working knowledge of computer-based (digital) audio as musicians should understand it.

If you are already familiar with Live, this book should feel like a souped-up reference manual with some powerful tips and musical ideas for you to incorporate into your Live vocabulary. This book should help you optimize Live's settings for speed and sound, which should translate into maximum musical output. *Ableton Live 7 Power!* covers some sticky but rewarding topics, such as Live's MIDI implementation, editing Live's mix automation, and using virtual EQs and compressors for professional audio results.

The Online Files

To get you going as quickly as possible, you can find online files included with this book containing custom-built Live Sets to illustrate the topics as you read about them. After all, what fun is it to read about music? It's much more fun to *hear* music.

To use these as you follow along in the book, you'll need to copy the Sets and Presets from the Web site at http://www.courseptr.com/downloads onto your computer. I recommend simply creating a folder on your desktop labeled "Live 7 Power" and copying the entire contents into it. Then you can load the files you need from there, the exact files you'll need, and where they are located as indicated in the chapters that follow.

2 Getting Live Up and Running

If you are accustomed to buying studio hardware gear, you may be like me—get the sucker home, tear open the box, and start making noise. Manuals are for other people, after all, and, well, who's got the time? When it comes to software, however, there is one fundamental difference: It is almost always up to you, the end user, to set up and configure the hardware properly, install the software the way it was designed, and set up the preferences so that the new application won't interfere with any legacy applications, cause strange hardware issues, or impair general functionality. In short, you become the final manufacturer. It is this sort of engineering control that is both the advantage and the disadvantage of personally transfiguring your computer into a recording studio, a performance sampler, or a Live sequencing instrument.

Before you dive in and start producing hits, it is important to take a moment to verify that your computer system is up to speed and that you've installed Live properly to ensure maximum performance potential. This chapter will provide more than a few recommendations to help you through the installation process, along with rarely mentioned tips for fine-tuning your Ableton Live studio. I'll cover both Mac and PC setup and talk about several methods for optimizing your system. Also, remember that Ableton's technical support is an excellent way to get to the bottom of anything not covered in this book, as is Ableton's online user forum (found at www.ableton.com/forum), which is usually rich with tips, tricks, and advice.

System Requirements

Listed below are Ableton's posted system requirements, dependent upon system make, and followed by my recommendations. As mentioned above, every computer is customizable, and this can lead to unforeseen problems. If Live is acting strangely—for example, if the audio is stuttering or if each edit is taking a very long time—try running Live completely by itself, with no other programs running on your system at the same time. Make sure that you are not running any other applications in the background, such as MP3 players, office suites, or third-party plug-in effects (which we will cover in Chapter 7, "Using Effects and Instruments"), as this can cause CPU performance problems.

Keep in mind that the vast difference between system requirements versus recommendations could mean the enviable difference between functioning and flourishing with your Ableton product.

Ableton Live's System Requirements for Macintosh

- Any G4 or faster

- 512MB RAM

- Mac OS X 10.3.9 or later

Ableton Live Power!'s Mac Recommendations

- Intel Mac processor

- 1GB or more RAM

- Mac OS X 10.4.8 or later

- Soundcard with MIDI interface

Ableton Live's System Requirements for PC

- 1.5GHz CPU or faster

- 512MB RAM

- Windows XP or Vista

- Windows-compatible soundcard (preferably with ASIO driver)

- QuickTime 6.5 or later

Ableton Live 7 Power!'s PC Recommendations

- As fast a CPU as you can afford

- 1GB or more RAM

- Windows XP

- ASIO-compliant soundcard with MIDI interface

Installing, Running, and Updating Live 7

If you are brand new to Live and haven't yet picked up a copy or have never installed audio software before, then this section is for you. Sometimes, a little background information helps make for a more rewarding software experience. Here are a few general tips about getting your hands on Live 7.

- Live can be purchased as a download or in a boxed retail version. The download version is sold only through the Ableton Web shop (www.ableton.com/shop).

- The boxed version of Live 7 includes the Essential Instruments Collection 2 (EIC2), a high-quality 13GB library of sounds for the Simpler (Live's built-in sampler instrument) or Sampler (a more sophisticated sampler, available as an add-on) containing piano, woodwinds, strings, drums, and more. If you decide you don't need this (or the printed manual), you can save some money by purchasing the download version instead.

- Live 7 can also be purchased as part of the Ableton Suite, which gets you all five add-on instruments (Operator, Electric, Tension, Analog, and Sampler) and the Drum Machines sample library. The boxed version of the suite also includes Session Drums, a beautiful collection of multisampled acoustic drums, and the EIC2.

- Sometimes people are surprised that Live doesn't ship with any loops. Because there are so many styles of music and so many types of loops available, Ableton has decided not to go this route, instead focusing on giving you tools for composing (like the EIC2), rather than pointing new users into any particular style by providing loops. Even if you don't get the EIC2, Live still comes with some basic drum sounds and waveforms to get you started. If you want prerecorded loops, there are countless libraries available for purchase.

Live Installation Tips (Mac OS X 10.3.9 and Up)

Installing Live 7 on Mac OS X is a breeze. Insert the Live installation disc, open the disc dialog, and drag the Live 7.x folder to the Applications folder on your hard disk. All pertinent files, including Live 7's manual, will be contained here. For quicker access to Live, you may want to install a shortcut onto the OS X dock (if you are using it). To do this, simply open your applications folder or the location on your drive where you decided to install Live and drag the program icon to the dock. An instant shortcut is made. To remove the item from the dock, drag it to the trash or to the desktop and watch it go "poof" and disappear.

Live Installation Tips (Windows XP and Vista)

Installing Live onto a Windows machine is much like installing any other Windows-based application. After you click on Setup and follow the instructions, Live's installer will ask you where you would like to place the Ableton folder and its files. I recommend using the installer's default setting, which will place Live in an Ableton folder in your computer's Program Files folder. You will want to pay special attention to where your VST plug-in folder exists. It is common practice to keep all VST plug-ins stored in one common location so that every VST-compatible application will be able to use them. For instance, if you have Steinberg's Cubase SX installed on your computer, you can instruct Live to look for plug-ins in the Steinberg shared VST folder, which is commonly located at Program Files → Steinberg → Vstplugins. Then you can set Live to use the same plug-in folder. After the installation, you will want to customize your preferences (see the "Setting Preferences in Live" section later in this chapter).

Mac Users Take Note The centralizing of plug-in folders is useful in both Windows and OS X, although OS X audio applications typically take care of this for you by installing VST plug-ins at the location Library → Audio → Plug-ins → VST.

Updating Live

To check what version of Live you are currently running under Mac OS X, click on Live → About. On a PC, go to Help → About Live. Both the version and serial number will be displayed (see Figure 2.1). Click anywhere on the pop-up screen to close this window. To see if there is an update for Live, you will need your serial number, although once you've created a User Account at ableton.com you'll be able to get updates just by logging in. You can also use Check for Updates in the Live Help menu if your computer is currently online. I recommend checking for updates as often as your time and interest allow. Ableton remains ambitious about tracking down even the smallest bugs in Live and posting software updates. Their user forum (click on "forum") is also of value and is a great place to pick up new tips, suggest ideas to Ableton, trade songs, and network with other Live users. Be sure to sign up for Ableton's newsletter to be alerted to all major updates and general Ableton news and events.

Figure 2.1 This screen will confirm which version of Live you are currently working in. After you update your copy of Live, follow the steps described in "Updating Live" to make sure that the new version is running properly. You may need to swap out old desktop or dock shortcut icons because they will continue to point to (launch) the old version of the product.

Copy Protection

Ableton uses a challenge-response authentication system to protect Live from software piracy. Many companies are employing this method now because of both its effectiveness in deterring illegal copying and its ease of use for the customer. I like it because it doesn't rely on clunky hardware dongles or the original system disk, which can become scratched or broken.

Here's how it works. After installing and launching Live you will be asked to enter a serial number. Live will then generate a unique (specific to your machine) number that coincides with your serial number. This new number is your challenge number. If you're connected to the Internet, simply click Unlock Online, and Live will handle all of the challenging and responding invisibly behind the scenes. Authentication can also be done via e-mail. If the computer you are using does not have access to the Internet, you can also obtain this information via fax or phone. Then you can manually plug Ableton's response number into Live when the authentication dialog box emerges.

Should you encounter problems authorizing Live, write a kind note to support@ableton.com, and you will get an answer soon.

Basic Computer Specifications

When buying a computer, you're often faced with a dilemma centered around brand, timing, processor speed, and a ridiculous number of options. You can spend your entire life chasing processor speeds. My feeling is that it is more important to get a functional machine rather than bleeding-edge technology that may or may not be 100 percent stable. In any event, here is a list of the most important considerations when buying a computer for using Ableton's Live software.

Processor Speed

It is in our very nature to want the fastest and most efficient processor available. Business folks want to spend less time waiting for massive data crunching, and musicians want to hear fewer digital "hiccups" in their music. However, although faster may be better, don't spend all of your time chasing processor speeds. Trust me, it can be an expensive proposition. Instead, try to set your sights just below the industry top dogs. Ableton Live doesn't necessarily require the fastest processor on the market to perform basic functions. Sure, there are limitations, and contrary to popular belief, there always will be. So instead of spending $3,500 (or more) on your next industry champion, take a step back, save several hundred dollars, and invest in a quality soundcard and a pair of professional speakers instead. Your music will be better for it.

Hard Drives

Fast hard drives, on the other hand, are essential. Say what you want about processor speeds; when recording audio, your hard drive spin and data throughput are terrifically important. One of the most important factors is RPM. Most drives run at 7,200 RPM these days, but be wary of buying one of those 5,400 RPM hard drives. As for seek time, 9 milliseconds or less is the maximum most users find acceptable. Laptop users should be especially aware of their hard drive specs, particularly if you want to buy a new laptop for use with Live. In an effort to conserve energy, many laptops ship with fairly slow internal hard drives, usually in the neighborhood of 4,200 RPM. This slow hard drive speed will limit the number of audio clips that you will be able to play simultaneously in Live. If the laptop manufacturer doesn't offer any hard drive upgrades at the time of purchase, you can usually have a third-party drive installed after the purchase. These days, some laptops have 7,200 RPM hard drives installed already, so these can offer nearly the same performance as a standard hard drive in a desktop computer. The downside is that these higher-power drives will usually drain your laptop's battery faster. That said, an internal 5,400 RPM drive will probably serve you just fine for most live performance applications, but you may find it wanting as your main recording/production drive.

RAM

In Live, most of your short samples (less than 5MB) will sit in RAM rather than on the hard disk. Any samples used in your virtual instruments must also occupy memory space. To start out with, 1GB should be adequate for any serious computer musician, although more is always better if you've got the cash. You can make it with less RAM for a short while, but more memory will help to ensure stability during live performances, and it will help if you have other applications or plug-ins running in the background or together with Live.

Audio Interface Specs

No piece of hardware is more important in determining the audio quality of your work than your audio interface. Almost invariably, the audio capabilities that come standard with your PC or Mac are lacking in many ways. Depending on your needs and budget, you will want to either replace your computer's audio hardware or add a second interface to your system. Audio interfaces can connect in several different ways. PCI cards for desktop computers and PCMCIA (CardBus) cards for laptops are thought of as internal soundcards, while USB and FireWire (IEEE 1394) soundcards can be thought of as external cards. Pro Tools TDM interfaces, in which the internal and external hardware are integrated, can be thought of as a combination of the two. Here are some items to consider when purchasing a soundcard.

What Type of Audio Interface Should You Get?

Desktop computer users have the greatest number of choices when shopping for audio interfaces. These computers can normally accept PCI and PCI-X audio cards, external USB and FireWire connected interfaces, and hybrid internal/external audio solutions. PCI and PCI-X cards, which fit into slots inside your computer, will offer the best performance of any format available. PCI offers high bandwidth and bus speeds, which allow greater amounts of data (digital audio) to be passed back and forth between the CPU and interface.

The increase in speed and reliability of laptop computers has made them very attractive candidates for hosting Live. By running live from a portable computer, you have the convenience of taking your instrument wherever you go, just like guitar, bass, saxophone, and harmonica players can. Also, since Live is a robust multitrack recording environment, a laptop gives you the ultimate remix and recording studio for the road or a bedroom studio. The laptop allows for and encourages spontaneous creativity, since your studio is never far from reach.

Laptops do not have room to accept PCI and PCI-X audio interfaces. Instead, most laptops are equipped with a PCMCIA or CardBus slot, which allows small format cards to be added when necessary. Most laptops also sport USB and FireWire ports to facilitate the connection of external audio devices. FireWire and USB 2.0 are currently your best choices for low-latency audio. PCMCIA comes in second, and USB 1.x comes in a distant third. External soundcards are portable and efficient, but many feel that USB 1.x is just not fast enough: USB 1.x can transmit only up to 12 megabits per second (Mbps), while FireWire and USB 2.0 cards push up to 400 or more Mbps per second (called *throughput*). Playback is usually decent on USB cards because you are often just listening to a stereo mix (two channels), but when recording multiple tracks (more than three or four), USB 1.x can have problems keeping up. You should consider carefully which applications (besides Ableton Live) you plan to use and then decide upon the best hardware platform. USB 1.x is fast enough for typical Ableton Live use, where "typical" is one or two inputs and a stereo output mix. Power users will want to take advantage of Live's multiple ins and outs (routing) to employ hardware mixers and outboard effects and will therefore need an interface to support it.

How Many Outputs Do You Need?

The advantage to multiple outputs is increased integration with the world outside your computer. For example, multiple outputs give you the ability to send drums to outputs 1 and 2 while sending the vocals to output 3. Then you could send these outputs to different channels on a hardware mixer to apply EQ and outboard effects. If you just have a single stereo output on your soundcard, all mixing has do be done inside the computer. Is this something you should necessarily be worrying about? Not at all! If you are just getting started, or you are not sure what all of this is about, then chances are there's no need for you to concern yourself too much about it at this point.

The exception to this rule is if you plan on performing with Live, in which case you will want to have a minimum of four outputs (two stereo pairs). This allows you to use one pair as your main output and the other for cuing (prelistening) to tracks or clips in your headphones, just like a DJ.

Once you've decided whether you need 2, 4, 6, 8 or more outputs, you may also want to consider what types of connecters the interface uses. For example, if you're always connecting to DJ mixers, it may be more convenient to have RCA outputs on your interface, rather than 1/4" or XLR. Ultimately, though, this shouldn't be a deal-breaker since you can always connect with the proper cables or adapters.

How Many Inputs Do You Need?

Like outputs, the number of inputs you need will narrow the list of interfaces to consider. Multiple inputs are a must if you're planning on recording multichannel sources, such as live drums. Generally, soundcards have a minimum of two input channels, a right and left input, used together as stereo. These can be RCA, XLR, digital (S/PDIF or AES/EBU), or others (such as ADAT Lightpipe). With digital formats, you'll want to be sure the interface you get will work with the other gear you are using or plan to use. For example, if you have a keyboard with a coaxial S/PDIF connection, you won't want to buy an interface with an optical digital input—the two are not compatible.

Keep in mind that for more than two channels of input, FireWire, USB 2.0, and internal PCI and CardBus cards will be a more efficient means than USB 1.x in delivering the large amount of multitrack audio data to your hard drive.

Roadworthy components, great-sounding analog-to-digital converters, and responsive tech support are the three most important qualities to consider when selecting your most vital piece of hardware outside of your computer—the soundcard. Here are a few tried and true soundcards suggested with quality, precision, and portability in mind.

M-Audio (www.m-audio.com)

M-Audio makes a wide variety of interfaces that will fit into almost any budget (see Figure 2.2). All of M-Audio's Delta series cards connect via PCI and support the leanest audio drivers (ASIO

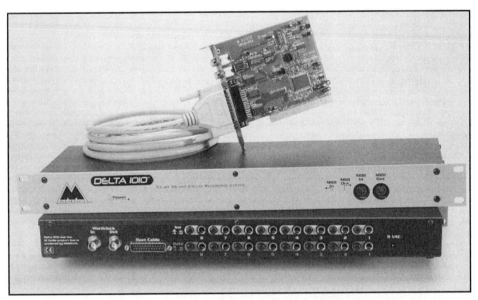

Figure 2.2 The Delta series of M-Audio audio cards are made with a variety of input, output, and MIDI options. The Delta 1010 is a powerful audio card with eight analog inputs and outputs and an additional stereo input via S/PDIF. The pictured rack portion of the unit connects to the PCI card inside your computer. M-Audio also manufactures less expensive cards without breakout boxes.

and Core Audio); M-Audio also makes a number of FireWire interfaces such as the Ozonic keyboard/interface (see Figure 2.3). FireWire is an excellent solution for laptop users, as it offers expanded bandwidth while maintaining the convenience of USB. Mobile users can now take advantage of multichannel audio for previewing tracks or routing outputs to a mixing desk. M-Audio used to be Ableton's U.S. distributor. Even though Ableton now self-distributes, they maintain a close relationship with M-Audio.

Figure 2.3 The FireWire Ozonic is a perfect all-in-one solution for Live. It is not only a 4 × 4 audio interface, it's also a 37-note velocity- and aftertouch-sensitive keyboard with knobs, buttons, sliders, and a joystick for control.

Echo Audio (www.echoaudio.com)

While Echo Audio makes a variety of interfaces, such as the Layla and Gina (PCI) and AudioFire (Firewire) lines, they also have an interesting product line for the space and budget conscious. The Indigo series (see Figure 2.4) is an inexpensive prosumer-level PCMCIA card that could easily support small clubs or informal editing sessions. The Indigo DJ is specially suited for use with Live, since its additional output allows you to preview clips before sending them to the dance floor. The Indigo I/O ("I/O" means the card handles both input and output) swaps the second output pair from the DJ for an analog input pair.

RME Hammerfall (www.rme-audio.com)

Hammerfall's series of FireWire interfaces (see Figure 2.5) turns up again and again as the soundcard line most preferred by laptop aficionados. If you are looking for a solid, professional solution and can afford to pay for it, you will not be disappointed with these interfaces.

Figure 2.4 Echo Audio's Indigo series audio cards provide consumer level audio support that is both inconspicuous and simple. No MIDI or digital transfer is supported, but what do you want for less than $200 bucks?

Figure 2.5 RME Fireface 400.

The Fireface 400 and 800 have an astonishing range of inputs/outputs and features, and RME's drivers are top-notch and offer some of the lowest latency times in the industry.

Apogee Electronics (www.apogeedigital.com)

One of the most exciting new products for Mac users looking for portability matched with superb sound quality is the Apogee Duet (see Figure 2.6). Long known for making some of the best digital converters in the business, Apogee has finally released a very affordable two-channel interface. However, since this is two channels only, it may not be the best solution for DJs or anyone who needs that extra headphone output. The good news is that Macs allow the creation of "aggregate devices," so you can create a virtual device (in the audio MIDI setup utility) that utilizes both the Mac's built-in output and the output of the Duet. Voila! Headphone mix problem solved.

Figure 2.6 The Apogee Duet.

Aside from the above-mentioned soundcards, many other companies make professional level soundcard products. It almost goes without saying that times change quickly, and new technology emerges. So keep your eye on the latest reviews in magazines such as *Computer Music, Music Tech, Remix, Mix, Electronic Musician, Keyboard, EQ,* and nonbiased industry Web sites such as Harmony Central (http://www.harmony-central.com) for fresh product info. Also, it is extremely important to continually check your soundcard manufacturer's Web site to be sure you have the latest audio drivers. Current and correct audio drivers can make a world of difference in how your software performs in your system. Don't just trust that the included CD that ships with your soundcard has the most recent drivers.

What Do You Need to Know About ASIO Drivers?

ASIO (Audio Stream Input/Output) was first invented by German software-slinger Steinberg (www.steinberg.de or www.cubase.net). Originally, ASIO drivers were created to help musicians and producers using Cubase to digitally record multitrack audio with a minimal amount of time lag within their digital system. This time lag can be a real buzz-kill and is called *latency*. Latency occurs because the sound you are recording is forced to travel through your operating system, your system bus, and host application to end up on your hard drive. Like bad plumbing, the signal may be coming down the pipe, but there are unnecessary clogs and corners that must be navigated along the way. The gist is that your computer is performing calculations (remember, it's all numbers for the computer) and, though they are blazingly fast, it takes a moment for the processor to finish, and the result is latency.

Live 7 supports ASIO on PCs (ASIO is unnecessary on Mac OS X, thanks to Core Audio). You'll be happy to know that most popular consumer- and professional-grade audio cards support the format, too. It has become an industry standard and can cut latency down to barely detectable levels. Properly installed, ASIO drivers will make Live as responsive as a hardware instrument with less than eight milliseconds of audio delay—practically unnoticeable. ASIO helps Live users hear the instantaneous results of MIDI commands, audio input/output, mouse moves, and keyboard commands. Someday, we'll all look back and laugh that latency was ever an issue, but for now, count your blessings that there is ASIO. See the "Setting Preferences in Live" section later in this chapter for more on the infamous "L-word."

ASIO 4 All If you're stuck using the internal soundcard of your PC or have an audio card that doesn't support ASIO, there still may be hope for you. Michael Tippach has programmed a freeware driver called "ASIO4ALL," which is available at www.asio4all .com. If you use it, you will have solved your latency problem, but you'll still want to consider a new audio interface because the converters in a pro interface will sound much better than those used in standard soundcards.

Choosing a MIDI Interface

Nothing makes playing Live more rewarding than cranking real knobs, watching virtual faders move, and hearing the results. You can move virtual knobs and faders, adjust the amount of effects and their settings, modify the tempo, and do just about anything else you can imagine, all by using a MIDI interface. Those wishing to exploit the power of Live's MIDI sequencing features will also require a good MIDI control device. In the next section, we will take a look at several portable, affordable, yet full-featured MIDI controllers—a product category that has grown exponentially over the last couple of years.

One controller commonly used by Live users is the Evolution X-Session controller (Figure 2.7). This compact device is especially suited for Live, as it sports a DJ-style crossfader among its 16 controls. The 10 programmable buttons also function perfectly as scene-select and -launch controls. You'll find it extremely easy to map filters, delays, feedbacks, and other parameters to the knobs for instant tweaking; plus, it will fit just about anywhere. Not only that, but it seems to be incredibly durable. We have dropped them many times but they never seem to break!

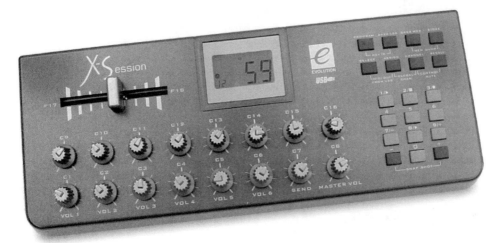

Figure 2.7 The X-Session is the choice for anyone seeking to dominate Live's crossfader.

The Faderfox controllers are so compact and functional you'd think they came from James Bond's arsenal of gadgets. No larger than a guitar stomp box, the Micromodul LV2 and LX2 (see Figure 2.8) are designed specifically with Live in mind, allowing control of the Session Mixer and Clip Slot Grid (both of which are discussed in Chapter 3, "Live Interface Basics").

Finally, let's take a look at the M-Audio Trigger Finger (see Figure 2.9), designed by one of the previous authors of this book (Chad Carrier of M-Audio). This controller was designed with Live foremost in mind and even contains a built-in preset for controlling two Impulse drum machines simultaneously. Along with the 16 velocity- and pressure-sensitive pads, you'll get eight knobs and four sliders that can be used to control additional parameters. I'll make reference to this controller time and time again throughout this book.

The above MIDI controllers begin to give you an idea of what is available for just a few hundred bucks (or less). As computers have become the dominant platform for music-making, the

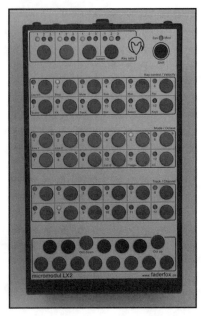

Figure 2.8   The Faderfox Micromodul LV2 and LX2.

Figure 2.9   The M-Audio Trigger Finger: 16 pads for you to bash upon to your heart's content.

controller market has exploded with an overwhelming number of options. The good news is that virtually any MIDI controller, including MIDI-based mixers, can work with Live. You can assign sliders, knobs, or buttons in an infinite number of creatively rewarding ways. In Chapter 4, "Making Music in Live," we'll explore specific ways of making a MIDI map. There are literally millions of possibilities. Imagine mapping these controllers to adjust panning, effects, tempo, crossfader, filters, EQ settings, and on and on.

Setting Preferences in Live

Optimizing Live's preferences is essential for smooth operation. Preferences are more than merely your personal whims about how you would like Live's interface to be colored, or where your files are automatically saved. Preferences are your primary control center for fine-tuning Live's ability to work in your particular computer/audio environment. From the Preferences menu, you will be able to control default loop traits, audio and MIDI interface settings, and audio latency settings. Sound like too much to manage? Read on, and let's tame this beast. To call up the Preferences dialog box on a PC, select Options → Preferences; on a Mac running OS X, select Live → Preferences. When you first open the preferences, you will see a small pop-up window with a number of tabs marked on the side, including Look/Feel, Audio, MIDI/Sync, File/Folder, Record/Warp/Launch, CPU, Products, and Live Packs. We'll have a look at each of these in turn.

The Look/Feel Tab

On the Look/Feel tab (see Figure 2.10), you'll first find a number of settings having to do with Live's appearance and the way it presents information to you. Let's look at all the settings.

The Language setting allows you to choose the language to use for Live's menus and messages. The internal help menus, interface text, and informational messages can be set to read in French, Spanish, and German, as well as English.

The "Don't Show Again" Warnings setting deals with the various warnings that come up when you first perform certain actions in Live. Typically, these warnings will only be seen the first time you perform a particular action, and then you won't see them again. If you want to bring back all these messages and restore Live to the state it was in when you first installed it, click Restore here.

The third option, Follow Behavior, determines the graphical style used when following the song position in the Arrange and Clip Views. When set to Scroll, the playback cursor will stay in place while the window moves smoothly under it. When set to Page, the window will stay stationary while the cursor moves. When the playback cursor reaches the right edge of the screen, the window jumps ahead so the cursor appears again on the left. The Scroll option is much harder on your CPU, so if you are experiencing dropouts or sluggish response, set this option to Page.

The next option here, Hide Labels, helps give you a little more screen real estate once you've memorized all of Live's components and don't need the labels anymore. When set to Show, the Live interface will look normal. When set to Hide, all of the little labels on the interface (such as Track Delay and Audio To) will disappear.

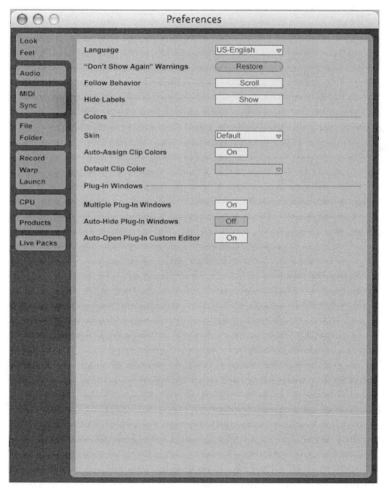

Figure 2.10 The Look/Feel tab in Live's Preferences.

Colors

In this next section of the Look/Feel tab, you'll find various settings dealing with Live's color scheme and appearance.

The Skin setting allows you to choose the skin for Live. This sets the overall color scheme. To find the scheme you like best, simply click the drop-down menu here and use the up and down arrows on your keyboard to scroll though the options.

Under the Skin drop-down selector, you'll also find the Auto-Assign Colors toggle switch and the Default Clip Color selector. With Auto-Assign Colors on, Live will randomly choose a color for each new clip or recording. (These color assignments can also be changed at any time for each clip in a screen called Clip View, which will be covered in depth in Chapter 4.) If Auto-Assign Colors is off, the Default Clip Color comes into play to determine which color Live will default to for all new clips. Of course, color will not affect the sound and is strictly a matter of preference.

Plug-In Windows

The three options in the next section of the Look/Feel preference tab determine how Live will display a plug-in's custom display window.

When Multiple Plug-In Windows is activated, you can open more than one plug-in window at a time. When this is off, open plug-in windows will be closed any time a new one is opened. Keeping this option off can help minimize screen clutter.

The second option, Auto-Hide Plug-In Windows, will make plug-in windows appear only for those plug-ins loaded on a selected track. For example, if you have a MIDI track loaded with an instance of Native Instrument's Battery and another MIDI track with LinPlug Albino, Battery will be hidden when the Albino track is selected, and Albino will be hidden when the Battery track is selected. This can also help minimize screen clutter, and thus is especially useful for laptop users.

The third option here is the Auto-Open Plug-In Custom Editor box. When active, the plug-in window will be opened immediately after the plug-in is loaded onto a track. This makes perfect sense, as you'll usually need to make some modification to the plug-in after you load it.

The Audio Tab

The next tab in Live's preferences, the Audio tab (see Figure 2.11), allows you to choose an audio interface to use in Live and make various adjustments to its performance. This tab's pull-down menus and options will depend largely on what kind of soundcard you have, whether it is correctly installed, and what operating system you are using. In the figure below, you will see that I am using a PreSonus FireBox on a Mac.

Audio Device

The first section of the Audio tab is labeled Audio Device. The first setting you can choose here is the Driver Type you want to use for your audio interface. On the PC, options will include MME/DirectX and ASIO, and in Mac OS X, you will see just one choice, Core Audio. After you select the Driver Type you want to use, you will have a selection of audio devices to choose from in the subsequent drop-down menus. As noted above, you will always get better performance with ASIO drivers, so you should always choose ASIO on PC if this option is available.

Next after Driver Type is the Audio Device setting, where you actually choose the specific soundcard you want to use. In Windows, you will see only a single menu choice here; in Mac OS X, you will see separate settings for Audio Input Device and Audio Output Device. Theoretically, you can choose different devices for input and output here; in practice, however, you will probably get the best performance by using a single audio interface at a time, so you'll probably want to choose the same device for both input and output. (If you are not recording, you don't need to choose an input device at all.)

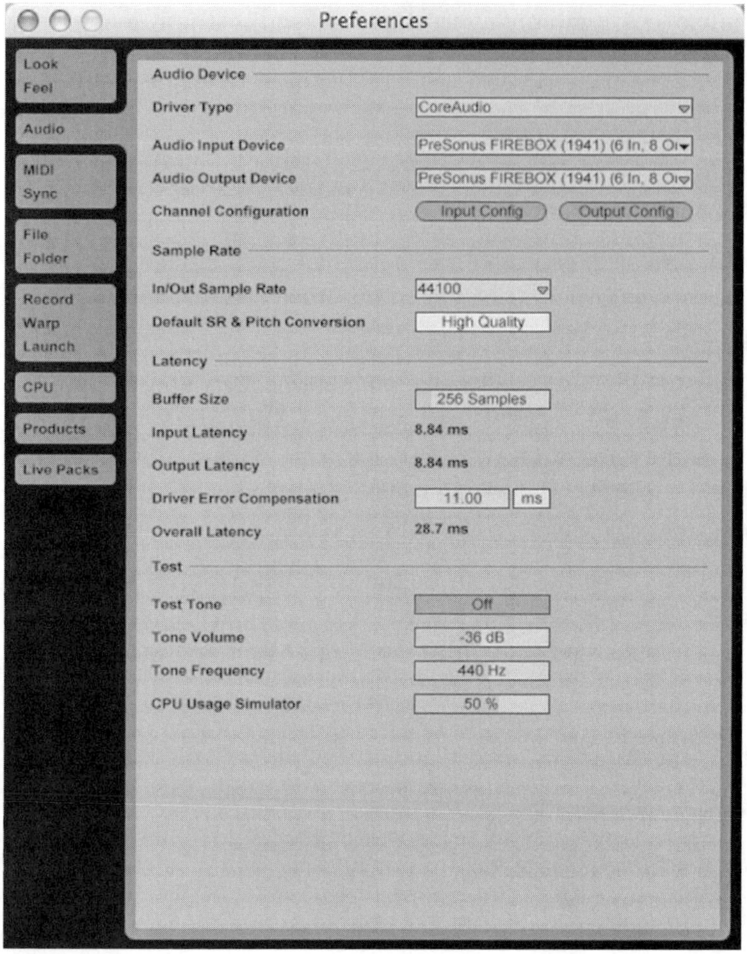

Figure 2.11 Live's Audio Preferences tab.

Note that you may not find the audio device you want to use when using certain driver types. For example, the built-in audio cards on laptop computers don't support ASIO, so you'll only find these cards listed when MME/DirectX is selected for Driver Type.

The Channel Configuration settings include two buttons, Input Config and Output Config. Clicking one of these opens another small pop-up window that enables you to activate various inputs and outputs on your soundcard for use in Live. Only those inputs and outputs that you activate here will appear in Live's other menus and selectors. If you don't need to use all of the inputs and outputs, you may want to leave them inactive here, as doing so will save you a bit of computing power. (In Chapter 12, "Playing Live…Live," we will talk further about how to capitalize on Live's cueing ability using multiple outputs.)

Please note that Live will always seek out the audio interface last saved in the preferences each time the program launches. If Live cannot find the soundcard—if, for instance, you have unplugged it or swapped it out—Live will still launch, but with no audio enabled. In this instance, you will see a warning message telling you that Live cannot find the audio card and that audio will be "disabled" upon startup. You will also notice a second red warning on Live's actual interface (after the program launches) that says, "The audio engine is off. Please choose an audio device from the Audio Preferences." In this case, you won't be able to play any sound in Live until you go to the Audio Preferences and select a new audio device.

Sample Rate

The In/Out Sample Rate setting in the Audio Preferences tab will determine the recording quality of both Live's output and recorded input. A good basic sample rate to start out with is 44,100Hz, or 44.1kHz. As you learn more about digital audio, or if you are a pro already, the Sample Rate drop-down box will give you further choices, depending on the capabilities of your soundcard. I never recommend using anything lower than 44.1kHz.

The higher the sample rate, the more high frequency detail in your sound, but the greater the strain on your computer's CPU. If your computer has power to spare, you might try experimenting with higher sample rates, but in practice you may find it difficult to hear much difference when you are playing live on a noisy P.A. system in a bar or club.

For achieving the best audio quality for recording/mixing situations, the primary rule of thumb is this: For a given Set, pick a sample rate and stick with it. Don't change sample rates once you've begun, and avoid using audio recorded at different sample rates in your Set. If you have to, convert the sample rate to the rate you are currently working at in an application with high-quality sample rate conversion, such as Bias Peak. While Live is certainly capable of performing sample rate conversion, its conversion engine is optimized for efficiency, not maximum sound quality. This is not necessarily a bad thing. Being able to drop any sound file you want into your DJ Set while flying to a gig is a huge convenience, but as I've already observed, trading a little sound quality in a live performance situation isn't a big deal; creating a pristine mix in a studio setting is a different story. If this is what you're doing, try not to do sample rate conversion in Live.

There is also another setting here labeled Default Clip S.R. Conversion. This affects the default sound quality setting for each new clip you create in Live. For best results you should set this to Hi Quality, although this will demand a bit more of your system resources. You can also opt to leave Hi Quality off as a default setting, yet still use it on select loops by double-clicking a clip and adjusting its settings. I'll say more on this subject in Chapter 5, "The Audio Clip."

Latency Settings

The next section of the Audio tab allows you to adjust a number of settings relating to the buffer size and latency of your soundcard. You may need to experiment with these settings a bit to get the best possible performance on your particular computer system. Before we get to the experimentation, though, let's make sure we understand the problem.

First, recognize that there is both output latency and input latency. There is a minimum amount of latency that must occur as signal passes through your A/D converters into your computer, just as there is also a certain amount of time that it takes for your computer to send audio to your soundcard and through the D/A converters. While this is a very short period of time, things are complicated somewhat by the fact that we need our audio to play back without interruption, while at the same time our CPU is being interrupted constantly, handling myriad other tasks while our audio is playing back. This is where buffers come into play.

Whether you realize it or not, you've almost certainly dealt with digital audio buffers before. When you listen to music on an iPod, there is a slight lag between when you select the song you want to play back and when you start to hear it. That's because before you hear anything, a certain amount of audio is loaded into the device's memory (the buffer), and then the audio is played back from the memory rather than directly from the hard drive. This ensures that if you knock the player around and cause the hard drive to skip, audio will continue to play back from the buffer while the device finds its way back to the place where it skipped. As long as the device can keep filling the buffer with data before it's all been played back, you'll never hear any problems, no matter how hard you whack it!

The same concept applies to your computer. A very small buffer necessitates a very fast CPU. It needs to work very fast in order to keep audio playback consistent while it also carries out background tasks for the OS, updates the display, and does whatever else it has to do. Occasionally, something will cause your CPU to momentarily spike, and if you don't have a big enough buffer, audio mayhem will ensue! This is why for live performances, you want to make sure you've got a big enough cushion to deal with whatever comes up. In the studio, you can go for lower settings because not only is latency more irritating when recording, but you also have the flexibility to experiment and correct things as you go along.

The first setting we'll look at is the Buffer Size, displayed as a number of samples, tiny bits of sampled sound. The lower your Buffer Size setting is, the less latency you'll experience, but the more potential problems can arise. In other words, too much buffer will increase the amount of undesirable latency, yet too little latency can result in your system choking and experiencing digital pops, audio dropouts, and the like.

You may or may not be able to adjust your soundcard's buffer size from this Preferences menu. While in Mac OS X you can usually just click here and drag up or down to adjust the buffer size, in Windows you will probably need to open your soundcard's own proprietary driver interface or control panel, which can be launched with the Hardware Setup button.

Next, we see the Input latency and Output latency values. *Output latency* is the amount of lag time between when you trigger a sound or action and when you hear it. Or if you add an effect, such as distortion or reverb, the extra time that it takes to actually hear that sound is Output latency.

Input latency arises for the same reasons as Output latency. Audio is buffered on the way into the computer, so Live receives this audio a little later than it should. Fortunately, Live knows it's behind, and it takes this into account when recording. The result is a take that is recorded in time. When Input latency starts becoming a problem, though, is when you try to monitor audio *through* Live. Now the audio has to pass through the input buffers, through Live and any potential effects that may be loaded, and back to the output buffers before it can reach your ear. Keeping your buffer settings as low as possible will keep this "double" latency to a minimum.

Round It Off While some soundcard drivers will allow you to adjust the buffer in increments of one sample, Ableton recommends that you set your buffer to one of the binary "round numbers" that we see so often on our computers: 64, 128, 256, 512, 1024, and so on.

You may well be able to set your latency time extremely low and have no discernible latency. It is there all the time, but it is often unnoticeable when using ASIO, WDM, or Core Audio drivers, which is why these driver types are preferred.

Most professional audio cards, like the ones mentioned above, also feature "direct monitoring," which helps alleviate some of the problems of recording with latency. Instead of having Live blend your input signal with its output signal and buffering it to the audio card, the audio card will blend your input signal with the output from Live so the input signal doesn't have to travel all the way through the computer and back out again. The result is instantaneous monitoring of your input signal—no latency. The drawback is that you will not be able to use effects on a direct monitored signal since the audio signal is not being sent through the computer. The audio interface simply routes the input directly to the output.

Audio interfaces are designed to report their latencies to Live so it can offset its operations properly. However, in practice, the reported amount is usually not completely accurate, and there is some additional latency that you must manually enter into the Driver Error Compensation box. The last parameter here, Overall Latency, shows the sum of the Input latency and Output latency. This is the total amount of latency you would hear from an input signal coming into Live.

Beating Latency To find out the exact amount of unreported latency that must be compensated for, look under the Help menu and select Lessons Table of Contents. Scroll down in the pane that opens up and find Driver Error Compensation under the heading Hardware Setup. This will provide you with superb step-by-step instructions and a custom Live Set for testing your hardware's latency.

The Diver Error Compensation value will only be used to correct the timing of recordings that are made with Live's monitor switch set to Off. (Using your interface's "direct monitoring" feature is one way to hear what you're doing when you don't monitor through Live.) What this means is that you will have to manually adjust the latency of recordings made while monitoring through Live. This can be done either by entering the Driver Error Compensation value into the Track Delay or by adjusting the clip's start point by that same amount.

Test

The Test section of the Audio Preferences allows you to generate a test-tone sine wave so you can test your system. You can also adjust the volume and frequency of the test tone using the other parameters in this section. Here are the steps for testing your system:

1. Turn on the test tone.

2. Set the CPU Usage Simulator to its maximum value (80%).

3. Decrease the buffer size until you start to hear crackling or dropouts in the test tone.

4. Increase the buffer size until these artifacts go away.

This test will yield a buffer size that will guarantee smooth audio performance in almost all situations. This will be a good value to use for live performance where stability is paramount. For situations where you need lower latency, you can test with a lower simulated CPU usage, or as long as you are working in the studio, just lower the buffer size as low as you want it and increase it if you have problems!

The MIDI/Sync Tab

This brings us to the third Preferences tab, the MIDI/Sync tab, shown in Figure 2.12. This is where you can specify which of your MIDI devices will serve as remote controls, MIDI inputs and outputs, and sources for synchronization.

The first part of this tab contains options for setting up natively supported control surfaces in Live. If you are using an interface that Live supports, you can use one of the drop-down choosers in the first column (labeled *Control Surface*) to select it from a list. Once selected, Live will have all the necessary information to support the device. You can also select the MIDI input and output ports for the device, although many MIDI controllers these days connect directly to your computer via USB.

Depending on which controller you are using, Live may need to do a "preset dump" to the device once you have selected it, in order to initialize it with the correct control values. In this case, the Dump button at right will become active (not grayed-out), and you need to click it once to do the dump.

The second part of this window shows a list of the MIDI input and output devices available on your computer. There are columns for the names of each MIDI port found by Live, plus columns

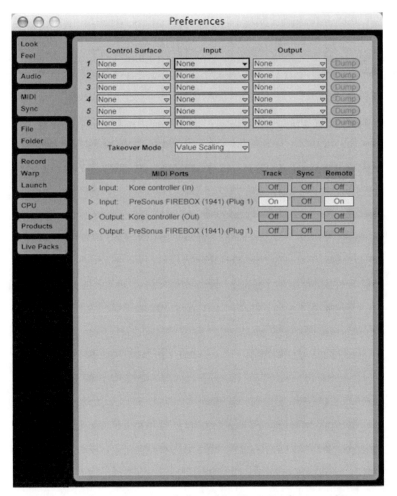

Figure 2.12   The MIDI/Sync tab found in Live's Preferences box.

named Track, Sync, and Remote. In order for a MIDI device to be usable, it has to be enabled as a Track input or output, as a Sync source, or as a MIDI Remote Control.

Enabling Track for a MIDI input device means that you can use it as an input to a MIDI track. This would be enabled for something like a control keyboard that you use for playing notes on a virtual instrument. Enabling Track on a MIDI output enables you to send MIDI data from a MIDI track output to an external piece of hardware, such as a sound module.

The Sync option enables the port as a MIDI Sync source. This will have to be enabled for at least one port for any of the Sync functions to work.

The last column, Remote, is especially nifty. By enabling a remote input, you can map any of Live's on-screen controls to a physical controller. Live also provides the ability to send feedback messages back to MIDI controllers with motorized MIDI knobs and faders, or those with light-up encoders, buttons, and so forth. If you have a control surface with these types of controls, you can enable Remote in the Output table for that device. Once you map a fader or knob to a MIDI control, Live will move the control anytime its value or position changes on-screen.

The File/Folder Tab

Next is the File/Folder tab (see Figure 2.13). Here you can set preferences for how your various files and folders are handled in Live. This tab also includes some preference settings dealing with effect and instrument plug-ins.

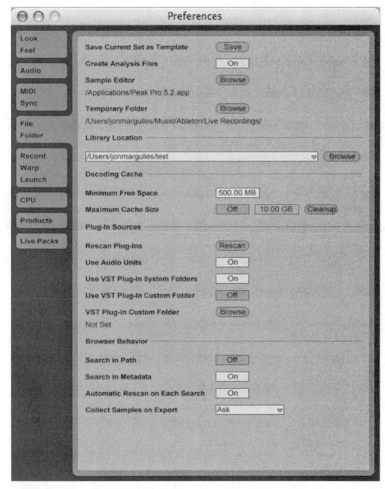

Figure 2.13   The File/Folder tab.

The first setting here, Save Current Set as Template, is used to save the current Live Set as the default or template Set that will be loaded each time Live is launched. This can be helpful for preconfiguring commonly used settings, such as MIDI assignments, input and output routings, and common effect patchwork (such as EQs on every channel). Note that you can save only one template in this Preferences tab. For additional templates, I recommend that you create a Live Set folder called *templates* and save empty, yet configured, Live Sets there.

The Create Analysis Files option lets you determine whether Live will save audio analysis data for quick loading in the future. The first time an audio file is used in Live, the program will create a waveform display and analyze the file for optimal warping. When this option is enabled, Live will store this information in a file on your computer's hard disk. The file has the same name as the sample it is associated with and has .asd as its extension. The next time the audio file is used in a Live Set, you won't have to wait for the graphical display to be rendered again, because the file analysis has been saved.

The Library Path setting will set the location of Live's Library, containing various effect and instrument presets and samples. This is Ableton's ingenious way of collecting all of its necessary support files into one place that can be easily accessed. The Library is installed automatically when you install Live, and this setting will already be pointing to its location on your hard drive.

A new feature of Live 7 is the capability to have multiple Library locations. This is useful because, particularly if you've purchased the Ableton Suite, the Library can become very large, and you may want to spread it across multiple hard drives. For example, you might want to keep a the standard factory Library on your laptop's internal drive, but store the Essential Instruments Collection 2 on an external drive.

Let's say this is what you want to do. The steps would be as follows:

1. In File/Folder preferences, browse to a folder where you would like the new Library to be created. Make sure to name it something meaningful like Live Library. All necessary subfolders will be created automatically.

2. With this location still selected in the File/Folder preferences, install the EIC2 (or any other Live Pack).

3. Whenever you want to use the EIC2, just go into your preferences and select this Library location. The Device browser will immediately be updated to show the presets available in the new Library.

The Sample Editor setting is for defining the location of your favorite wave editor, such as Sonic Foundry's Sound Forge, Steinberg's Wavelab, Bias Audio's Peak, or Syntrillium's Cool Edit Pro. Your preferred editor will launch when you press the Edit button in an audio clip. For a more detailed look at wave editors, please refer to Chapter 13, "Live 7 Power."

Temporary Folder allows you to set a location to temporarily store any files Live needs to create in the course of its operation. Again, in most cases, you won't need to change this from its default setting. This is the folder into which Live places all new recordings made before a Set is saved for the first time.

Decoding Cache

In order for Live to play MP3-format files, they must first be decoded/decompressed into standard WAV files. These resulting files are stored in the Decoding Cache. The parameters in this section determine how Live will handle the creation and cleanup of the decoded files.

The first option, Minimum Free Space, is the amount of free space that you always want available on the hard drive. If you set this to 500MB, Live will stop increasing the size of the cache once there is only 500MB available. This can be extremely important if you only have one hard drive on your entire computer system (which is frequently the case for laptop users). This setting will ensure that a minimum amount of space is available on the drive for swapping files and other housekeeping tasks. Alternately, Maximum Cache Size can be used if you would rather set a hard limit for the Decoding Cache. For example, you might want to make sure the cache never gets bigger than 10GB, regardless of how much drive space you have left. When either of these limits is met, Live will begin to delete the oldest decoded files to make room for new ones.

You'll notice that if you add an MP3 to your Set and Live decodes it, Live will not have to decode the file again if you drag the same MP3 into a Set at a later time. This is because the decoded file is still in the cache. If the decoded file gets deleted, you'll have to wait again for the previously decoded MP3 to be decoded again. The larger your cache is, the less this will happen.

Active Sources

The VST plug-in folders can be set to any folder on your machine that holds VST effects and instruments compatible with Live. Audio Units (Mac OS X only) are stored in Library→Audio→Plug-Ins→Components. The only sure way to know if Live is compatible with a plug-in is to try it out. To do this, place the plug-in in the appropriate folder and click the Rescan button. If you can see the new device listed in the plug-in section of Live's browser, then chances are Live will at least be able to load the plug-in. If it doesn't work properly, remove it from the VST folder and drop a friendly note to both Ableton and the plug-in developer about the problem you encountered.

Browser Search

This section contains settings relating to the Search function in Live's browser. The Search in Path option includes folder names as well as files when you do a search. The Search in Metadata option tells Live to search through audio file metadata (for example, the artist/track name info in the header of an MP3 file) as well.

If the Automatic Rescan on Each Search option is activated, Live will do a new indexing and rescan of files in the search location every time you do a search. This can be useful if the contents of a folder have been changed since the last search by an application other than Live, in which case, Live may no longer see the contents correctly.

Collect Samples on Export

This preference affects Live's behavior when clips are dragged from the Session or Arrange View into the browser in order to create new Sets or Live clips (see Chapter 3). If it's set to Yes, Live will always copy the underlying samples into the new location, along with the new Sets or Live clips you are creating. Otherwise, these new files will just refer to the original locations of the samples. If you're not sure what all of this is about, I recommend setting this preference to Ask so you can learn by doing.

The Record/Warp/Launch Tab

As you might guess, this tab contains settings dealing with Live's recording, launching, and clip launch functions (see Figure 2.14). Let's look at each of these in turn.

Record

The Record section allows you to make various default settings relating to how Live records audio.

Any time Live attempts to record, either through resampling or from a live input, it will use the record parameters you set here. First, you can record in WAV or AIFF format. I usually prefer the WAV format because it is readable by both Mac and Windows applications.

I also recommend setting the bit depth to 24 when recording (the Record Bit Depth option) if your audio interface supports it. This ensures the maximum detail for newly recorded sounds. You can always render a file downward (to 16-bit), but you cannot upsample later to add detail that is not there. Think of it this way: A color photo can be degraded to black and white easily, but the reverse—changing black and white to color—is much more difficult!

The next option in this section is Count In. When set to None, Live will begin to record immediately when the transport is engaged. If you select a value here, such as 1 Bar, Live will provide one bar of count-in time (the metronome will sound, but Live will not be running) before it begins to record. This is useful if you're recording yourself and you need some time to get to your instrument after you've engaged recording.

The Exclusive buttons are used to determine the Live Mixer's behavior when engaging solos and arming tracks for recording. For example, when Solo Exclusive is on (yellow), only one track may be soloed at a time. If you click the Solo button of another track, the previous track's solo status will turn off. The same is true for Arm Exclusive. Only one track can be record-enabled when this button is active. To solo more than one track at a time in Live, simply hold down the Ctrl (Cmd) key and click away. You can also arm more than one track at a time for recording by using the very same method.

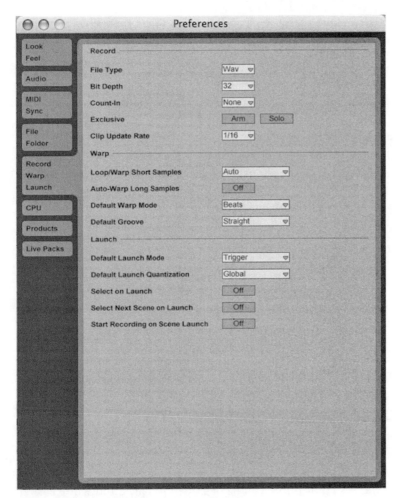

Figure 2.14 The Record/Warp/Launch tab.

The Clip Update Rate is the frequency with which Live recalculates changes to the clip. For instance, if you transpose a clip in Live while the Clip Update Rate is set to 1/32 note, you will hear nearly instant changes to the pitch of the loop in the clip. Conversely, choosing a Clip Update Rate of 1/4 note or the even slower rate of Bar (meaning one update per measure) will result in changes occurring more slowly. This is meaningful during a live performance, in which changes may need to be heard as they happen instead of after the fact.

Warp

This section includes various settings relating to Live's Warp functions, used to warp the time flow of a given clip.

The Loop/Warp Short Samples menu is used to determine the default state of a new audio clip, be it a loop or a one-shot sound. The Auto setting will cause Live to try and determine the nature of an imported loop on the fly and set its loop and warp settings accordingly.

The next option relates to Live's Auto-Warp feature. When the Auto-Warp Long Samples option is on, Live will attempt to determine the tempo of the imported audio file and will place Warp Markers into the audio clip automatically. This will only happen on long samples—files that Live assumes to be complete songs. Auto-Warp works better with some kinds of material than others (for example, dance music with clear tempo and transients), so what you do with Live will determine whether or not you want this setting enabled.

Default Warp Mode, the next item on this tab, is another story entirely. There are five Warp modes. Here is a DJ-style breakdown of the five Warp modes in Live. This is a topic central to understanding how Live works and will be revisited in chapters to follow. Remember, these are merely the defaults; all can be changed after the clip is loaded in Live.

- **Beats:** Beats mode is the original Live Warp mode. The program automatically breaks up the loop into sections determined by the Transients settings. For instance, Live can divide a loop into 1/32 notes, 1/16 notes, 1/8 notes, 1/4 notes, 1/2 notes, and full measures. As long as the sound is rhythmic, Live does an excellent job of making the loop sound as though it were recorded at your project tempo. Drum loops, dance grooves, and percussive instrument loops (bass, short synth, turntables, or funk guitars) can all be stretched convincingly in Beats mode.

- **Tones:** This is the mode for bass and keyboard lines, melodies, and pitched sounds that are not necessarily grooving in perfect time with a metronome, such as a legato horn line, a harmonic chord progression, or even vocals.

- **Texture:** For sounds more complex than melodies and rhythms, Ableton has brought us Texture mode. This is the mode to use for ambient effects, atonal pads, and indefinable sounds. Texture mode bears the distinction of further tweaking possibilities with Grain Size and Flux (fluctuation) controls. These two parameters determine the intensity, severity, and randomness of Live's resynthesis. This can be an excellent sonic deconstructing tool for any kind of loop, in addition to the ones mentioned.

- **Re-Pitch:** If you're not looking to independently adjust the speed and pitch of your samples, Ableton's Re-Pitch mode defeats all pitch correction and adjusts the tempo as you would with a turntable's pitch control or an old-school hardware sampler.

- **Complex:** This fifth mode utilizes an extremely high-quality algorithm for warping, optimized for signals that contain multiple characteristics of the other Warp modes. The benefit of this mode can be heard best when applied to a fully mixed song. The downside is that the algorithm is about 10 times as CPU intensive as the other Warp modes.

Also, you can turn all of the above modes off entirely. This means that the sample/loop is played back exactly as is, at its original tempo and pitch. This no-warping mode can be activated by deselecting the Warp button in the Audio Clip View.

The Default Groove setting lets you choose a straight or swing feel when you create new clips; if you choose a swing feel, you can choose from 1/8, 1/16, or 1/32 note variations. See Chapter 4 for a detailed explanation of how to get your Groove on.

Launch

When triggering a clip to play, Live gives us some options called *Launch modes*. The full rundown on these modes can be found in Chapter 4. For now, I recommend leaving the mode on Trigger or Toggle.

The next setting, Default Launch Quantization, determines the default point at which new clips will be launched in relationship to the time grid. Any time you launch a clip in Live, you have the option of launching it on the first beat of the next bar or every second bar, every fourth bar, every eighth bar, or by picking a note quantifier to begin playback on the very next 1/32, 1/16, 1/8, 1/4, or 1/2 note after you trigger the clip. Of course, this is a grand selection of choices, and the right selection can depend upon the type of sound you are launching. For instance, an orchestral or ambient guitar sound might not need to be quantized as strictly as a conga or cowbell loop. You can also opt to turn Quantization off by default by selecting None from this drop-down dialog box, or select Global, which is the safest bet for novice or careful Live musicians and will assume the same quantization setting as the project—a good way to keep every sound in line.

The Select Clip on Launch setting will cause the Clip View or the Track View (effects) of a clip to be displayed immediately when it is played. You'll stay in whatever view you're currently in when you launch a new clip. In other words, if you're already in the Clip View for a clip, and you launch a new clip, you will be taken to the Clip View of the newly launched clip.

Select Next Scene on Launch greatly simplifies the performance of Live sessions. Any time a scene is launched by keyboard or remote control, Live will automatically advance the scene selector to the one below it. If you've already laid out the sections of your song in a top-to-bottom arrangement on the Session Grid, you can progress through the song with just one button.

Start Recording on Scene Launch determines if clips will begin recording when launched by a scene. Having this option off will allow you to play an instrument live (track is armed for recording) while navigating through scenes. If this option is armed, a clip will begin to record in an armed track when the scene is launched. This can be powerful when used live by triggering a recording at a particular point in a piece. The recorded part can be looped instantly for building compositions in real time.

The CPU Tab

The CPU section of Preferences has only two settings (see Figure 2.15).

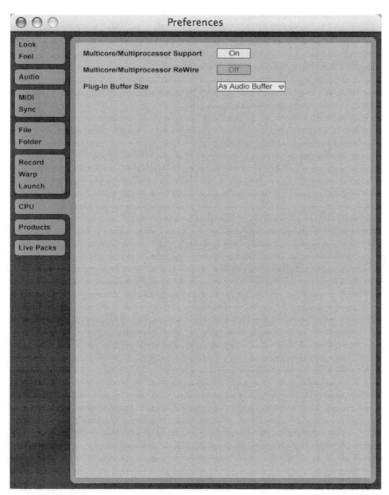

Figure 2.15 The CPU tab.

The first, Multicore/Multiprocessor Support, should be turned on if you are using a Mac or PC that has multiple or multicore processors, such as the MacBook Pro with its Intel Core Duo chip. There is also another option to enable Multicore/Multiprocessor support when you are using Live in ReWire mode.

The Plug-in Buffer Size setting sets the buffer size used when Live passes audio to and from external plug-ins. Normally, this option should be left on As Audio Buffer. Setting this option lower will result in your plug-in responding a little more quickly but can easily overburden your CPU. Make sure to save your work before changing this value, in case you choose a setting too low for your computer to handle.

The Products Tab

The Products tab in Preferences shows you a list of Ableton products and their status (see Figure 2.16).

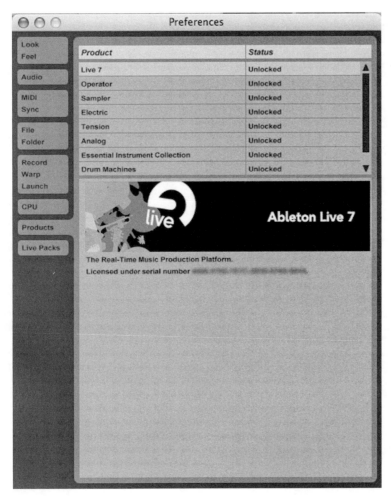

Figure 2.16   The Products tab.

More specifically, this tab shows you whether or not you have unlocked each product. To unlock a product, you need to purchase it from Ableton, click the individual product name here, and then click the Unlock button. You will be asked to enter the serial number you received from Ableton, and then you will be offered options to authorize the product online or offline. Authorizing your products directly online is easy and convenient, but offline options are offered as well, in case you are using a computer without an Internet connection.

The Live Packs Tab

The Live Packs tab shows you which Live Packs are installed on your machine (see Figure 2.17). Live Packs are collections of presets, lessons, and Live clips for you to use. You can also search for additional Live Packs to install from this tab or uninstall packs that are already present. You can download additional Live Packs from Ableton.com as well.

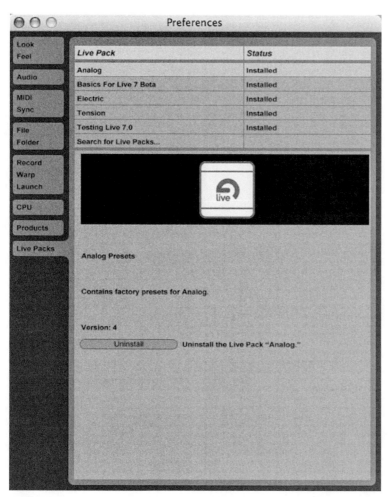

Figure 2.17   The Live Packs tab.

The goal of this chapter has been to get you up and running with Live and to give you a general idea about how the Preferences settings will affect your workflow. As you move through this book, I will direct you back to the Preferences discussion in this chapter again and again. In Chapter 3, we will complete your introduction to Live's two primary views.

3 Live Interface Basics

One of the crowning achievements of Ableton's software development is the creation of Live's simple but elegant interface. Only two views are needed to accomplish everything in Live: Session View and Arrangement View. Session View is geared for use in live performance, for loop experimentation, and as a quick multitrack recording sketchpad, while Arrangement View facilitates automation editing, audio and MIDI sequencing, and song arranging. Each subsection of Live's pared-down interfaces is intuitive and easy to maneuver and contains built-in help to remind you of any on-screen buttons or features that might be unclear in the heat of a mix. Ableton's Zen-like approach to audio software provides solid relief in a world full of gargantuan multitrack applications that have gaggles of resizable pop-up windows and confusing setup and routing schemes. Instead, Live is a breath of fresh air, boasting streamlined controls with easy-to-read menus and discernible mixer and effect settings. Even with the fog machine blowing and lights down low, Live lets you get into the mix, rather than trying your patience with unnecessary system customization.

In the next few sections, we will break down each section of Live's two primary landscapes, as well as point out some timesaving ways to maneuver in Live. Later in the chapter, we'll look at some of Live's more customizable viewing features, a few pertinent file-saving schemes, and the permanent parts of Live's screen real estate. Feel free to skip around if you need help in a particular area.

Session View

Live's Session View (see Figure 3.1) is where you will spend the greater part of your performing and composing time. Once you've had some practice with it, Session View can take on a musical life of its own and may well be the software world's first "jam-friendly" songwriter's sketchpad. Even better is that after the jam, Live permits an infinite amount of additional recording, editing, and arranging, which we will get to later in this chapter. There are four main sections contained within the Session View:

- Clip Slot Grid
- Scene Launcher

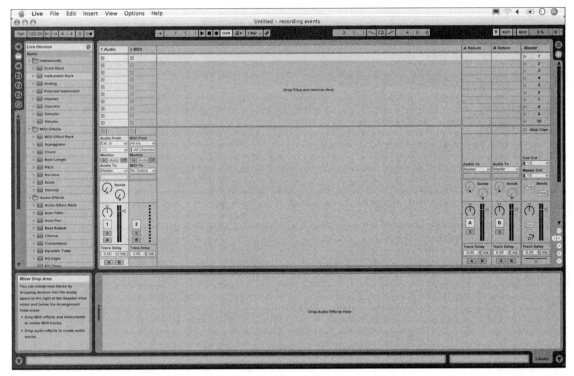

Figure 3.1 Pictured above is Live's Session View. This is the window used for live performance. Each clip slot (represented as rectangles beneath the track Title Bar) is a placeholder for audio samples, loops, and MIDI sequences.

- Session Mixer
- Input/Output Routing Strip

The grid-like display in the upper portion of the screen is the actual Session View, while the side and bottom retractable rectangle views (such as Browser, Info View, and Track/Clip View) are present in any view when you want them to be. Session View is where most people experience the creative spark in Live, so if you should create something worth saving while you are working through this chapter, go to File → Save Live Set As and name your new sketch. We should also point out that while we will cover each element in the interface, the Browser and Info View will be explained later in the chapter, while Track and Clip Views will be saved for Chapter 4, "Making Music in Live."

This ordinary-looking grid will be the launchpad for many a Live jam. Each cell—Ableton calls them *clip slots*—can contain a clip. A clip is a musical part that can be triggered to play or stop via the mouse, computer keyboard, or MIDI controller, depending upon your settings. Each clip can even be played in similar fashion to an Akai MPC, drum machine, or similar phrase sampler. For example, you can lay out several sampled drum hits across the 16 pads of a drum controller like the M-Audio Trigger Finger and then play them with the comfy rubber pads. Live's clip slot grid, which we will explain in detail below, is similar in design and can house an unlimited number of loops, samples, one shots, and MIDI parts.

Clip Slot Grid

Session View's clip slot grid (see Figure 3.2) is actually the first tool you will use to organize your musical parts (clips) into a song. Live uses these rows and columns, referred to as "scenes" and "tracks," respectively, to give you different levels of control. What's important is that you begin to think of Live's clip slot grid as a palette upon which to place your sonic colors (in this case musical parts composed of audio files and MIDI data) for later sonic "painting" and further color exploration (sound combining).

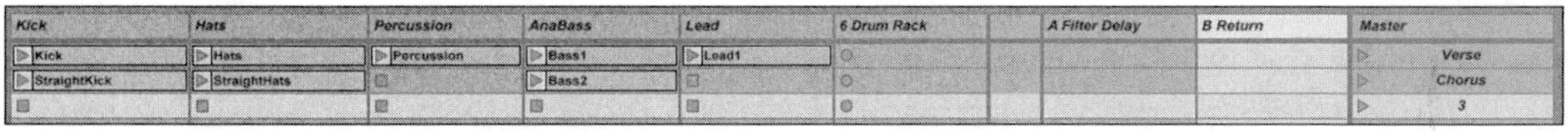

Kick	Hats	Percussion	AnaBass	Lead	6 Drum Rack	A Filter Delay	B Return	Master
Kick	Hats	Percussion	Bass1	Lead1				Verse
StraightKick	StraightHats		Bass2					Chorus
								3

Figure 3.2   The clip slot grid with a few clips loaded in some slots.

Along the bottom of the clip slot grid are the Clip Stop buttons. Clicking the square in one of these slots will cause any clip playing on the track above it to stop. Also, there is another box labeled Stop Clips in the Master track at the right. This button, as its name implies, will stop all clips—both audio and MIDI—when triggered.

Space Out   The spacebar starts and stops audio in Live as it does in most other audio software applications.

By loading clips into the clip slot grid, you are arming Live with musical ammo. Next steps could be anything from firing off parts in a live performance to creating new musical combinations (songs) to switching to the Arrangement View for more editing.

Knobby Digital   To adjust any of the virtual knobs found in Live, click the knob and move the mouse forward and backward just like a fader. In other words, moving the mouse sideways is a waste of time. Don't feel silly practicing how this feels; after all, it's your "sequencing instrument."

Some Live users prefer to build their entire song in Live by using several small yet simple loops and then utilize Live's Session View to organize, improvise, or compose. Other artists may show up to the gig with a blank slate along with a stash of well-organized clips and practice building their mix from the ground up in a more gradual, yet still improvisational way.

The Scene Launcher

As mentioned previously, the rows in the clip slot grid are referred to as *scenes*. Since Live can play only one clip at a time in each track, it makes sense to put each one you want to play in a horizontal line across the grid. Live then offers you a way to launch all of the clips in the scene using the Scene Launchers (see Figure 3.3) found on the right side of the clip slot grid in the Master track. As you get deeper into the program (especially in the next chapter), you'll see how using scenes offers you a quick way of arranging and performing a song.

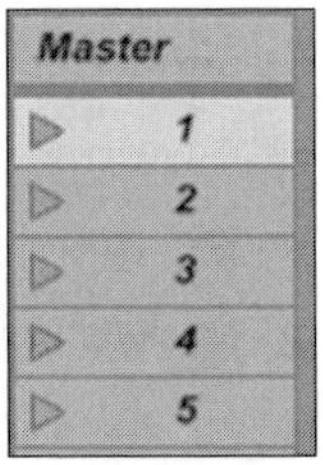

Figure 3.3 Click the triangle to launch all the clips in the scene (row).

The Session Mixer

Live's Session Mixer, seen in Figure 3.4, approximates a hardware mixer in both concept and design, but since it's a software mixer, it is also completely automatable, MIDI-mappable, and expandable. Similar to its hardware cousins, Live's Session Mixer utilizes a set of individual channel controls and a Master section.

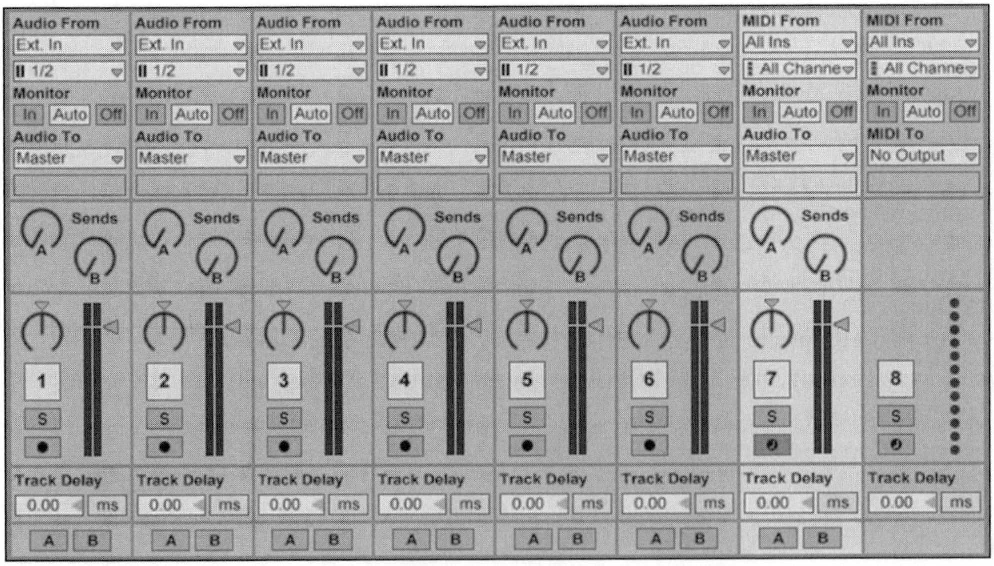

Figure 3.4 Live's Session Mixer looks similar to most other virtual mixers. Each vertical strip represents a channel with individual values for volume, panning, and routing.

If you click and drag on the top edge of the Session Mixer, you can resize the mixer so as to better see what you are doing when editing and mixing. Ableton calls this enlarged view the Pro Session Mixer (see Figure 3.5). When you make the mixer a bit bigger than the standard size, you will also see level meters, tick marks, and legends appear, all of which scale with the height of the mixer. You will also see a Peak Level/Overload button that indicates the maximum level reached during playback. Widening the mixer by dragging at the upper right-hand corner of a track's Title Bar also reveals a numeric decibel scale next to the meter.

Figure 3.5 The Pro Session Mixer gives you additional controls and readouts for better control of your final mixdowns.

Audio Tracks and Their Controls

The track shown in Figure 3.6 is an audio track. This type of track has been with Live since the beginning. You can use audio clips and audio effects (both described in detail later) on this type of track, and you can use it to record new audio clips.

The audio track outputs an audio signal that is fed into an audio channel of the Session Mixer below it. The audio channel controls give you control of the output volume, pan position, and

Figure 3.6 The audio track can house audio clips and process them with audio effects. The controls available on audio track are Volume, Pan, Mute, Solo, Record Arm, and Sends.

effect sends for the track. The buttons include the Track Activator (the large button containing the track's number), which enables the track when it's green and can also be used to mute the track; the Solo/Cue button, which routes the track to the Pre-Listen Bus; and the Record Arm button, which enables the track for recording, as well as monitoring for tracks set to Auto (monitoring will be explained in a few sections).

MIDI Tracks and Their Controls
A MIDI track without a virtual instrument inserted (Figure 3.7) does not output audio; thus, there are no Volume, Pan, or Send knobs for them in Session Mixer. You still have the Track Activator, Solo/Cue, and Arm buttons, which function the same way as their audio track counterparts. When a virtual instrument is loaded onto the track (see Chapter 7, "Using Effects and Instruments"), the full audio track controls explained previously will appear instead.

Return Tracks and Their Controls
The Return tracks (see Figure 3.8) output audio, but unlike their audio track cousins, they can't hold any clips. What good is a track that can't hold clips? While they may not add new parts to your song, they can still hold effects and can receive input from both the Send knobs and Audio Output routing. These can be used for send-style effects like reverbs and delays or to group

Figure 3.7 The MIDI track does not have a Volume or Pan control if there is no virtual instrument loaded into its Track View.

tracks together by routing the individual track outs to the Return track. Since clips can't be used on Return tracks, there is no Record Arm button. See Chapter 7 for a full explanation of Return tracks and their uses.

You Send Me Notice that even Return tracks have sends. However, by default, the sends on Return tracks are disabled. To enable them, right-click the Send knob and select Enable Send. Any send in Live can be disabled by right-clicking (Ctrl+Click Mac) it and choosing Disable Send. The Send control will now appear grayed out.

Function's Function Your computer's first eight function keys (F1 through F8) double as channel-mute shortcut keys for Live's Session Mixer. F1 works for channel 1, F2 for channel 2, and so on up to channel 8. This is an exceptionally handy tool for live performance

Figure 3.8 The Return track is basically an audio track without clip slots.

when you are looking to mute and unmute parts in a hurry—a technique employed by many DJs and electronica artists. Those using Mac laptops will need to hold the Fn key to use the function keys in this fashion or enable "Use the F1-F12 keys to control software features" in the Keyboard & Mouse System Preferences pane.

Master Track and Its Controls

The Master track, shown in Figure 3.9, is the granddaddy of them all. All tracks outputting to Master will pass through this track on their way to your speakers. You can't make or destroy the Master track, and like the Return tracks, it cannot house clips. In place of the clip slots are the Scene Launchers explained earlier. The Master track provides you with one final place to treat your mix: It has a Track View that can be loaded with effects such as mastering EQ and compression. You'll also find the Solo/Cue volume knob here, which adjusts the pre-listen level for browsing audio files and also sets the volume of the metronome.

Figure 3.9 Your entire mix will pass through the Master track, so it's a good place to add any final effects to your song.

Solo/Cue The Solo/Cue volume knob and function button are here in the Master track. The knob controls the volume of all pre-listening functions, such as soloing tracks and previewing audio files in the Browser. If you've selected unique outputs for your Cue Out (see the Audio Tab section in Chapter 2), the Solo button above the knob may be switched to Cue. When Cue is active, the Solo buttons on the audio tracks will turn to Cue buttons (little headphone icons). When you press one of these Cue buttons, Live will route that track to the Cue output without muting the other tracks. You can use this feature to listen to a track before bringing it into the mix.

Track Delay

The Track Delay feature (see Figure 3.10) is a godsend when synchronizing loops and external MIDI gear. With this feature, you can manually nudge entire tracks ahead of or behind the current

Track Delay	Track Delay	Track Delay	Track Delay
-10.00 ◀ ms	5.00 ◀ ms	68 ◀ Smp	0.00 ◀ ms

Figure 3.10 The Track Delay feature is a handy way to compensate for sluggish MIDI gear.

play location. This is handy if, for example, you have a piece of external MIDI gear that responds sluggishly. (This is more common with older MIDI devices.) If you dial in a negative Track Delay value for the MIDI track, Live will send the MIDI data to the external device just a little earlier than normal. The result is that you'll hear the external device play in time instead of sounding a little late. This parameter can also be used creatively to make a part rush or drag a bit.

New to Live 7, Track Delay can be set in samples as well as milliseconds, allowing for extremely minute adjustments. This may be particularly useful when correcting for inaccurately reported latency from plug-ins. Note that in order to hear the effects of Track Delay, Delay Compensation must be activated under the Options menu. To make the Track Delay setting visible at the bottom of each track, select the Track Delay option under the View menu.

The Crossfader

Live also features a MIDI-mappable DJ-style crossfader. (Live calls it just a plain old *crossfader*.) For over 20 years now, analog crossfaders have been making magicians out of DJs by enabling them to mix two or more tracks together, juggle those mixes, and break up monotonous loops with one simple gesture. Scratch DJs have also taken crossfader technique to incredible levels. The Live adaptation of the analog crossfader is the humble-looking horizontal slider just below the Master Volume section (see Figure 3.11). To make the crossfader visible if you can't see it, select Crossfader from the View menu.

Figure 3.11 Live's crossfader adds a whole new set of performance (and mix) tools to Live's Session View. The A and B buttons assign their respective tracks to one side of the crossfader or the other.

To use the fader, you will have to assign Session Mixer channels to either the A (left) or B (right) side of the crossfader. If you are new to crossfaders, think of it as a double-sided volume fader. As you move to the right (to increase the volume of all channels set to B), you decrease the volume of all channels set to A. The reverse holds true when you come back to the left—A channels get louder, while B channels get quieter. Any tracks assigned to neither A nor B will be played back regardless of the crossfader position. To get an idea of what you can do with this, try assigning a drum groove to A and an alternate groove to B while leaving all other parts unassigned. Now gradually flip back and forth on the crossfader.

■   By mapping a MIDI controller to control Live's crossfader, you can add a whole new performance element (see Chapter 4 for instructions on mapping). If you don't have a controller with a crossfader, you can use the modulation wheel on a keyboard, a standard fader, keys,

Figure 3.12 The crossfader is different than most of Live's controls in that it has three separate areas that can be mapped to MIDI controllers or the computer keyboard.

buttons, or even your computer keyboard. When you enter one of the Map modes (by pressing the Key or MIDI button in the upper right-hand corner), you will see that the crossfader has three sections (see Figure 3.12). Mapping the center section to a MIDI controller will give you access to the entire range of the fader, while the outer edges let you map the absolute left and right positions for fast cuts. This way, you can have a crossfader that is controlled by a single MIDI fader, three individual keys, or any combination thereof. Welcome to the future!

■ Right-clicking (Ctrl+click Mac) on the crossfader will reveal the crossfader modes. These control the volume curve that will be used when transitioning between A and B. Constant, Dipped, and Intermediate are curves that slowly change the volume across the entire range of the crossfader. With all three of these modes, you will notice a gain reduction to both sides in the center position (Dipped reduces gain the most, Constant the least). This compensates for the volume overload you get from mixing together two powerful sources like dance tracks. Fast Cut, Slow Cut, and Slow Fade have both sources at maximum amplitude before the center position is reached. Slow Fade provides the largest amount of transition between the two, with Fast Cut providing almost none, and Slow Cut is between the two.

Hideaway Live can feel a little constricted with its profusion of virtual controls. You can hide sections of the Session View by clicking the small icons to the right of the Master Volume slider. You can also turn the same sections on and off by selecting them in the View menu.

Track Input and Output Routing

Live's Session Mixer is even more flexible once you get under the hood. The Input/Output Channel Routing is capable of routing any input imaginable into a Live track from external audio and MIDI sources, ReWire clients, and other Live tracks by merely clicking the menus (see Figure 3.13) and

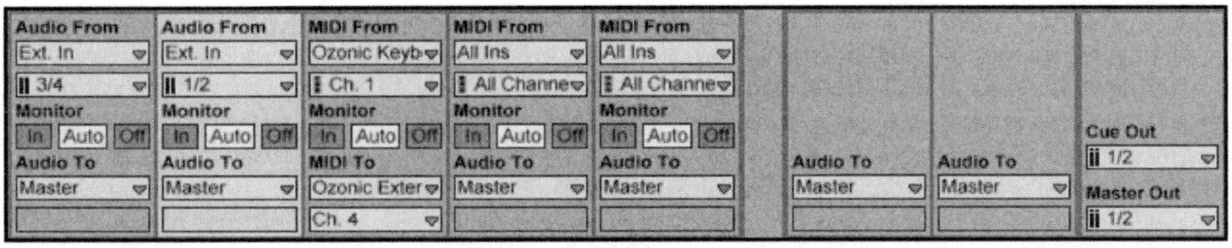

Audio From	Audio From	MIDI From	MIDI From	MIDI From				
Ext. In	Ext. In	Ozonic Keyb	All Ins	All Ins				
II 3/4	II 1/2	I Ch. 1	I All Channe	I All Channe				
Monitor	Monitor	Monitor	Monitor	Monitor				Cue Out
In Auto Off	In Auto Off	In Auto Off	In Auto Off	In Auto Off				II 1/2
Audio To	Audio To	MIDI To	Audio To	Audio To	Audio To	Audio To		Master Out
Master	Master	Ozonic Exter	Master	Master	Master	Master		II 1/2
		Ch. 4						

Figure 3.13 The Input/Output Channel Routing strip. In Live, you have the choice of configuring input type and channel, as well as output type and channel for audio and MIDI tracks. Return tracks only have the output options.

picking your source. The input source is labeled *Audio From,* and the output destination is labeled *Audio To.* Any multichannel input, such as an eight-channel soundcard or multiple-output software such as Propellerhead's Reason, can have inputs routed to correspond with any given channel. If, for example, you want Microphone Input number one to be recorded on Session Mixer channel one (or any other), the drop-down menus will accomplish this.

Mixer routings have been made even more flexible by the addition of Pre FX, Post FX, and Post Mixer options (see Figure 3.14). These new options will appear in the mixer's input section whenever you have selected another track as the track input.

Figure 3.14   The new Pre FX, Post FX, and Post Mixer options give you more control over internal mixer routings.

Any ReWire applications currently residing on your computer will also be seen in the Audio From drop-down menu. (ReWire is a software-linking technology invented by Propellerhead that allows Live to run, control, or be controlled by programs such as Reason, SONAR, Cubase, and Pro Tools. See Chapter 11, "ReWire," for the lowdown.) By routing a ReWire application through Live's inputs, you will be able to monitor and record that application's audio output as you would another audio source.

You will also see Resampling in the Inputs section. This is available in case you want to send Live's own output to itself—for instance, if you have finished a track and want to render your song in real time, or if you want to make a quick submix of more than one track. These various inputs and methods will be covered in the next three chapters.

Cloning and Grouping Tracks Live's Input/Output section can be used to feed audio or MIDI from one track to many other tracks. For example, you could send one MIDI clip to multiple tracks and trigger different instruments to create a layered sound. It's also possible to send the output from multiple tracks into a single track. This could be useful for creating a submix from a group of individually miked drum tracks.

Splitting one track's output into multiple tracks is done by setting the input source on the receiving tracks to the source track. To send a group of tracks into a single track, set the output destination of each track to the track you want to group them into. Set the monitor switch to In on the destination track in order to have the audio or MIDI from the source pass through it.

Arrangement View

Beginners may think of it as merely Live's "other" window, but Arrangement View (seen in Figure 3.15), is the place for recording and editing your Live Session View jams, performing overdubs, automating additional effects, and rendering your final track. If Session View is the spontaneous right-brain-tickling creative screen, Arrangement View is the analytic left-brain-stimulating, "finishing touches" side of Live. You may notice that Live's Arrangement View closely resembles many other multitrack applications' Arranger screens. Many other programs, such as Digital Performer, SONAR, Cubase, Logic, and Pro Tools, are based on horizontal, left-to-right audio arrangers (also called *linear-based arrangers*). If you like this method of working, you will be right at home making music in Live's Arrangement style.

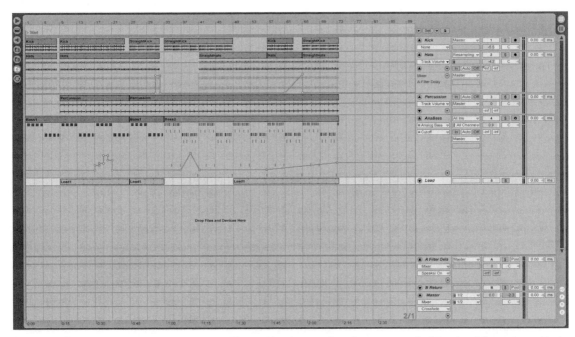

Figure 3.15 Live's Arrangement View will contain the results of your recorded Session View songs. Each horizontal line in Arrangement View represents a track that corresponds to a vertical channel in the Session Mixer.

For those who didn't read the figure caption, here it is again: Each track in Session View corresponds precisely to its track counterpart in Arrangement View. If you have eight tracks in Session

View, you will have eight tracks in Arrangement View. You can add a track in either view, and it will appear in the other as if you were working on the same project—because you are.

There is, however, a very important distinction between Session View and Arrangement View. Once you record your music from Session View into Arrangement View, you will hear your new arrangement (playing from Arrangement View) until you override it by executing a control in Session View or by actively moving a previously automated control.

This is actually a great feature, but it can baffle those making the switch from a traditional linear-based sequencer application. The idea rests on Session View being a palette for your musical "painting" in Arrangement View. You can record a single run-through (a take) and then move to Arrangement View to edit your song to completion. Or you can do multiple takes or punch-ins by again activating Global Recording and overdubbing additional song parts into Arrangement View from Session View. This is also a great method for touching up previously recorded automation data.

This is an extremely important concept to grasp, so let's look at it a bit more closely by loading up the example Set titled Automation.als. After you have loaded the file, which can be found in the Examples → Chapter 3 folder in the online examples (see http://www.courseptr.com/downloads), follow the steps below.

1. When you load Automation.als, you will be looking at a simple song in Live's Arrangement View. Press the Tab key on your computer keyboard to switch to Session View.

2. Take a look at the Session Mixer and notice all the red markings. These markings mean that the knob, fader, or button has associated automation data in the Arrangement View. (Automation data consists of the recorded movements of every fader, knob, or button you moved when you did your Live recording.) Press the spacebar and watch all these controls move automatically as the song plays.

3. Now move the volume slider on Track 2. Notice that the red blip on this control turns gray, and the red light on the Back to Arrangement button (in the Control Bar) lights up. You have now told Live to ignore that specific fader's automation and use your manual setting. This fader will no longer move automatically as you play the song.

4. To reinstate the automation—so you can listen to the song's original recording settings—simply press the red Back to Arrangement button on the Control Bar to the right of the Record button. Notice how Track 2's fader level jumps back to its original position.

Session or Arrangement? Important: Any time you move a control that has been automated, Live ceases playback of that particular control's automation. The same holds true for clips: Any time you launch a clip from Session View, it will override the clip that was playing back on the corresponding track in the Arrangement View. If you flip to the Arrangement View you'll see that the clip on the corresponding track is now faded out, indicating its inactivity.

Bear in mind that you can only be sure that you are hearing the mix from Arrangement View when the Back to Arrangement button is unlit (Figure 3.16). You should always double-check exactly what you are hearing (either your recorded arrangement as-is or Arrangement clips and automation combined with Session clips and manual settings) if Live seems to be "misbehaving."

Figure 3.16 Whether you are in Arrangement View or Session View, you can always revert to the Arrangement View's mix settings, which usually contain automation, by pressing the Back to Arrangement button.

This view-dependent mixer setting concept constitutes a drastic difference from other recording applications you may be used to. The reasoning here is simple: You will want to hear entirely different settings on your improvised remix or jam than you will on a finished piece of music. It can be handy to remove the automation or, if you are in Session View, to hear the automation at a moment's notice. For this reason, and others we will delve into later, remember that Arrangement and Session View track settings are not always the same mix—hence, they will not necessarily sound the same.

Icon Flip In the upper-right corner of the Live window are two icons: one with three vertical lines and one with three horizontal lines. These icons can be used to switch between the Session and Arrangement Views. You access the Session View using the icon with the vertical lines (tracks in the Session View are oriented vertically) and the Arrangement View using the other icon with its horizontal lines.

Track Settings and Contents

The Arrangement View's track settings are located on the right side of the screen and take up about one-third of the working portion of the Arrangement View, as seen in Figure 3.17. To maximize (view) a track, click the downward-pointing triangle. Any clips on that track will reveal their contents and several hidden track settings.

Each Arrangement track is still bound by the same rules as the tracks in Session View. Only one clip can play at a time in an Arrangement track. You can add clips to Arrangement tracks the same way you added them to the Session View. Simply drag the desired file from the File

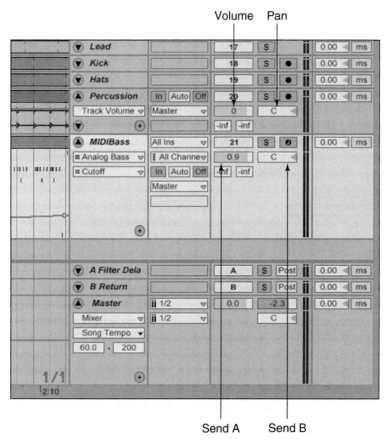

Figure 3.17 Each track in Arrangement View has the same controls as the tracks in Session View. This makes sense since the Arrangement tracks and Session tracks are actually the same.

Browser into an Arrangement track. The clip will appear, and you will be able to move it, copy it, lengthen or shorten it, and perform other editing features described in the Arrangement section of Chapter 4.

Volume, Panning, FX Sends, Solo, Mute, Arm for Recording, and the same track routing features found in the Session Mixer are still accessible in Arrangement View. The only difference is visual: The controls have been turned on their sides and are represented by values instead of graphical controls. The Session Mixer's Master Settings are located on the bottom line of Live's Arrangement View.

Relation to the Session View

Though the Arrangement and Session Views seem like two different sections in the Live environment, they are actually closely related to one another. In Live, there are two places to arrange and play clips: the Arrangement View and Session View. However, there is only one mixer in Live, and this means that the Arrangement and Session Views need to share it. Just as only one clip can be playing on a track at a time, only one track—either from the Session or Arrangement View—can be fed into a mixer channel at a time.

If you are playing clips on a track in the Session View, they will override any clips in the associated track of the Arrangement View. When you press the Back to Arrangement button, the tracks in the Arrangement View will take over, and all clips in the Session View will stop.

This relationship between the two views means that you can arrange a song in the Arrangement View but begin improvising in the Session View. When your improvisation is done, press the Back to Arrangement button, and your preset Arrangement View will take over.

Overview

Standing tall above Live's Arrangement/Session Views and just below the Control Bar is the Overview of your Live Arrangement (see Figure 3.18). The Overview, which resembles a musical staff, is there purely for navigation and reference to show you where you are in your arrangement. So long as you have clips in Live's Arrangement View, it offers a bird's-eye view of your entire composition. You will see tiny colored lines representing your clips in the Arrangement View. You can hide the Overview by pressing Ctrl+Alt+O on a PC, or Option+Cmd+O on a Mac.

Figure 3.18 Live's Overview is a view from above.

To use the Overview to move to a new location, place the cursor over the portion of the Overview bar you want to move to, and the magnifying-glass icon will appear; click once, and you will be moved to the corresponding location in the arrangement. To zoom in and out, hover over the Overview bar, depress the mouse button (left on PC), and move the mouse up and down to zoom in and out, respectively. Clicking and moving the mouse left or right will move the visible area of the arrangement. You can skip quickly from the beginning to the end with one click of the mouse—though we should point out that you will still need to place your cursor in the desired location and then press your spacebar to start playback. Try this a couple of times, because it takes some getting used to.

Tab = Flip To see Live's other screen, simply press the Tab key; for example, if you're in the Session View, press Tab, and the Arrangement View window will appear. Press Tab once again to return to Session View and then, just for fun, hit F11 to see Live's full screen view (or F11 again to go back to Live's previous dimensions).

Note that Mac users with Exposé enabled will have to use Ctrl+F11 to enter full screen view. Or you can enter your Exposé settings (in the System Preferences) and reassign the F11 function to another key.

The Live Control Bar

Headlining each of Live's two working views (Session and Arrangement) is Live's own version of a transport bar. Typically, transport bars function as the start/stop mechanism and song position finder all in one. Although transport bars are often free-floating in many other applications, in Live the Control Bar (see Figure 3.19) is fixed to the top of your screen. Still, most power users default to keyboard shortcuts such as the spacebar for starting and stopping playback, rarely using the icons at the top of the screen. Also, many Live aficionados map Live's Control Bar functions to MIDI or computer keyboard controls. We will cover this in detail later in this section.

Figure 3.19 Live's Control Bar remains constant at the top of both of Live's main views. Here you will find standard symbols for Stop, Play, and Record, as well as time/tempo information and other project parameters.

In the Control Bar, you will find pertinent song information, such as time signature, tempo, and processor load (a vital stat for the computer-based musician). The Control Bar will also help you pinpoint your exact location within the song and determine Live's Master Quantize settings, and a Tap Tempo and metronome make recording your Live projects from scratch just a tad more manageable.

Tempo, Time Signature, and Groove Controls

On the left side of the Control Bar, you will find settings for song parameters (see Figure 3.20). The buttons are (from left to right): External Sync Switch, External Sync Indicators, Tap Tempo, Tempo, Tempo Nudge, Time Signature, Groove Amount, and Metronome.

Figure 3.20 This subsection of the Control Bar is devoted to time, including MIDI Sync, Tempo, and Time Signature.

You won't see the External controls unless you've already set up an external sync source or destination in the MIDI/Sync Preferences tab (see Chapter 2, "Getting Live Up and Running"). You'll need to do this if you want Live's tempo to be set by an external device or if you want Live to control the tempo of a drum machine, synth, or sequencer. The External Sync switch engages or disengages Live's MIDI synchronization to an outside source, while the monitoring lights announce that the MIDI sync signal is being sent or received.

The Tap Tempo button is a handy song-starting feature in Live. For a quick test drive of one of Tap Tempo's features, click the button four times, and your project will begin at that tempo. This is a handy feature if you need to sync up with your drummer or match another device such as a turntable or CD player. You can also use Tap Tempo to help map out songs and align groove clips better. Sound confusing? Don't worry, Chapter 5 and Chapter 6 will clear it up.

Next up are Live's project Tempo and Time Signature settings, which are found just to the right of the Tap Tempo button. Live can handle tempos ranging form 20 to 999 BPM (beats per minute) and time signatures with numerators ranging from 1 to 99 and denominator choices of 1, 2, 4, 8, and 16—a huge range of possibilities.

Moving to the right of Time Signature, you come to Tempo Nudge Down, followed by Tempo Nudge Up. These controls are used to momentarily change Live's master tempo in order to bring it into sync with another source, much the way a DJ beat matches two tracks by physically dragging the record back or speeding it up slightly before letting go of it. Tapping these controls will yield very slight tempo changes (less than 1 BPM), while holding them down can be used to slow the tempo to a third of its original value or speed it up by as much as two-thirds. Releasing either control immediately returns Live to its original tempo.

Next comes the Global Groove control, a number between 0 and 100. This allows you to set the global "swing" amount as a percentage, the amount by which all MIDI and audio clips will be played back in a swing rather than a straight feel. This function is explained further in Chapters 5, 6, and 7 in the sections about MIDI and audio clips.

Finally, we come to Live's Metronome button. When this button is engaged, you will hear a click (metronome) that can serve as a guide for new recordings and help with loop editing. The volume of the click can be adjusted by using the Solo/Cue volume knob in Live's Master track (the same knob you use for adjusting the preview volume when browsing for samples).

Data Entry All numeric controls in Live, such as the tempo, can be adjusted in two ways. You can click on the control and type in a value, or you can click and drag your mouse up or down. The Tempo control also has a nifty shortcut available. To adjust the Fine Tempo (the values to the right of the decimal point), hold down the Cmd key (Ctrl on the PC) while dragging.

Transport, MIDI, and Quantization Controls

Most starting and stopping in Live is best handled with the spacebar (tap it once to start, tap it again to stop); however, the second area of Live's Control Bar (Figure 3.21) has Start and Stop buttons. You will also find the Arrangement Record, MIDI Overdub, and Back to Arrangement buttons here, which you will use during the track-editing process.

Figure 3.21   Here is the second element of Live's Control Bar. Keep your eye on the Quantization menu. This is the key to sounding like a pro when you fire off your loops.

Other points of interest include the Arrangement Position box and the Global Quantization menu. The Arrangement Position box provides a continuous readout—in measures, beats, and subdivisions—of where you are in the song, whether you're listening or recording. You can manually enter a start time value into this box or drag up and down with the mouse to change the setting.

The Quantization menu, to the right of the Record button, sets the launch timing for clips that are set to Global Quantization (more on this in Chapter 4). You have the option of selecting 1/32, 1/16, 1/8, 1/4, 1/2, and multiples of the full bar. What this means is that each clip triggered in the Session View will "fire" at the very next subdivision you have selected. For instance, at the Bar setting, your "fired" clip will not begin to play until the first beat of the very next measure. If your setting is 1/16, your clip will begin playing at the next 1/16 note. You can imagine how this quantitative correction tool will clean up your performance. This can be a huge help and a very cool trick for guiding rapid-fire sample sections or just ensuring that your next scene launches right on the first beat.

If you want your music to breathe more, or you're working in a context where referring to a master tempo is undesirable, you can also set this menu to None for no quantization at all. Any clip (set to Global) will sound the instant it is launched.

Punch In/Out and Loop

This section of Live's Control Bar, shown in Figure 3.22, is used in conjunction with the Arrangement View. The outermost controls are the two loop points: the start and the end. They also double as the punch-in and punch-out locations. In the center of this section is the Loop switch. When depressed, Live's playback will loop (the defined start/end length) continuously, as opposed to playing though to the end of the song. If the two punch points (located next to the start/end controls) are activated, Live can be set to record a select length of audio or MIDI without you having to worry about accidentally going over sections you want to leave alone. We will cover recording in detail in later chapters, so don't worry if this description seems a little brief.

Figure 3.22 Live's Loop Start and Loop End controls also double as the punch-in and punch-out locations.

Computer Keyboard, Key and MIDI Assigns, System Performance, and MIDI I/O

The fourth segment of the Control Bar (see Figure 3.23) is the system-monitoring and Key/MIDI setup area. The keyboard icon on the left turns MIDI input from the alphanumeric computer keyboard on and off; this is a feature that allows you to use your computer's keyboard as a MIDI

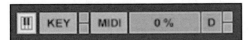

Figure 3.23 Pictured above is the fourth segment of Live's Control Bar. From here, you can monitor your hardware (CPU load and MIDI input/output action) and set up your Key and MIDI controls.

input device, which can be handy when working on a laptop on the go. We will cover the many ways to configure MIDI and computer-keyboard triggering and controls in Chapters 4, 5, and 6; however, we should point out that the Key (Key Map Mode switch) and MIDI (MIDI Map Mode switch) buttons are your entrance points to controlling Live without using your mouse. Ableton was ingenious enough to make sure that all MIDI and keyboard mapping could be done on the fly, without ever stopping playback—no small feat.

Knowing how much gas is left in the tank—or whether you're running on fumes—is important in the computer world. Here to help, Live's CPU Load Meter continuously shows the amount of strain on your system for audio processing. If this bar approaches 100 percent, you may begin to experience performance degradation or audio dropouts. The Hard Disk Overload Indicator (the letter "D") just to the right of the CPU meter will flicker red if your computer is not able to get data from the hard drive quickly enough. This will also result in dropouts and usually occurs because your hard drive is too slow for the number of audio clips you are trying to play back simultaneously.

Midi Prognosis The last two indicators, just right of the Disk Overload Indicator, represent MIDI input and MIDI output signal presence by lighting up (turning colors) when Live is sending or receiving MIDI signals.

The two similar indicators between the MIDI Map Mode and Key Map Mode buttons will illuminate when an incoming message is assigned to a MIDI Remote function.

Live's Custom Views

Live also hosts several windows that can be hidden and are accessible in both Session and Arrangement Views. These secondary windows enable you to explore your loops and files, Live's devices, plug-in effects, and Live's integrated Info menu. Unlike most configurable software applications, these windows pop up or close with the click of a single triangle-shaped icon (see Figures 3.24 and 3.25). For instance, if you are working on a song arrangement, you will not need to have the File Browser open; or, if you are familiar with Live, you can close the Info View to give more space to the Clip and Track Views. After some experimentation, you will discover your favorite working views in Session or Arrangement View. The idea is that you may want to hide collapsible windows in order to maximize screen real estate.

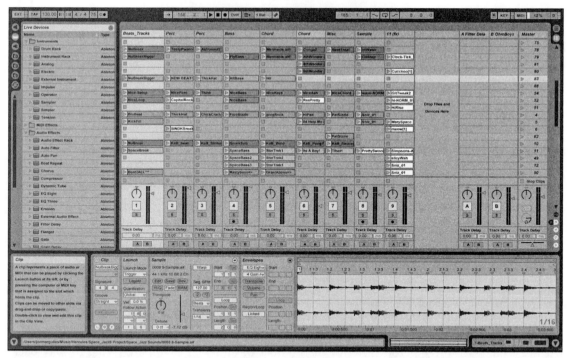

Figure 3.24 Live's Session View with the Browser, Info, and Clip View (Chapter 5) maximized (open).

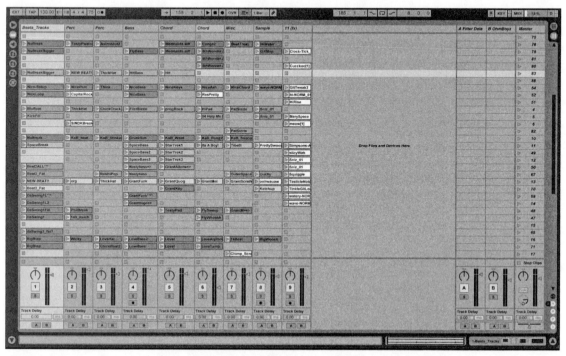

Figure 3.25 With Browser, Info, and Clip View closed, Live's screen is wide open. You'll be able to see a greater number of tracks and clips this way.

The Browser

The Browser window (see Figure 3.26) provides the means to access all of the prefab elements you will add to a Live Set. It provides quick access to three different locations on your hard drive for finding samples and MIDI files; it houses all of your Live Devices and their presets; and it provides a listing of all external plug-in devices located by Live. The Browser is retractable and located in the upper-left section of either the Session or Arrangement View. By clicking the leftward-pointing triangle-shaped arrow, you can hide this window. Conversely, if the arrow is pointing toward the right, simply click once to view the Browser.

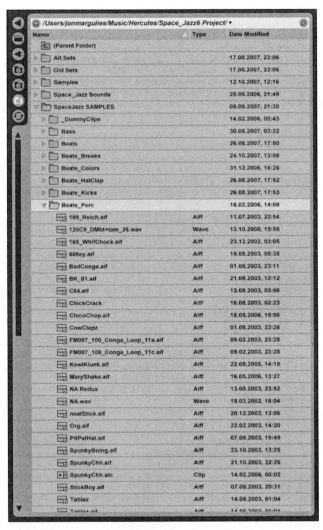

Figure 3.26 Located on the far and upper left-hand side are Live's internal Device, Plug-in, and File Browsers.

File Browsers

Warning! Do not underestimate the power of Live's Browser. With it, audio and MIDI can be previewed in real time at the project tempo. There are a few other audio sequencers that can pull this off, such as Cakewalk's SONAR and Sony's Acid Pro, but most other programs require some preformatting before they can provide this kind of preview. Previewing can be toggled off and on by clicking the miniature set of headphones that are uppermost on the left side of the Browser. When Preview is on, simply click a file in the Browser, and Live will begin previewing it on the next downbeat. Please note that this tiny headphone button will only be visible at the top of the Browser when one of the File Browser folder buttons is selected.

Cuing the Mix You can adjust the volume of loops heard via Live's pre-listening feature by rotating the virtual Solo/Cue volume knob on Live's mixer. In Session mode, you will see this control near the bottom of the master channel in the lower-right corner of your mixer. In the Arrangement View, the Solo/Cue volume appears as a number in a blue box located to the right of master channel output.

When the Solo/Cue switch is set to Cue, the pre-listen output will be routed to the Cue Out instead of the master, enabling you to preview files during a performance. Whether you do this or not all depends on how you like to work. Some people don't use the Browser during a performance at all—they already have all of their files in the Session View.

Drag and Drop

If you happen to like the sounds you are hearing when previewing loops, simply drag and drop the part(s) into either the Session or Arrangement View. You can place the loop in a clip slot in Session View or onto a track (at any point you like) in Arrangement View. The sound file can then be accessed immediately in Live's Clip View.

Conversely, if you like a clip that you've created using Live's clip settings and effects, you can drag the clip from Live back into the Browser to store a new *Live clip* there. You will then have access to this new clip in any project you work on in the future. When you drag it back into an empty track in another project, the original effects and instruments associated with the clip will automatically be loaded into the track. You can also perform this trick on multiple clips simultaneously. If you select a group of clips and drag them over to the Browser, Live will create a new Live Set in this location with tracks for all the clips you're saving.

Another feature of the File Browser is the ability to drag portions of Live Sets, or even entire Sets, into your current project. When you see a Live Set in the Browser (indicated by the Live icon and the file extension .als), you will see a small triangle in front of it, just like you see in front of the folders. You can click this triangle to "unfold" the Live Set so you can see the individual tracks in the Set. You can drag any of the tracks or the entire Set right into your current project. Additionally, if you drag these new elements into empty tracks or into the empty space in the Session or Arrangement View, Live will reload all of the effects and instruments associated with the parts.

On top of all this, the Live Browser works almost identically to Explorer (on the PC) or Finder (on the Mac). You can drag and drop files and folders from one location into another, use the Copy, Cut, and Paste commands (Ctrl/Cmd+C, Ctrl/Cmd+X, and Ctrl/Cmd+V, respectively), as well as rename and delete files. Right-clicking [Ctrl+clicking on Mac] on a Live Set or other file in the Browser will bring up a contextual menu with options for searching, renaming, deleting, and creating folders and clips.

Navigating the Browser

The default position of Live's File Browser will be the same position that you were searching when you last closed Live. To facilitate faster manual searches, Live enables you to set up shortcuts within three different File Browser placeholders (seen in Figure 3.27). These will save you time, as well as aid in the time-consuming process of organizing your loops for a live show

Figure 3.27   The File Browser placeholders. They may be tiny, but they are a mighty big time saver.

At the top of the Browser, just below the Tap, Tempo, and Time Signature information, is the title bar (Figure 3.28). You will see a set of headphones at the upper-left corner; this is Live's Preview button, which allows you to preview clips (see above). The title of the window will be either one of Live's default locations, such as the Library (Live's preloaded library of samples presets), or the path of the folder you are currently browsing. This is followed by a small down arrow; click here to view a list of other locations on your computer and jump to them quickly. In addition to the default locations, you will also see a list of folders you have bookmarked, allowing you to jump to them quickly. You can bookmark a folder in the Browser by right-clicking (Ctrl+clicking on Mac) and choosing Bookmark Folder from the context menu that pops up.

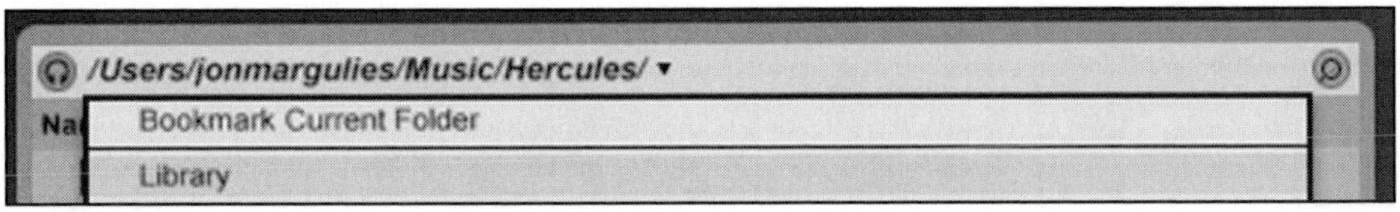

/Users/jonmargulies/Music/Hercules/ ▾	◎
Na	Bookmark Current Folder
	Library

Figure 3.28   The Browser's header bar and drop-down menu.

Further to the right in the title bar, you will also see a small magnifying glass symbol; clicking here will cause the Browser's search box to appear, allowing you to search the folder you are viewing for a particular file or clip.

You can navigate the Browser more easily by setting important locations in advance. Since you have three separate File Browser Choosers, you can set three different locations. Here's how to do it:

1. Open Live's Browser and click one of the File Browser Choosers (the file folder icons numbered 1, 2, and 3).

2. Next, click into the folder you would like to browse sounds from by cycling down the file folder tree. You may need to click through several folders to get to the one you are after.

3. Now double-click on the folder you would like Live to default to for this File Browser. You can also right-click on the folder and Set as Root from the context menu. This location will now be opened whenever you select this Browser. The path to this folder will also appear in the title bar of the Browser.

4. If you change your mind or want to go back to a folder that you cannot see, double-click Parent Folder at the top of the Browser to work your way up through the hierarchy. Alternately, you can click the small down arrow just to the right of the path name and select All Volumes to work your way down from the top.

Searching for Files

You can also search for files in Live 7 using the Search function in the Browser (see Figure 3.29). This will allow you to find files in your collection by typing in keywords for your search. You can search within the current root folder by clicking the small magnifying glass at the upper-right of

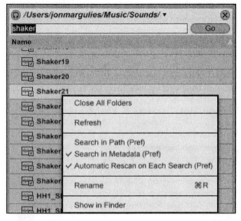

Figure 3.29 Search preferences can be adjusted by right-clicking in the search results.

the title bar; you can also search within a given subfolder by right-clicking (Ctrl+clicking on Mac) on the folder you want to search and choosing Search in Folder. In this case, Live will only search within that folder for your desired sounds. This can help speed up or narrow your search by limiting the scope.

The first time you try to search for something, it may take longer than usual because Live is building an index of your files. On subsequent searches, Live will reference the index file and render faster search results, as long as Automatic Rescan on Each Search is turned off in the File/Folder tab of your preferences. Live can keep the index up to date as long as files are moved to and from the search location through the Browser, but if files are changed outside of Live, the index will be out of date, and new files will not be found. When Automatic Rescan is turned off, the Stop/Go button next to the search field becomes the Rescan button, so you can force a full rescan of the search location and find any files that may have been missed.

Organizing Your Files

In an effort to keep workflow smooth, you can rename your clips and samples right inside the Browser. This can be an enormous time saver and creative tool when composing in Live. To rename a loop, simply highlight the loop in the Browser and then press keyboard shortcut keys Ctrl/Cmd+R. You may also do this via the menu by highlighting the loop and selecting Edit → Rename, or by right-clicking on the file and choosing Rename from the context menu. Press Return to complete renaming the file or ESC to cancel and revert to the file's original name.

It is a good idea to develop a system of organizing your loop/sample collection that works effectively for you. It is important that your naming scheme is informative and promotes creativity. For instance, if you name every drum loop sequentially, drumloop1, drumloop2, drumloop3, etc., this may be definitive, but it will ultimately not be inspiring to work with. We try to come up with short titles that give us a brief idea of what we were thinking when we first made a given group of loops. For instance, bigloudDR1 and bigloudDR2 would be a couple of big loud drum loops. A method I like to use is to create folders for each category of samples and MIDI clips we have. We have folders titled Bass, Drums, Chords, Effects, and Vox. This makes it easy to find the parts I'm looking for.

The Device Browser

Live's Device Browser (see Figure 3.30) contains Ableton's own brew of effects and instruments. Each device type has its own folder in the Browser, one each for instruments, MIDI effects, and audio effects. Each device also has its own folder(s) containing presets. The Device Browser is accessed through the button with the box icon at the left edge of the Browser window.

We will explain each of Live's wonderful devices and how you can incorporate AU/VST effects and instruments in Chapter 8, "Live's Instruments." For now, it's enough to know that when you double-click one of Live's devices, you'll instantly add (or plug in) an instance of the selected device into the channel you have highlighted.

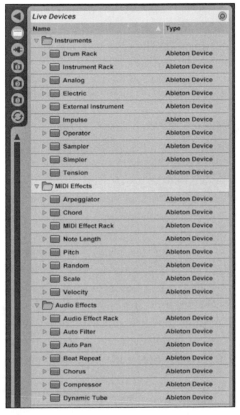

Figure 3.30 Live's Device menu. To add an effect or instrument, highlight the track you want to receive the device and then double-click the device in the list.

The Plug-in Browser

The Plug-in Browser allows you to access your third-party software effects and plug-ins. You can use a wide variety of third-party plug-ins with Live, in either VST (PC/Mac) or AU (Mac only) formats.

On the PC side, all of your VST plug-ins need to be in the VST folder that Live searches at each startup. If you've been following along, you already set this folder up when you read about Live's Preferences in Chapter 2. We recommend giving Live its own VST folder and simply copying all VST plug-ins you would like to run in Live into that folder. Any Live-compatible plug-ins in this folder will be visible when you click on the small power-plug icon to the left of the Browser window, as shown in Figure 3.31. See Chapter 8 for the rundown on using external plug-ins in Live.

If you are using a Mac, you don't need to worry about the location of your plug-ins, because the Mac OS will always store them in the same default location. You can find your plug-ins and see what you have installed by checking the folder Macintosh HD → Library → Audio → Plug-ins. Within this folder, the Components subfolder holds your AU (Audio Unit) plug-ins, and the VST folder contains your VST plug-ins (duh!). If you delete a plug-in from one of these folders, you won't see it any longer in Live.

Note that there is also a small magnifying glass in the top bar of the Plug-in Browser, enabling you to search for a specific plug-in by name. This can be a helpful feature if you have a very large number of plug-ins installed on your system!

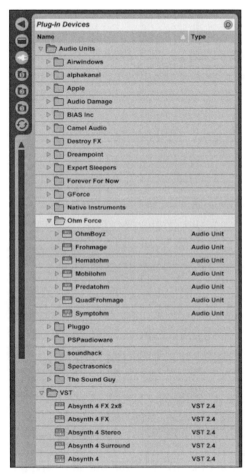

Figure 3.31 The Plug-in Browser will look different for everybody since it reflects your own unique collection of effects and instruments.

I Want My VST If a particular VST plug-in cannot be seen via Live's Browser, then it cannot be used in Live—even if it is located in the correct directory on your PC or Mac. Be sure to move (delete) these plug-ins out of the VST folder that you told Live to look in when you set up Live's File/Folder preferences. As a result, Live will start up faster. Also, if you notice a plug-in not working properly in Live, you should also take it out of the plug-in directory, write down the settings or combination of events that created the error, and send Ableton and the third-party plug-in manufacturer the feedback. By doing so, you may just help some small software developer zero in on a problem that would otherwise take them months to figure out on their own.

The Hot-Swap Browser

This Browser allows you to exchange samples and try different combinations of sounds in Ableton's Simpler, Impulse, and Sampler instruments. (See Chapter 7 for more on these instruments.) This works much the way hot-swapping effects presets does. When the mouse hovers over a sample slot in one of these instruments, a small Browse or "hot-swap" button will appear. Clicking this will take you automatically to the Hot-Swap Browser; here you can click on an individual sample's Browse button to swap the samples.

Saving Your Work

If you are a Pro Tools or Logic veteran, you know that calling up last week's session from a CD you burned that night might not be so simple. Live features an enhanced file-saving scheme sure to reduce at least some of the frustrating missing file searches and "which version am I working in?" blues.

Saving the Live Set

Live offers four ways to save project files: Save Live Set, Save Live Set As, Save a Copy, and Collect All and Save. If you are familiar with common computer documents, such as word processor applications, Save and Save As work in exactly the way you'd expect. Save, which can be done by pressing Ctrl/Cmd+S, saves the document (in this case a Live song file called a *Set*) in its present state, under its present file name. This is the most common way you will save while you are working on a new song, especially when you like the results.

Save Live Set As, done using Ctrl/Cmd+Shift key+S, is the command for saving the current song file in its current state under a *different* name and is usually done only when you want to begin a new song or modify an existing song without changing the original version. To do this, select File → Save Live Set As, select the location where you would like to place the file, and type the song's newest name.

If you are modifying a song but would like to preserve a copy of it in its current state, use File → Save a Copy. This command is the same as Save As in that it allows you to save the file under a new name, but instead of opening the newly named copy, the Save a Copy command will keep the version you are currently working on open, while simply saving the new copy to disk.

The first time you save a set under a particular name, Live 7 will automatically create a folder with that name + *Project* to hold all the files associated with the Set.

Collect All and Save

The most comprehensive save method is undoubtedly Collect All and Save. (For you Live veterans, this is the same as Save Set Self-Contained in earlier versions of Live.) It is a terrible inconvenience (to put it mildly) to lose a file. Collect All and Save eliminates this problem by guaranteeing that all files related to a given project are copied into a new folder labeled (Your Song Name) + *Project*. This includes all the audio and MIDI files you may be using.

Sounds great, doesn't it? Imagine never ever having a problem again locating a file, opening a song on a different computer, e-mailing a track to a buddy, or just coming back two days later and not having any trouble recalling your song just as you had left it.

To save your Live Set this way, select File → Collect All and Save and then navigate to the folder where you would like to place the song (and all of its related files).

Even though saving your files this way does sound all-encompassing, and it does work wonders for keeping all your files in the same easy-to-locate folder, keep in mind that any external plug-ins (VST and AU) used in a given song will not be saved inside your file. This means that if you transport your song to a different computer, all of the plug-ins used on your song must be present on that computer as well. Unless you know you'll have all the necessary plug-ins on the system you are moving to, it's a good idea to freeze plug-in dependent tracks before moving your session (see Chapter 4).

Collect All and Save is the best method for saving any Live song. You can try just saving the file and keeping your audio where it is, but my experience and that of many expert audio users is that if you do so, you will inevitably be referring to the next section of this book at some point.

Saving multiple versions is an essential part of any experienced producer's process. How often you save a new copy is up to you. The important thing is to leave a "breadcrumb trail"—a record of what changed when. Having done this, you can recover previous settings in case they are accidentally lost, or you can simply decide you don't like the direction you've gone in and go back and try again.

Managing Files

No matter how careful you are, it's going to happen—files will get lost or misplaced, or you're going to occasionally get confused about where all those great sounds from last year's project came from. The good news is that Live's File Manager is here to help you get a handle on what's going on.

Select Manage Files from the File menu to open the File Manager. When it opens, you'll be given the option to manage either the current Set, the current project, or the Live Library.

- **Manage Set:** This will present you with options and information pertaining only to the current Set. You can locate missing samples, collect external sample files into the project folder, or simply view all of the samples in your Set.

- **Manage Project:** Remember what we just said about saving multiple versions? When you've done this, using the Manage Project feature is very useful. For example, it can tell you how many external samples you have for every version of your Set and collect them into the project folder, so you can make sure your project is self-contained for each and every version of your Set that you have saved.

- **Manage Library:** This feature will give you information about all of the presets and samples stored in your Live Library. It can be used to get your Library back into shape if files have gotten moved or lost.

Manage Set

Let's take a look at what happens when you choose Manage Set. Figure 3.32 shows the window entitled Current Live Set that opens when you choose this option. Like all of the File Manager's windows, it's broken into several sections, each with a small triangle to the left that can be used to hide or show the section. The first section is View and Replace Samples. Clicking the View Samples button will reveal a list of all of the samples used in the Set (see Figure 3.33). The Location column next to the sample name will tell you if the file is located within the project folder, in an external location, or is missing. Clicking the Edit button to the left of the sample name will open the file in the audio editor you have specified in the File/Folder tab of the Preferences screen.

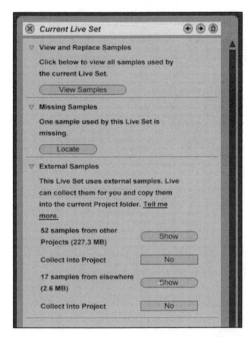

Figure 3.32 Manage Set gives you information about the locations of the files in your set.

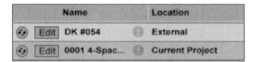

Figure 3.33 View Samples reveals the sample list, which shows you the name and location of the samples in your set. You can replace samples or open your audio editor from here as well.

Clicking the Hot Swap button to the left of the sample name will reveal the file's location in the File Browser. While the Hot Swap button is highlighted, any file you double-click in the File Browser will be used to globally replace that sample in your Set. That means that any clip that is based on this sample will be updated to use the new sample. All of the other properties (such as loop points and transposition) of the clip will be retained. Another way to globally replace samples in your Set is to simply drag a file out of the File Browser and drop it into the File Manager—directly on to the sample you want to replace.

Looking at the title bar of the File Manager (see Figure 3.32), you'll notice a set of three Web Browser style buttons in the upper right-hand corner. You can use the Back button (the left-pointing arrow) to return to the Set Management overview. If at any point you want to return to the main File Manager window, you can use the Home button on the far right.

Finding Lost Files
Below the View and Replace Samples section of the Manage Set window (see Figure 3.32) is the Missing Files section. Clicking the Locate button in this section will bring up a list of missing samples in the Set (see Figure 3.34). Instead of having a Hot Swap button next to these samples, there is a Search button, which can be used to execute a search for the file in the Browser. Before you use the Search button, make sure to select the Hot Swap Browser first (see the section on the Browser earlier in this chapter) and navigate to the location where you want to search for the file.

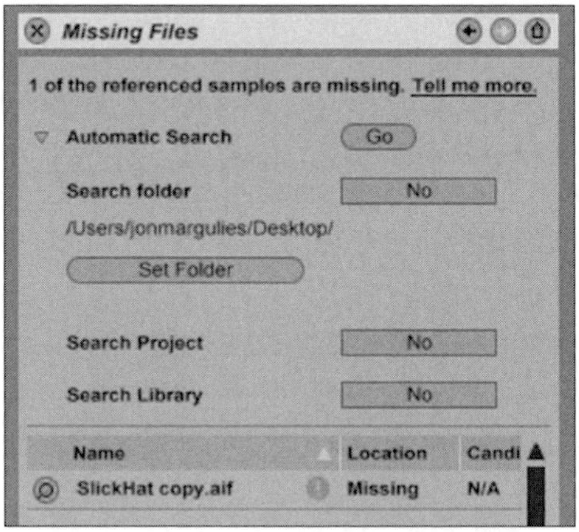

Name	Location	Candi ▲
SlickHat copy.aif	Missing	N/A

Figure 3.34 The Missing Files window can be used to identify and replace individual samples, or automatically search for all lost audio files.

The other way to replace missing samples is to use the Automatic Search feature in the Missing Files window (see Figure 3.34). What's nice about this feature is that it lets you search for all of your missing samples in one shot, instead of one at a time. Here's how it's done:

1. Set the Search Folder switch to Yes, unless you only want to search your project folder and the Live Library, in which case you can skip to Step 3.

2. Click the Set Folder button and navigate to the folder you want to search. Any sub-folders in this location will be searched as well.

3. Set the Search Project and Search Library switches to Yes if you believe your files may be in the current project folder or the Live Library.

4. Click the Go button at the top of the window.

When the search is completed, Live will tell you how many "Candidates" (how many potentially correct files) were found and how many samples it was able to automatically replace with the candidates it found. The missing samples list will now be updated to show the replaced files, changing their location status to either Project or External. There will be two main reasons a file does not get replaced automatically. Either the missing file cannot be found at all, or more than one file has been found that matches the name of the missing file. In this case, the location will read Candidates, and the number of possible replacement files found will be listed in the Candidates field (see Figure 3.35).

Figure 3.35 When more than one file with a matching name is found, Live needs you to intervene and pick out the right one.

Clicking on the ? button will reveal a list of all the matching files in the File Browser. You have a few choices to determine which is the right one. First, you could simply enable the Preview button and decide by ear. Another option is to view the Path and Date Modified columns in the Browser (see Figure 3.36). If these aren't visible, you'll need to right-click in the header column and select them from the context menu to show them. You'll probably also want to make

Figure 3.36 Showing additional columns in the Browser can help you identify which files to use.

the Browser a bit wider, so you can see everything you need. Once you've found the right file, you can double-click or drag and drop as described earlier.

External Samples

The final area of the Current Set window is the External Samples section (see Figure 3.32). If all of your samples are already within the current project folder, this section will be empty. If not, the first Show button will allow you to view all samples that exist outside of the current project folder, but that are within the main folder of other projects. The other Show button will reveal samples in other locations. Note that Live considers the Library to be a "project," so any files from the Live Library are considered to be contained in another project.

Below the two Show buttons are switches that will allow you to collect (copy) these external samples into your project folder. These differ from the Collect All and Save command, in that they allow you to specify what samples should be copied into the project. You can differentiate between files that are in other project folders and files elsewhere. To actually copy the samples and save the current Set, use the Collect and Save button at the bottom of the File Manager.

Manage Project

Manage Project contains several features that are identical to Manage Set (except that they act on all Sets in the project), so I'll just focus on the features that are different here.

The first area of the Manage Project window is the project location—it just shows you the path of the current project. After that is the Project Contents section, which tells you the number of Sets, Live Clips, Preset Files, and Samples in the project. Clicking any of the Show buttons will reveal the referenced files in the File Browser (see Figure 3.37).

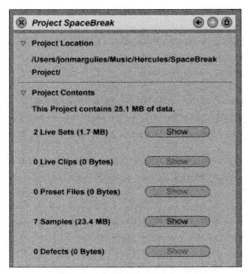

Figure 3.37 Project Contents tells you about all sorts of different files that exist within your project.

Upper Management What if you want to manage files for a project or Set other than the one you have open? Fear not. Even though the Manage Files command opens the current Set/project by default, there's a way to get to others without closing your current Set. Simply navigate to a Live Set in the File Browser and right-click it. Select the Manage File option that appears in the context menu, and it will open in the File Manager. If you want to manage a project instead, right-click the project folder and choose Manage Project from the context menu.

Here's another trick that may save you some time. The next time you want to replace a sample, right-click the waveform in the Clip View and choose Manage Sample File from the context menu. The File Manager will open with that sample highlighted in the samples list.

The next area of interest is the Unused Samples section (see Figure 3.38). When working on a project, it's possible to generate many extra audio files that don't end up getting used. These could be multiple takes of a live performance or earlier versions of a loop before you effected and resampled it to perfection. This section differentiates between files that were recorded into the Set, created with the Freeze command, created with the Consolidate command, and files not created by the current project. Clicking the Show button will reveal these unused files in the File Browser, where you can choose what you want to do with them. While we heartily recommend getting rid of unnecessary files to recover disk space, I strongly recommend backing up the entire project first, extra files and all, before deleting anything. Bad things can happen. Like a lot of what I have to say, this recommendation is based on a true story!

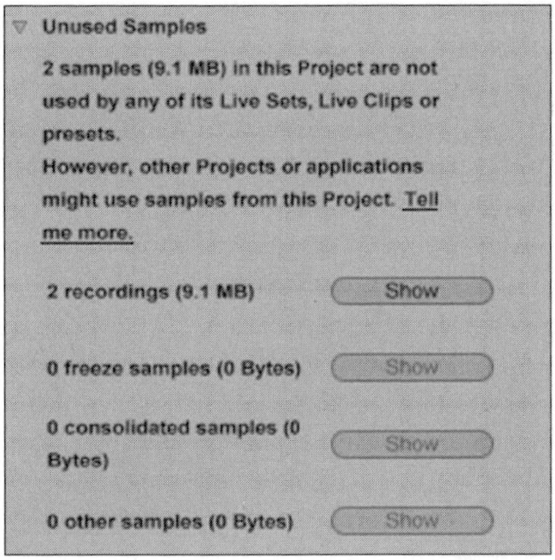

Figure 3.38 Getting rid of unnecessary audio files can reclaim a lot of disk space.

The final two sections of the Project Manager window contain one button each. The Packing section lets you create a Live Pack from your project. A Live Pack is a convenient way to transport your project (see Figure 3.39). It's a compressed archive file containing everything in the project folder. The final option, Export to Library, will copy all of the files from your project into the Live Library so they can be easily accessed from other projects. This isn't something you're going to use a whole lot, but if you end up with a project containing a bunch of useful presets and loops, you can use this to get them into the Library.

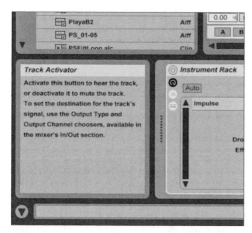

Figure 3.39   The Info View can be hidden or expanded to give you quick bits of pertinent Live wisdom. In this case, the mouse is hovering over a Track Activator.

Getting Help

The software world is big on searchable help menus, online help files, and gazillion-page PDF manuals. Between Google.com and online forums (such as Ableton's), the challenge is in the sifting.

The Info View

The quickest way to get help in Live is the Info View, a retractable and informative window in the lower-left corner of the Live window that will discuss whatever topic correlates with the control your mouse is hovering over (see Figure 3.39). You can show or hide this window by selecting Info from the View menu or clicking the small triangle icon in the lower-left corner of the Live screen. This won't always provide enough information to satisfy the power user you are becoming, but in a pinch or sudden memory lapse, it is the perfect thing to remind you: "Oh yeah, that's what this button is for."

Feel free to pop this baby open any time you are unsure about a specific element of Live. You can easily hide it again, to protect your reputation, when your friend looks over your shoulder.

Getting Help Online

We all know the Internet holds an amazing amount of random and erroneous content. Precisely what you are after can be more elusive than Elvis's ghost. Thankfully, Ableton knows this better than most and remains faithful to its customers by providing the Live user forum and reliable technical support. You can also feel free to drop corporate headquarters a note and tell them what a great job they've done.

All you need to do is click on Live's Help menu, and you will see these options:

- **Lessons Table of Contents:** This will open up the Live Lessons View and will present you with a list of the excellent interactive tutorials.

- **Read the Live Manual:** The manual is in Adobe PDF format and only takes up about 11 megabytes of hard drive space.

- **Visit ableton.com:** Ableton's Web site is easy on the eyes and full of neatly organized goodies. If you are looking for some helpful distraction, the Artist page hosts scores of interviews, loops to download, and insightful hardware and setup tips. You'll also notice that Ableton prides itself on acknowledging bugs as they are reported instead of denying their existence. After all, bugs are a part of software, and Ableton's admissions and frequently provided workarounds will tell you that you are not alone with your problem.

- **Join the User Forum:** Ableton Live users are some of the more savvy audio software heads on the planet. Try posting your question and set the option for e-mail notification. (You'll get an e-mail message when someone responds to your post.) Nearly all sensible inquiries are answered, even if they are repeats or misnomers. In fact, once in awhile, real live Ableton employees will jump in on the discussion. Now that's team spirit!

- **Get Support:** Every so often, the user board isn't fast enough, or a problem is just plain weird enough that you really need a direct line to the author. Realize that Ableton, like most specialized software houses, is small, and they may need a couple of days to get back to you.

- **Check for Updates:** How handy is that? Ableton puts a shortcut right to the download section of their Web site so you can check if you have the latest version of Live. For added convenience, Live will automatically enter your serial number into the Web site, saving you the tedium of tracking down the serial number and typing in the string of hexadecimal values.

4 Making Music in Live

At last, the time has come to begin making music in Live. In this chapter, we'll cover how to analyze and prepare files for use in Live. We will explain the common areas of the Clip View and, through practical examples, discover some of the most common ways music is made in Live. We'll also take a look at software configuration and general working methods for the Live-based computer musician.

Whether you are playing a popular hot spot or working in the privacy of your own home, the basic Live configuration and performance concepts are the same. However, upon examining the working methods of either power-users or casual dabblers, you'll discover that nearly everybody is using Live just a little bit differently, depending upon musical style and live performance needs. DJs demand different things out of Live than producers working in studios do. Film and television composers may be looking for different kinds of sounds than a musician playing Live in a band. As you read this chapter, think about how you want to use Live and focus on the areas that make sense for your situation. After all, there is no reason a DJ can't borrow techniques from a film composer and vice versa. As we proceed through the various ways to work in Live, take a minute to try some of the provided examples. As with learning any musical instrument, discovery will lead to inspiration, additional detail will bring delight, and a little practice never hurts, either.

I will warn you now that this is a long chapter, covering a lot of information. You'll find it interesting, though, as each concept I explain will introduce the next. This parallels the way Live's working process is based on a hierarchical structure of principles, starting from smaller musical pieces and working up to a finished masterpiece. The basic procedure goes like this:

- **Create individual musical parts:** Record bass parts, guitar riffs, keyboard lines, drum grooves, and MIDI instruments, or import samples and MIDI sequences. These become *clips*.

- **Create song sections:** Arrange the clips side by side in the Session View to make *scenes*. Each scene represents a section of your song, such as intro, verse, chorus, bridge, and outro.

- **Record an Arrangement:** Live will record your actions in the Session View while you trigger the scenes on the fly to record your song into the Arrangement View.

- **Finalize the song:** Edit the Arrangement, add effects to the mix, layer additional parts, finalize the automation, and render the song to disk.

Each element of Live's interface is optimized for one of these tasks. You'll see that clips are manipulated in the Clip View, scenes in the Session View, song arrangements in the Arrangement View, and mixes in the Session Mixer and Track Views. This logical approach and use of only one window make Live a streamlined composition environment. Furthermore, the same tools you use for writing are available for performing—there's a blurry line between composing and performing in Live.

You'll notice that the steps above are not numbered. This is because the creation process can always be in flux when using Live. You can record multiple layers of a part in the Arrangement View and bounce the results to a clip in the Session View. You may begin mixing the song as you're composing it. In any case, Live is flexible enough to suit your style.

Working Methods

One of the remarkable things about Live is that no two people use it the same way. Some musicians come to use Live as a quick and flexible multitrack recorder that allows them to explore their own music in deep and original ways. Other artists use Live as a way to integrate their samples and loops quickly into a performance or group environment. Some use Live for the entire production process—concept to mixdown. DJs like Sasha and Gabriel & Dresden are using Live to play their favorite tracks, as well as to integrate their own material and preproduced loops. In other words, DJs are producing and remixing full-length tracks on the fly, while producers are acting more and more like DJs all the time by mixing unusual textures, rhythms, and styles into a single track. Live is quite popular with remix and dance music producers, who take a preproduced track, break it down, and rebuild it in another musical style. Let's take a closer look at each of these methods to better understand each perspective and see how Live can be the perfect application for each of these approaches.

Using Live to DJ

Today, DJs play music using CDs, MiniDisc players, MP3 players, turntables, and computers. Their artistry involves selecting their own mix of music or musical components (beats, samples, etc.) to entertain, explore, or make something altogether new. Live fits into the DJ world perfectly, as it allows for songs to be synchronized to other tracks and other playback devices. Additional parts, such as beats and basslines, can be made on the fly using MIDI instruments, which also lock perfectly to the beat. Many DJs use Live in conjunction with turntables, CD players, and other computers. Often, they will spend a good deal of time configuring their songs for use in Live. This can involve editing tracks in a wave editor, mapping any necessary Warp Markers (see Chapter 5) in Live's Clip View to time-align the track, or merely cropping their favorite portion of a larger track to be used as one in a collection of many time-synced loops. The bottom line is that DJs are benefiting from the flexibility and choices Live offers. DJs can use different parts of the same song looped against one another at the same time or take advantage of multiple tracks (as opposed to being limited to a finite number of turntables, CD players, or mixer channels). Besides, a digital DJ doesn't ever have to worry about wearing out precious vinyl and irreplaceable acetates or scratching a CD surface.

Using Live with a Band

The organic nature of bands may seem like an unfit environment for computers. Every gig has a different energy, and playing to the same old backing track every time could end up sucking the life out of a stage performance. Many bands have a free-form approach that doesn't follow a preset number of bars in a song arrangement. Whatever the case, Live has some exciting news for you: The parts from the computer *can* be different every time and can be placed under full control of the band.

- Some performers feel that using a sequencer removes a level of freedom that is essential to live music. Many times throughout this book (with more to come), we've referred to Live as a sequencing *instrument*. Live can be played in a live setting, and it leaves the musical arrangement completely under the user's control. Perhaps your band always practices a song with an eight-bar solo section for your guitarist. When you are playing the show, your guitarist catches fire, and you all feel that the solo needs to be longer. By having the song arranged as scenes in the Session View, you can extend the solo section by *doing nothing*, thus allowing the solo section clips to loop and naturally extending the section. You finally trigger the next section once the guitarist signals to move on.

- The Tap Tempo features of Live will keep Live playing to the band, rather than the band playing to the sequence. A drummer could assign a trigger pad or foot pedal (anything that outputs MIDI) to the Tap Tempo button and could tap out quarter notes from time to time to keep Live in time with the band. Starting a song is also under the drummer's control since he can issue four taps while he counts off the song, resulting in the band and Live starting together.

- When playing a gig, it may be necessary for some of the musicians to hear a click track from Live, possibly when the song calls for two bars of silence with everyone (including the computer) then coming in together. Live can provide this by means of its cue and multichannel output functions (see the following note).

Click Track A click track is nothing more than a metronome that a band or musician plays along with, just like the one in Live's Control Bar. Usually, the click is piped into the headphones of whoever is recording. By playing along with the click track, the musician performs the musical parts in sync with parts of the track that have been previously recorded. In the studio, click tracks are sometimes replaced by percussive loops, which are less monotonous and generally more musical. This can easily be accomplished with Live by assigning a track with a fitting loop to Cue (see "Audio Tracks and Their Controls" in Chapter 3, "Live Interface Basics").

Multitracking

Crafting songs by multitracking can be one of the most rewarding and creative activities a songwriter can take part in. Whether you are a solitary artist composing a demo in your bedroom or a band with limited input channels, multitrack recordings allow you to add many layers of music to the same piece without erasing previous tracks. In today's age of unlimited audio tracks, you might take for granted the power of layering ideas on top of one another and auditioning different digital arrangements. Live can be a perfect composition tool or arrangement auditioning tool. When songwriters see Live's ability to rearrange a song easily and musically (whether it was recorded to a click or not), their eyes often grew wide with disbelief.

Producing and Remixing Music

Since the beginnings of computer-based music, remix and dance music producers have been the driving force behind many of the industry's most impressive innovations. Of course, "producer" is a loose term that usually refers to any remix artists, consultants working with bands or vocalists, or musicians with a penchant for hard disk recording and editing. Whether they are set up in a fancy studio or holed up in their college dorm room, producers using Live may be the largest and most feature-savvy group of them all. Many producers have already tapped into the exciting prospect of remixing another artist's work, as well as creating new music, when using Live's instant time-stretching and unprecedented sample-manipulation ability. Producers want to compose, make music, put together unusual elements, and find the "right" hooks. Live allows them the creative freedom to stick to the task at hand while keeping the process simple enough to remain focused on the music.

Scoring for Video

They say timing is everything. Nowhere is this more evident than in scoring music for the moving image. Whether you are adding sound effects or mood music or creating a complete soundtrack, Live's ability to stretch audio in sync with MIDI makes it the perfect tool for the job. Live 7 brings the ability to import QuickTime video files directly onto a track in Live, so this has become much easier. As we begin to discuss Live's unique "elastic audio" ability in the next few sections, you will see how Live is built to make sound behave in ways that were simply not possible before. Film and television music composers often run into problems when trying to synchronize audio and video. For instance, the audio track may need to speed up and then slow down; the music then must reflect this tempo change. Movie and TV music also need to be done quickly, and Live's ability to be played, rather than just programmed, is a huge advantage.

While we have pointed out some of the typical ways creative people like you are making use of Live, we have by no means covered them all. New uses for Live continue to emerge. In fact, you will invent a few of your own. Check out "Fair Use," a brief excerpt from an interview with film composer Klaus Badelt from the Ableton Web site.

Fair Use New ways to use Live are popping up all the time. Here are a couple of ideas by film music maestro Klaus Badelt.

"Ever since Live came out, it changed my life. It enabled me to use our whole library of percussive loops. I'm not talking about loops (only) in the sense of just electronic loops, but all kinds of orchestral or ethnic percussion loops. I'm finally able to use them all very quickly and try them out in tempo. It makes it possible to work much faster, especially when you only have a few days to write a whole score.

"I don't actually use (Live) in the way it was originally intended. I'm playing it from my sequencer. I trigger the program from the other computer as Live runs on its own machine. It holds the library. I drag in the loops I'm using and trigger them from the keyboard. I use the effects in there, but basically submix and then send to the mixer. I basically use it as a synthesizer."

—*Klaus Badelt is credited with* The Thin Red Line, Mission Impossible 2, Hannibal, Pearl Harbor, Pirates of the Caribbean, *and many other award-winning films. (Taken from www.ableton.com.)*

In the next section, we are going to take a brief but important sidestep to explore the more practical side of Live's interface, Clip View and Track View, as well as several tips for working with loops and samples. Later in the chapter, we will return to the idea of working methods and different approaches for using Live. The combination of both practical knowledge and tried-and-true examples should put you well on your way to discovering your own particular way of harnessing the power of Live.

Live's Musical Building Blocks: Clips

Within a musical composition, the parts involved can be broken into smaller pieces, such as verse 1 bassline, chorus backing vocals, intro percussion, or whatever terms you might use. Each of these pieces is suited perfectly for a *clip*—the basic musical building block in Live. Everything in Live is based on the creation, editing, arrangement, and playing of clips. By having the pieces of your song assembled in clips, you can then arrange the song on the fly and intermix different sections, whether for a live performance or as a means for programming the Arrangement View.

What Are Clips?

Clips are the colored rectangles scattered throughout the Session View (see Figure 4.1a) and the Arrangement View (see Figure 4.1b). Each one plays an audio file or MIDI sequence. Playing clips in the Session View is done by clicking the small play triangle at the left side of the clip. Clips in the Arrangement View will be played when the *Now Line* (the thin vertical line that moves from left to right when Live is running) passes over them.

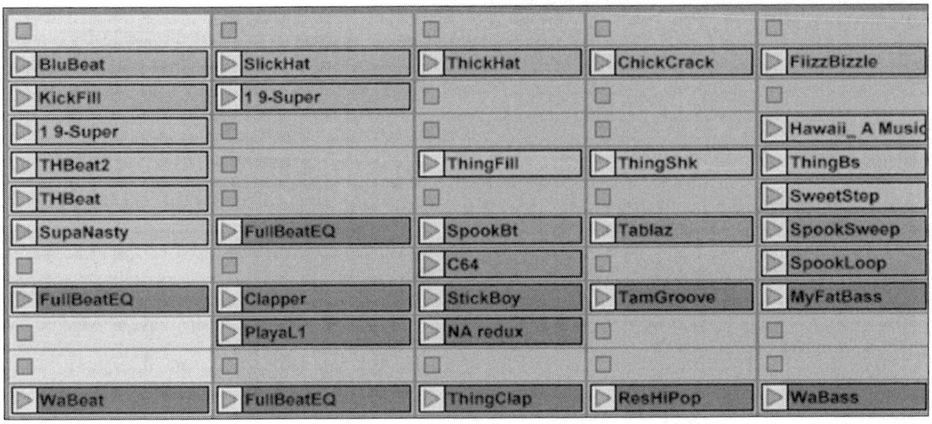

Figure 4.1a   Clips as they appear in the Session View.

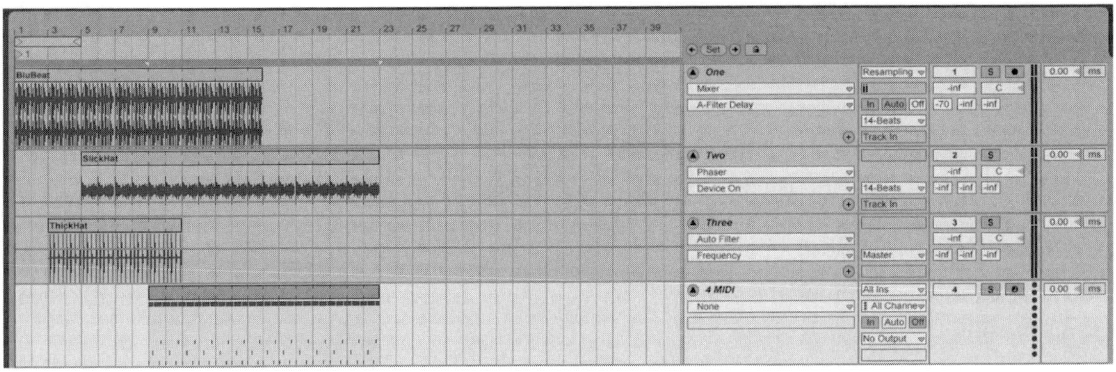

Figure 4.1b   Clips in the Arrangement View can be resized to change how long they will play.

Think of clips as small, independent MIDI sequencers and audio samplers that all play in relation to one another. This is similar to pattern-style sequencing, except that the patterns can all be different lengths. This offers the convenience of creating anything from small musical units to larger evolving parts and using them together in any combination.

While a clip can be copied from one place to another, either by copying it from the Session View to the Arrangement View (or vice versa) or by creating multiple instances in both views, each resulting clip is independent from the others, even if they contain the same musical data and share the same name and color. This means that a clip that was recorded into the Session View can have its parameters modified in the Arrangement View while leaving the original Session View clip intact. This separation will become clearer as you look more closely at the Session and Arrangement Views later in this chapter.

What Do Clips Contain?

Clips come in two forms: audio and MIDI. Audio clips (see Figure 4.2a) contain references to audio files, while MIDI clips (see Figure 4.2b) contain MIDI data for playing MIDI instruments (either virtual or hardware instruments).

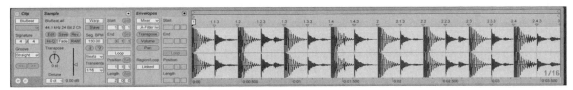

Figure 4.2a   An audio clip plays an audio file on the computer. A graphical representation of the audio can be seen in the Clip View waveform window.

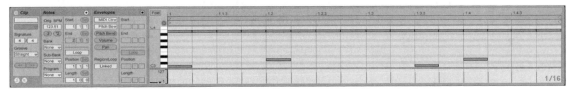

Figure 4.2b   MIDI clips contain sequences of MIDI notes and data, which can also be seen in the Clip View.

What Audio Clips Don't Contain While you can easily think of all the little clip boxes as containing audio loops and such, remember that the audio file used in those clips is not actually part of the clip or Live Set. A clip merely contains the information necessary for Live to play an audio file from disk—it is a pointer to your sample.

Should that file (sample) become altered by another application, such as a wave editor, each clip that used that file will now play with the same alteration. If you delete the sample that is referenced by a clip, the clip and any other clips that used that file won't play anymore! See Chapter 3 on how to save your set as a self-contained project using the Collect All and Save commands to keep the audio files you use in a safe location.

Where Do Clips Come From?

Clips are created in two ways: either by adding an audio or MIDI file from disk to the Session or Arrangement Views or by recording new audio and MIDI performances into Live. When first learning how to use Live, you'll more than likely begin with audio clips created from pre-existing audio files on your computer. If you need to get your hands on some loops, there are sample libraries from companies such as East West, Big Fish Audio, Native Instruments, M-Audio, and more, to arm you to the teeth with audio loops for musical inspiration. Of course, Live can work with audio files that aren't loops—any audio file (in WAV, AIFF, SDII, MP3, Ogg Vorbis, Ogg FLAC, or FLAC format) on your computer is fair game for manipulation in Live.

What's also great is that you can make new clips by recording audio from external sources. If you've found a drum loop and bass loop that you want to use as the foundation for your song, you can plug in your guitar and record your own riffs on top, which are instantly turned into clips.

The same is true for MIDI clips. Tracks from MIDI files can be added from file Browsers, or new performances can be recorded directly into the session or arrangement. Unlike audio clips, the MIDI information in a MIDI clip is saved in the Live Set file itself. Even MIDI clips created from MIDI files will be independent from the original files.

Because the methods for recording audio and MIDI clips are different, they will be covered separately in the next chapters. What's important to understand at this point is how clips work and how they integrate into the production process in Live. Whether they came from a sample CD, your own voice, a General MIDI file, or from your MIDI controller, both audio and MIDI clips behave the same; most importantly, once you fully understand how to use clips, you'll be able to record better clips yourself.

The Clip View

While there are two distinctly different types of clips in Live (MIDI and audio), there are a number of behaviors and settings that are common to both types of clips, all of which will be discussed next. The common behaviors of MIDI and audio clips help blur the line between audio and MIDI in the Session and Arrangement Views. After all, when you're performing, you don't really care whether a piano part is coming from an audio file or being triggered by a MIDI instrument. When you launch the piano clip, you expect to hear the piano part with nothing else to worry about.

Obviously, your understanding of clips will have a tremendous impact on your ability to use Live. If clips are not set up properly, many of Live's other functions, such as the ability to play multiple clips in sync, will be compromised. The settings determining clip behavior are accessed and edited through the *Clip View* (see Figure 4.3), which appears at the bottom of the Live window whenever you double-click a clip.

There are different sections within the Clip View that can be accessed with the icons in the lower-left corner of the window. A few of these sections are common to both MIDI and audio clips. Those common properties will be explained in this chapter, while the type-specific parameters and features will be explained in detail in their own chapters (see Chapters 5 and 6).

The sections you'll be concerned with at the moment are the Clip and Launch sections, as well as the Loop settings found in the Sample window (for audio clips) or Notes window (for MIDI clips).

Clip Name and Color

The first two settings in the Clip section (see Figure 4.4) are purely cosmetic—they have no impact on the behavior or sound of the clip. The first field is the Clip Name, which can be

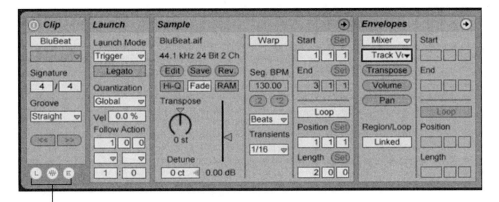

Use these three icons to hide
or show the different sections
of the Clip View.

Figure 4.3 The Clip View contains multiple sections that can be shown and hidden using the icons at the lower-left corner of the window. Turn them all on now so that you can see all the options in Clip View.

Figure 4.4 Give your clips useful names so you can remember what they are when you're performing. You can also give similar clips the same color to help organize your views and change the width of tracks in the Session View, giving your clips greater visibility.

any name and as many characters as you want. You'll see only about the first nine letters in Session View clips when using the default track width, but you may see more of the name if you widen the track or extend the clip in the Arrangement View.

Clips are automatically named when they are created and given a color based on your default preferences. If you create a clip by dragging a file in from the Browser, the clip will be named the same as the file. When you record a new clip, it will be given the name of the track it is created in. To help keep multiple takes (recordings) in order, Live tacks a number on in front of the clip (and file) name as each new one is created.

You can change the name of a clip by selecting it in the Session or Arrangement View and clicking the Name field at the top-left corner of the Clip View. You can also simply right-click the clip or Ctrl-click on the Mac to select Rename from the context menu. Using this technique, you'll be able to rename the clip right within the Session and Arrangement Views, speeding things up tremendously.

When changing the name of an audio clip, you should be aware that the name of the associated audio file is not changed. If you drag a file from the Browser called DnB Loop07 (168 BPM) into the Session View, the resulting clip will have the exact same name. If you change the clip name to something more useful, like MainBeat, the original audio file on your hard drive will still be named DnB Loop07 (168 BPM).

Time Signature

The clip's Time Signature (labeled Signature) determines the numbering of the Grid Markers and Quantizing Grid (discussed separately in Chapters 6 and 7, respectively). It also affects the Launch Quantizing behavior, which we'll explain in a moment.

Clip Groove

The Groove section is probably one of the more mind-blowing features you'll ever witness in an audio program. Using the Clip Grooves and the Global Groove Amount value in the Control Bar, you can add a shuffle or swing feel to the individual clips in your songs. The idea of morphing between straight and swing feels is not new. Many classic drum machines, like Roland's TR-909, have a shuffle control. The shuffle control delays certain beats of a sequence to create a swing or triplet feel—the further the control is turned, the more dramatic the effect.

While a swing control on a drum machine isn't news, swinging audio tracks is unheard of, or should we say, *was* unheard of. Since Live already has the whole time-stretching thing down pat, it's not really surprising that it can make such a surgical change on the fly to an audio file. After all, if MIDI sequencers just delay certain beats, Live can similarly delay portions of an audio file (using short expansions and compressions of time) to yield the same results. Indeed, Live can swing your audio and MIDI performances in perfect sync with each other.

Choosing your Clip Groove within the Clip View will determine which beats get delayed. The Global Groove Amount (see Figure 4.5) will set the intensity of the shuffle from 0 to 99. Start out by setting it to 50. The Swing 8 setting is for 1/8-note swings and shuffles, while the Swing 16 setting will take a straight sixteenth feel and delay the even numbered 1/16 notes, resulting in a nice swing to get everybody dancing. Any clip with Straight selected for the Groove will be

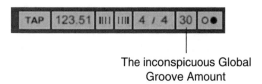

The inconspicuous Global
Groove Amount

Figure 4.5 The Global Groove Amount is the tiny, unlabeled number in the left section of the Control Bar. Click and drag, type in a number, or assign it to a MIDI control to change it.

impervious to the Global Groove Amount setting. Of course, you don't have to set the Global Groove Amount to 50. Smaller amounts will make the swing less pronounced and less machine-like at the same time. For the swing timing found in most dance music, dial in a Global Groove Amount of 65. Going beyond 65 will give your clip a crazy hip-hop over-swing that you'll want to hear for yourself!

One of These Clips Is Doing Its Own Thing   While the Global Groove Amount value sets the intensity of the swing applied by Live to your clips, remember that each clip has its own Clip Groove setting. If you're increasing the Global Groove Amount but are getting weird results, be sure that all of the playing clips are set to the same Clip Groove. If some clips are set to Swing 8 while others are set to Swing 16, the time shifts will not be in sync with each other, which can result in strange polyrhythms (of course, if this is what you're after, don't mind me).

It may seem strange that Ableton didn't just use a Global Groove setting; however, by having each clip follow its own Groove settings, you have much more flexibility. Let's say you want to match a loop that has no swing feel to one that does. In this case you would set the loop with the swing to Straight so its timing isn't affected. Then you would set the straight loop to use one of the swing modes and adjust the Global Groove Amount until they match up.

Clip Nudge Controls

Next are the Clip Offset Controls, which are comprised of two buttons in the lower-left corner of the fully opened Clip View. These controls allow you to offset a clip easily by a quantized value, or to sync clips manually without quantization. These work differently than the Tempo Nudge controls. Clip Nudge changes the offset of a single clip relative to Live's master tempo, while Tempo Nudge momentarily changes the master tempo and thus the playback tempo of all clips.

Pressing the two arrow buttons (the Nudge buttons) will perform the shift (the clip should be playing when you do this). Each time you press an arrow, the start and playback positions of the clip will change by an amount determined by the Global Quantize setting. (Don't confuse this with the clip's Launch Quantization, which will be explained next.) If the Global Quantize is set to 1 Bar, the clip's start location will be shifted by 1 Bar with every click of the Nudge buttons. If you want to offset by a smaller amount, select a smaller Quantize value. With Global Quantize set to None, the Nudge buttons will offset the clip by minute increments, allowing you to make your clip sit just the tiniest bit ahead of or behind the beat.

For an example, let's say you're DJing with Global Quantize set to 1/16, rather than 1 Bar, in order to occasionally offset a track to create a new groove. The Clip Nudge controls could be used while pre-listening to correct the placement of a track that was launched a little too early or too late, or to experiment with different offsets before bringing the track in. Or you could launch a track with Global Quantize set to 1 Bar, then change it to None, and nudge the clip until it feels just right.

The Third Control While it looks like the Nudge controls are limited to only two buttons, there is a third control that can be accessed only through MIDI assignment. When you enter the MIDI Map mode (Ctrl [Cmd]+M), you'll see a tiny box appear between the arrow buttons. Click this box and twist a knob on your MIDI controller. Now you can twist the knob to perform the nudge. We recommend using an endless encoder knob for this, allowing you to offset the clip over a wide range of time.

Keep the Groove Once you've nudged a track to perfection, you may want to be able to recall exactly how much you've nudged it so it can be played back exactly the same the next time you launch it. To do this, select Capture and Insert Scene from the Insert menu. This will make a copy of whatever clips you currently have playing back and create a new scene with just those clips in it. Any tracks that you've nudged will have their Start markers moved by the amount they were nudged.

Quantize

You can perform two types of quantizing with Live. One method lines up stray notes in a MIDI clip. This is called *Note Quantization*, which will be explained in the "Quantizing Your Performance" section of Chapter 7. The other method is *Launch Quantization*, the topic of this section. (Note: In order to see the Launch controls of the Clip View, you must click the small L icon (Show/Hide Launch Box) at the bottom of the Clip control box.)

Launch Quantization determines when a clip will start playing or recording after it has been triggered. Proper Launch Quantization settings ensure that clips will start on time and in sync with each other, even if they are triggered a little early by us sloppy humans. The default setting for this value is set in the Preferences. Most people choose either Global or Bar as the default values.

The available choices for Launch Quantization range from 1/32 notes up to eight bars and are selected from the drop-down menu shown in Figure 4.6. There are also two additional settings, Global and None, which will cause the clip to follow the Global Quantize setting (in the Control Bar) or ignore quantization, respectively. Any clips set to Bar will only start playing on the downbeat of a measure, even if they were triggered before that. This means that you can click (launch) a number of new clips, but they won't start playing until the next measure.

Figure 4.6 The Quantize settings for a clip.

You can therefore launch a new bassline, drum part, and guitar riff halfway through the bar, and Live will wait until the downbeat before playing them all.

When you trigger a clip before its quantize setting will allow it to start, its green Play triangle (the *Fire button* or *Play button*) will start to blink, indicating that the clip is standing by to play. Once the beat for the quantize setting is reached, the Play icon will turn solid green, and the clip will begin playing. It's at this point that the previous clip playing in the track (if there was one) will be cut off in favor of the new one.

Of course, you may not want to start a clip on the downbeat of a measure. In these cases, a smaller quantize setting can be selected. A setting of 1/4 will force a clicked clip to start on the next beat rather than waiting for the bar. Any clip set to None will start playing the instant it is launched.

Bar Length *Bar* is another term for measure, which is the length determined by the time signature. In the case of 4/4 time, a measure (bar) is four beats long, with the 1/4 note equaling one beat. 12/8 is 12 beats long with the 1/8 note equaling one beat. This means that the length of time determined by a Bar quantize setting depends on the time signature.

If the time signature is 3/4 and Quantize is set to Bar, you'll be able to launch new clips every three beats (each measure is three beats long). When the time signature is 4/4, you'll be able to launch the clips every four beats.

A special condition can arise when you're using clips with time signatures different from the Live Set. If your project is set to 4/4 but your clip has a time signature of 3/4, a setting of 1 Bar in the Clip View will allow the clip to launch every three beats. This means that while 4/4 clips will launch on the downbeat, the 3/4 clip will launch on bar 1, beat 1; bar 1, beat 4; bar 2, beat 3; and bar 3, beat 2. In this case, the length of the Bar setting is determined by the clip's time signature.

If, on the other hand, the 3/4 clip has Quantize set to Global, the quantize setting in the Control Bar will be used. If this value is set to Bar, the 3/4 clip will launch every four beats (on the downbeat with the other 4/4 clips) because the length of the Global Bar setting is determined by the project's time signature (4/4 in this case).

Launch Controls

To add more creative possibilities when using clips, Ableton has given you four Launch modes (see Figure 4.7) to add extra control to your performances. In all of our descriptions so far, launching a clip has caused it to start playing (once the quantize time has been reached), at which point it continues to play indefinitely (if looped) or through its entirety (when unlooped). This is the default behavior for clips, and one that makes quite a lot of sense, but times may arise when you want a different level of control.

Figure 4.7 Launch modes: Choose, but choose wisely...

Launch modes will change not only the clip's playback state when the clip is launched (either by clicking with the mouse or pressing an assigned key or MIDI note), but will also determine the action taken (if any) when the mouse or key is released. The four available Launch modes are as follows:

- **Trigger:** The most common Launch mode for use in most performance situations is Live's Trigger mode. Each time you fire a clip, it will launch. Once a clip is launched and playing, you will be able to stop its playback only by pressing one of the Clip Stop buttons located in the same track. This mode ignores the up-tick (release) of the mouse button, computer keyboard key, or MIDI note. Each clip can be fired as rapidly as the quantization will allow, and each time the clip is fired, it will restart the clip from the beginning, even if it was already playing.

- **Gate:** When triggering a clip in Gate mode, you will hear the sound only for as long as your mouse or keyboard key is depressed. This is an excellent setting for dropping in snippets of sound without playing the entire clip. In short, holding down your left mouse button (or MIDI/computer-keyboard key) will play the clip continuously until you let up.

- **Toggle:** With Toggle mode engaged, the Fire button basically turns into an on/off switch for the clip. If you launch a clip that is playing, it will stop. Launch the stopped clip, and it will begin playing. This also works at the scene level if you trigger a scene with clips set in Toggle mode. Each time you trigger the scene, clips that are playing will stop, and stopped clips will start. Bear in mind that stopping of the clip will respect the current quantization, just the way launching does.

- **Repeat:** Repeat mode is a way of retriggering a clip by holding down the mouse or assigned key/MIDI note. Any time the mouse or key is held, the clip will continuously restart itself at the rate specified by the clip's Quantize setting. If the setting is 1/4, holding down the mouse/key will cause only the first beat of the clip to play over and over again. When the mouse or key is released, the clip will play through its entirety like normal. This mode can create fun stutter effects but should be used sparingly—probably not a good choice for default behavior.

Velocity

Just below the Quantization box is the Clip Velocity scale setting (see Figure 4.8). This value works only for clips launched by MIDI. It uses the incoming velocity level of the MIDI note to set the playback volume of the clip. At 0%, the velocity has no effect on clip playback volume—it plays at its original level. At 100%, the clip will respond as a velocity-sensitive clip. For settings in between, lower velocities will have less of an attenuating (quieting) effect. This works for both audio and MIDI clips.

Figure 4.8 Velocity scaling based on the MIDI velocity of the clip's trigger note.

Follow Actions

Live's Follow Actions allow an amazing level of automation within the Session View. Basically, using Follow Actions, you can set rules by which one clip can launch another. Any particular clip can launch clips above and below it, replay itself, or even stop itself—all based on odds and a time period that you can program. You can think of Follow Actions as a virtual "finger" that presses Clip Launch buttons for you. While that may not sound that impressive yet, it's just another example of Ableton's ingenuity in bringing simple, generalized tools to its users that can unleash the imagination. In fact, Follow Actions open up so many creative possibilities that you'll find a long list of potential applications listed in Chapter 13, "Live 7 Power."

Follow Actions work on groups of clips, which are clips arranged above and below one another in the same track (see Figure 4.9). An empty clip slot inserted between two clips divides them into separate groups. Follow Actions will allow automatic triggering of other clips in the group and cannot be used to trigger clips in different groups or tracks.

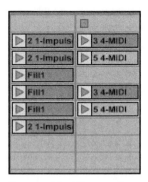

Figure 4.9 The track on the left features one group of clips, while the track on the right has two groups.

The time and conditions for a Follow Action are set in the three sections at the bottom of the clip's Launch window (see Figure 4.10). The first section, the Follow Action Time, determines how long the clip plays before it performs the Follow Action. If the time is set to 2.0.0, the clip will play for two bars before "clicking" on another clip.

Figure 4.10 These parameters determine the Follow Action behavior of the clip.

Instead of just doing the same action over and over again, Ableton gives you the ability to create two different possible Follow Action scenarios for each clip. Live will randomly choose between the two actions selected in the drop-down menus in Figure 4.11 (one on the left and the other on the right). The possible Follow Actions and their effects are the following:

- **No Action:** The empty menu selection refers to No Action, and it is the default action for all new clips. In fact, clips are always performing Follow Actions; however, with No Action selected in both menus, Live will never trigger any other clip.

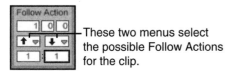
These two menus select
the possible Follow Actions
for the clip.

Figure 4.11   The left Follow Action will trigger the clip above this one, while the right Follow Action will trigger the clip below this one.

- **Stop:** This action will stop the clip (after it has played, of course).

- **Play Again:** Essentially retriggers the clip just as if you'd clicked on it again with the mouse.

- **Previous/Next:** These options will trigger the clip either above or below the current one. If the clip at the top of a group triggers the Play Previous action, it will "wrap around" and trigger the bottom clip of the group and vice versa.

- **Play First/Last:** These will trigger the top or bottom clip in a group, no matter how many clips are in the group. If the top clip in a group triggers the Play First action, it will retrigger itself.

- **Any:** This action will trigger a randomly chosen clip from the group. Live might retrigger the same clip with this option.

- **Other:** This action will trigger a *different* randomly chosen clip from the group. The same clip will not be triggered.

Which Follow Action the program chooses to perform is based on the odds set in the numerical boxes below each Follow Action. By default, the odds are 1:0, meaning that the Follow Action in the left menu will always be performed. Odds of 0:1 will cause the right Follow Action to always be performed. Odds of 1:1 will give you a 50-50 chance of either the left or right Follow Action being performed. You can put in any values you like, such as 2:3 or 1:200.

Above the action drop-down lists is the Follow Action Time. This specifies how soon after a clip is launched the Follow Actions are evaluated. By default, this is set to one bar, meaning that one bar after the clip is launched, the odds will be calculated and the Follow Action performed.

Playing the Odds   Note that odds are calculated afresh every time a Follow Action is performed. If you have a clip with Follow Action odds of 1:1 and Live chooses the left Action the first time, it does not mean that Live will choose the right Action the next time. Just as it is possible to roll the same number on a die time after time, it is quite possible for Live to choose the left Follow Action five times in a row, even with 1:1 odds.

When looking at the Follow Action choices, some of you may be scratching your heads at the Play Clip Again selection. What is the point of this one? To explain, let's look at a practical example.

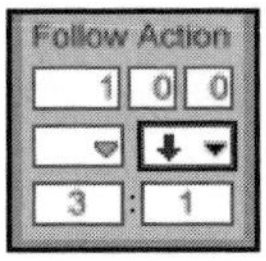

Figure 4.12a   Here, if the left Follow Action is chosen, the clip will loop indefinitely.

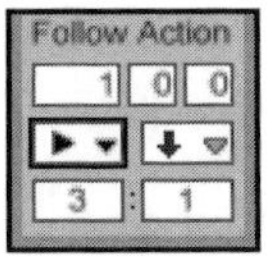

Figure 4.12b   In this example, when the left Follow Action is performed, it will relaunch this clip, causing the Follow Action to be performed again after the specified time.

You have two drum loops. One is the standard beat, while the second is a variation of the first. You really like the standard beat, but from time to time, you want the variation thrown in to keep things from getting too repetitive. Consider Figures 4.12a and 4.12b. Both may appear to be the proper setups for this situation, but one has a flaw.

Follow Actions are performed only after the Follow Action Time has passed since the clip was launched. Thus, in the case of Figure 4.12a, the clip performs the Follow Action one bar after the clip was launched. If the option on the left (No Action) is chosen, no Follow Action will be performed, and the clip will keep playing (infinitely if it's set to loop). Since the clip hasn't been relaunched, the Follow Actions never get evaluated again, because the Follow Action Time has already elapsed. In Figure 4.12b, when the left option is performed, the clip will be retriggered, causing the Follow Action Time to start counting down again. After the specified time, Live calculates the odds and performs the appropriate Follow Action. Using Play Clip Again loops the Follow Action.

Tempo Settings

A clip's tempo is used to determine the timing grid for the clip. This timing grid affects the Grid Markers and Warp Markers in an audio clip and the playback speed of a MIDI clip. This tempo is also what Live uses to keep clips in sync with each other. (If Live doesn't know the original tempo, it won't know the proper amount to speed up or slow down the clip to match the rest of your project.)

The tempo settings work a little differently in the Audio and MIDI Clip Views. For one, tempo is available in audio clips (see Figure 4.13) only when the Warp feature (see next chapter) is engaged. If Warp is off, Live will simply play the audio at its original speed and perform no time-stretching on the clip; therefore, its original tempo is irrelevant. However, with Warp engaged, Live will be able to warp the audio to match the tempo of the Set. Second, an audio clip's tempo and the position of the Grid Markers and Warp Markers are related. As you make

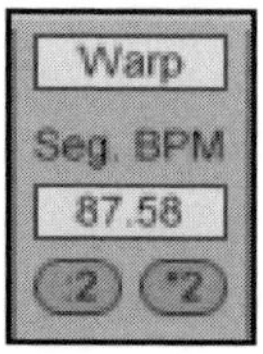

Figure 4.13   A clip's tempo setting is crucial to the proper operation of Live. Without the proper value here, the clip will not match the speed of other clips in the project.

timing adjustments with the Warp Markers, you may notice the Seg. BPM change to compensate for the change in file playback speed. We will delve into this further in Chapter 5.

MIDI clips do not have Warp Markers, so the original tempo is controlled solely by the user. When you create a new MIDI clip, it will take on the current tempo of the Live Set. This is usually sufficient, and you probably won't need to change it; however, if you do need to (perhaps an imported MIDI clip is playing at the wrong speed), changing the tempo value will scale all of the MIDI data in the clip accordingly to make it play back faster or slower.

Below the tempo value are two icons. The left Divide by 2 and the right Multiply by 2 buttons will quickly double or halve the playback speed of both audio and MIDI clips. If the original tempo was 120 BPM, then pressing the Divide by 2 button will result in a new tempo of 60 BPM. If the tempo of the Live Set is 120, then Live will play the clip twice as fast to bring the 60 BPM up to 120 BPM. The Multiply by 2 button will effectively cut playback speed in half. We use this all the time when writing drum and bass tracks, which are usually in the 170 BPM range. When you drag in a drum loop at that tempo, Live often mistakes the loop as being a half-tempo loop, thus importing at 85 BPM. A simple click of the ×2 button brings the tempo of the drum loop back up to 170 BPM.

Tempo Master/Slave

If you are in the Arrangement View, you will see another control just above the Seg. BPM: the Tempo Master/Slave switch. (Note that this control is not present in the Session View.) This allows you to designate any clip as the tempo master by toggling its Master/Slave switch to Master. You can set as many clips as you want to as tempo masters, but just as in the world of Christopher Lambert's *Highlander* films, "there can be only one" when it comes to being the tempo master in a Set. If more than one currently playing clip is set as the tempo master, the bottom-most, currently playing clip in the Arrangement View will take precedence.

The current tempo master clip will always play as if Warp were *off*, and all of the other clips in the Live Set will be warped so that they play in sync with the master. The Warp Markers set in the current tempo master clip will act as tempo automation to the entire Set while the tempo master clip is playing. (You will also notice that Live disables the Tempo field in the Control Bar.)

If you toggle the Master/Slave switch back to Slave or delete the clip, the Master track tempo automation will stop, and the former tempo will resume. If you want to keep the tempo information from the clip, right-click (or Ctrl-click) on the Control Bar's Tempo field and choose the Unslave Tempo Automation command. All clips will then be set to Slave, but the tempo automation will remain in place.

When Live's *EXT* switch (visible only when an external tempo source is enabled) is enabled, the Master/Slave switch has no effect and will appear disabled in all clips.

Clip Start/End

The size of the data in a clip versus the size of the portion that you actually choose to use can be vastly different. In other words, you may have a four-bar clip but decide to use only the first bar of the part. You may have a five-minute song from which you isolate a great drum fill in the middle. Clip Start/End defines the area and length of the sound played within a clip. In the following example (see Figure 4.14), I am using only a portion of a larger sample. To do this, I constrained the length of the loop by setting the Clip Start and End Markers (shown as markers with little triangular flags) to the locations I wanted. You can make these adjustments while you are listening, or even recording, in Live.

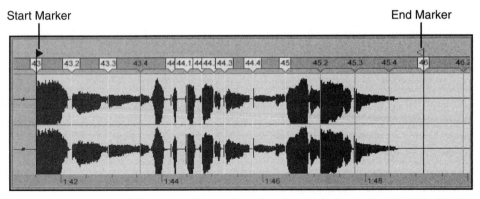

Figure 4.14 You can define a smaller section of a clip to use by setting the Clip Start and End Markers.

Remember, Live is streaming audio files from disk, as opposed to playing them from RAM. This means that using 10 seconds of a 10-minute file is no different from using all 10 seconds of a 10-second file. Don't worry about chopping off the ends of an audio file that you're not using—those sections are never loaded into RAM (like a sampler would do), and you may want to use those parts in another song in the future. Moving the Start and End Markers around your desired section is all that's necessary.

Loop Settings

While the clip's Start and End Markers are shown as small left- and right-facing triangles, the Loop region is shown with a pair of connected markers (see Figure 4.15). If a clip's Loop button is on, the clip's play position will jump to the Loop Start every time it reaches the Loop End

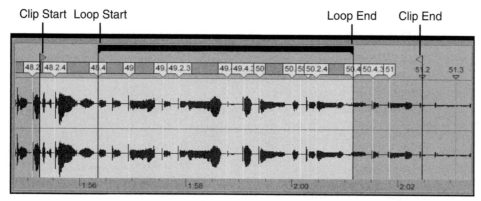

Figure 4.15   There are four markers in a clip now: Clip Start, Loop Start, Loop End, and Clip End.

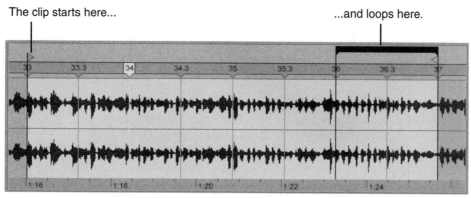

Figure 4.16   You can now loop a subsection of a clip.

Marker. When Loop is turned off, the clip will be allowed to pass the Loop End Marker and play until it reaches the Clip End Marker.

This means that you can have a clip that plays normally through its first three bars before it begins to loop infinitely on its last bar (see Figure 4.16). I find this to be particularly useful with drum loops that begin with crash cymbals. Instead of looping the entire clip, resulting in the crash cymbal sounding every time the clip repeats, you can specify a loop area after the crash cymbal. This way you'll hear the crash the first time you trigger the clip, but you won't hear it again until you relaunch the clip.

As you'll discover, this loop procedure is quite handy when DJing. That's because Live not only lets you set these loop points by hand within the Clip View, but also lets you define these loop points on the fly by pressing the Loop Position Set and Loop Length Set buttons while the clip is playing (see Figure 4.17). This makes the clip behave like a DJ's CD player where you can instantly grab perfect loops out of songs or other types of clips.

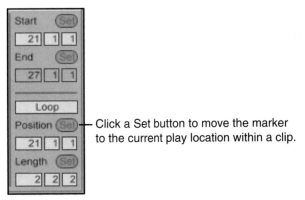

Click a Set button to move the marker to the current play location within a clip.

Figure 4.17 The Set buttons will cause the associated markers to jump to the current play position.

Red Digits When loading new clips, you may find that some of the numbers in the Loop Setting's display are red. This means that the number displayed is not exact. For example, if a clip length is listed as 1.4.4 with the last 4 in red, the clip may actually be 1.4.45 beats long. Since Live cannot display values smaller than the sub-beats, the digits show up red when there are further numbers that can't be seen. Resetting the Warp Markers (see Chapter 5) will fix these red digits by defining the exact size and timing of the clip.

Loop Start Offset

Like a sentence, the point from which you start a musical phrase can make a huge impact on getting your meaning across. Because the clip's Start and End points are completely independent of the clip's loop points, it is entirely possible to start a looped clip from a point other than the beginning. If you place the clip's Start Marker after the Loop Start, the clip will begin playing in the middle of the loop when launched. In fact, it's possible to set the clip's Start Marker to a position after the Loop End Marker. In this case, the clip will never loop, even if Loop is turned on (see Figure 4.18).

Clip Transport You can start playing a clip from any point you choose without having to move the Start Marker. To do this, simply hover the cursor over the waveform or MIDI data of the clip until it turns into a speaker icon (this will happen in the lower-half of the waveform). When you click the waveform, the clip will begin playing from this location. This makes it easy to jump to any point in a track, even during a performance, since the jumps are based on the Global Quantize Setting.

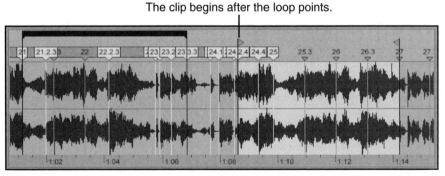

Figure 4.18 Even though this clip is set to loop, it won't because it begins playing after the Loop Markers.

Editing Multiple Clips

You can also edit multiple clips simultaneously. When you select multiple clips, part of the Clip View will be hidden from view. The controls that remain are those that can be changed for all of the selected clips.

Some of the options, such as Clip Name and Clip Color, will be set identically for all clips—if you change the Clip Name to Hot Drums, all of the selected clips will take on the same name. This same behavior is true for nearly all of the available fields when editing multiple clips.

There are a couple of settings, however, that aren't copied identically to all of the clips: the Transpose, Detune, Velocity, and Volume settings. Changing these controls will change all of the selected clips by the same relative amount. For example, if the Transpose setting of one clip is −2 and another is +3, turning up the Transpose knob 2 ticks while selecting both clips will result in the first clip being set to 0 while the second clip is set to +5. This is extremely handy because you can select multiple clips and transpose them all at once while maintaining their relative tunings. If you decide to change the key of your song or need to create a section that is modulated a full step higher, you can do it in a snap.

What the **?** When selecting multiple clips, you may see that some of the fields contain an asterisk (*) instead of a value. This means that this value is different for each of the clips selected. (This is more than likely what the Clip Name and Clip Color fields look like, as most clips have different names and colors.) When you change one of these settings to a specific value, all of the selected clips will inherit the same value, and the asterisk will disappear.

Warping Multiple Clips

The Clip View also gives us the ability to warp multiple clips at the same time. Whenever a number of clips of equal length are selected simultaneously, any Warp Markers applied to one clip will be applied to all of them. This is very convenient when you are working with a number of tracks that have the same rhythm and you want to alter the timing of each of them in exactly the same way. A common use for this function would be on a multitrack recording of a band's live performance where the musicians are all playing in time with one another but they are not in sync with any external clock.

This has been a much-requested feature and will make it a lot easier for you to edit and mix live multitrack recordings! Just select all the tracks and apply Warp Markers across the track with the most obvious rhythms, like the drum mix track or even the bass drum track if you have it on a separate channel. After setting Warp Markers on the drum track, all of your selected tracks will be warped and played back in perfect sync with the Tempo Grid.

The Track

Moving up the totem pole from the clip is the *track*. The track is a pathway for signals, audio or MIDI, to enter a channel of the Session Mixer and is also a place to arrange related clips for playback. There are four different types of tracks in Live (see Figure 4.19), and each one serves a specific purpose in the way audio flows through your Live project.

The Audio Track

An audio track (the leftmost track shown in Figure 4.19) is where you will place audio clips so they can be routed through effects and fed into the Session Mixer. As we've mentioned before, only one clip can be playing at any time on a track, therefore it is wise to place similar clips that won't need to play simultaneously on the same track. For example, Verse Gtr and Chorus Gtr are two guitar parts from different sections of the song. They won't be played at the same time, so putting them on the same track makes sense. You can trigger the verse guitar part, and it will play until you trigger the chorus part. This gives you instant control of the arrangement since you can switch between the verse and chorus parts with a click of the mouse (or push of a button, if you've assigned external control).

To create a new audio track, choose Insert Audio Track from Live's Insert menu. You can also press Ctrl (Cmd)+T for the same results. Double-clicking an audio track will display its Track View. It is here that you'll place plug-in effects for processing the clips as they're fed to the Session Mixer. (Chapter 7 explains the usage of effects in Live.)

The MIDI Track

A MIDI track is the same as an audio track, except it holds MIDI clips, MIDI effects, and virtual instruments. When you create a MIDI track (Insert → Insert MIDI Track or Ctrl (Cmd)+Shift+T), it will output MIDI information, which can't be fed into the Session Mixer directly. Instead of seeing the normal volume and pan controls in the Mixer, you'll see only a status meter. These MIDI

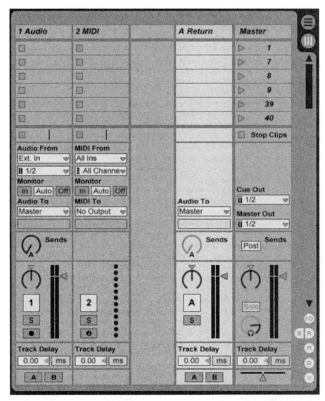

Figure 4.19   The Session View with one of each type of track.

tracks can send their data to external devices, such as sound modules, or to other MIDI tracks using the Input/Output Routing section.

Double-clicking a MIDI track displays its Track View. MIDI effects can be added to this view for performing operations on the incoming MIDI data. More important, virtual instruments such as Live's built-in Simpler and Impulse can be placed on the track to convert the incoming MIDI data to audio. Once an instrument has successfully been added, you'll see that the MIDI track now has audio controls in the Session Mixer. This essentially turns the MIDI track into a hybrid MIDI/audio track, one that functions as MIDI from track input through the clip slots and into the Track View, but functions as an audio track from instrument output through the Session Mixer. This means audio effects can be added to the Track View anyplace to the right of the virtual instrument.

The Return Track

A Return track does not hold any clips, audio or MIDI, but can host audio effects. Each Return track is fed by a mix of the Send knobs corresponding to the Return track (see Figure 4.20). As

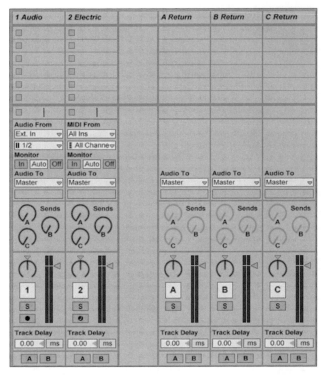

Figure 4.20 The Return track has a corresponding Send knob in each audio channel of the Session Mixer. Here we have three Send knobs for three Return tracks.

you'll discover in Chapter 8, "Using Effects and Instruments," the Return tracks allow you to add additional effects to multiple tracks without overly taxing your CPU.

By default, there are two Return tracks in a new Live Set. You can add more, up to 12, by choosing Insert → Insert Return Track from Live's menu, or by pressing Ctrl (Cmd)+Alt+T on your computer keyboard.

The Master Track

The final track, the Master track, is created automatically with every new Live Set and cannot be deleted. By default, new tracks send their output to the Master, although it is possible to route audio directly to physical outputs on your interface and bypass the Master track.

The Master track has its own Track View, and this is a fitting place for master compression or EQ to put the final touches on your mix (see Chapter 7). Also, the Master track will not hold clips but instead houses the Scene Launchers, which we'll explain in a moment.

Track Freeze

The Track Freeze function will help you manage your CPU load by "freezing" tracks so that they can still be launched but don't require all their processing to be performed. Live does this by rendering the clips on the track through all its instruments, effects, and whatever else is on the track and placing these clips back onto the track. To do this, simply right-click or Ctrl-click the name of the track you want to freeze and select Freeze Track from the context menu. You'll have to wait a moment while Live processes all the clips through the track's effects—obviously, longer clips will take longer. When finished, the track will turn an ice-blue color. Now, when you launch one of these frozen clips, you'll be playing an audio file from disk, as opposed to the CPU-intensive instruments and plug-ins that were running before.

What's so great about this is that, after rendering the new clips, Live automatically disables all the plug-ins on the track, thus freeing up valuable CPU resources. It does *not*, however, delete or remove these plug-ins—they merely lie dormant.

So what's the catch? Saving CPU must come at some sort of cost, right? Indeed it does, but a manageable one. Since Live has rendered the clips into temporary audio clips, you can no longer make any real-time tweaks to your sounds. The only thing you can do is launch the various clips in the track, which is still pretty cool because you keep real-time control of the song arrangement, even when the tracks are frozen. Additionally, you will still be able to alter the mixing controls on frozen tracks, such as Volume, Mute, Pan, Solo, and In/Out Routing.

If you find that you do need to tweak the sound, you can unfreeze the track (again, right-click or Ctrl-click the track and select Unfreeze Track), at which point Live will discard all of the temporary audio clips and will re-enable all of the plug-ins on the track. You can now use the track as normal. When you've completed your tweaks, you can refreeze.

This means you can make more parts in your song than would normally be possible by running everything in real time. Furthermore, it means slower computers now have the ability to create more complex compositions, using sounds from instruments and effects that normally wouldn't be able to run simultaneously.

You can perform cut, copy, paste, duplicate, and trim operations on frozen clips in addition to working with automation and clip envelopes. You can consolidate clips (Ctrl (Cmd)+J) and even drag frozen MIDI clips into audio tracks to create new clips!

In the Arrangement View, each track will keep playing until any effects you may be using, such as delay or reverb, die out. This is represented in the Arrangement as a crosshatched region immediately following the

(Also note that the new samples generated by the Freeze Track command are stored in your default temporary recording folder until you save your Live Set. When you save, these samples will be moved to the project subfolder Samples/Processed/Freeze.)

The Session

You'll quickly find the Session View to be the most spontaneous section of Live. It is here that tracks are arranged side by side and broken into tiny cells called *clip slots*. This clip slot grid

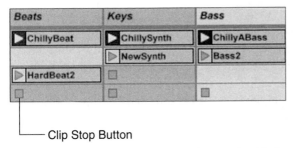

Clip Stop Button

Figure 4.21 Launching the second scene in this Session View example will allow the first clip (Chilly-Beat) to keep playing, while launching new synth and bass parts.

(see Figure 4.21) becomes a huge organizer for your musical ideas (all nicely encapsulated in clips) where you can begin to create the structure of your songs, as well as perform live arrangements.

Clip Stop Buttons In Figure 4.21, you'll see that only some of the empty clip slots have small squares in them. These are the Clip Stop buttons. If you click or trigger one of these buttons, it will stop the clip playing on that track. The clip will stop according to the Global Quantize setting.

Removing Clip Stop buttons from a scene will leave any playing clips on the track untouched when the scene is launched. (No new clip will start, and any playing clip will continue.) You can toggle a Clip Stop button on and off by selecting it (or a group of them) with the mouse and pressing Ctrl (Cmd)+E.

Adding Clips to the Session

Adding new clips to the session is as easy as dragging a file from the Browser into one of the clip slots. Audio files are dragged into the clip slots of audio tracks and MIDI files into the clip slots of MIDI tracks. You can also grab multiple samples from the Browser (hold Shift to select an area or Ctrl (Cmd) to select individual files) and add them as a group to the Session View. By default, the clips will be created on the same track. In fact, you'll see transparent versions of the clips as you drag them into the session. To have Live arrange the samples in the same scene, press and hold Ctrl (Cmd). You'll see the transparent clips change their arrangement into a horizontal fashion, and you can then choose their final destination.

You can also drag parts from the Browser and drop them onto empty areas of the Session View (where there are no tracks). When you do this, Live will automatically create the appropriate type of track and will place the new clip there. And you can create new clips directly in the session by recording your performances, either audio recordings or MIDI recordings. Recording new clips is covered in the recording sections of Chapters 5 and 6.

Drag-and-Drop Techniques

Clips can be added, moved, and duplicated in the Session View by using a variety of key and mouse combinations. You can move a clip already on the grid to other slots just by clicking and dragging it and then releasing the mouse button once the clip is in the desired location. Move groups of clips by first selecting the area of clips you want to move and then dragging your chosen group to a new location in the grid. You can select groups by dragging an area around the clips with the mouse. If there isn't any room around the clips, you can click one corner of your desired area (selecting the clip) and then click the other corner while holding the Shift key. Defining the corners of the area you want selects all clips within that area.

You can also duplicate a clip by selecting it (click once) and dragging the new copy to the desired location while holding the Ctrl (Option) key. By holding the Ctrl (Option) key when you click and drag, the original clip will stay in its original location. This is the same as selecting a clip, choosing Edit → Copy from the menu, clicking the destination, and choosing Edit → Paste. This duplicating technique also works with groups of clips like above.

Editing Commands

The clips in the Session View (and Arrangement View, for that matter) all respond to the standard Cut, Copy, Paste, and Delete editing commands. You can select a group of clips, choose Cut (Ctrl (Cmd)+X) to remove them, and then paste them (Ctrl (Cmd)+V) in a new location. You can also copy (Ctrl (Cmd)+C) clips and paste new versions elsewhere in the session. If you merely want to create a new copy of some clip to be moved later, you can use Duplicate (Ctrl (Cmd)+D) to instantly create a copy of your clips below the originals. Of course, you can always select clips and press Delete to erase them.

Using Scenes

Scenes are horizontal rows of clips in the Session View you can trigger all at once, meaning that you can trigger several clips with a single action. Musical arrangements in Live often work best if you think of your music as starting in Scene 1 (the top row) and then progressing downward, scene by scene (row by row). In other words, Scene 1 may be an intro section, Scene 2 may be a verse, Scene 3 may be a chorus, and so on. Of course, don't get caught up in the idea that your song has to work this way—you can set up and skip scenes in any manner you see fit. As you read on, this concept will begin to make sense.

Notice that in Live's Session View, the Scene Launcher is located just to the right of the clip slot grid. By pressing the sideways triangles in the Scene Launch strip (under the Master Track column), you can launch simultaneous playback for all clips in a given scene. If there are any Clip Stop buttons in the scene, they will stop any clip in their track. The Scene Launch buttons prove useful when composing live, on-the-fly arrangements, during which you may want to jump from one song section to the next and then back again. Figure 4.22 shows a single scene (row) in Live's Session View.

Scene Launch ──
Button

Figure 4.22 Scenes can be used as song sections, such as the verse, chorus, or bridge.

Two Scenes Are Better than One When working on a song arrangement, it can be really useful to make a copy of an entire scene and use it to create some variations. The Duplicate command will insert a new scene directly below the scene you are working in and will copy all present loops—a huge timesaver! To do this, select a Scene Launcher and press Ctrl (Cmd)+D.

Inserting and Naming Scenes To insert an additional scene (row) in Session View, or to insert a scene at a given point, select the scene above the desired location where you would like the new scene to appear and press Ctrl (Cmd)+I. You can also add additional scenes by choosing Edit → Insert Scene. If you create a new scene in the wrong place, see the "Moving Scenes" Tip. You can name or rename a scene by right-Ctrl-clicking it next to the Launcher button, accessing a pop-up context window.

Moving Scenes To move a scene, simply grab the scene's title with the mouse and drag it up or down to the preferred location. All clips in the scene will be included in the move.

Each row can house whole musical sections, new song directions, or merely a slight modification in the piece currently playing. Many Live users think of their songs from top to bottom, advancing their song as they move down the grid, one row at a time. The fact that a track can play only one clip at a time, rather than being a limitation, is actually a tool you can use to your advantage in a couple of different ways. For instance, by using variations of the same drum loop—each in its own Clip slot, stacked in the same track—you can make interesting drum fills and rhythmic turnarounds. This is also a great method for organizing other instrument tracks that change parts when moving from scene to scene (such as two different bass guitar loops, one for the verse, the other for the chorus). By dedicating a single track to variant clips of one particular instrument (one track for drums, one for bass, one for piano, etc.), you will create a more common mixer setup, one that feels more like an actual recording studio.

Channel Strip Live's Session Mixer approximates its analog cousin in a couple of important ways. For starters, any mix, panning, or effect settings on a given channel will be applied to any sound on that channel. If you plan carefully, you can take advantage of this by keeping similar instruments on the same track. For instance, if you apply an EQ to Track 1 and boost the highs, all highs on all clips on this channel will be boosted. As you move from scene to scene, verse to chorus, the settings remain the same. You will see in later chapters that Live's Arrangement View allows you to automate effects or toggle them on and off in the middle of a song, among other options.

You can therefore set up Live's Session Mixer to resemble an analog studio mixer: Track 1 is designated for drums, Track 2 is designated for guitar, and so on. The difference is that you will have several drum clips vertically aligned on the same track in each scene. Here is a more complete song (see Figure 4.23). Notice how the same loop is copied multiple times on each track (in multiple scenes).

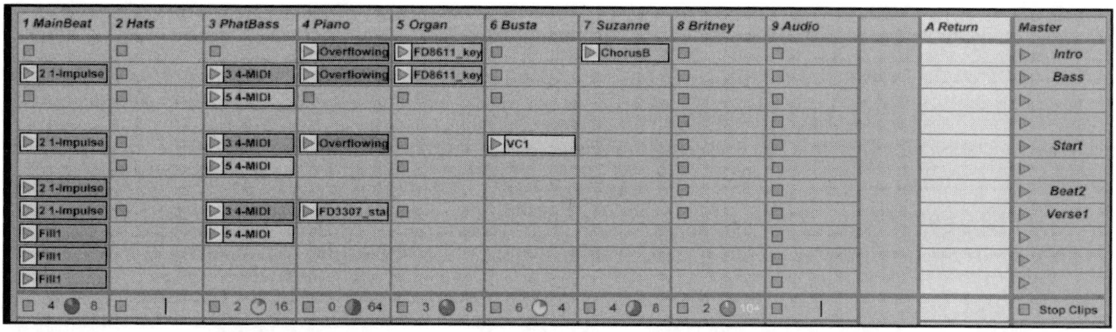

1 MainBeat	2 Hats	3 PhatBass	4 Piano	5 Organ	6 Busta	7 Suzanne	8 Britney	9 Audio		A Return	Master
			Overflowing	FD8611_key		ChorusB					▷ Intro
2 1-Impulse		3 4-MIDI	Overflowing	FD8611_key							▷ Bass
		5 4-MIDI									▷
											▷
2 1-Impulse		3 4-MIDI	Overflowing		VC1						▷ Start
		5 4-MIDI									▷
2 1-Impulse											▷ Beat2
2 1-Impulse		3 4-MIDI	FD3307_sta								▷ Verse1
Fill1		5 4-MIDI									▷
Fill1											▷
Fill1											▷
4 8		2 16	0 64	3 8	6 4	4 8	2				Stop Clips

Figure 4.23 This more complete-looking clip slot grid shows how a more developed song might work. You will move through the song sections by clicking the scenes, which are named in the Master column. As you can see, you don't need to use every row—scenes can skip rows if you like.

Ram Tough All of these copied loops will not strain your CPU more than the one instance of the loop playing. Live "knows" that the clips all reference the same file for playback.

There are a number of different ways to launch and move between scenes. In addition to pressing the Scene Launch button (with mouse, computer keyboard, or MIDI keyboard), you can also trigger a scene by pressing the Enter (Return) key so long as the scene number/name is highlighted. Changing the highlighted scenes can be done with the arrow keys and then triggered again with the Enter (PC) or Return (Mac) key. Live also features a Preferences setting (Select Next Scene on Launch—see Chapter 2) that will automatically move down one scene every time you press the Enter key. Note: If you select another clip slot or parameter on the mixer, you will need to highlight the scene again to begin triggering with the Enter/Return key.

Capturing Scenes

When experimenting with random combinations of clips in the Session View, you'll come across combinations that work well together. You can press Ctrl (Cmd)+Shift+I, or select Insert → Capture and Insert Scene, to create a new scene that is populated with the currently playing clips. You can quickly build a collection of potential scenes this way that you can experiment with to build a song arrangement.

Naming Scenes

Scenes can be named and renamed as many times as you like (the default name is simply a number). Many Live users label their scenes by song section, such as verse, chorus, bridge, or breakdown, in order to remind them what section they are triggering. To rename a scene, click its current name or number, press Ctrl (Cmd)+R, or choose Edit → Rename; then type in whatever you like. Press Enter (Return) to accept the new name or Escape to leave it as it was.

Programming Scene Tempos and Time Signatures

From time to time, you may want to make instantaneous jumps to different tempos while in the Session View. By naming a scene using a special convention, you can cause Live to change tempo when the scene is triggered. To switch the tempo to 85 BPM, just include "85BPM" in the name of the scene and launch it. The scene can be empty; you don't need to trigger any clips when you launch this scene if you merely want to change tempos. You can remove all the Clip Stop buttons (select them and press Ctrl (Cmd)+E so that none of your clips are stopped.

One instance where programming scene tempos is particularly helpful is when you're organizing a large batch of clips into a Set so that a single Live Set contains multiple songs. One group of scenes may belong to one song at a given tempo, while another group of scenes represents a different song and tempo and so on.

Scenes can also be named to create changes in the time signature. Time signatures are represented as fractions with the numerator (number of beats per bar) being any value from 1 to 99, and the denominator (type of beats) being 1, 2, 4, 8, or 16. Scene names can contain both time signature and tempo changes as long as the two values are separated by at least one character (see Figure 4.24).

MIDI and Computer Keyboard Control

There sure is a lot of mouse clicking going on in Live. Thankfully, you can offload a lot of these tasks to a much more intuitive interface, such as your MIDI keyboard or your computer's keyboard. Once you get Live under external control, you'll really be able to feel the musical power at your fingertips.

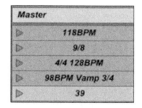

Figure 4.24 This more complete-looking clip slot grid shows how a more developed song might work. You will move through the song sections by clicking the scenes, which are named in the Master column. As you can see, you don't need to use every row—scenes can skip rows if you like.

Controlling Live from external devices is called *remote control*. Before you start, select your desired control devices in the Remote Control section of the MIDI/Sync Preferences pane (see Chapter 2). Live will remember these settings, but loading Live without one of your devices connected may require you to reselect it when it's available again.

First, click the MIDI Assignment button in the upper-right corner of the Live window or press Ctrl (Cmd)+M (see Figure 4.25). You'll see a bunch of blue squares and rectangles appear above Live's clip slot grid, Session Mixer, effects, and a variety of other parameters, such as Tempo and Groove in the Control Bar. You'll also see a MIDI Mappings window appear at left, containing a list of all MIDI mappings currently active in your Live Set.

Click here to enable MIDI mapping.

Figure 4.25 Clicking the MIDI Assignment button exposes the MIDI layer where control can be assigned to elements of Live.

The superimposed blue squares indicate controls that can have a MIDI message assigned to them. If you click on one of your clips in the clip slot grid and press a key on your MIDI keyboard, you'll see a white box appear in that clip slot showing the MIDI channel and note assigned to that slot. Clicking the MIDI Assignment button again will exit Assignment mode and return Live to normal. Now, when you press the assigned key on your MIDI keyboard, the clip will launch, just as if you'd clicked it with the mouse.

You can also assign knobs and sliders on a MIDI controller to the knobs and sliders you see on Live's screen. If you like, you can assign a knob to control a slider and vice versa—whichever suits your style. To assign MIDI controllers, press the MIDI Assignment button, click on the dial or fader you want to control, and then twist or move the control you want to use. Exit MIDI Assignment mode, and you'll be ready to go.

With the Push of a Knob Live will allow you to assign MIDI knobs and sliders to its buttons, as well as assign MIDI buttons to its sliders and knobs. In the first case, the button in Live will turn on when your MIDI control passes 64. It will switch off when you move the control back under 64. If you assign a MIDI button or key to a slider or knob, pressing the button or key will make the slider or knob toggle between its lowest and highest settings.

Just to the left of the MIDI Assignment button is the Keyboard Assignment button. This works the same way as the MIDI button, except it assigns Live's controls to keys on your computer keyboard instead of the keys on your synthesizer or other MIDI control device. Press Key (or Ctrl (Cmd)+K), and orange highlight boxes will appear, and a Key Mappings window will be displayed at the left. This window shows all of your currently active key mappings. Click and press a key to assign it a task, and then exit Key mode.

Min/Max Live allows you to constrain the movement of MIDI knobs to a smaller range of values. Normally, the relationship between a MIDI knob and a knob in Live is 1 to 1. This means the knob on-screen will follow the same movements of the associated MIDI knob.

This can prove troublesome from time to time, however, if you want to make only minute changes to a parameter. For example, if you assign a MIDI control to the volume of the track, you may not want the track ever to pass a certain volume because it would overpower your mix. To prevent this, you can assign minimum and maximum values to a control while making a MIDI assignment. After you've clicked on the knob while in MIDI Map mode, you'll see two number boxes at the bottom of the screen. Here, type in the minimum and maximum volumes you desire. When you leave MIDI assignment mode and attempt to crank up the volume of the track using the MIDI control, you'll find that the volume goes up to your maximum value only when the MIDI control is moved to its maximum position.

For even greater creativity, Live will allow you to place a higher number in the Minimum field and a lower number in the Maximum field. This essentially switches the polarity of the MIDI control, where turning up the MIDI control lowers the value of the control in Live and vice versa.

Also note that these minimum and maximum values affect only the way in which a MIDI knob or slider controls a value in Live. If you use your mouse on the Live control, you'll still have full range of motion.

Key and MIDI assignments are saved in each Live Set, so every song can have a different control scheme. If you find yourself always making common assignments, such as buttons for the Transport, you can assign them and save them as part of your Live template (see Chapter 2 for more on creating templates).

The Arrangement

Even though we've been touting Live's unique on-the-fly arranging style possible in the Session View, you still have the Arrangement View to consider. We've hinted a few times at what the Arrangement View does and how it shares channels on the Session Mixer with the Session View, but how does the Arrangement View augment your compositional workflow in Live? Some of you may think that the Arrangement View is a step in the opposite direction from Live's real-time capabilities; however, because of the unique interrelationship between the Session and Arrangement Views, you'll find the Arrangement View is just as creative a space to work in as the Session View, and it can be used to enhance a live performance.

Look Both Ways You can zoom and scroll through the Arrangement View using the same method as navigating the waveform display of the Clip View.

Anytime your mouse turns into a magnifying glass, you can click and drag to change your view—dragging up and down changes the zoom setting, while dragging left and right pans the view.

You can also use the condensed overview, located at the top of the Arrangement View, to locate sections of your arrangement. You can drag the left and right edges of the Overview box to choose the area you want to view.

What Is an Arrangement?

Briefly, an arrangement is a predetermined playback scheme of clips and mix automation (to be explained in a moment). The Arrangement View (see Figure 4.26) has horizontal tracks (unlike the vertical track layout of the Session View), and clips are placed in these tracks so they can be played in order from left to right. The Arrangement View is almost exactly like the timeline views of other sequencer packages such as Pro Tools, Logic, and Cubase. For those with experience in those programs, the Arrangement View will be instantly familiar.

Just like other sequencer programs, the Arrangement View has a playback cursor that shows the current playback location. When you press the Play button in Live's Control Bar, it will start the Arrangement running. In fact, *anytime* Live is running, even when just playing clips in the Session View, the Arrangement will be running as well.

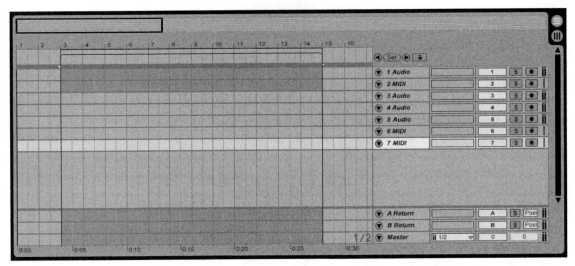

Figure 4.26 The Arrangement View is where you can start putting the arrangement of your song into stone.

When you start Live's transport, the Arrangement will start playing from the beginning of the song. If you want to start from a different position, click on an empty spot in the Arrangement to place the Start Marker (see Figure 4.27). Now, when you start the transport, Live will begin playing from the Start Marker. If you press Stop and then press Play (or if you press the spacebar once to stop, followed by another press to start again), the Arrangement will restart from the Start Marker. If you double-click Stop, the Start Marker will be removed, and the Arrangement will play from the beginning. If you want to have the arrangement restart from the point where you stopped it, you'll need to hold down Shift while you press the spacebar. The Shift+spacebar command means continue instead of start.

Click on an empty spot in the arrangement
to place the Start Marker.

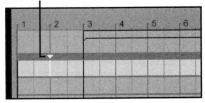

Figure 4.27 The Start Marker is signified by the small orange triangle at the top of the Arrangement View.

Another method for changing the start location of the Arrangement is to type in a new start time in the Control Bar. Also, if you click on a clip in the Arrangement, the Arrangement will start playing from the beginning of that clip the next time you start the transport.

The final method for controlling the transport involves mousing over the marker lane of the Arrangement (see Figure 4.28). When your mouse turns into a speaker icon, you can click, and Live will immediately begin playing from this location. You can even do this while the transport is running to jump to a different position in the Arrangement.

Click in this area to jump to different places in the arrangement.

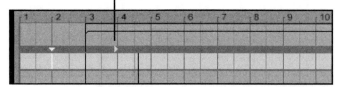

Figure 4.28   Click in this lane to make the Arrangement jump to that location.

Recording from the Session into the Arrangement

Because the Session and Arrangement Views are so closely related, it's possible to program the arrangement by recording your performance from the Session View. With the Session View open, press the Global Record button in the Control Bar (see Figure 4.29) and then perform your song as usual. When you're finished, press Stop and take a look at the Arrangement View (press Tab). It will now be filled with an arrangement of clips. Press Play, and the arrangement will begin to play. You'll hear your entire performance played back for you exactly as you recorded it, including all control movements, such as tempo changes, volume adjustments, and effect tweaks. Easy!

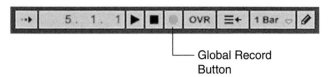

Global Record
Button

Figure 4.29   Global Record captures your every move into the arrangement.

Back to Arrangement   Since the Session and Arrangement Views share the same channels in the Session Mixer, it is possible to override what has been programmed into the Arrangement by launching clips in the session. These newly launched clips will play in place of what you've programmed into the Arrangement. When this happens, the Back to Arrangement button (see Figure 4.30) will light up red. Clicking this button (turning it back to gray) will stop any clips playing in the Session View and will re-engage the tracks in the Arrangement. If you're working on an arrangement and find you're hearing something different from what you see in the Arrangement View, check this button and be sure it's gray.

In the case of an empty Arrangement View, *anything* you do in the Session View will cause the Back to Arrangement button to light. This is because you're hearing something different from the arrangement—which is silence. You'll see that if you click the Back to Arrangement button in this situation, all of your clips will stop in order to play the silence programmed into the arrangement.

Figure 4.30   You can see that the Back to Arrangement button is lit. You can also see that Track 3 of the arrangement is not playing because the track is slightly transparent. Clicking the Back to Arrangement button will make Track 3 solid again so you can hear it.

If you find you like a different selection of clips in the Session View better than what you'd programmed into the arrangement, you can press the Arrangement Record button, and the Session clips will begin replacing the contents of their Arrangement tracks. This is just another way Live makes it easy to experiment and capture your ideas quickly without stopping the flow of music.

Adding Clips to the Arrangement

While recording from the Session View is one way of quickly filling the Arrangement View with clips, you can create new clips manually by using the same methods employed in the Session View. You can either drag files from your Browser to create new clips, or you can record new clips from external sources.

Drag a file from the Browser into an Arrangement track. *Voilà!* A new clip appears. This is exactly like dragging a file into one of the clip slots in the Session View. You can double-click this clip to see its Clip View where you can make all of your adjustments just like in the Session View. Indeed, clips in the Session View and Arrangement View are identical. One does not have more functions than the other; however, one thing you can do with an Arrangement clip is determine its play length. When a clip is added from a file, it will appear as only one repetition of the file (e.g., a one-bar drum loop will appear as a clip that is one bar long). By clicking and dragging the right edge of the clip, you can lengthen it, which will cause the clip to repeat as it's played. This works only for clips with Loop engaged. If your clip is not extending past a certain point, check the Clip View and make sure that Loop is enabled.

Session to Arrange (And Back Again) As you work on your masterpieces, you'll sometimes want to manually drop a Session clip into the Arrangement View. To do this, click a clip and hold down the mouse button while pressing the Tab key. Now you can drag that clip to wherever you want it in your arrangement and drop it in. The same technique also works for dropping clips from the arrangement into the session.

Editing the Arrangement

By editing the contents of the arrangement, you can fix mistakes you may have made while recording your performance. Perhaps you launched a clip a bar early when recording from the Session View. Maybe you coughed during the middle of a vocal take. You can remedy these mishaps using the techniques explained below.

You can also use the tools of the Arrangement View as a step in the creative process as well. You can use the meticulous editing and manipulation available at this level as a stylistic element of your music. In fact, the arrangement View often serves as a "cutting table" for assembling new clips for use in the Session View. You can splice together beats to create new clips or roll multiple vocal takes into one perfect take.

Viewing Tracks

There are two ways to view tracks in the Arrangement View: folded and unfolded (see Figure 4.31). A track can be unfolded by clicking on the downward pointing triangle next to the track name. Holding down Alt while clicking here will fold or unfold all tracks in the arrangement. The unfolded track can be resized easily by dragging up or down at the bottom edge of the track's Mixer section. While keeping tracks folded is convenient for getting an overview of your arrangement, many editing operations require that the track be unfolded. When you move your cursor over a clip in an unfolded track, it may change into a Pencil tool, indicating that Draw mode is enabled. For the editing features we're about to discuss, you'll want to turn off Draw mode by clicking on the pencil icon in the control bar so that it's not highlighted.

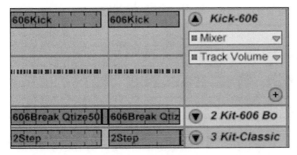

Figure 4.31 Fold and unfold tracks by using the arrow button next to the track name.

Cut, Copy, Paste, Duplicate, Delete

The standard Cut, Copy, Paste, Duplicate, and Delete commands work as expected in the Arrangement View. Copy (Ctrl (Cmd)+C) will copy the selected clip(s) to the computer's clipboard. You can then place a copy of the clip(s) at a new location on the timeline by first clicking the destination location for them in the desired track. Use Paste (Ctrl (Cmd)+V) to copy the clip(s) from the clipboard to this new location. You can also copy clips by holding down Alt while dragging a clip to a new location.

The Cut command (Ctrl (Cmd)+X) works like the Copy command, except that it removes the selected clip(s) from the source pane. You can then use Paste to place the clip(s) in a new location in the arrangement. Duplicate (Ctrl (Cmd)+D) simply takes the selected clip(s) and makes a new copy directly to the right of the selection. This is handy for repeating a section. If you want to remove a clip or clips without copying to the clipboard, select the clip(s) and press the Delete key.

If you want to perform one of the above actions on just a portion of a clip, you'll have to unfold the track first. Once the track is unfolded, you can click and drag in the clip's overview to highlight just a portion of it and then perform the editing action you want.

Dragging and Resizing

When a track is folded, you can move a clip (or group of clips) by clicking anywhere in the clip and dragging it to a new location. When the clip is unfolded, you'll have to click on the title bar (above the waveform display) of the clip before dragging it. Select a group of clips and click-drag one to move the whole group. You can even drag the clip(s) to a different track if you want. Furthermore, you can change the length of a clip by moving your mouse to its left or right edge. When your mouse turns into a bracket ( ]), click and drag the clip to your desired length. You'll be able to extend the clip beyond its original length only if the Loop button for the clip is on.

Splitting and Consolidating Clips

You can break a clip into smaller clips using the Split function. To do this, you'll need to unfold the track first. Once the track is unfolded, you can find the point at which you want to split the clip. Now click the location for your cut and press Ctrl (Cmd)+E. The clip will be split into two clips (see Figure 4.32). These new clips will be completely independent of one another, meaning they can have their own unique Transpose, Gain, Warp, Loop, and Envelopes.

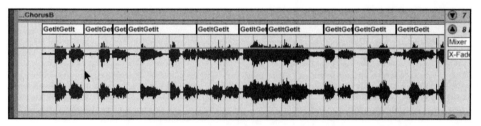

Figure 4.32 Just click and split to break clips into smaller ones for independent editing.

After breaking clips into smaller ones for editing purposes, you can rejoin the clips into one clip for easier use. Select the clips that you want to join and select Consolidate from the Edit menu, or press Ctrl (Cmd)+J. Live will quickly render a new clip containing all the parts you had selected. When Live consolidates a clip, it creates a new audio file in your project folder, in *Samples → Processed → Consolidate*.

Cut, Paste, Duplicate, Delete, and Insert Time

While copying and manipulating clips are achieved with the Cut, Copy, Paste, and Delete functions, you can use the Cut Time, Duplicate Time, Delete Time, and Insert Silence commands to make broad edits to the whole arrangement. When using these commands, you need to select (by click-dragging) only the area of time you want to manipulate. These commands work on all tracks simultaneously, selected or not.

The Cut Time command (Ctrl (Cmd)+Shift+X) works like the regular Cut command, except that it cuts an entire section of the arrangement away to the clipboard and moves the rest of the arrangement over to fill the gap that would be left by the clips that were cut. You can place the Cut Time in a new location if you want by clicking the desired insert point in the arrangement and selecting Paste Time (Ctrl (Cmd)+Shift+V). Just like the Cut version, the Paste Time command will move everything over to make enough room for the section of time you are pasting in.

Duplicate Time (Ctrl (Cmd)+Shift+D) will duplicate a section of an arrangement and insert it directly to the right of the original. Delete Time will remove a section from the arrangement without copying it to the clipboard.

Insert Silence (Ctrl (Cmd)+I) will insert an amount of silence where you click-drag an area. Selecting the first two bars of an arrangement and executing Insert Silence will shift the entire arrangement to the right by two bars, thus giving you two bars of silence before the song starts.

Automation

Along with the clips are tracks of *automation*. Automation is programmed or recorded movements for controls in Live's mixer, devices, and plug-ins. For example, if you want to fade out the volume at the end of your song, you would *automate* the Master Volume so Live will perform the fade every time it reaches the end of the song.

Just about every parameter in Live can be automated. One exception is the Solo/Cue switch in the mixer. Ableton conceived of this control as a tool for isolating tracks in the studio, or pre-listening on the gig, so automation for this control has never been possible.

Recording Automation

The simplest and most intuitive means of automating your arrangement is by recording the desired control movements in real time while the song plays. For example, to program the fade-out explained above, you'd activate the Arrangement Record button in the Control Bar and press Play. When the song reaches the point where you want to fade out, start moving the Master Volume control downward. You can either click and drag with the mouse or use an external MIDI controller—both methods will be recorded the same way. When you're done with the fade, press Stop. You'll now see a red dot in the Master Volume control. This red dot appears over any control that has recorded automation in the arrangement. You can go back and repeat the recording process as many times as you like to build your automation in layers. For instance, you can control the volume of a synth part on the first pass and then make another recording to automate the pan. Live will perform the previous pass of volume automation while you make the new recording of pan movements.

Viewing Automation

You can see the automation for a track by first unfolding the track and then selecting the parameter you want to view. The parameter is selected by using the two menus in the track: The first menu (the Device Chooser) selects the general category of automation, such as Mixer, Send, or any of the track's plug-ins. The second menu (the Control Chooser) selects a specific parameter from the general category selected. For example, to see the track's volume automation, you'd select Mixer in the first menu and Track Volume in the second menu. If an Auto Filter effect is loaded onto the track, you can view its Cutoff automation by choosing Auto Filter and Cutoff Freq.

Automation is displayed as a line-graph superimposed over the clip's data (see Figure 4.33). The meaning of the line shown in the automation track is determined by the parameter being controlled. In the case of level controls such as Volume or Send, volumes increase as the line moves

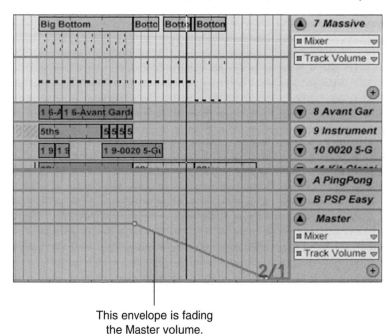

This envelope is fading
the Master volume.

Figure 4.33 You can see the final fadeout of the song represented by the downward-sloping line in the Master track of the arrangement.

toward the top of the track. For other controls, such as Pan, a line in the center of the track represents a center pan position. Lower values move the pan left, while higher values move the pan right.

As of Live 7, it is now possible to view more than one lane of automation at a time. The easiest way to view all of a track's automation is to right-click on the track name and select Add Lane for Each Automated Envelope from the context menu (see Figure 4.34). Note that Ableton uses the terms *Automation* and *Automation Envelopes* interchangeably. Clip Envelopes are a different entity and will be discussed in Chapter 5.

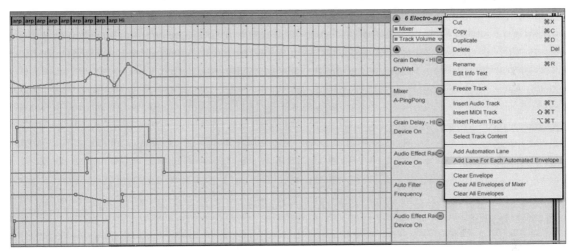

Figure 4.34 Use the plus and minus icons in a track's title bar to add and remove automation lanes.

If you want to view only certain envelopes, you can click the plus sign below the track name. This will add a new lane for whatever envelope you are currently viewing on the track. To add additional lanes, select a different envelope from the Device and Control Choosers, and click the plus sign. Conversely, each automation lane has a minus sign that can be used to remove the lane. Instead of removing lanes, you may just want to hide them. This can be done with the additional Fold button that appears at the bottom of the track's title bar.

Editing Automation

You can change the shape of the automation graph by using two techniques. When Draw Mode is off (toggle Draw Mode with Ctrl (Cmd)+B), you will be creating *breakpoint envelopes* (see Figure 4.35). The automation will be displayed as lines with little circles at each "elbow," known as *breakpoints*. You can click and drag these breakpoints to new locations to reshape the graph. You can double-click a circle to delete it, or you can double-click a line to create a new breakpoint in that location. You can also select an area of the automation graph (click and drag the desired area) and then move a whole section of automation around with the mouse.

Maintain Ctrl When editing automation curves, you'll frequently be making only small modifications, such as increasing volume by 1 dB or making a mute happen a little sooner. By holding the Ctrl (Cmd) key while moving points of the graph, your mouse movements will be minimized, allowing you to make subtle and specific changes with ease.

By switching Draw Mode on, you will be working with Live's Pencil tool. By drawing with the pencil in the automation graph, you'll create flat "steps" that are each the same width as the current grid setting (see Figure 4.35). This will allow you to create tempo-synced automation effects, such as volume gates or timed effect sends. The pencil will overwrite any ramps that may have been made in the breakpoint mode in favor of its flat-step style.

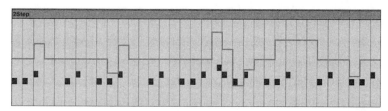

Figure 4.35   Using the Pencil tool, you can create tempo-synced steps in your automation graphs.

Quantize Keys You can change the value used for the quantize grid with these keystrokes:

Ctrl (Cmd)+1: Makes the quantize units smaller.

Ctrl (Cmd)+2: Makes the quantize units larger.

Ctrl (Cmd)+3: Toggles triplet mode on and off.

Ctrl (Cmd)+4: Toggles the quantize grid on and off. When the grid is off, you will be able to draw values anywhere.

You can also select different Adaptive or Fixed Grid modes by right-clicking (Ctrl-clicking) a track in the Arrangement View.

Locators and Time Signature Changes

In simple terms, locators can be used to mark different sections, such as flagging the start of a verse, chorus, or bridge. However, Ableton did not stop there—it has given you the ability to jump around to different locators in your arrangement, thus allowing you to perform custom arrangements right in the Arrangement View.

Creating Locators

Creating a locator is about as simple as it gets: Click the Set button in the upper-right corner of the arrangement at the point where you want to drop the marker (see Figure 4.36). Like all things in Live, the locator will be placed at the nearest beat specified in the Quantize menu. Locators can also be created by right-clicking in the Scrub area (the area directly above the topmost track) and selecting Add Locator from the context menu.

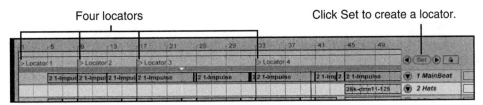

Figure 4.36   Every time you click Set, a new locator will be created at the current play position.

Moving and Renaming Locators

Each time you make a locator, it will be given the name Locator followed by a number. To give the locator a more useful name, right-click (Ctrl-click) on the locator and choose Rename. You can also click the locator to select it; then press Ctrl (Cmd)+R to rename.

You can change the locations of locators after you've made them by clicking the locator and dragging it to a new location in the timeline. If you want to remove the locator, click to select it and then press Delete.

Jumping to Locators

The best part about locators is the ability to jump between them seamlessly while the arrangement is playing. All you have to do is click on a locator (it will begin to flash green) and playback will jump to that location, subject to global quantization. You can also use the two arrow buttons to the left and right of the Set button to jump to the previous or next locator.

Ableton really hit the mark, though, by allowing you to assign MIDI messages and computer keys to these locators, just like any other control in Live. This means that the arrangement is now nearly as flexible as the Session View in that you can repeat sections of the song at will or jump to other areas as you see fit. Even the most complex of arrangements is now opened up for your experimentation, thanks to these locators.

Time Signature Changes

Time signature changes can be created by right-clicking in the Scrub area, choosing Insert Time Signature Change from the context menu, and typing in the time signature you want (see Figure 4.37). Editing and deleting a time signature change is done from the context menu as well. Just right-click on the time signature change and select Edit to alter the time signature or Delete to remove it.

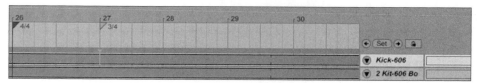

Figure 4.37 Time signature changes in the Arrangement View.

Looping and Punching

The Loop Start and Loop Region Length values serve two purposes. In addition to specifying the Arrangement loop points, they also mark the start and stop points for automatic recording (punching).

Creating a Loop

You can loop, or repeat, a section of the arrangement by placing the Loop Brace around the desired area and clicking the Loop button in the Control Bar (see Figure 4.38). You can start the arrangement anywhere you like, but if playback reaches the right Region Marker, it will jump back to the position of the left Region Marker. To the left of the Loop button is a numerical display indicating the bar and beat that the region begins, while on the right you will see another numerical display showing the length of the region. If you prefer, these values can be edited directly instead of moving the Loop Brace.

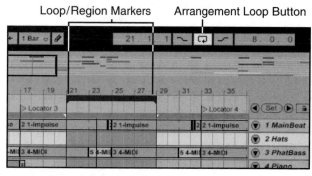

Figure 4.38 Playback will loop repeatedly between the Region Markers while the Loop button is engaged.

You can move the Loop region while the arrangement is playing. Playback will not follow the Region Markers as you move them, but the song will begin to loop again once it reaches the new location of the right marker. This means you can loop one section and then just move the markers to the new location after all the desired repetitions are played. After Live reaches the next region, it loops. This can help you zero in on problem spots, automate mix settings, or merely give a section a good listen. If you happen to move the Loop region to a position to the left of the current playback location, playback will continue until the end of the song.

Instant Loop Often, you'll find that you want to set your loop points to match the exact length of a clip, or a series of clips, in your arrangement. To do so, select the clip(s) and then press Ctrl (Cmd)+L, which is the shortcut for Loop Selection. This will automatically set the Loop Brace to the position and length of the selected clip(s).

Punching In and Out

In the next two chapters, we will discuss recording audio and MIDI into Live. The process is nearly identical for both audio and MIDI clips. We will cover how to record both into the Session View and the Arrangement View.

When recording to the Arrangement View, Live can be set so that it automatically begins recording at a specified point in the arrangement and stops at another. This is the second function of the Loop Brace. This auto-recording function is referred to as *punching* and is enabled by the two buttons on either side of the Loop button (see Figure 4.39). Punching in occurs when you start recording; punching out occurs when you stop. Normally, punching is used when you need to replace only a section of a recording, as you might after recording a good take with a few weak passages.

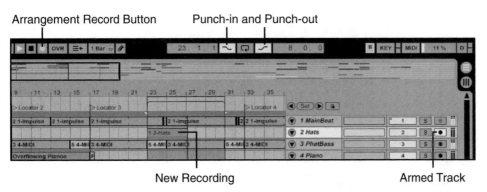

Figure 4.39 Here we've placed the Region Markers around the bar right before the last chorus. With the Punch-In and Punch-Out buttons, we can start playback before the bad measure, but Live will only record the section in between the markers.

As you can see, the Punch-In and Punch-Out buttons can be set independently. This means you can have Live start recording at a specific point and continue until you stop it. This will allow you to punch in partway through the song and record until the end. You can also have Live stop recording in the same spot every time. This is helpful when trying to nail down a tricky intro part.

Export Audio

After you have finished your Live song—and you like the way it sounds—it is time to get it out of your computer, burned to CD, and onto the streets. Before you can start burning CDs, though, you need to render your arrangement to a stereo audio file. Figure 4.40a shows the Export Audio/Video dialog (formerly known as Render to Disk) that appears when you press Ctrl (Cmd)+R. Figure 4.40b shows the only difference in this dialog when it is invoked from the Session View: the Length value.

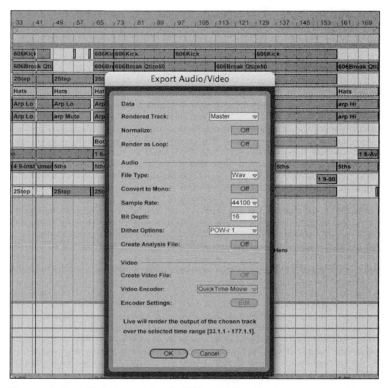

Figure 4.40a   The Export Audio/Video dialog in Arrangement View.

Figure 4.40b   The Export dialog in Session View differs only in that the length of the output file must be specified in the Length field.

In both the Session and Arrangement Views, the Render to Disk menu presents several important decisions to make. To begin, you will need to know the exact length of the section of audio you are rendering. If you are rendering from Session View, then you are likely rendering only a four-, eight-, or sixteen-bar section, whereas in the Arrangement View, you may well be rendering an entire song and can select the amount of desired rendering time by highlighting the portion of the arrangement you want to render (or its entirety). For instance, if you want to render a four-minute song, simply drag (highlight) the entire length of the song on any track.

Note that you also need to select which output to render, selected in the Rendered Track box. For creating a final mix, you would select the Master output. You also have the option to render any of the individual tracks or the Render All Tracks option, which will render each of your tracks individually all at the same time. This last option can be extremely useful if you want to export split tracks for mixing in another audio sequencer such as Pro Tools or Logic.

Remember that rendering the Master output will include only the output that is routed to the Master track. If you want to create a submix of a few tracks, you can solo those tracks, and only those will be heard in the final mix. Also, don't forget that if you have any tracks bypassing the Master and being routed directly to outputs on your audio interface, they won't get included at all.

To render from Session View, the steps are as follows:

1. Determine how long you want your loop or rendered audio section to be. There is no need to render more than one repetition of the audio segment; however, you can often make your music more interesting by embellishing the repeated loop and then rendering both the original and the varied loop as two loops.

2. Launch all of the clip(s) you want to be rendered. Once you've got them all playing, stop the sequencer.

3. Select File → Render to Disk to call up the Export Audio/Video dialog and type in the length of the file to be rendered, as determined in Step 1.

4. Click OK or press Enter, and select the drive/folder where you want to save your new loop.

To render from the Arrangement View, do the following:

1. Select the portion of the arrangement that you want to render. This selection can be made by click-dragging on any track, clicking on a clip, Shift-clicking to select a series of clips, or adjusting the loop brace to the desired length and clicking on its top bar.

2. Select File → Export Audio/Video to call up the Export dialog. Note that the range you have selected in Step 1 is displayed at the bottom of the dialog.

3. Select the Rendered track. Select Master to create a final mix, select an individual track, or select All Tracks to export all tracks individually.

4.   Click OK or press Enter, and select the drive/folder where you want to save your new loop.

Normalize

When the Normalize setting is set to On, Live will raise the level of the highest peak to the maximum level possible without distortion. I recommend leaving this setting off for full songs and relegating all mastering/normalizing tasks to your wave editor (or mastering engineer!). Most wave editors, such as Sonic Foundry's Sound Forge, Bias's Peak Audio, and Steinberg's Wavelab, have a good deal more flexibility than Live in the matter of normalizing; however, if you are merely rendering a quick loop or small selection of audio, you may switch on Live's Normalization setting to save time.

Render as Loop

Upon first glance, Render as Loop may seem like an insignificant option; however, this is a very important box if you have used any reverbs or delays in your soon-to-be-rendered loop. Typically, you want to render any audio file with delay or reverb such that you can hear the entire "tail" of the effect. In other words, you want to hear the reverb or delay decay until the sound completely dissipates. In a looping context, this creates a problem because the very end of the decay actually needs to occur at the *beginning* of the loop. By activating the Render as Loop option, Live will render the file twice—once placing in the effect tails, and twice to actually render the sample(s). Without this option enabled, delays and reverbs will be heard to end abruptly when the audio loops back to the beginning.

File Type

When rendering, you have a choice between saving your audio in either AIFF or WAV file format—either of which is capable of being burned to CD. When in doubt, stick with WAV files—they are readable by both Macs and PCs, while AIFFs are not natively recognized by Windows. When it comes time to actually burn your music onto a CD, you will need to use Apple's iTunes, Microsoft's Windows XP burning utility, or a third-party CD-burning utility.

Sample Rate

Always render at the sample rate of the audio with the highest sample rate in your set. In other words, when rendering, don't have Live reduce the sample rate of your audio unless absolutely necessary. If you have recorded or imported audio with a sample rate of 96,000, you should render at 96,000 and use a program optimized for sample rate conversion to reduce the sample rate to 44,100 (the CD standard rate).

Typically, you will use sample rates only of 44,100Hz and up. For most applications, a sample rate of 44,100 is adequate, while rates of 48,000 and 96,000 will provide more accurate sampling at the expense of hard disk space and CPU drain. The lower sample rates (22,050 and

32,000) are most often used for creating lo-fi special effects popularized by older first- and second-generation hardware samplers.

Bit Depth

The Bit Depth drop-down menu gives you three choices: 16, 24, or 32 bit. If you are making a CD, your audio will eventually have to get down to 16-bit, but this doesn't necessarily mean you should always render to 16-bit. Live's internal architecture is 32-bit, which means that even if you start out with a 16-bit loop, once you've added effects and automation, the resulting audio is 32-bit. Therefore, strictly speaking, 32-bit is the safest bet for maintaining maximum audio quality when rendering.

However, rendering 32-bit audio is not always practical. Not only does it take up a lot of disk space, 32-bit is not currently a common standard and may not be supported by other audio software, not to mention the fact that you can't burn a CD from it. The bit depth you choose will end up being based on what you are going to be doing with the resulting file. If you are going to have your audio professionally mastered, render at 32-bit or ask the mastering engineer what format is preferred. If you're rendering audio that's going to be imported back into an arrangement, go with 32-bit to avoid any loss in quality. If you are going straight from Live to CD, then 16-bit is the way to go. But 24-bit is the safest bet when rendering tracks to be imported into another sequencer such as Pro Tools or Logic.

Dithering Options

Dithering is a process that adds low-level noise to digital audio to hide the distortion that occurs when reducing bit depth. While it is outside of the scope of this book to have an in-depth discussion of dithering, there are a few things you need to know. First, whenever you are rendering below 32-bit, some sort of dithering should be used. The three POW-r dithering modes are for final mastering. Use one of these when you are preparing your audio for CD, but never when there is going to be additional processing done to the audio. The rule of thumb is that dithering should not be applied more than once. However, there are cases where this is necessary, such as rendering 24-bit audio to import into another sequencer. Eventually, this audio will be dithered to 16-bit. In this case, you should use Triangular dither when rendering at 24-bit.

Create Analysis File

Each time Live sees a WAV or AIFF file, it has to draw a visual waveform, determine the positioning of the Warp Markers, and analyze the pitch and tempo. To do all this, Live uses a small, pertinent secondary file called an *Analysis File* that will retain the master sample or loop's file name with the added file extension .asd. When this setting is activated, Live will also create an ASD file in addition to the rendered audio file. This is helpful when creating loops that will be reimported back into Live. Otherwise, it is really not necessary to create the added file.

Convert to Mono

Although this heading is fairly self-descriptive, I want to point out its usefulness. Many Live musicians have found that Mono loops/samples are preferable when working in a limited environment, such as a laptop computer setup. The reason is that stereo loops are actually two channels of audio running on a single track. Therefore, they require roughly twice the system resources of a mono file—I say roughly because Live can forego all Warp Marker and file analysis since it has already been done for one side/channel of the file.

Watch the Levels As you are adjusting and automating your mix, pay close attention to Live's Master Level meters. They will tell you when your overall levels are peaking. (As an added visual cue, the meters turn red any time a wave gets clipped.) Any peaking on the output channels will result in a nasty digital glitch or distortion. To remedy the problem, simply decrease the Master Volume. Don't worry if you see other channels in your Session Mixer entering the red. Live has an extreme amount of headroom that will allow your individual channels to enter the red without distorting. The only channel you really need to be worried about is the Master.

Scoring to Video

While Live 6 created a lot of excitement by adding video support, Live 7 has taken things a step further by giving us the option to export video as well. Here's how it works.

Importing Video

Getting video into Live is simple: Just locate the video file you want to import in the File Browser and drag it into your Live Set. The audio will be loaded on an audio track in Live, and the video will appear in a special floating video window. Only video files in QuickTime format (.mov, .mp4, or any other format playable by QuickTime) are supported.

You can only work with video in the Arrangement View. If you drop a movie into the Session View, the clip will load as audio only. Once loaded, the video clip will look like any other audio clip in Live, except that you will see virtual "sprocket holes" in the top of its title bar to show that it has video associated with it (see Figure 4.41).

Video clips in the Arrangement View behave more or less just like audio clips. Thus, by dragging a video clip into the arrangement and aligning it with the beginning of the first measure, you can quickly start scoring to picture and creating a soundtrack. You can use Live's FX and audio editing tools to edit the video clip's associated audio in the Arrangement View, just like any other audio clip. (You will find that Consolidate, Crop, and Reverse operations will cause your video clip to be replaced by an audio clip.)

Figure 4.41   A video clip in the Arrangement View; you can also see the associated Video window.

The Video Window

The Video window will always be visible, as shown in Figure 4.41, as long as you are using the video clip in your arrangement, and the video will follow playback when activated by Live's transport. You can drag the Video window around wherever you want. You can resize it by clicking on the lower-right corner or expand it to full-screen mode by double-clicking on the video itself.

Keeping Sound and Video In Sync

The most common application for video in Live will probably be creating a new soundtrack for a video clip of a given length. In this application, the most important thing is not to disturb the timing of the video inside Live. To maintain sync, simply drag your video clip to the beginning of the Arrangement View and then make sure that you have the video clip's Master/Slave switch set to Master. This makes the video Live's tempo master, meaning that any changes to the Warp Markers in the video will change Live's master tempo—not the playback speed of the video. This allows you to define hit points in the video, which will affect the playback speed of the other clips in your session. Changing the speed of the video to match your music will not make you a very popular film composer!

Saving/Exporting

After you have finished your new soundtrack, you will want to save your work either as a new movie or as an audio file to be turned over to a film editor. If you're just exporting audio, there are a few things to bear in mind. First, the safest bet for turning in your soundtrack to an editor is to make an audio file the exact length of the video you were given, so the start points line up exactly and there won't be any confusion about where your sound cues go. Second, if you're exporting audio only, don't forget to mute the audio on the video track; otherwise, you'll get a file containing both the dialog and the music.

To create a video, select File → Export Audio/Video and turn on Create Video File in the bottom section of the dialog. The menu below allows you to choose the type of video encoding you desire. If you need to customize the video settings in any way (to optimize it for Internet streaming, for example), use the Edit button next to Encoder Settings.

As you will probably notice once you start working with video clips, any audio editing commands that you apply to the audio track hosting your video clip will affect the video playback as well. In other words, you can use all of Live's Warping and editing functions to create video as well as audio edits. So get busy taking advantage of Live 7's video export capabilities to create some warped video mashups—YouTube awaits!

Summary

We covered quite a lot of topics in this chapter—everything to bring your song from the tiniest musical fragments to fully arranged compositions. It is appropriate, therefore, to summarize the process once more just to help solidify it in your mind.

Here is a *general* idea of how a song is built in Live:

1. You start, for example, in the Session View by making a MIDI track named *Drums*. You load an Impulse instrument (see Chapter 8) onto the track and quickly build a drum kit from samples on your hard drive. You program a MIDI clip for the main groove of your song and set it to loop.

2. You might then make an audio track titled Bass. You pull out your P-Bass and plug it into the instrument input 1 of your audio interface. You select input 1 of your interface on the Input/Output Routing strip and arm the track. You can now hear your bass blended with the drums, although you're not recording anything. You fool around for a moment on the bass until you come up with a part you like. You click one of the record buttons in a slot on the track and start playing on the next downbeat. You put down the jam along with the drums. When you're done, you click again on the clip, and it begins to play. You move the clip's right Loop Marker to the left since you didn't stop the recording on the downbeat (your hands were full playing the bass).

3. You keep recording new clips, such as guitar and MIDI synth parts. You search your loop libraries for things that augment the song. Once you find a good combination, you use Capture and Insert Scene. You now have one scene in your session.

4. You record a new bass part for the next section of your song. You write some new drum clips. You record the parts of other members in your band. You start tweaking clips with envelopes. You keep building more and more sections and capturing them as scenes.

5.   Once you have a pretty good set of scenes to build a song from, you start listening to them and reordering them on-screen into a songlike structure. (It's okay if you don't use all the scenes you captured.) You enable Record in the Control Bar and start performing the song as it's arranged in the Session View. You can, of course, trigger any scene in any order that you want (you don't *have* to go top to bottom) and can also launch any clip you want individually.

6.   You'll have a skeleton of your song in the Arrangement View. You now start making multiple passes over the song to program volume fades, mutes, pans, effect modulations, and any other automation you want in your song. You also edit the clips in the Arrangement View, changing their length, volumes, and so on, and splitting and rearranging them.

7.   Throughout this process, you are adding effects to the mix and bouncing the results to new clips when necessary.

8.   You then start to experiment with new parts against your arrangement by launching new clips in the Session View. You try out some new synth loops and record new guitar riffs—they'll all play synchronized with the arrangement. When you want to hear your original arrangement again, you click Back to Arrangement.

9.   You finalize your song's arrangement, putting the last tweaks on your mix. You render the final arrangement to a WAV file. In Wavelab, you apply mastering plug-ins and maximize the quality of your song. You render the results to a 16-bit, 44,100Hz stereo file, which you burn to CD. You take the CD and put it in your car and drive all around town with it turned up as loudly as possible!

Of course, the process of creation in Live is entirely up to you. You may decide that, instead of building the song from little pieces, you're going to multitrack your whole band playing at once, thus capturing the song in one pass. You then use the creative editing and mixing features of Live to finalize the mix. Afterwards, you may take those large recordings and split them into small clips so you can make a live remix in the Session View. The creative flow is all up to you. Isn't that nice?

5 The Audio Clip

The audio clip has been the basic building block in Live since version 1 and is basically a reference to an audio file on your hard drive. When you trigger an audio clip, it plays the referenced audio file according to the settings contained in the Clip View. The parameters available to you are plentiful yet simple to understand. Using the tools of the audio clip, you can make any audio file play back in perfect sync with your song, as well as play it in the proper key. You can also use the audio clip settings to mangle your sounds and generate new ones.

In addition, you can record new audio clips from virtually any source. You can use the inputs of your audio interface for recording vocals, guitars, drums, pianos, horns, and synths—anything that can be picked up with a microphone or connected directly to the audio interface is fair game. You can also record from other computer programs or other tracks in your Set or even re-record Live's own output. Live's Launch Quantizing allows you to play around with sounds precisely, such as recording perfect loops on the fly.

Before you start recording hordes of audio clips, take a moment to familiarize yourself with their unique parameters. Drag an audio file from the Browser into a Clip Slot, or load one of Live's Demo Sets so you can follow along and try tweaking some of the parameters that follow.

Audio Clip Properties

The properties of an audio clip are edited through the Clip View (see Figure 5.1). Double-click an audio clip to see its contents at the bottom of the screen. The properties of an audio clip are organized into four boxes: Clip, Launch, Sample, and Envelopes. Every clip in Live has the Clip,

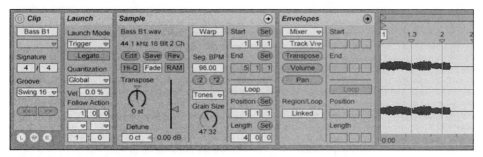

Figure 5.1 The Clip View for an audio clip.

Launch, and Envelope properties, but the Sample box is unique to audio clips. In this chapter, I'll explain those areas unique to audio clips. You'll get the rundown on MIDI clips in the next chapter.

Buttons

In the Sample window (Figure 5.2) is a group of six buttons that are used to manage the sample used in the audio clip.

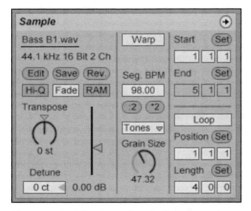

Figure 5.2   The Sample window contains controls concerning audio file playback speed, pitch, volume, and loop region, plus the settings for the Warp Engine.

Edit

Clicking the Edit button will open the audio file in the sample editor you have selected in File/Folder Preferences. Audio editors are useful for performing a variety of operations on your audio files, particularly when you want to edit *destructively*. Now, this may not sound very appealing at first, but there are times that you want to make a change that permanently affects the audio file itself. Modifying the Sample properties in Live only changes that audio file's playback characteristics. In other words, it is what is called *non-destructive editing*. If you have a file that has an ugly digital click that you never want to hear again, you may want to go chop it out with an audio editor.

While you are editing your sample file, the Clip View's waveform display will say Sample Offline. When you finish editing, just save your changes and return to Live. The newly edited sample will be loaded into the clip.

Save

When adjusting the parameters of a clip, you may want your changes to become part of the audio file. For example, if you have to warp a certain beat every time you load it into a clip slot, wouldn't it be nice if Live could remember the Warp Markers the next time you import the file? By pressing Save, information regarding the playback settings of the audio file will be saved in a special file with the extension .asd. The ASD file contains the peak information of the audio file (used for the Clip View waveform display), but it can also contain information regarding Warp Markers, Tempo, Tuning, and Warp modes. Pressing Save updates the ASD file with the clip's current settings. Next time you create a clip from the file (by dragging it from the Browser), the Warp Markers will already be in place, and the proper Tuning and Warp modes will be set.

Reverse

Live's sample reverse feature (the Rev. button) is not instantaneous—don't expect it to be. It is, however, a whole lot of fun when used properly. Click the Reverse button and Live will create a new audio file—a reversed version of the original. This new audio file will be named the same as the original but will have the letter "R" added to the end.

Okay, so it's not truly a Reverse button, as in "play the sample backwards." Instead, the Reverse button means "play a backward version of the sample." This means you'll have to wait for the "R" file to be made the first time you reverse, but from that point on, Live will just choose the original or reversed file to play, allowing you to switch directions almost instantaneously. Because of the nature of the Reverse feature, you may want to avoid using this button during live performances. Instead, I recommend you make two clips: one normal and one reversed.

Hi-Q

This button simply switches the audio clip between high-quality and low-quality interpolation (used for transposition). If this button is on, the clip will play using better pitch shifting and resampling algorithms, but it will also place a slightly heavier strain on your CPU. I recommend leaving this option on for all clips (setting it to "on" in the Default Preferences) and turning it off only if you have a slower computer and you need to save every bit of CPU power.

Fade

To help an audio file loop seamlessly (no clicks or pops when the file loops around), Live can perform a quick (4ms) volume fade at the ends of the clip. I recommend leaving this option on as the default, unless the downbeat transient seems too quiet. It is possible that the fade can soften the initial attack of the downbeat (for instance, shaving the attack of a one-shot sample), so you may need to turn this off from time to time.

RAM

As I've mentioned before, Live streams audio files from disk as they play. With each additional audio clip that plays, the computer will have to stream another file from disk. Your hard disk can stream only a finite amount of data per second, and when Live requires more than the disk can provide, you get audio dropouts. When you hear audio problems, check to see if the Hard Disk Overload Indicator (the letter "D") in the right-hand corner of the Control Bar is lighting up.

To alleviate this, you can load audio clips into your computer's RAM, which is accessed much faster than the hard disk, by pressing the RAM button. The clip will cease streaming from the hard disk.

Remember to be conscious of the size of the files you're loading into RAM. If you have five clips that are four minutes long and two clips that are loops of only a few seconds, it would be better to load the short clips into RAM. Even if you're using only 10 seconds of an eight-minute file, Live will still load the whole file into memory if you press its RAM button! Unless you have multiple gigabytes of RAM available on your system, you should try to load only short files into RAM.

Transpose and Detune

When adding a previously recorded audio clip to your Live Set, more than likely it will not be in the right key. If you're writing a song in the key of E but you import a clip that's in B-flat, the new clip will be out of tune with the rest of the set, even though it's playing in sync tempo-wise with the song. The Transpose and Detune controls (see Figure 5.3) change the playback tuning of the clip (without changing its playback speed) so that it matches the key of the song.

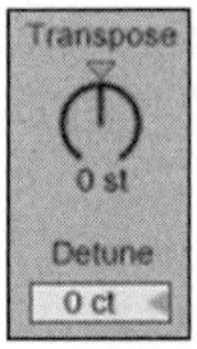

Figure 5.3 The large Transpose knob will shift an audio clip up or down in semitone amounts. The Detune value below the knob can make microadjustments to the tuning by moving it up or down within 50 cents (100 cents = 1 semitone).

You'll use the Transpose knob to shift the playback pitch of the audio clip. In case the audio clip is still slightly out of tune, the Detune knob can be used to fine-tune the pitch by raising or lowering it in small steps known as *cents*. Cent means one-hundredth, which is why a centimeter is one-hundredth of a meter. In music, a cent is one-hundredth of a semitone.

Going Way Out Although the tuning features of an audio clip are generally used to make a loop match the key of your song, don't forget that new sounds can be found by tweaking the tuning up or down by multiple octaves while playing with different Warp modes. Once a sample is altered this much, new textures and sounds can emerge. Take time to experiment!

Gain

The Gain slider is used to adjust the individual volume of a clip. If you grabbed three different drum loops for a song, it's possible that the loop for the bridge is quieter than the other two.

Instead of trying to automate a volume change at the bridge, you can simply turn up the volume, or *gain,* of that clip to match the others. This is a very convenient way to balance audio levels.

When you adjust the gain, you'll see the waveform display change to reflect the new playback volume. Know that the original file has not changed. You're just telling Live to play the file at a different volume. Keep an eye on your levels as you increase the gain of the clip since it's possible to turn the volume up so much that the audio will begin to distort.

Cranking up the volume also provides you with a way to zoom in vertically on a waveform. You can always extend the Clip View window vertically (see Figure 5.4), but it still may not show enough detail.

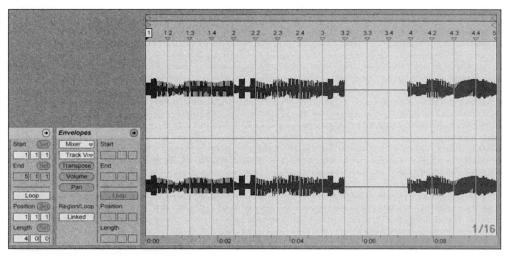

Figure 5.4 You'll see the waveform in better detail if you drag the top edge of the Clip View upward. Raising the gain of a clip can be used to make a waveform larger, too, but it also makes it louder!

If enlarging the Clip View still doesn't show enough detail, turn up the gain to get a larger waveform to edit in the waveform display. When you're done editing and adjusting, don't forget to turn the gain back to its original level, or the clip may be very loud (watch those ears!).

Tweak That Clip You can assign MIDI and key controls to various parameters of the audio and MIDI Clip Views. Engage either MIDI Map or Key Map mode, and boxes will appear over various controls in the Clip View. Click the control; then move or press the desired control to link them.

One thing to be aware of is that your MIDI and Key assignments in the Clip View do not stay stuck to a particular clip. Instead, the assignments work on whatever clip, or clips, you have selected. Therefore, if you use a MIDI knob to transpose a clip, you can click on another clip, and the same MIDI knob will now transpose the new clip.

Warp Control

Warping is the term used to describe Live's time-stretching and compressing technique. The technique of warping an audio file to match the tempo, groove, and pitch of a song involves many parameters, but the most important of these is the Warp button (see Figure 5.5). With Warp off, the clip plays at the audio file's original tempo and pitch unless you tweak the speed with the Transpose knob (which will adjust the tempo and pitch simultaneously, like a record). However, once Warp is engaged, a whole world of possibilities opens. You can change the playback speed and pitch of the audio clip independently, as well as make adjustments to its timing and groove.

Figure 5.5 Here are the Warp controls. Depending on the Warp mode, different controls appear. Notice that the Master/Slave switch only appears for clips in the Arrangement View.

Seg BPM

This value box is similar to the operation of Warp Markers, which I'll explain in the "Warp Markers" section later in this chapter. "Seg" is short for *segment,* which is what Ableton uses to refer to a section of audio between two Warp Markers. When you have multiple Warp Markers in a clip, the Seg BPM window will display the BPM from the selected Warp Marker to the next one to its right. If you have four Warp Markers in a clip and you click on the second one, the Seg BPM window will show the tempo between Warp Markers two and three. When you click on the third Warp Marker, you'll see the tempo from marker three to four.

You'll see that when adjusting grid and Warp Markers, the tempo listed here will change. This is helpful because, after setting the Warp Markers appropriately, Live will be able to determine the exact BPM of the clip. Quite often, this is not a round number, like 120 BPM, but more like 119.72 BPM.

This value is used by Live to set the playback speed of an audio clip in BPM. If the Project tempo is 120 BPM and the clip's Seg BPM is 120, then Live will not change the playback speed of the clip. If the project tempo is 100 BPM, Live would know from looking at the Seg BPM value that it needs to slow down the clip so that it will match the rest of the song.

Half/Double BPM

The two buttons below the Seg BPM window will either double or halve the tempo of the clip. Pressing the *2 button will multiply every Segment BPM by two. The result is that the clip will play at half speed. This may be counterintuitive, but remember that you're not telling Live to "play this clip at twice the speed," but rather you're telling it "this audio was recorded at twice the speed you thought it was." Pressing :2 will have the opposite effect and make the clip play back twice as fast. This is helpful when Live incorrectly guesses the length and tempo of a new audio clip. Loops at a drum and bass tempo of 170 BPM will frequently import as 85 BPM clips. A click of the *2 button will fix this immediately.

Warp Modes

As mentioned earlier, Live's Warp modes allow for cleaner, more musical warping. The Warp mode affects the way in which Live approaches stretching and pitch-shifting your audio clips. Five different Warp modes are available in the audio clip's Warp section: Beats, Tones, Texture, Re-Pitch, and Complex. Each mode also features a special set of controls that will appear below it in the form of a Transients drop-down menu, Grain Size box/knob, and Flux box. We will cover these in each subsection below. Also, don't forget that you can simply turn off Live's Warp Engine altogether and play the sample at its default speed and pitch. Here's what kinds of different sounds you can expect when choosing among these five Warp modes.

Beats

Beats mode is a great mode for rhythmic loops, percussive samples, and even entire songs. You will usually want to use Beats mode with percussion, drums, drum machines, and sounds characteristically containing minimal decay (sustain). When importing songs (or long wave files), the same rules apply. Occasionally, if the sound is too textured or lacks rhythmic definition, you may hear artifacts. Artifacts happen when Live tries to warp a nonpercussive file, such as a drone or a flute melody. Live's Transient settings, just below the Warp mode settings, allow you to zero in on busier patterns or relax the Warp Engine for sparser-sounding loops.

Definition of Transient The Transient setting is a critical element of Live's beat-warping functionality. But what is a transient to begin with? A transient is the short, sharp attack portion of a sound. An acoustic snare has a huge transient, which is the "crack" you hear (and see, as in Figure 5.6) right when the stick hits the drum. The soft attack of strings has no transient.

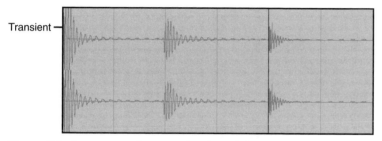

Figure 5.6 Drum parts have easily identifiable transients.

You'll choose the proper setting for the transient value based upon the rhythm of the audio file. If the beat doesn't have anything smaller than an 1/8-note subdivision, set Transients to 1/8.

Beats mode looks at your audio as a series of transients, the size of which is determined by the Transient setting. If you have a one-bar loop with the Transient value set to 1/16, Live's default behavior will be to treat the file as if it were sixteen equally sized segments (see Figure 5.7). Live then plays these chunks back as if they were sixteenth notes at the current tempo.

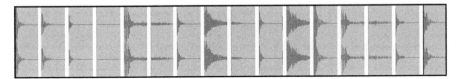

Figure 5.7   How live "sees" a one-bar drum loop when Transients is set to 1/16.

The unique thing about Live, however, is that the chunks don't have to be of equal duration—each one can be as long or as short as you like. By adding Warp Markers and moving them around, you can make each segment of the file a little bit stretched or compressed, such that each transient occurs where you want. If the second sixteenth comes a little too early, make the first segment a tiny bit longer. Or, if you want the snare drum on the third beat of the bar to come a little earlier, just make the segment before it a little shorter. Starting to get the idea? Don't worry if it takes a little while. Learning warping is strange at first. We'll get into it in more detail when we discuss Warp Markers.

If the beat being warped needs to be sped up to match the tempo of Live, the segments will be moved closer together. As this happens, Live will time-compress the end of each segment, making the duration of each drum hit slightly shorter, so the decay doesn't get cut off due to the faster tempo. If the beat is getting slowed down, Live will stretch out the playback of each segment. When slowing down the tempo of a loop by a large amount, this will tend to give your audio a strange glitchy sound. Generally speaking, it is easier to speed beats up without noticeable artifacts than it is to slow them down.

However, if you specify a Transient setting of 1/8, the beat will be cut into only eight pieces. Since this beat has 1/16-note transients, each segment will contain two 1/16-note transients each (see Figure 5.8).

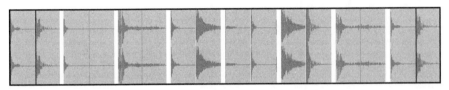

Figure 5.8   How Live will view the same drum loop when Transients is set to 1/8.

Take a look at Figure 5.8 and imagine what would happen if the segments delineated by the heavy lines were moved closer together. The space between the two transients *within* each segment would stay the same, but the distance from the second transient to the first one on the *next* segment would get shorter. This means that the original timing of the 1/16 notes in the audio file would be lost since the space between *every other* 1/16-note changes. If you do this right, you can turn a straight beat into a swinging beat! Check out the "Beats mode" example in the Chapter 5 folder of the CD-ROM materials to hear how this is done.

The technology behind Beats mode is a special form of granular synthesis. Instead of using miniscule *grains* of audio, Beats mode uses larger segments, and instead of repeating each grain to fill the space between pieces that are moved apart (slowing down a file), Beats mode loops only the last portion of the slice—the fading sound of the transient. This means that the wrong setting for the Transient value, such as 1/8 for a 1/16-note loop, can have weird, undesirable effects as Beats mode will loop the second transient on the slice in an attempt to fill the space.

Tones

Tones mode is standard granular resynthesis. As a file is played back, it is broken into grains. The idea is that when you loop a grain, you get a continuous tone that represents that sound "frozen in time." By splitting the audio into grains and spreading the grains apart, Live slows down the tempo of the audio playback; however, since each grain is still played at its original pitch, there will be empty space between each grain. Looping each grain fills space to time-stretch the file.

Of course, looping each grain isn't necessary when speeding up playback of a file. As the grains are brought closer together, they will overlap one another. Each grain will therefore cut off the one before it, resulting in a continuous sound, but one playing faster than before. For this reason, you'll probably find that you have better success speeding up loops or transposing them down (both methods use the same process) than slowing them down or pitching them up, which requires looping the grains.

With careful setting of the Grain Size value, you can achieve nearly transparent warping. Tones such as bass guitars, synthesizers, vocals, keyboards, or other long-sustaining instruments will usually sound much less processed when playing in Live's Tones mode. You can adjust Live's Grain Size to help reduce undesirable audio artifacts.

Texture

Texture mode is built for using orchestral samples, field recordings, thick keyboard pads, and similarly dense audio textures. Like Tones mode, Texture mode is based on granular resynthesis. In an effort to cloud the repetitive artifacts from looping grains, a Flux value is added that, when increased, allows Live to randomly change the Grain Sizes used in the process. This also adds a sense of stereo imaging to mono files.

Re-Pitch

Re-Pitch mode is more like true vinyl DJing—Live will alter the pitch of the sample according to the playback speed. This mode produces no artifacts and thus usually sounds the best, especially if the warped, looped, re-pitched sample is played close to its original tempo. Re-Pitch basically turns off the granular resynthesis and merely alters the file playback speed, which results in pitch changes. Since resynthesis is off, you will not be able to use the Transpose adjustments in this mode.

Complex

Complex mode is another enhancement aimed straight at DJs but has value for all types of users. The Complex mode employs an extremely high-quality algorithm to stretch and shift audio clips. This requires more effort from your CPU, but the end results can be gorgeous. Designed for use on entire songs, this Warp mode will match the audio clip with nearly no noticeable artifacts. It sounds quite good on nearly any kind of material. If your computer is having a tough time keeping up with the added load of the Complex mode, you can use the Freeze Track option from the Track Context menu (right-click on PCs or Ctrl-click on Macs to open it), or you can resample the warped clip into a new clip that doesn't need Complex mode.

Master/Slave

The Master/Slave button (available only in Arrangement View) allows you to select whether this clip will act as the Tempo Master for Live. What this means is that Warp Markers added to a Master clip will affect the tempo of the Set rather than the playback speed of the clip.

Let's say that you have a piano recording that you want to add some additional programmed parts and loops to. It's a well-played part with a mostly steady tempo, but since it wasn't recorded to a click track, there is some natural variation to the time. One way you could use warping in this context is to straighten out the timing of the piano track by adding Warp Markers so the piano lines up perfectly with the sequencer tempo. However, if the piano has a nice feel, this could make the whole recording feel rigid and dull.

Instead, you could add a Warp Marker to the downbeat of each bar in the piano part and set the clip to Master. Now, Live's tempo will breathe with the pianist's rhythm, and all of your MIDI clips and warped loops will breathe along with it!

Warp Markers

I've mentioned Warp Markers time and time again throughout this book, so it's about time we explain what they are. The principle behind Warp Markers is simple but still manages to confuse some longtime users; however, using them properly has a profound effect on Live's ability to lock your audio clips together and your ability to unlock Live's creative potential.

Purpose of Warping

In a nutshell, you use warping to alter the playback timing of an audio file, usually to match the tempo of your song. You've already witnessed how Live can quickly change the playback tempo of an audio file, dependent on the Session Tempo. When you lowered the tempo, the audio files slowed down immediately. Since Live is performing all its warping in real time, it can respond to instant changes anywhere during audio playback.

If you have an audio file that has improper timing, such as a drum part where the drummer played a beat late (see Figure 5.9), you can fix the timing by using small changes to the warp parameters. If the snare drum on beat 1.2 is late, playing through the first beat of the file at an increased rate will cause the snare to move earlier. Playing the second beat of the file slower will allow the rest of the file after beat 1.3 to stay in the same place. By adjusting these two speeds, you can correct the timing of individual beats in a file. Fortunately, you don't have to alter these playback speeds numerically. They are computed for you as you manipulate Warp Markers.

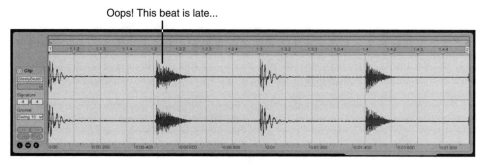

Figure 5.9   The snare drum hit on beat 1.2 is late. Curse those human drummers!

Auto-Warping

One occasion that may require numerous Warp Markers is synchronizing an entire song to your Set. DJs have to do this with all of their files before playing them in Live. A function called Auto-Warping will save you a lot of time, although it is not perfect and often requires adjusting the Warp Markers' timing by hand to get the beats to sync just right.

Whenever you import a long audio file, Live will run it through its Auto-Warping scheme, thus making the file immediately ready for use in your Set. (If you don't like this behavior, you can turn it off in Preferences.) The process of auto-warping is fairly quick, and you can initiate it manually if you desire. Right-click (Ctrl-click) a marker and select one of the Auto-Warp options from the context menu:

- **Warp from Here:** This tells Live to auto-warp the clip starting at the selected Warp Marker and continuing to the right. Everything to the left of the selected marker will remain intact.

- **Warp from Here (Start at *Tempo*):** This option is the same as above but uses the current project tempo as a starting point for the auto-warping algorithm. If you've already determined the approximate tempo of the audio file using the Tap Tempo, this option should yield good results. Identifying a ballpark tempo is helpful because Live can calculate BPMs that are twice as fast or slow as they should be. For example, a one-bar loop at 62 BPM is the same length as a two-bar loop at 124 BPM. By providing a starting tempo in the neighborhood of 60 or 120 BPM, Live will know how to evaluate the clip.

- **Warp from Here (Straight):** This mode attempts to set the tempo of the clip using one Warp Marker only. This should be used only when warping electronically produced music that has a fixed tempo.

- **Warp Tempo from Here:** This simply sets the current Warp Marker to the project tempo. If there are any Warp Markers to the right, they will be erased in the process.

- **Warp as X-Bar Loop:** If you already know that the file you're working with has an even number of bars, you can select this option to automatically turn the clip into an even loop. The number shown here will depend on the current project tempo. If Live determines that it will have to do the least amount of warping to turn the clip into a one-bar loop, as opposed to a two-bar loop, the program will display 1 in place of X in the menu item above. If you increase the project tempo by almost double, Live will see that it is now easier to make the clip a two-bar loop and will suggest that by showing 2 in place of 1 in the menu option.

Note that there are also a number of other options in this context menu to help you work with your sample files, including:

- **Set 1.1.1. Here:** This command will reset the very first Warp Marker at the point indicated.

- **Crop Sample:** This command will crop your sample to the length you have set with the Loop Brace in the waveform display. You will see a progress bar at the bottom of the screen as the truncated sample file is written to your hard drive.

- **Manage Sample File:** This will show you the audio file in the File Manager (see Chapter 2, "Getting Live Up and Running").

Manually Creating and Erasing Warp Markers

While in the Clip View, click the Sample window in the title bar to view the clip's markers in the waveform display. The markers show where Live thinks the beats are in an audio file. The lines that appear with numbers above them are the Grid Markers. The lines with the green handles at the top are Warp Markers. Any Grid Marker can be turned into a Warp Marker by double-clicking its beat number (see Figure 5.10). Double-click a Warp Marker to switch it back to a gray Grid Marker.

The difference between Warp and Grid Markers is that Warp Markers will stay where you place them. When you create a Warp Marker, you can click and drag it to a new location in the waveform

Double-click here to create a Warp Marker.

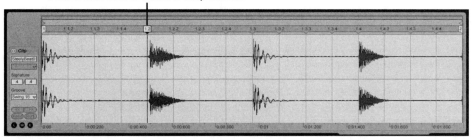

Figure 5.10   There is always at least one Warp Marker in an audio clip when the Warp mode is engaged. It's the marker at beat 1. You can make others by double-clicking Grid Markers.

display. The Warp Marker will stay in this location even if you move other markers around it. Grid Markers will always stay evenly distributed between neighboring Warp Markers (see Figure 5.11). Moving a Warp Marker will make all the surrounding Grid Markers move as well.

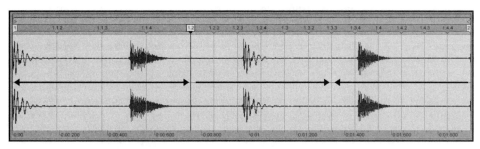

Figure 5.11   As Warp Marker 1.2 is moved right, the Grid Markers to its left spread apart while the markers to its right get closer together.

Correcting Timing Errors

If you turn Grid Marker 1.2 into a Warp Marker and move it right so that it's lined up with the beginning of the snare drum, you are telling Live the new location of beat 1.2 in the file (see Figure 5.12). Since you are showing Live that the second beat is later in the file, Live will play the file faster up until this point to make sure that it reaches this later transient on beat 1.2.

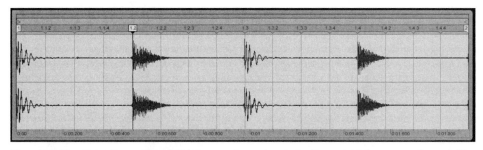

Figure 5.12   Creating a Warp Marker and moving it in line with the snare drum will cause Live to play this section of the file in time.

When you move the Warp Marker over to its new location, all the Grid Markers to its right will move as well. This means beat 1.3 now needs to be lined up. Changing Grid Marker 1.3 into a Warp Marker and moving it left to the proper location fixes this (see Figure 5.13). Since the location of beat 1.2 is now closer to beat 1.3, Live will play that section of the file more slowly so it doesn't arrive at the third transient early.

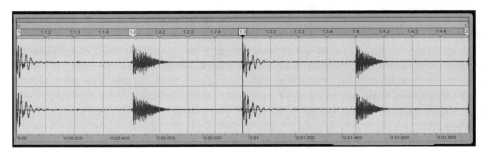

Figure 5.13   Moving Warp Marker 1.3 into position with the third transient corrects the rest of the file.

To fix all of the timing errors in a file, you may need to make a lot of Warp Markers (see Figure 5.14). In cases like this, you'd probably want to click the clip's Save button so the Warp Markers will be loaded in future imports of the file.

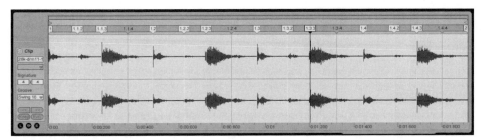

Figure 5.14   You can manipulate Warp Markers down to small subdivisions to correct multiple timing problems.

Keep in mind that all the usual editing commands and techniques work here. You can, for example, click on a Warp Marker and press Ctrl (Cmd)+A to select all of the Warp Markers. You can then slide them around as a group or delete them. You can also select a range of markers by clicking one of them and then clicking another while holding the Shift key. You can then move or delete only that specific range of markers.

Creating New Rhythms

If you can use Warp Markers to align audio to the proper beat, can you use them to align audio to the improper part of a beat? Of course! You can change your beat by having Live play the snare later in time, perhaps on beat 1.2.2. If you remove Warp Marker 1.2 and create Warp

Marker 1.2.2, you can align this new marker to the transient of the snare (see Figure 5.15). By doing so, you have told Live that the snare drum falls on beat 1.2.2. Live will now play the audio file from 1 to 1.2.2 much slower than normal to get to the snare at beat 1.2.2. Since the snare was pushed so far back in time, Live will now have to play quickly from 1.2.2 to 1.3 in order to keep the rest of the file aligned.

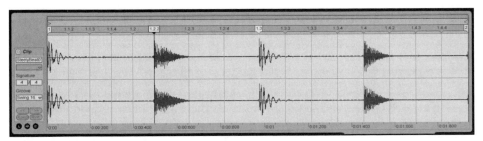

Figure 5.15   Though the waveform hasn't changed, this beat will sound significantly different because the new Warp Marker (at beat 1.2.2) has pushed back the snare beat.

Setting Warp Markers for Multiple Clips

If you have two or more clips based on audio files of exactly the same length, Live will allow you to set Warp Markers across multiple clips simultaneously. This is especially convenient when you are working with a multitrack recording of a performance, and you want to give all the tracks exactly the same warp timing. You can do this quite easily by simply selecting all of the clips you want to work with in the Arrangement View and then making your warp adjustments to any one of them. The Warp Markers you set here and their timing will automatically apply to all of the other clips you have selected as long as they are all of equal length. (This last point is crucial; all of the clips you are working with must be exactly the same length or you cannot use this function.)

For example, here's a good technique you can use for syncing up a live band recording with Live's Tempo Grid. First, import each track from your original multitrack recording onto a separate audio track in Live, and then make sure that they are all exactly the same length. Select all of them in the Arrangement View. Then find the track that is rhythmically simplest and clearest to insert your Warp Marker settings. Using a separate bass drum track often is the easiest way to go; a stereo drum mix will work as well. Once you have set the timing of this track, all of the other tracks also will follow Live's Tempo Grid, as if by magic!

Beat Slicing

Live 7 has added two new important features that offer a totally different way to change the playback tempo of your source audio. REX file support gives us the ability to work natively with files generated by Propellerhead's ReCycle software, and Beat Slicing allows us to chop up and play back our audio at different speeds without using Live's Warp Engine at all.

REX File Support

REX files are a special type of audio file developed by Propellerhead Software for their revolutionary program ReCycle. ReCycle was developed as a tool for chopping up loops so they can be played back at different tempos. REX files contain slicing information that specifies where each transient in the file occurs, as well as rhythmic information indicating when each slice should be played. You could think of a REX file as a package containing a bunch of samples (the slices of the loop) *and* a MIDI file that's programmed to play the samples back.

As of Live 7, you can drop a REX file (they have an extension of either .rex or .rx2) directly into Live. When REX files are played back, they are not processed by Live's Warp Engine, so rather than seeing a choice of Warp modes, you'll just see REX displayed in the Clip View (see Figure 5.16). The REX file's self-contained slice and timing information will be used to match it to the current tempo. Even if you don't use ReCycle, this is a great feature, as there are numerous loop libraries in REX format available.

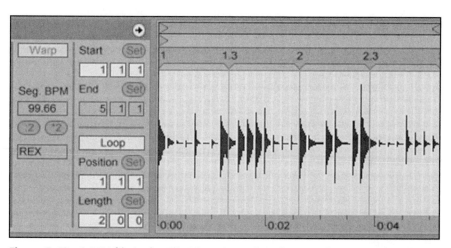

Figure 5.16   A REX file in the Clip View. Note that the waveform overview displays lines to let you know where the slices are.

Slice to New MIDI Track

Okay, strictly speaking this isn't just about audio clips. Instead, it's a technique for turning audio clips into MIDI clips. Slice to New MIDI track works very similarly to ReCycle, creating a new track containing a MIDI clip that triggers an instrument containing the slices of your loop.

To invoke this new command, right-click on a clip and select Slice to New MIDI track from the context menu. Next, you'll be presented with a dialog offering a couple of options (see Figure 5.17). The first menu allows you to choose how many slices your audio should be divided into. A good value to start with here would be whatever value you would use for the Transients setting in Beats mode. If the beat is based on 1/8th note divisions, try slicing at this value. There's also an option to slice at Warp Markers. This means that anywhere you've created a Warp Marker, a slice will be

Figure 5.17 The Slice to New MIDI track dialog. Make sure to experiment with the different slicing presets!

created. In other words, you can control how many slices are generated by adding Warp Markers before doing the slicing.

The next menu gives you a few presets that will affect the MIDI track that gets created. To fully understand these options, you'll need to know a bit about Drum Racks, so you may want to explore Chapter 7, "Using Effects and Instruments." The presets are as follows:

- **Built-In:** This is the standard procedure for slicing. The end result is a MIDI track containing a Drum Rack. Each slice of the loop will be mapped to a pad in the Drum Rack, and a MIDI file will be generated to play the slices back.

- **Built-In 0-Vel:** Same as Built-In, but the Drum Rack is configured such that the pads are not velocity sensitive. This is useful if you want to preserve the exact dynamics of the loop you've sliced, regardless of MIDI velocity.

- **Chord & Stutter:** This preset also slices to a Drum Rack and generates a MIDI file. The difference here has only to do with the configuration of the Drum Rack itself. Some MIDI effects have been included in the Rack, and some nifty macros (the eight knobs at the left-hand side of the Drum Rack) have been set up to control these devices to generate chords and create some weird stuttering.

- **Slice to Single Sampler:** For owners of the Sampler instrument, this will map each slice to a zone in a Sampler instrument instead of a Drum Rack.

After you've clicked OK and waited for a few seconds, you'll have a brand new MIDI track all loaded up and ready to go (see Figure 5.18). Just launch the new MIDI clip, and you'll hear your loop playing back just as if it were the original audio clip. This is where things get interesting. Try rearranging, deleting, or adding MIDI notes, or try creating a brand new clip and using individual slices to program a beat! Also make sure to check out the macros that have been programmed for you in the new Drum Rack.

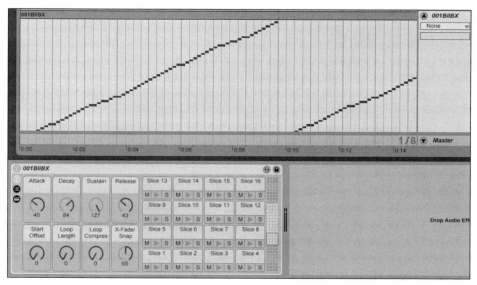

Figure 5.18 A newly created MIDI clip, and a Drum Rack full of loop slices—all courtesy of the Slice to New MIDI track command!

One scenario in which you may find this technique useful is when you need to slow down a drum loop by a large amount. While warping has a tendency to create stretchy-sounding artifacts when slowing down drum loops, slicing to a new MIDI track can be much more transparent, especially if you add Warp Markers first telling Live where to put the slices. Each drum hit will be played back exactly as is, without Live stretching it to fill extra space.

Slice to New Midi track may not sound as good as warping when working with loops that are very smooth or have a lot of ambience. In cases like this, slicing may produce choppy sounding results, and the Warp Engine's granular synthesis technology will be better at keeping the audio "glued together."

Clip Envelopes

The final window in the audio Clip View is the Envelopes window. To see the Envelope View, you must click the small "E" icon underneath the clip properties (bottom-left)—the Show/Hide Envelope Box button.

Before we go too far, some of you may be wondering what an envelope is. To start with, it's nothing that you will put in a mailbox. Rather, it's a graphical representation of values, such as positions of knobs and faders, which change over time. The envelopes appear as a line graph superimposed over the audio waveform and represent anything from volume and pitch changes to effect tweaks. To understand how envelopes function, it helps to actually manipulate them and hear the results, so play along here by opening the "Clip Envelopes" example in the Chapter 5 folder of the CD-ROM materials.

Volume

The easiest Clip Envelope to understand is the Volume Envelope (see Figure 5.19). In the figure below, the envelope is the ramp that rises from the bottom-left corner of the display window to the upper-right corner. When you play this clip (labeled Volume Up in the example Set), its volume rises over its two-bar length. When the clip repeats, the volume immediately jumps to silence and begins to rise again.

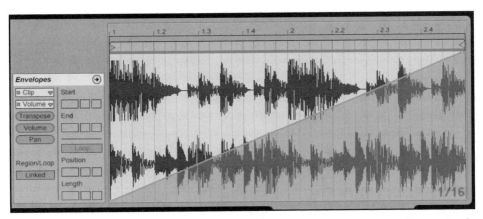

Figure 5.19 The upward ramp causes the clip's volume to rise over two bars as it plays.

To access the Volume Envelope for your clip, press the Volume shortcut button in the Envelope window. The Volume Envelope will superimpose itself over the clip.

When you first make a clip, its Volume Envelope will look like the one in Figure 5.20. Clip Envelopes are always working, so this "fully up" envelope allows you to hear your clip. This means there's no such thing as a clip without a Volume Envelope—it's just set to full level so it

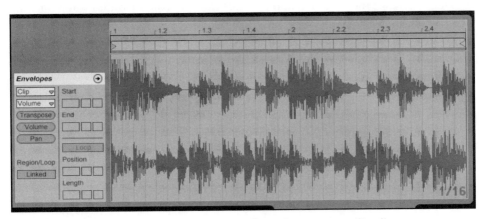

Figure 5.20 This is the default Volume Envelope for a new audio clip.

appears to have no effect. In other words, all the envelopes are always present, but by default they're set to do nothing.

You can freely edit this envelope to hear the effect it will have on the clip. Click on the Pencil tool in the Control Bar so its icon is on. Then click in the Envelope window to create some steps like those shown in Figure 5.21. You'll hear Live adjust the volume of the clip according to these steps when you play it.

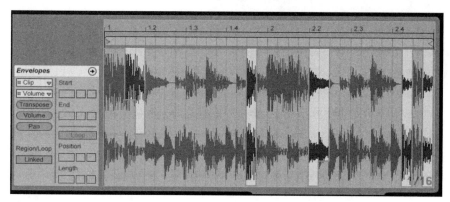

Figure 5.21 These steps change the playback volume of the clip.

It's important to realize that the Volume Envelope (as well as any other Clip Envelope) is affecting the playback volume in a relative way. If you look closely at the Gain slider in the Sample window, you'll see a small dot by it that moves up and down along with the volume changes. This dot shows the volume of the clip based on the Volume Envelope. I like to think of this dot as the envelope's "finger" on my controls showing me what it's doing. If you change the Gain amount, you'll hear an overall volume change while the steps drawn in your Volume Envelope continue to incrementally change the volume. You'll notice that the volume didn't jump back up to its previous location because of the envelope. Instead, the envelope scales its range based on the location of the Gain slider. This is because the Clip Envelopes work relative to a control's current position. This way, you can create repetitive volume patterns but still adjust the overall level of the clip in the mix.

Pan

Another simple envelope to master is the Pan Envelope, which is accessed with the Pan button in the Envelopes window. Instead of seeing a "full up" envelope like you saw for Volume, you'll see a flat line going through the middle of the window (see Figure 5.22).

Remember how we said that Clip Envelopes work relative to a control's current position? In the case of the Pan Envelope, the flat line down the middle means no panning left or right. If the envelope is above this center line, the pan position of the track will be moved right. The track will pan left when the line is below center. This means creating a ramp from the upper-left

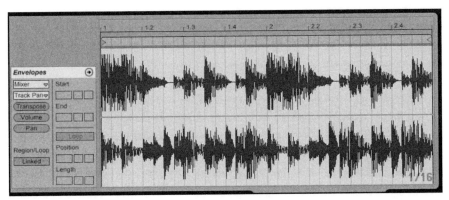

Figure 5.22 The Pan Envelope doing nothing, meaning a track would play evenly from right and left.

corner of the window to the bottom-right (see Figure 5.23) will cause the clip to pan from right to left as it plays. Launch the Ramp Pan clip to hear this in action.

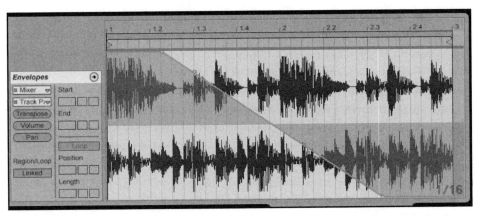

Figure 5.23 This ramp causes the track to pan from right to left during playback.

If you turn the Pan knob in the Session Mixer to the left, you'll hear that the panning doesn't start fully on the right. It now starts partway to the left and continues fully left. This is because the Pan Envelope is changing the pan position relative to the current location of the Pan knob. In fact, if you look closely, you'll see a colored indicator appear around the Pan knob as the envelope changes its position (see Figure 5.24). This is how the envelope's "finger" is represented on a knob.

Transpose

The third envelope accessible through shortcut buttons is the Transpose Envelope. This envelope will modulate the location of the Transpose knob, allowing you to program pitch changes, slides, or entire harmonic progressions for the clip.

The envelope begins as a flat line, just like the Pan Envelope. Every line above zero is one semi-tone up, while every line below zero is a semitone down (see Figure 5.25).

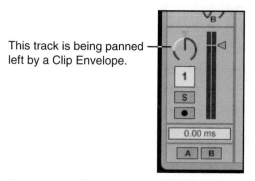

This track is being panned left by a Clip Envelope.

Figure 5.24   The colored section of the Pan knob shows the actual output position as a result of the Pan Envelope.

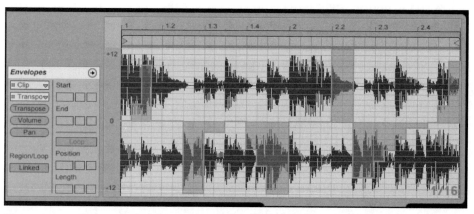

Figure 5.25   The Transpose Envelope transposes the clip up and down as it plays.

The envelope affects the Transpose knob in a relative way, meaning that after you've programmed in your progression, like Figure 5.25 above, you can still select the root note of the scale with the Transpose knob.

Sample Offset

There are only three shortcut buttons in the Envelopes window, yet there are many more envelopes available for you to program. In fact, there's a Clip Envelope for nearly every parameter of the clip and its containing track.

To select an envelope other than the three available as shortcuts, you use the two drop-down menus at the top of the Envelopes window. These menus work in a similar fashion to the pairs found in the Input/Output Routing section. In the top menu, you can choose the device you want to view, and in the bottom menu, you can select the parameter. One of these additional Clip Envelopes takes a little explaining—the Sample Offset Envelope. This envelope can be found by selecting Clip in the top menu and then choosing Sample Offset in the lower menu. This option is available only for clips in Beats mode. If this option is grayed out, switch to Beats mode or find another clip that's in Beats mode already.

The Sample Offset Envelope (see Figure 5.26) is another one of those flat-liners like the Transpose and Pan Envelopes above. You can think of it as a step sequencer for your beat. Each line above zero is worth +1 1/16 note. Each line below is worth −1 1/16 note. Compare the two clips named Normal and Offset in the CD-ROM example Set to hear how the Sample Offset works.

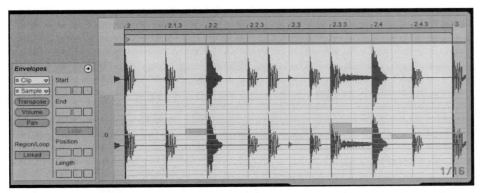

Figure 5.26 The Sample Offset programmed above in the Offset clip will cause the snare drum on beat 2.2 to play on 2.1.4 as well. The snare at 2.4 will play at 2.3.3, 2.3.4, 2.4, and 2.4.2.

Remember how Beats mode treats an audio file as if it were multiple segments? Well, when playback of an audio clip reaches a non-zero value in the Offset Envelope, it signals Live to jump to a different segment of the file relative to the current location. In Figure 5.26, there is a value of +1 at beat 1.1.4. When playback reaches this point, Live will play the segment of audio located 1/16 note ahead of the current position, which is the segment for beat 1.2. So, when playback reaches 1.1.4, you'll hear the snare that occurs on beat 1.2. On the next beat, 1.2, the Offset Envelope is zero. This means Live plays the audio segment at its current location. In this case, you'll hear the snare on beat 1.2 again. The additional steps around beat 1.4 will cause two hits before 1.4 and one after. By creating patterns of offset motions, you can rearrange the segments of an audio file into any order you want. Try it—take the Pencil and scribble all over the Sample Offset Envelope and listen to the random results.

Since the Sample Offset Envelope rearranges the segments in a Beats mode clip, the Transient setting for the clip will determine the smallest offset that can be performed. If Transient is set to 1/4, you will be able to offset the beat only on the quarter note. This also means that the finest possible resolution for the Sample Offset is 1/32 (the clip's Transient setting can't get any smaller). However, if you're looking to do some meticulous micro-editing of your beats, using the Sample Offset Envelope may not be the best solution, but it can definitely get you started. Really tight and complicated edits are still better suited for the Arrangement View (see Chapter 13, "Live 7 Power," for the "Beat-Wreckin' Clinic").

Sends and More

Another fun Clip Envelope is the Send Envelope. Select Mixer in the top device menu and then choose Send A in the lower menu. With this envelope, you can control the level of signal sent to the various Return tracks.

The Send Envelope (see Figure 5.27) is a "full-on" envelope like Volume. This makes sense because the Send knobs are just special volume controls themselves. Editing the envelope will scale the output level of the associated Send knob. In the envelope below, the Send works only on beat 2.4. In the example Set, we've already placed a Reverb on Return A. Turn up Send A on the Drums track and launch the Send A clip to hear what happens.

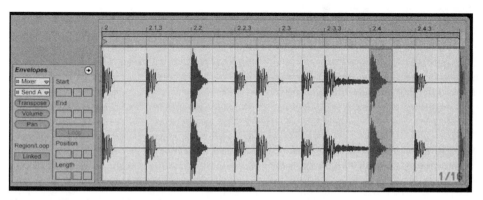

Figure 5.27   The Send Envelope sending on beat 2.4 only.

To hear this work, you'll need to have an effect loaded onto the Return track (see Chapter 7) and the Send knob for the track turned up. Since the Send Envelope is relative, the track has to have its Send turned up at least a little before the envelope can scale the level. The result is that the Send knob will actually send on beat 1.4 only. The rest of the time, it will be muted, even though the Send knob is up.

You'll find even more Clip Envelopes as you explore the drop-down menus in the Envelopes window. In fact, as you add effects to the track (see Chapter 8, "Live's Instruments"), envelopes for the plug-in's parameters will also appear in this list so you can modulate them. That's quite a lot of modulation available at your fingertips!

Unlinking Envelopes

Until this point, we've been talking about editing loops of a given length. After all, a loop is, by definition, a repeating sample or phrase. That is just what loops do—they loop. And by default, each envelope in a clip is the same length as the clip itself, allowing you to create repetitive modulation patterns that recur every time the clip repeats itself.

Sometimes, you may want to extend a given loop beyond its original borders. For instance, you have a repetitive two-bar drum loop, and you really wish that you had an eight-bar loop to make it sound more lifelike and less repetitive. One way to accomplish this is by *unlinking* the clip's envelopes. By changing the length of a Clip Envelope so that it is different from the length of the clip that contains them, you can introduce just this kind of variation to your loops.

Anytime you click the Unlink button (see Figure 5.28), the audio peak data is removed from the waveform display. This is because the envelope is now an independent entity with its own Start, Stop, and Loop points. These points are adjusted using a Loop Brace and the familiar looking Start and Stop Markers—but in this case you're affecting the envelope only, not the sample. Feel free to make an unlinked envelope of eight bars over a two-bar loop, or one that starts on beat one, goes for four bars, then goes into a two-bar loop. You can also create some very unusual envelopes using the technique described next.

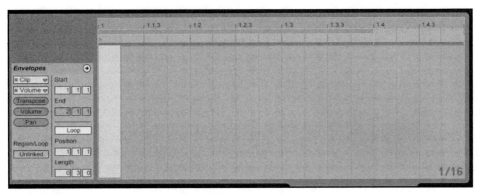

Figure 5.28 Unlinking the Clip Envelope will allow you to create more random-sounding modulations because the various envelopes can repeat independently.

If you have a one-bar clip and you unlink its Volume Envelope and then set its envelope length to three beats, you'll end up with a Volume Envelope that repeats sooner than the clip itself. If you've muted the volume at any place in the envelope, as in the figure above, this mute will begin to occur at different places as the clip loops. The envelope shown above will remove one 1/16 note every three beats. This means that beat 1 will be missing, and then beat 1.4 (it's three beats later, see?), followed by beat 1.3 the next time through the clip. The third time through the clip, beat 1.2 will be muted. With the fourth repetition, the pattern starts again. It therefore takes three bars for the Volume Clip to repeat itself; thus, the resulting clip also repeats in a pattern three bars long. Launch the Unlinked clip to hear this firsthand.

To make things more complicated (and fun), other Clip Envelopes can be unlinked and set to their own unique lengths. If a pan pattern is programmed into an envelope that is set to be 3.3 beats long, it will take seven bars for the pattern to repeat itself. Most of your listeners would probably think the motion was totally random, especially with mutes occurring every three beats.

Breakpoint Editing

In these examples, you edited the envelopes using the Pencil tool. The Pencil tool creates steps that are as wide as your quantization setting. Alas, step-style modulation is not always proper. For example, you may want to make a smooth panning ramp to create the effect of swirling sound. You can create ramps by turning off Draw mode and editing the envelope Breakpoint style.

When in Breakpoint mode, each "elbow" in the envelope will be marked with a tiny circle, or *breakpoint*. Breakpoints are created by double-clicking on the envelope. Double-clicking an existing node will remove it (see Figure 5.29). By moving the nodes around, you can create complex modulation curves.

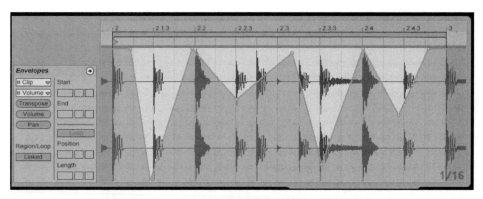

Figure 5.29 Double-click to create and remove nodes. Click and drag to reposition them. The clip shown here is the Breakpoint clip in the example.

It's possible to select an area of the breakpoint curve by click-dragging across the envelope and moving all the selected nodes together as one unit. You can also click and drag segments of the envelope by dragging the lines instead of the breakpoints themselves, causing its attached nodes to move as well. With a little clicking around, you'll quickly learn how to create your desired ramps.

Control the Levels If you like the timing of your envelope and you just want to change the level of a node or segment, hold down the Ctrl (Cmd) key while dragging it. Your moves will be restricted to the vertical plane and will also be more precise.

Recording New Audio Clips

Now that you've got a grip on audio clips, you can really start putting them to use. While audio clips will sometimes be created by dragging an audio file into Live from the Browser, you can also record audio input directly into a new clip.

...In the Session View

You can record new audio clips in the Session View, even while the others are playing. First, select the source you're recording from in the track's Input menus. The top menu lets you select the source device, which includes options such as Ext. In (the inputs of your audio interface), Resample (for recording Live's Master output), ReWire applications (for recording the output of external programs such as Reason), and the outputs of the individual tracks in your Live Set. When you arm the track for recording, all of the Stop Clip buttons in the track's clip slots will turn to circles (see Figure 5.30). These are individual Clip Record buttons—click one of them to start recording a new clip in that location. You do not need to use the Global Record button in the Control Bar to record new clips in the Session View. You can stop recording by either clicking the clip again (if you've set Toggle as your default in Record/Warp/Launch Preferences), clicking the Stop button in the Control Bar, disarming the track, or stopping the sequencer.

Figure 5.30 Select an active audio input, arm the track, and then click one of the circular Clip Record buttons in the clip slot grid. Recording will commence at the time specified by the Global Quantize setting in the Control Bar.

What's fantastic about recording in the Session View is that Live can create perfect loops from the recordings with ease. Just as a clip will wait for the Launch Quantize setting before playing, clips will also wait for the same setting before recording. If you have Bar selected as the Global Quantize value, Live will wait until the downbeat of a measure before it begins to record. If you click the red Play button in the clip while it's recording, it will stop recording on the downbeat of the next measure. Furthermore, if your default Launch mode is Trigger, the clip will immediately start looping when recording ends.

Please keep in mind that recording will stop following the Global Quantize setting only if you click the clip's Play button while recording. If you press Stop in the Control Bar or disarm the track, the recording will stop immediately.

Sound on Sound Since Live makes recording perfect loops so easy, you can build sections by doing multiple layers of recorded loops. For example, you can begin by recording some congas for four bars. When you stop recording, the clip immediately starts to loop. Move the clip to an empty audio track, and it will continue to play. You can then trigger another recording in the first track and play along with the congas. Perhaps you want to record a shaker part for the second loop. When you stop recording, the congas and shaker will both be looping in sync with one another. You can keep layering additional clips in this fashion and then resample the output into one final clip when you're done.

Doing multiple takes (repeated recordings of the same part of the song) is as easy as triggering additional Clip Record buttons in the track. Every time a new recording starts, the previous one ends. You can then go back and listen to each take individually to find the best one. You can also move the clips to the Arrangement View to combines the best parts of each take into one perfect "supertake."

Of course, the nicest thing about this workflow in the Session View is that it allows you to quickly build layers and sections of a song without ever stopping Live. You can then audition all of your new clips and capture scenes to start arranging the sections of your song.

On the Level Before you start recording, check your input signal level to make sure it's not too high or too low. The track's meters will show the volume of any incoming signal as soon as the track is armed. Play as loud as you plan to play during the recording while watching Live's meters. If the signal is too loud (the meters reach the top), it could distort, or clip, the recording. If the level is too low, your sound may become grainy when turning it up to match the rest of your song. If you're recording at 24-bit or more, you can record at lower levels and still have excellent audio quality. At 16-bit it's more important to get the loudest level possible without clipping.

...In the Arrangement View

To record an audio clip directly into the Arrangement View, select the channel input and arm the track just like setting up recording in the Session View. This time, instead of pressing one of the Clip Record buttons, press the Arrangement Record button in the Control Bar (see Figure 5.31). When you start Live's Transport, it will begin recording a new clip into the corresponding track of the Arrangement View while playing back the other tracks in the Live Set. Stop the Transport, disarm the track, or turn off the Record button in the Control Bar to end recording.

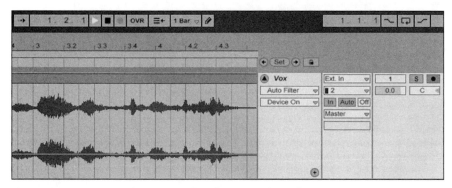

Figure 5.31 To record a new audio clip in Track 2 of the Arrangement, you need to arm the track for recording and enable Record in the Control Bar.

Get Ready, Get Set, Go! The Count In feature is found on the Misc tab of the Preferences. When this is active, Live will wait the specified number of bars before it starts recording. This works only if the Live Transport is stopped when you initiate recording. (If the Transport is already running, Live will ignore the Count In setting.) During the count off, the metronome will sound so you can "get into the beat" before it's time to play. This feature works in both the Session and Arrangement Views.

You can also automate Arrangement recording using the Punch-In/Punch-Out values in the Control Bar. Set the Start and End Markers around the area you want to record. Engage the Punch-In and Punch-Out buttons (see Figure 5.32), and press Record and then Play in the Control Bar. Live will start running but will wait for the punch-in time before it starts to record. It will continue recording until it reaches the punch-out point. You may, of course, use either Punch-In or Punch-Out by itself if you choose.

Recording Effects If a track's monitoring is set to Auto while it's armed for recording, Live will play the incoming audio through the Session Mixer and out to your speakers or headphones. You can place effects onto the track for real-time processing of your input, but Live will still record the part without these effects.

If you want to record the sound of your incoming part *with* the effects, you'll need to use another audio track. On the second track, set its audio input to the first track. The sound of your incoming audio will be processed by the effects on the first track, which you can then record on the second track.

Figure 5.32 Live will automatically begin recording at bar 3 and then stop recording at bar 7. This leaves your hands free to play your instrument instead of trying to trigger the recording.

Editing Audio Clips

After you've recorded your new clips, you may need to edit them. Perhaps you rushed a part or breathed too loudly between your vocal lines. There are a variety of ways to alter your clips after recording them, and these are a few you'll want to check every time.

Clip Timing and Rhythm

Whether you create an audio clip by dragging a file into Live or by recording something new, the method for fixing the timing of the file is the same: Warp Markers. After you've recorded your part, you may be inclined to first look at the waveform and the Grid Markers to determine if the timing needs adjusting. Don't do this. First, *listen* to the file and make an assessment, based on how it sounds and feels. If it sounds off, then look it over to see where the warp adjustments need to be made. Later when you are matching your recording to other loops and recordings, you may hear discrepancies in the timing that you will want to correct, but always lining everything up to the grid can make music feel rigid and lifeless.

After you've fixed any mistakes, check your Warp mode and set it to something appropriate for the audio file, as explained at the beginning of this chapter. Press the Save button in the Sample window so your markers and tunings are saved with the audio file, in case you use it in another project. Make a habit of doing this now to help keep future creative sessions running smoothly.

Editing in the Arrangement

While you're in the Session View to record new pieces of audio, you can also use the Arrangement View as a "splicing block" for editing multiple clips together. If you want to use the first two bars of Vox A and the last bar of Vox B, you can arrange them as such on an Arrangement track and then consolidate the clips into one new one (see Figures 5.33a and 5.33b).

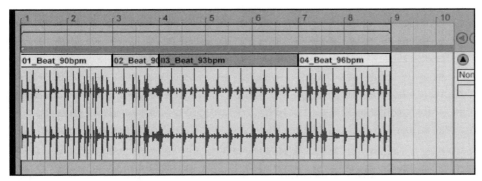

Figure 5.33a You can arrange and edit an assortment of clips on a track.

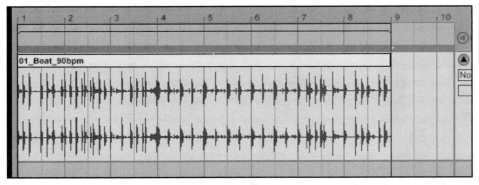

Figure 5.33b Choose Consolidate from the Edit menu to render the track into one new clip, which can be moved back to the Session View.

The resulting clip will contain the parts from Vox takes A and B all wrapped up in one convenient audio clip. You can copy this clip from the Arrangement to the Session View for use in the developing song structure. If you need to re-edit, the original audio clips remain, so you can always do it again.

Tips for Great Loops

Looping audio files is an art form all its own. You're trying to make something that was played once sound natural and in perfect time with the rest of the parts in your song. While Live does an exceptional job of looping imported files (especially loops that are already cut to the right lengths), there may be times when Live is unable to determine the proper tempo and length of a file, especially in the case of a long audio file, like a whole song. When Live fails to identify a loop, you can quickly tell it where the loop points should be and figure the original tempo. The tools to do this are simple, and the concepts are just as easy:

- **Set Warp Marker 1:** Always be sure that the loop is actually beginning on the downbeat of the sample. Zoom in at the beginning of the sample (see Figure 5.34) and make sure there is no silence before the sound starts. If there is, slide Marker 1 over to change the start location.

- **Do the same zoom-in check at the end of your sample:** Make sure there is no extra silence at the end or noise or from a following beat (see Figure 5.35). Just like above, move the last marker in line with the very end of the last beat.

- **Check the beats in between:** If the Start and End Markers are in the right places, there's still no guarantee that every beat of the loop will be locked in with the rest of your parts (see Figure 5.36). Check all the major beats and be sure that the sounds are lined up properly. Create Warp Markers to compensate when necessary.

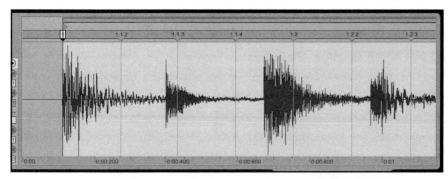

Figure 5.34 Make sure there's no dead air before the sample starts.

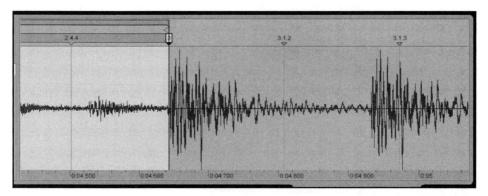

Figure 5.35 Check the end of the loop for any extraneous noise that shouldn't be there.

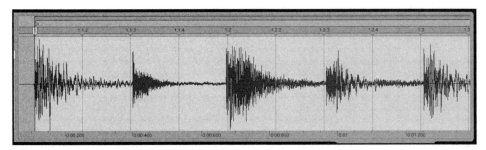

Figure 5.36 You can see that the sub-beats of this loop are not lined up, even though the first and last markers are in the right place. Additional Warp Markers will be necessary to fix the timing of this loop.

- **Make sure that the Fade button is on:** This will perform a quick fade at the beginning and end of the audio loop to remove any "clicks" that can occur at the loop point.

- **Experiment with all of the Warp modes:** While Beats mode will be rhythmically accurate, it may cause sonic artifacts that outweigh the rhythmic precision. You may find that some of your loops sound better in Tones mode. Don't forget to check Re-Pitch mode as well— this will often sound better and clearer for some kinds of material.

- **Play with the Warp Markers:** The elastic audio possibilities of the Warp Engine are staggering. While you can fix timing errors with Warp Markers, try messing things up a bit by "shifting" some beats. Is there a Warp Marker on beat 1.2? What happens if you put the 1.1.4 marker there instead? The sound will now play a 1/16 note early! Use this in combination with the Sample Offset Envelope in Beats mode to reorder the slices in your loop. Then layer a Transpose Envelope, then an unlinked Pan Envelope, and then whatever other parameters you dare to experiment with.

WHO'S USING LIVE? Pr0teus *When we happened to stumble across a bootleg Psytrance mix of the song "Toxic" by Britney Spears, we were quite interested in who pulled it off. The man behind the mix is Fernando Arquines, a.k.a. pr0teus. This guy has played all over the world, and here's what he had to say about using Live:*

The complexity of Psytrance makes a truly live performance difficult to achieve. I've been searching for the best way to perform my music "live" for years. I wanted a way to trigger, layer, and manipulate sounds on the fly, which led me to purchase the M-Audio Trigger Finger. It wasn't until then that Ableton Live came into the picture. I could have sworn the Trigger Finger was specifically designed for Live as I began to notice that they complemented each other perfectly.

Now I have complete control over my live sets. I'm constantly changing my Live setup, but here's a good example of one I used recently: I Warp-Marker all of my tracks and set them aside in a couple muted "queue tracks." I used one of the Trigger Finger's faders to control the crossfader on two main tracks, which I use much like a DJ setup. I have an EQ Three on each of these tracks, which are controlled by computer keyboard assignments. Now the fun starts: I have two loop tracks, which I use for drum, percussion, and synth loops. I use more faders on the Trigger Finger to control the track levels. My main loop track is fed to an EQ Four, Auto Filter, Compressor II, and finally a Chorus. I've got a set of Trigger Finger knobs that are assigned to control the Auto Filter Cutoff and Resonance and another set of knobs that are assigned to control the Chorus Modulation Amount and Rate. This setup is great for mangling my loops to get weird sounds. I also set up another track to sprinkle vocal samples here and there.

The other main part of my Live setup integrates the 16 pads on the Trigger Finger. I use my last Trigger Finger fader to control the level of a MIDI track set up to control Native Instruments' Battery. I assign a sound to each pad, grouping them ergonomically for efficient triggering. For example, a group of pads for hand drum samples, another group for staccato FX samples, another for longer spacey samples, etc. Then I just fade it in and jam out with the track, layering whacked-out FX and percussion on top of the mix. One wicked trick is to take a short sample in Battery, such as a snare, and set it to loop. I assign it to one of the Trigger Finger's pads and set the pad's pressure to send its MIDI CC to control the loop length. When I press the pad lightly, it will retrigger the snare slowly. As I press harder, it speeds up to create an insane motor sound. I just go wild!

I also use the same MIDI CC to control the pitch of the sample, too. I can then assign one of the Trigger Finger's knobs to control the pan and toss the sound across the stereo field. The possibilities are simply mind-boggling! I've been using Live along with the Trigger Finger for a while now, and I find the two inseparable. I see the difference on the dance floor, and after my set, I hear the enthusiastic response from the dancers. This is only the tip of the iceberg!

6 The MIDI Clip

As you might expect, the implementation of MIDI in Live is based on the concepts embodied in Live's audio clips. Just like audio clips, every MIDI clip has launch properties, envelopes, and groove settings, as well as independent start, stop, and loop points. Just like audio clips, MIDI clips are completely independent of one another, allowing you to generate collections of infinitely varied clips effortlessly.

The good news is that MIDI clips are actually simpler to manipulate than their audio clip cousins. MIDI clips don't use any files on the hard drive for playback. Instead, the MIDI data for the clip is saved in the Live Set project file itself. Unlike audio files, MIDI data does not need to be fed through any sort of Warp Engine when matching its playback speed to the project tempo, so you won't have to worry about Warp modes or any of the related settings, such as Warp Markers; nor do you have to worry about Hi-Q interpolation, RAM modes, locating audio files, or hard drive speeds.

However, you'll soon see that the apparent simplicity of the MIDI clip actually belies an extreme amount of power. In addition to all of the typical MIDI commands you would expect to be able to execute, MIDI clips also have much of the power of their audio cousins, since they both behave the same in regard to Launch modes, Launch Quantization, Follow Actions, and Envelopes. For this reason, using a combination of audio and MIDI in a Live Set is a pleasure—audio and MIDI clips look and respond the same in both the Session and Arrangement Views. The differences aren't apparent until you start digging into the Clip and Track Views. In Chapter 4, "Making Music in Live," we discussed a good portion of the Clip View, such as naming and coloring clips, defining loops, and using Follow Actions. These properties exist for both audio and MIDI clips. We also covered the additional areas of the Clip View that were unique to audio clips in Chapter 5, "The Audio Clip." Now it's time to look at the unique sections of the Clip View for MIDI clips.

MIDI Clip Properties

The list of unique properties for a MIDI clip is abbreviated compared with audio clips. As explained previously, manipulating MIDI information is not limited to the same constraints found when dealing with audio files. In the MIDI world, pitch is not related to time. You can speed up a MIDI clip without causing the MIDI notes to rise in pitch. The opposite is also true—you can transpose the notes in the MIDI clip without changing its playback speed. Because all these changes are possible by editing the MIDI data, there is no need for special functions in the MIDI Clip View like the Transpose and Warp functions in an audio clip.

Furthermore, MIDI and audio clips approach controlling sound differently. While audio clips manipulate an existing sound (an audio file), MIDI clips are simply containers for MIDI messages that will only create sound if used to trigger a sound-creating device—be it an external device or a virtual instrument.

Best of Both Worlds If there is an audio clip–specific function that you want to perform on your MIDI part, such as reversing the sound, you can record the output of the MIDI instrument into an audio clip in an audio track and then tweak this new clip.

The MIDI Clip View is somewhat smaller than the audio Clip View. The only properties that are unique to the MIDI clip are the Bank, Sub-bank, and Program selectors (see Figure 6.1). Bank

The Bank and Program Selectors

Figure 6.1 The above settings will recall the twentieth sound in the ninth bank of the associated Wavestation instrument. When you're using the factory default sound bank, these settings will load the Sub Stick sound.

and Program Changes are used to recall particular sounds on the destination MIDI device. If you're going to be working mostly with virtual instruments, you may not need to mess around with these parameters too much. However, if you're working with hardware synths, or you want to have the greatest amount of flexibility with your software synths, you'll need to understand how these parameters work.

Most MIDI devices have the ability to save their settings, such as filter parameters, LFO speeds, and modulation sources. These saved settings are referred to as programs, patches, presets, sounds, or instruments, depending on the manufacturer's nomenclature. Regardless of what the company calls its saved sounds, they are almost always accessed with MIDI Program and Bank Change messages. By setting the Program and Bank values in the Clip View, each clip can recall a different patch from the same instrument when it is launched.

A Program Change is a MIDI message with a value between 0 and 127 and refers to a memory location in your MIDI device's sound bank. The way a manufacturer maps the Program message to the memory slots is entirely up to them, but generally a Program Change of 0 will cause the first sound on the instrument to be loaded. In the case of a General MIDI synthesizer, this will load a piano patch. (The General MIDI specification includes a predefined list of standard instruments and their associated program numbers that manufacturers should adhere to.) So, using the Program Change message, you can recall a sound from our instrument's 128 choices. But what if your device has more than 128 sounds? That's where the Bank Change message comes into play. A bank holds 128 programs. So you can recall any sound in your MIDI device by first specifying the containing bank followed by the program number.

Again, the way instrument manufacturers choose to assign sounds to banks and programs is entirely up to them. For example, Waldorf's MicroQ has three banks of 100 sounds. This means that MicroQ doesn't use Program Changes 100 through 127. Furthermore, the first sound is labeled as Bank A Sound 01. This means that a Program Change of 0 will recall sound A01. A Program Change of 15 will recall A16. Therefore, if you wanted to use sound B01, you'd first have to send a Bank Change message to switch from bank A to bank B and then issue a Program Change of 0 to recall the first patch in that bank (number 01).

You will probably have to consult the manual for your MIDI instrument to find out how the manufacturer is using the Bank and Program Change messages. Some will even require that the Bank Change be done with two numbers, thus the presence of the Sub-bank setting in the MIDI clip properties.

While this may sound confusing, figuring out how your MIDI instruments respond to these messages will open up a level of flexibility where each clip in a MIDI track can "sound" different. This is because a new sound will be loaded when you launch a new clip. When using the Waldorf mentioned above, you can make one MIDI clip that is a string part, while another clip (in the same track) is an arpeggiated blip sequence. If you do not want to change the patches of your virtual instruments during a song, you can just load the patch you want directly in the instrument's interface, and Live will recall it each time the Set is loaded.

Recording New MIDI Clips

To harness the power of MIDI clips, you'll need to make some first. The easiest way to make a new MIDI clip is to simply double-click on an empty slot in the MIDI track. You can also create a MIDI clip by recording it from a MIDI device, such as a keyboard, EWI (electronic wind instrument), MIDI guitar, or a controller. It's also possible to record the MIDI output of other MIDI tracks and external sequencers. You'll need to have a MIDI interface (discussed in Chapter 2, "Getting Live Up and Running") to record an external MIDI source. Some audio interfaces include MIDI ports, making them especially handy in this situation. After you have your MIDI device connected and selected in the Preferences, you're ready to record.

...In the Session View

In the Session View, recording a new MIDI clip is almost identical to recording an audio clip. The fact that the procedures are similar means there is less for you to learn and remember about Live. It makes the composition process more transparent because you'll use the same motions every time you record, be it audio or MIDI.

To begin, make a MIDI track (Ctrl (Cmd)+Shift+T). Then specify the MIDI input you'll be recording. This is done in the Input/Output Routing strip, shown in Figure 6.2, by selecting the MIDI input device followed by the channel you want to record. Live has a setting called All Ins that will record any MIDI data entering the selected input, regardless of the MIDI channel assigned to the data. If you have only one device connected to the MIDI device you selected, then All Ins will be an appropriate setting. If you have multiple instruments entering the selected MIDI port, you may want to specify the channel you want to record to prevent data from another instrument being recorded in your clip. Of course, in order to hear your MIDI data,

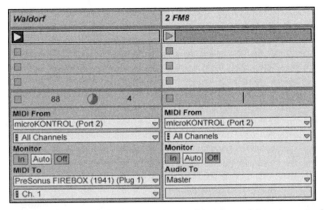

Figure 6.2 The Korg MicroKontrol keyboard has been selected as the MIDI input device. On the first track, the keyboard will end up controlling channel 1 of our Waldorf MicroQ, which is hooked up to the MIDI Out port of the FireBox. The second track has an FM8 softsynth loaded. Notice how this track shows an audio output instead of MIDI.

either you'll need to select an output destination for the MIDI track to route it to an external hardware device, or you'll have to load a virtual instrument.

In the example above, the input and output have been specified for the track, so we can set the track for recording by activating the Arm button in the Session Mixer. With Monitor set to Auto, we'll now be able to play the MicroQ from the keyboard. (MIDI data enters the track from the keyboard and is then immediately sent out to the Waldorf.) The track is now ready to record.

You'll notice that all the Clip Stop buttons in the track have changed to circles. Clicking one of these circles will begin recording a new MIDI clip in that slot. Just like audio clips, MIDI clips will wait to record until the time specified by the Global Quantize setting. Once recording has commenced, start playing. Everything you do, including pitch bends, aftertouch, knob tweaks, and so on, will be recorded into the MIDI clip. When you're done, click the play icon in the clip to stop recording. (If your default Launch mode is Trigger, the clip will begin playing back your new recording.) You can start recording additional takes by clicking the circles in any of the other clip slots.

...In the Arrangement View

If recording MIDI clips resembles recording audio clips in the Session View, you can probably already guess how to record MIDI clips in the Arrangement View. Indeed, it is the same procedure used with audio clips in the Arrangement View. You'll need to set up your MIDI input and output first, as explained in Figure 6.2. You'll also arm the track, but instead of using the circles in the clip slots to start recording, you'll click the Record button in the Control Bar. When you press Play in the Control Bar, Live will start playing your arrangement while recording your new MIDI clip (see Figure 6.3). If Live is already playing, recording will begin the instant you press the Record button. By arming multiple tracks, you can record multiple clips simultaneously, allowing Live to work as a multitrack MIDI recorder. You can, of course, also record multiple audio clips at the same time, too!

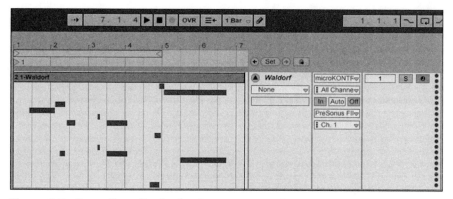

Figure 6.3 Recording clips in the Arrangement View.

Multirecording Can't seem to arm more than one track at a time for recording? Don't worry, you're just being stopped by Live's "arm-exclusive" behavior. To arm multiple tracks, hold down the Ctrl (Cmd) key and then click the Arm buttons. This is just like selecting multiple files on your computer. If this behavior annoys you, you can turn it off in the Preferences (see Chapter 2).

Quantizing Your Performance

Nobody's perfect. We can't always play our instruments with the rhythmical precision of a drum machine, but with judicious use of quantizing, Live can make you sound like you're dead on the beat. *Quantizing* is the process of aligning events to a timing grid. In the case of Launch Quantizing used in the Session View, you're making sure your clips start playing on a division of your timing grid. When quantizing a MIDI clip, you're making sure *every note* is aligned to the grid. Quantizing can be done either while you record or after the fact.

If you want to quantize while recording, you'll have to visit the Record Quantization submenu (under the Edit menu). After you select a quantization value here, any recording you make will be perfectly aligned to the rhythmic subdivisions you have selected. Figures 6.4a and 6.4b show how this works. This is a dream come true when programming drumbeats since every recording will be rhythmically tight. Live can quantize notes to a grid of 1/4 notes, 1/16-note triplets, or anything in between.

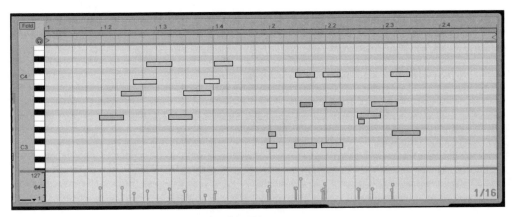

Figure 6.4a Here are some unquantized MIDI notes.

Of course, not every style of music demands strict rhythmic quantization. In fact, many musicians prefer to keep the natural feel of their performances in their takes. You can turn off Live's automatic quantizing by choosing No Quantization from the Record Quantize menu.

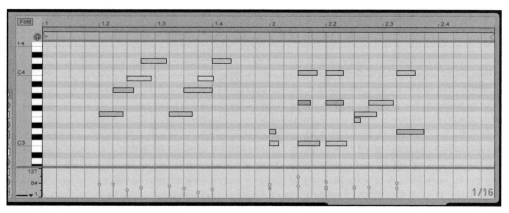

Figure 6.4b The same part recorded with quantizing. Notice how each note's left edge is aligned with one of the grid lines.

The Undo Two-Step When Live is set to automatically quantize a recording, you'll still be able to undo the quantizing in case you left it on by accident. The first time you press Ctrl (Cmd)+Z after recording, the recorded notes will move to their original, unquantized locations. The second Undo will erase the clip, allowing you to make another.

If you decide later that you do want to quantize the part, press Ctrl (Cmd)+U to open Live's Quantizing dialog box (see Figure 6.5). You'll have to be in the Clip View for the clip you want to quantize before trying to open this dialog. The first value at the top sets the quantize grid. You must set this to the smallest subdivision that occurs in the part. If you have played a part with 1/16 notes, you'll need to select 1/16 here. If you select 1/8, the Quantize function will move the 1/16 notes to the closest 1/8 note, therefore screwing up the part.

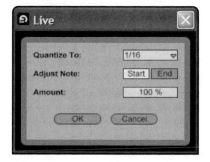

Figure 6.5 Live's Quantize dialog box will tailor the method by which Live quantizes your notes.

Below the Quantize selection is the Adjust Note selection, with two buttons labeled Start and End. By default, only Start is enabled. This means that Live will change only the start location of a note when it quantizes—the length of the note will remain the same. If you enable End as well, Live will make sure that the note ends on a grid subdivision, too. This is handy for rapid-fire synth bass sequences, as each note will be on beat *and* the same length. If you wanted, you could deselect Start, making Live fix only the end of each note.

The last parameter in the dialog box is the Amount value. Normally, this is set to 100%, which forces every note to the nearest grid subdivision. If you set this value to 50%, Live will move the notes only halfway to the proper place. The result is a tighter performance, but one that is not completely rigid.

Partial Quantizing Sometimes you may not want to quantize an entire clip. Maybe part of it feels just right, but one passage is a bit off, or maybe one section needs to be quantized to straight 16ths and another section to 16th-note triplets. In this case, just select the notes you want to quantize by click-dragging over them in the Clip View or Shift-clicking on individual notes. Now quantization will be applied to these notes only.

Overdub Recording

Overdub Recording is a function available only for MIDI clips; it records additional MIDI data into a clip without erasing what's already there. This is an awesome feature when it comes to programming drumbeats, since you can build them one piece at a time. You can make a two-bar loop with a hi-hat and then play the additional parts (kick drums, snares, cymbals) layer by layer as the clip continues to loop.

To enable MIDI Overdub Recording, click the OVR button in the Control Bar (see Figure 6.6). When you launch a clip, it will start playing, and its play triangle will be green. After you arm the track for recording, the MIDI clip will keep playing, but its play triangle will turn red. This signifies that the clip is playing *and* recording at the same time. Anything you play at this point will be added to the current MIDI clip (and quantized on the fly, too, if you enable Record Quantization), and each iteration of the loop will contain the new data you recorded.

Combined with the drag-and-drop techniques of the Session View, programming variations of beats can be accomplished in moments instead of minutes. You can start with a simple drum pattern (perhaps just kick drum and hi-hat for the intro of your song), drag-copy (use the Ctrl (Cmd) key while dragging) the clip to a new location, and then use the MIDI Overdub to layer the snare hits on top of the kick and hi-hat. Now you'll have two MIDI clips: one with just kick and hats and the other with a snare added. You can drag-copy the new MIDI clip and layer on an additional part, such as a shaker or congas. Using this technique, you can build a collection of drum variations quickly for your song that you can then trigger on the fly.

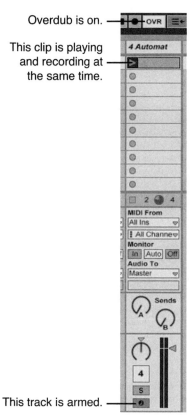

Overdub is on.

This clip is playing and recording at the same time.

This track is armed.

Figure 6.6 MIDI overdub recording allows parts to be built in layers while a MIDI clip is playing. Note that recording occurs for any clip playing on an armed track.

Of course, you can use Overdub Recording for more than drums. If a piano part is really tricky, you could record the left-hand and right-hand parts separately. Perhaps you'll perform the left-hand part on the first pass and then overdub the right-hand part on the next pass.

Editing MIDI Clips

One of the most attractive features of MIDI is the ability to edit the MIDI data in order to create a perfect part. Recorded notes can be effortlessly transposed to different pitches, extended or shortened, and moved to a different location in time. This can make recording MIDI parts a little easier because you don't have to worry about getting the part *exactly* right. You just need to get it close so you can make final adjustments to the MIDI data.

When you edit MIDI clips in Live, you not only have the ability to change the notes that are recorded, but also to create new ones by hand. In fact, many producers prefer to draw parts directly into the clips instead of playing them, when programming drum parts, for example. It allows them to create specific performances, such as perfectly repeating 1/16 notes that are all the same duration and velocity. Editing data by hand also allows you to create precise automation, such as perfect volume fades and quantized filter modulations.

Adjusting the Grid

All editing in a MIDI clip is governed by the timing grid. Anytime a note is created or moved, it will snap to the grid values. If your grid is set to 1/4, you'll be able to align the MIDI notes only to the 1/4 note of the clip. You can, of course, change the grid settings, allowing you to make more precise rhythmic adjustments. You can even turn the grid off completely for free-form editing.

Live has two grid modes: Adaptive and Fixed. The grid mode can be selected by right-clicking anywhere in the Note Editor and selecting from the context menu. Adaptive mode, the default, simply changes the grid value according to the zoom level. The grid values get smaller the more you zoom in on your MIDI notes. Fixed grid keeps the resolution at the value you select, regardless of the zoom level. Changing the Fixed grid resolution can be done with the key commands outlined below. As you execute these key commands, you'll see the quantize value change in the MIDI data window (see Figure 6.7), reflecting your modification. Note that before using the following key commands, you must click on the grid to select it; otherwise, you might be adjusting the Quantize menu in the Control Bar.

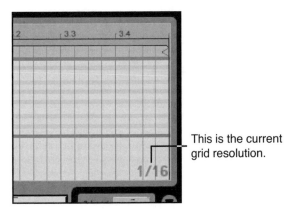

This is the current grid resolution.

Figure 6.7 The current grid setting is 1/16. This means that all notes you manipulate will snap to 1/16-note timing.

- **Ctrl (Cmd)+1:** This will decrease the value of the grid. If the grid was set to 1/16 before, it will be 1/32 after using this key command.

- **Ctrl (Cmd)+2:** This has the opposite effect of the command above. A grid value of 1/16 will change to 1/8 after using this command.

- **Ctrl (Cmd)+3:** This key command toggles Triplet mode on and off. A previous setting of 1/8 will turn to 1/8T (1/8-note triplet) after pressing these keys. Use this key command again to switch Triplet mode off.

- **Ctrl (Cmd)+4:** This turns the entire grid on and off. When the grid is off, the grid value display will turn gray. You will be able to place MIDI data anywhere you like while the grid is off. To re-enable the grid, use this key command again.

Editing Notes and Velocities

After you've got your desired grid timing selected, you're ready to start manipulating MIDI notes. Live displays MIDI notes in a style known as a *piano roll*. This term comes from the old player pianos that were programmed using rolls of paper. These rolls had small slots cut into them, each representing a specific note on the piano keyboard or one of the other instruments mounted inside. A note that played for a long time was triggered by a long slot in the paper. As the paper rolled by mechanical sensors, it triggered servos to play notes on the piano.

Viewing MIDI Data

The Piano Roll View in Live features a lane for each note on the MIDI scale. When looking at Figure 6.8, you'll see an image of a piano keyboard at the left side of the window. From each of these keys is a lane extending to the right where notes can be placed. Notes placed in these lanes trigger their corresponding key in the scale.

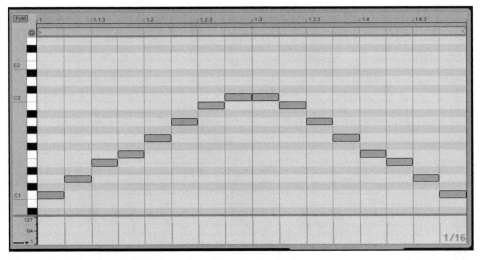

Figure 6.8 The MIDI data here is a C-major scale. You can see that only the white keys are being triggered by the MIDI notes.

You can zoom in and out of the vertical piano keyboard, thus allowing you to see more or less of the 128 possible notes in the MIDI scale. Zoom in by moving your mouse over the piano keyboard at the left of the window. When the mouse changes to a magnifying glass, you can click and drag to zoom. Since the view is vertical instead of horizontal, the zooming moves have also been turned on their side. Dragging the mouse left and right will now adjust the zoom, and dragging up and down allows you to scroll through the piano keyboard. If you zoom out too far, the piano keyboard will disappear. Zoom in to see it again.

Into the Fold Live's MIDI display has a unique feature that hides any lanes that don't contain MIDI data. When the Fold button (located just above the Piano Roll display) is activated, the display will be condensed, and you'll see only the lanes that contain notes in the clip. This is perfect for programming drums since many synths and keyboards map their sounds over a wide range of octaves. You may be using a kick drum sound at D1, while using a hi-hat sound three octaves higher at E4. So, instead of scrolling up and down repeatedly to see the two parts, you can press Fold, and you'll see only the lanes for D1 and E4, making editing a snap. Turn Fold off to see all the lanes again.

Previewing MIDI Notes

You will see a tiny little headphone icon right above the keyboard shown in the piano roll. The headphone icon looks like the Preview icon found in the Browser and has a nearly identical function. When this button is on, each MIDI note that you click in the editing grid will also be sent out to the connected MIDI instrument. This allows you to hear every note that you add and edit, which can help keep you from editing the wrong note or placing a note in the wrong lane. Additionally, you can click on the keys at the left edge of the grid to preview the sounds.

Editing MIDI Data with Draw Mode

There are two methods for editing MIDI data: with or without the Pencil. When the Draw mode is on (activate it in the Control Bar or press Ctrl (Cmd)+B), you can quickly add notes to the MIDI note window and set their velocities. Clicking in the grid will cause a note to appear that is the length of the current grid setting. If you continue to hold the mouse button after you create the note, you can drag up and down to set its velocity. If you click and drag horizontally (see Figure 6.9), the Pencil will create a series of notes in that lane, which is great for hi-hat patterns.

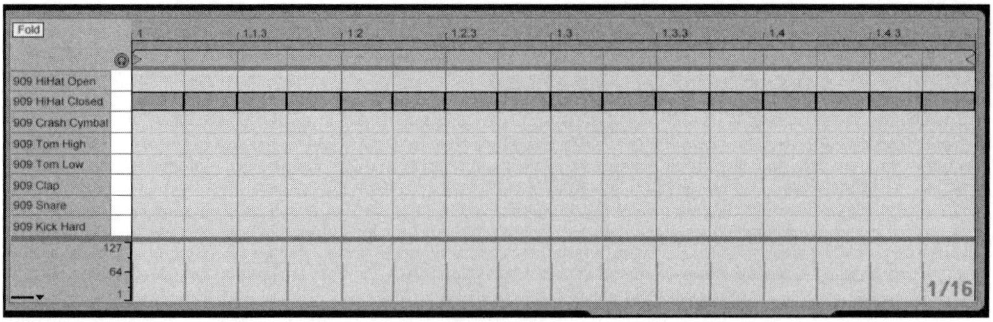

Figure 6.9 Draw mode makes it easy to quickly draw in a series of 1/16 notes.

(You can also drag up and down to set the velocities of the whole group.) Clicking an existing note with the Pencil will erase it.

Editing MIDI Data Without the Pencil

While writing notes with the Pencil can be extremely efficient, there are a few things that can't be done with the Pencil, such as changing the start time and length of a MIDI note. These advanced edits can be performed by switching the Pencil tool off (click the icon in the Control Bar or press Ctrl (Cmd)+B to toggle it). When the Pencil is off, your mouse will appear as a standard arrow.

To create a MIDI note in this mode, double-click an empty slot. After the note has been made, you can click and drag it to a new location. This will let you change the pitch and time for the note in one maneuver. When you move the mouse to either end of the MIDI note, the mouse will change to a bracket (it will look like [at the beginning of the note and] at the end). Clicking and dragging in this location will stretch the MIDI note, making it either longer or shorter. Double-clicking the note again will erase it.

To adjust the velocity of a note when you're not using the Pencil requires exposing the velocity lane in the MIDI note window. This lane can be viewed by dragging the lower boundary upward (see Figure 6.10). The velocity of each note is represented by a vertical line with a small circle at the top. The taller the line, the greater the velocity will be. Since multiple notes can occur in different lanes at one time in a MIDI clip, it's possible for the velocities of multiple notes to be stacked on top of one another. As you move your mouse over one of the circular handles at the top of the velocity lines, you'll see its corresponding note become highlighted in the upper window, showing you which note you're about to edit. I actually recommend doing the reverse, however, by selecting the note in the upper portion of the window first to ensure that you're editing the right velocity. If you decide to use the Pencil tool in the velocity lane, you will not be able to specify which note to edit when two or more occur at the same time (vertically aligned). Instead, you'll end up setting these notes to the same velocity.

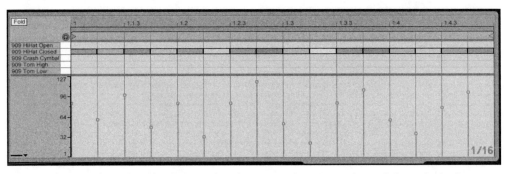

Figure 6.10 By dragging the bottom border upward, we've enlarged the velocity lane.

Another benefit of using the arrow is that you can select groups of MIDI notes to edit. You can click and drag around the area of notes you want, or you can select them individually by holding Shift and clicking. Once you've selected them, you can perform edits on multiple notes at once. You can drag the notes to a new location, changing their pitch and timing. You can lengthen or shorten them as a group. You can copy them using all the standard Cut, Copy, and Paste commands (even the dragging techniques of the Session View work here), or you can scale their velocities all at once in the lower window.

MIDI Clip Envelopes

After your MIDI notes are straightened out, it will be time to look at your Clip Envelopes. These envelopes will be used for creating controller data to be sent to your MIDI devices. When effects and instruments are loaded onto the MIDI track, the Clip Envelopes will be able to control those devices, too.

MIDI Ctrl Envelopes

In a MIDI track with an empty Track View, the only category of envelopes that will be available is the MIDI Ctrl Envelopes. These are controllers such as Pitch Bend, Modulation, Volume, Pan, and Sustain, and all are shown as graphical envelopes in the Clip View (see Figure 6.11). These envelopes generate values that are translated to MIDI data and then sent to the destination MIDI device. Remember, you can view the envelopes for your MIDI clip by clicking on the tiny E icon to show/hide the Envelope box.

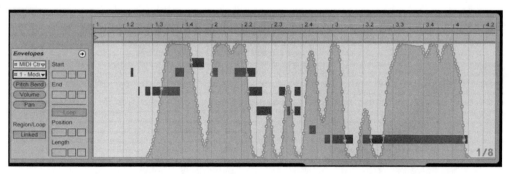

Figure 6.11 The movements of the mod wheel are represented by an envelope that bears a striking resemblance to a roller coaster.

When you look through the list of available MIDI controllers, you'll see some of them have already been named, such as Volume, Breath, Pan, and Expression. This is because part of the MIDI standard defines certain controller numbers for certain musical tasks. Controller 10 is generally Pan. Controller 7 is usually Volume, and so on. Whether these controllers actually have any effect will be determined by the MIDI device on the receiving end. If you have an old analog synth with MIDI, it may respond to notes and pitch bend, but it might not be able to pan.

Other devices may not respond to Controller 7 for volume. You'll need to look at your MIDI device's manual, specifically the MIDI implementation chart (usually at the end of the manual), to see a list of the MIDI controllers and messages for the instrument.

Mixer Envelopes

If you happen to load a virtual instrument onto your MIDI track, a few more envelope categories will be available for your tweaking. Once the virtual instrument is in place, the track now behaves like an audio track. You'll see that you have a Mixer category available with Volume, Pan, and Send Envelopes. There will also be a category for the virtual instrument you loaded. This means you can modulate the parameters of the virtual instrument while it plays. Furthermore, any audio or MIDI effects loaded into the track will be available for tweaking.

Shortcut to Confusion The Volume and Pan shortcut buttons do different things, depending on whether you are working with a virtual instrument or a hardware synth. If there's a virtual instrument loaded, these buttons will link you to the Volume and Pan envelopes for the Mixer. If you are routing your MIDI track to an output port, however, the buttons act as shortcuts to MIDI Volume (CC 7) and MIDI Pan (CC 10).

Virtual Instruments and Effects

You can draw and edit envelopes for parameters of the Live devices and plug-ins loaded onto a track by selecting them from the Clip Envelope menus. The top menu will select the device or plug-in, which can be an instrument or an effect (both audio and MIDI effects). For each device selected in the top menu, you'll get a list of parameters that can be edited. The exact list you'll see here depends on what instrument or effect you have loaded.

Is This Thing On? All controller values are represented as envelopes in Live. If the parameter you are controlling is a switch, values above 64 usually turn it on, and values below turn it off. You'll need to make sure your envelope passes above 64 only when you want your parameter on.

Importing and Exporting MIDI Files

Live stores all MIDI data and parameters for MIDI clips within the Live Set. You can see the individual MIDI clips and tracks within the Browser. While audio clips must play a specific audio file stored on a hard disk, the MIDI clips don't require any sort of external support file that you need to keep track of. When you import a MIDI file, Live copies the data from the MIDI file into the Live Set. Live will never use the original MIDI file again, so should that file be changed or lost, the Live Set will still play perfectly.

Importing Standard MIDI Files

Live imports MIDI parts from Standard MIDI Files (SMFs), which come in two flavors: Type 0 and Type 1. Unless your MIDI file has only one part in it, Type 0 won't do you any good in Live—all the parts are squished into one track. Type 1, on the other hand, has the MIDI parts split into separate tracks for each instrument. There will be a track for the bass, some for the drums, and tracks for any other part in the song, all of which will be displayed below the MIDI file when you open it in the Browser (see Figure 6.12). Live lets you import these tracks into new clips by dragging the tracks into your session or arrangement like regular clips.

Figure 6.12 This MIDI file has multiple tracks that can be added to the Live Set individually.

If you've got a song in another software, or perhaps something stuck in an older hardware sequencer, and you want to transfer it to Live, SMFs will usually take care of the job. The format has been around for a long time, so you can be assured of compatibility; however, SMFs don't necessarily retain *everything* from a computer project. When exporting songs done in other programs, you may have been utilizing application-specific features that are beyond the scope of MIDI. These could include mixer and effect automation, as well as the port and channel assignments of the MIDI tracks. This kind of information gets saved in the application's native file format but usually won't appear in an SMF export.

Exporting Standard MIDI Files

If you need to take the MIDI part from a clip and send it to another Live Set or a different program, you can export the MIDI data as an SMF. Select the clip and choose Export MIDI clip from Live's File menu. You'll be prompted to give a name and destination for the exported data. Choose a location and name and click Save.

Using the Live Clip Format

Note that you can save your MIDI clips along with the virtual instrument you used for it, including any MIDI and audio effects that were in use. This allows you to save your MIDI part easily as a musical idea in your collection of clips. When you add the clip to a new track in another song, it will load up the instrument and necessary effects automatically.

To export this kind of clip, simply click the clip and drag it into a Browser. It will appear there, and you will immediately be able to give the clip a new name. Press Enter when you're done renaming to save the clip.

You can differentiate these enhanced clips from regular clips by the icon that precedes the clip in the Browser (see Figure 6.13). Additionally, these clips have an .alc file extension, which stands for Ableton Live Clip.

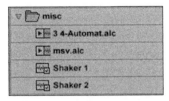

Figure 6.13   You can see that the top two files have a special icon in front of them that indicates they are Live Clips.

Now that you have a handle on the ins and outs of audio and MIDI clips and how to arrange them, it's time to start adding effects. The next chapter will show how effects, if used properly, can add another dimension to your music by introducing elements of sound design. You'll also learn how to use virtual instruments and put them fully under hardware control.

7 Using Effects and Instruments

Effects can profoundly change the impact of your music. They can be used in a variety of ways: to remove unwanted frequencies from an audio track (EQ), to create the sound of a room for a vocalist (Reverb), or to completely destroy and mangle a sound into something totally new (Distortion). Effects put a lot of power at your fingertips. Those people who are new to these toys will more than likely run hog-wild the first few times they get their hands on them. Hey, effects are fun—we all know that. As with all things, practice will help you determine which type of effects will help your mix the most. Don't forget that sometimes having no effect on a sound is the best decision. In this chapter, we'll look at how to use plug-in audio and MIDI effects in your Live Sets. We'll also have a brief peek at how to use virtual instruments in Live as well, since they are also plug-ins. We will discuss how to work with Live's built-in instruments in much greater detail in the following chapter.

Using Effects in a Session

In the simplest sense, an effect is a device that takes an input signal—either audio or MIDI data—performs calculations upon it, and spits the result out the other end. For example, a delay effect will take a sound into its input and then wait a specified amount of time before sending it to the output. A filter effect can take a sound and remove all the frequencies below 500Hz. You can chain multiple effects together for even more power by having the output of one effect feed the input of another, and so on.

The Track View

In Live, the graphical layout of an effect chain is surprisingly simple and logical. Double-click a track name—either at the top of the Session View or at the right side of the Arrangement View—and you will see its Track View appear at the bottom of the Live window. Effects are placed in the Track View side by side to form a chain (see Figure 7.1). A signal enters the leftmost device and proceeds through each until it comes out the right-hand side.

The Big Picture As you can probably see from Figure 7.1, it's very easy to add enough devices to a track that they can't all be seen at one time. When this happens, the devices will simply scroll off to the right. At the lower right-hand corner of your screen, you'll see a

Figure 7.1 An arbitrary arrangement of audio effects in the Track View. The input signal is processed by each device in order from left to right.

miniaturized image of all of the devices in the track with a black rectangle indicating the devices that are currently in view. Just like in the Arrangement View, you can slide the rectangle around to view different parts of the device chain.

My favorite trick for keeping devices in view, however, is folding them. Just double-click in a device's title bar, and it will collapse sideways, taking up a fraction of the screen space it did before. It's easy to keep your devices folded and just unfold the one you're working with at the moment.

The Effect Browsers

You gain access to your collection of effects through the two Browser icons seen in Figure 7.2. The top icon activates the Live Device Browser (the built-in effects and instruments), while the lower icon activates the Plug-in Browser (your external VST and Audio Units effects and instruments).

Figure 7.2 These two buttons are located in the upper-left corner of the Live window. Click the top button to gain access to Live's built-in effects and instruments. The bottom button displays a list of all the plug-ins, both VST and Audio Units, currently available to Live.

The Live Device Browser contains three folders, which can be opened to view the built-in audio effects, MIDI effects, and instruments. We'll discuss those individually later. The folder layout of the plug-in Browser, on the other hand, depends on the current configuration of your system and the plug-ins that are available to Live.

Adding an effect from one of the Browsers is as easy as it gets. In fact, there are three different ways to load these devices onto a track, all of which may be used interchangeably:

1.   Click and drag a device from the Browser to the desired track, as shown in Figure 7.3. This will add the new effect to the right side of the effect chain if there are any pre-existing devices on the track.

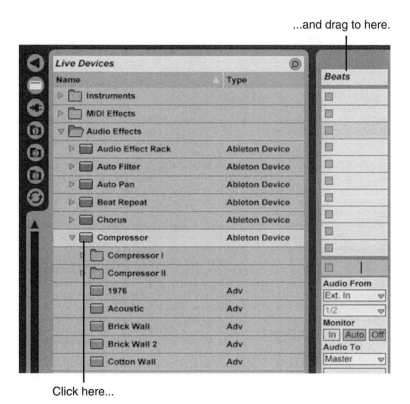

Figure 7.3   Click and drag an effect from the Browser to the title of a track. When you release your mouse button, the effect will be loaded into the track.

2.   Select the destination track by clicking on the track's name, and then double-click the desired device or plug-in shown in the Browser. Just as above, the selected effect will be loaded into the far-right position in the track's effect chain.

3.   Double-click the name of a track to expose its Track View. You may then drag and drop effects from the Browsers directly into the Track View (see Figure 7.4). The benefit of this method is that you may choose where in the device chain the new effect will be loaded instead of always defaulting to the last position, as in the previous two methods. If you decide that you need some EQ before your compressor, you can simply drag it into this location.

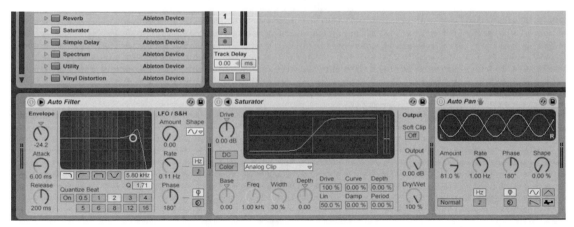

Figure 7.4 By dragging devices straight into the Track View, you can choose to insert them at any point in the chain that you want.

All three methods explained above work identically in both the Session View and Arrangement View. Just remember that in the Session View, the track names are found at the top of the window, while in the Arrangement View they are found on the right side.

Plug-In Types

There are three types of plug-ins in Live: Audio Effects, MIDI Effects, and Instruments. As you would assume, audio effects process and alter only audio signals, while MIDI effects perform calculations on passing MIDI data. MIDI effects can't be used on audio tracks. Audio effects can, however, exist on MIDI tracks—as long as the MIDI track is being used to host an instrument (see Figure 7.5). The only way you can have an audio effect on a MIDI track that's controlling external hardware is if the hardware is being accessed via an external instrument device. Don't worry, external devices will be discussed in Chapter 8, "Live's Instruments."

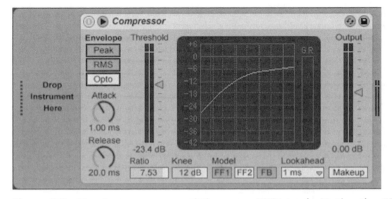

Figure 7.5 Here's a compressor sitting on a MIDI track. Notice the "Drop Instrument Here" message before the device.

Audio Effects

Audio effects have existed in Live since the program's first release. Audio effects can be used to correct tone problems, add ambience to sounds, or shape noise into completely new textures—the possibilities are staggering. Audio effects include equalizers, delays, choruses, pitch shifters, flangers, compressors, phasers, gates, distortions, and limiters. There may be a few more esoteric effects not categorized here for sure, but the majority of audio plug-ins will be of these types. Live 7 includes a collection of 25 audio effects for your perusal, use, and abuse. A complete dissertation on these audio effects appears in Chapter 9, "Live's Audio Effects."

Instruments

When Live tells you to "Drop Instrument Here," it's not directing you to drop your keyboard. Instead, it is referring to an *instrument* plug-in. While you probably wouldn't consider an instrument to be an effect, instruments still reside in your effect chain (see Figure 7.6). You can think of an instrument as an extremely lightweight sound module. It takes MIDI input and spits out audio, but it lives inside your computer and doesn't require a power cable!

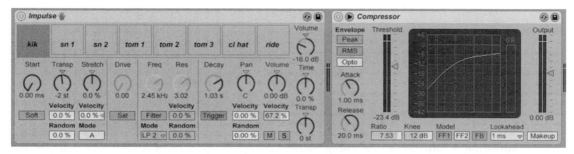

Figure 7.6   Here we've added Live's Impulse instrument to the track. The compressor will now compress the output of Impulse.

Live comes with two built-in instruments of its own: Impulse, a simple drum sampler, and Simpler, a very basic sampler that can play back and manipulate individual samples. Ableton also makes five additional instruments for Live 7, but in order to use these you must first purchase an unlock code separately for each instrument. (See Chapter 8 for the scoop on these.) Live will also support any plug-in instrument conforming to the VST standard, while Mac OS X users also have the ability to use Audio Units instruments.

By adding an instrument to a MIDI track, you end up converting it into a hybrid audio/MIDI track. You can see the result when looking at the I/O routing section of the Session Mixer (see Figure 7.7).

Figure 7.7 The I/O section on the left is for the track in the examples above. Adding the Impulse has caused the router to change the output format of the track from MIDI to audio. The track on the right does not have an instrument loaded, so MIDI is never changed to audio. The right-side track still outputs MIDI.

MIDI Effects

The last type of effect used in Live is the MIDI effect. Placing one of these on a MIDI track will alter the MIDI messages being passed through the effect chain. These alterations can range from subtle, such as smoothing out velocity response, to drastic, such as remapping notes to different pitches or using the Arpeggiator. Keep in mind that MIDI effects alter what you hear by changing what an instrument is told to play. For example, consider the following example.

You load your favorite piano plug-in onto a MIDI track. You record a short riff into a clip and set it looping. You then load the Pitch effect onto the track right before the piano plug-in. As you turn up the Transpose knob on the Pitch effect, the notes being sent to the piano plug-in are shifted upward. The result is that the piano plug-in now plays the part in a higher register. You'll also notice that as you continue to turn up the Transpose knob, the piano will play higher and higher *while still sounding natural*. This is because you are not shifting the sound of the piano upward—you're moving the MIDI notes used to trigger the piano upward. It's exactly as if you'd moved your hands to a different part of the keyboard and played the part again.

Now remove the Pitch effect and record the piano part into an audio clip. As you transpose the audio clip higher, there will be a point at which the piano starts sounding artificial. This is the difference between changing pitch in the MIDI and audio domains. The Pitch effect changes what the instrument plays, which results in a more pleasing transposition.

This distinction also has "gotchas," which can result in seemingly confusing behaviors for MIDI effects in certain scenarios. If you use the Pitch effect (see Figure 7.8) to transpose up the MIDI messages sent to the Impulse by one semitone, you won't hear the drums sounding higher in pitch—you'll hear different drums playing the same pattern. That's because each drum in the Impulse is mapped to a single MIDI note. If you transpose the incoming MIDI up by more than an octave, you won't hear any drums at all! You've raised the pitch of the MIDI notes to the point where it's outside of the range of notes the Impulse responds to.

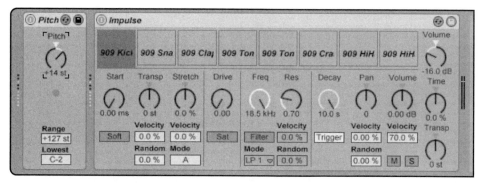

Figure 7.8 The Pitch device is transposing the MIDI data out of the operating range for Impulse. You can see the MIDI data entering the Impulse on its left, but there's no audio exiting on its right.

To get a better handle on this, take a look at the MIDI Pitch example provided in the Chapter 7 folder from the CD-ROM. When you first run it, the beat will play normally. Try adjusting the Pitch knob in the MIDI Pitch effect, and you'll hear the result.

Third-Party Plug-ins

While Live offers an impressive collection of 35 devices right out of the box, you may still prefer to use plug-in effects and instruments from other manufacturers. Live fully supports the VST and Audio Units (Mac OS X only) plug-in standards, allowing limitless expansion possibilities for your virtual studio.

While all of Live's plug-ins can be edited entirely from their graphical interfaces in the Track View, the nature of VST and AU plug-ins and their fully customizable graphical interfaces require that a separate window be used to display the effect. When you load an external plug-in, Live displays a generic X-Y object in the Track View (see Figure 7.9), allowing access to more detailed functions.

Click here to open the
plug-in's editor.

Figure 7.9 A VST or Audio Units plug-in shows up as a generic placeholder. Clicking the wrench icon opens up the plug-in's custom graphical interface.

Reordering and Removing Effects

Live allows you to change the order of effects easily within a chain. This ability provides a way to experiment with different device arrangements. Does it sound better to run a vocal through a reverb and then into a delay or the other way around? To find out, just drag and drop the pre-existing effects within the Track View to change their order (see Figure 7.10). You'll hear the results immediately. When dragging an effect between existing effects, you'll see a dark line appear, indicating the insertion point for when the mouse is released.

...and drag to here.   Click here...

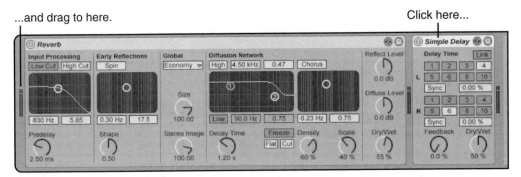

Figure 7.10 Click and drag the Simple Delay to the left side of the Track View. When you release the mouse button, the two effects will switch positions.

With or Without You If you want to compare the sound of a track with and without an effect, click the effect's power button, located in the upper-left corner of the effect's window. You can toggle the effect on and off without having to delete it. When the effect is off, audio will bypass it and continue through any other effects in your chain.

If you no longer need an effect or loaded it by accident, click on the effect title bar to select it and press Delete on your computer keyboard. The effect will disappear, and any effect that may have been to the right will shift to the left to fill the space left behind.

Managing Presets

Software effects and instruments come with preset sounds and settings built into them, and in most cases you can save your own presets as well once you have come up with a particular combination of settings that you like. Live deals with these presets somewhat differently, depending on whether the effect/instrument in question is one of Ableton's built-in devices or a third-party effect/instrument in VST or AU format. Let's look at each of these types in turn.

Managing VST Plug-In Presets

The preset management scheme for third-party VST plug-ins is straightforward and similar to the methods employed by other DAW programs. Live can store the current settings of a plug-in using the preset icons at the top of the plug-in window (see Figure 7.11).

Open an effect bank.

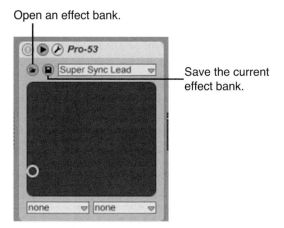

Save the current effect bank.

Figure 7.11 Preset management buttons found in each VST plug-in's title bar.

The drop-down menu in the plug-in window contains a list of previously stored presets for the effect (or instrument), including those provided as starters from the manufacturer. Selecting a preset from the menu will load it and replace the settings currently being used by the plug-in. If this menu is inaccessible, it's because the manufacturer has integrated preset management directly into the graphic interface of the plug-in (accessed with the wrench icon in the upper-left corner of the plug-in window).

While presets for Live devices are automatically stored in the Library, VST presets can be saved anywhere you want. Just click in the floppy disk icon (see Figure 7.11) and choose a location on your hard drive. It's probably a good idea to choose a centralized location for these preset files so you don't lose track of them.

Warnings. By using a third-party plug-in, you are incorporating a new piece of program code into Live. This is very much like receiving an organ transplant—it may work just fine or it may be rejected. Plug-ins are available from a wide range of sources. Waves, Cycling '74, and iZotope are a few companies that make terrific effects. Native Instruments, LinPlug, Arturia, and VirSyn peddle some of the most cutting-edge software instruments around. A curious Web surfer can find an even greater offering of plug-ins to try, many of which are available as freeware downloads. In any case, the quality of programming put into the plug-in will determine its effectiveness and stability within Live. It's safer to use plug-ins from major companies because they have the resources to develop, diagnose, and improve their products quickly. Plug-ins that some guy developed in his basement may be the most imaginative of the breed, but they commonly suffer from lack of optimization (use huge chunks of CPU power) and instability (crash at the most inappropriate times). I'm not saying that you shouldn't use these freeware and shareware plug-ins—quite the contrary. I just want to impress upon you that problems may arise in this situation, so be ready (and save often!). Most important, never use a brand-new plug-in for the first time at a gig. Who knows what it may do? Take the time to thoroughly test the plug-in at home before trying it live.

Tips. When experimenting with new plug-ins, there are a few precautions to take. These hints can help keep you from losing your work, crashing the system, and destroying speakers.

- **Save your Live Set before loading a new plug-in you've never tried before:** Live is generally very good at recovering from crashes, but better safe than sorry.

- **Backup the new Set:** Once you have a new plug-in running, save a copy of the Set under a new temporary name, possibly the name of the song with "-test" added to the end. Then quit Live and start back up again. Try loading the test Set to be sure the plug-in initializes properly. I've seen a few cases where the plug-in worked when added manually, but the program crashed when trying to load the whole Live Set. After you are sure that the plug-in will load dependably, you can then resave your Set under its original name.

- **Watch your volumes:** Anytime you add an unproven plug-in to your Set, turn down your speaker and headphone volumes. A bad plug-in initialization can leave your computer outputting full-spectrum digital noise sometimes, which could rip both your speakers and eardrums to shreds.

- **Organize your plug-in collection:** We like to use the custom plug-in directory (in the File/Folder tab of Preferences) to keep a collection of plug-ins that are confirmed to work with Live separate from the slew of freeware and demo plug-ins that exist in the standard shared plug-ins folders. By having only a small collection of plug-ins for Live to use, you will significantly reduce the boot-up time for Live since the program performs a plug-in scan during every startup. A shorter list is also easier to navigate.

Crash-Start If you find yourself trying to load a Live Set that keeps crashing, it could be one of the song's plug-ins causing the problem. Try removing (or at least relocating) the plug-ins from your folders one at a time until the song loads successfully. When the song does load, Live will tell you that it is unable to load one of the plug-ins (because you hid it), but at least you'll be able to open the Set and keep working. Try using a similar plug-in to replace the problematic one (e.g., try using Live's Reverb if a third-party reverb gives you problems).

Managing Presets for Audio Units and Live's Devices

Live devices and Audio Units differ from VSTs in that preset management is done via the Device Browser. For example, click the Live Device Browser icon and open the Audio Effects folder by clicking the little triangle in front of the folder. You'll find Live's built-in audio effects inside. If you look closer, you'll see that there are little triangles in front of these effects, too. If you click the triangle in front of Chorus, for example, you'll see a list of the built-in presets for the Chorus effect, as well as any new presets you may have made yourself.

You'll find that the presets for Audio Units are handled very similarly to those of the Live devices. Any presets you save will appear just like presets for Live devices do. However, for factory presets, the behavior varies from manufacturer to manufacturer. With most manufacturers, you won't be able to see the factory presets in the Browser before you've added the plug-in to a track. After that, the presets will show up in the Browser when you use the Hot Swap button. With some plug-ins, however, this doesn't work, and you'll have to use the plug-in's custom interface to access the factory presets.

Hot-Swap Button. There's a little icon located in the upper-right corner of each VST/Audio Unit and Live Device window that looks like two arrows in a circle. This is the Hot-Swap button (see Figure 7.12). When you click this button, it will turn orange, and you'll see an identical icon appear in the Browser next to the current preset. You can now double-click on another preset to load it into the device.

Note that the Hot-Swap icons may not be visible in the Browser list. If you can't see them, you may need to expand the horizontal view of the Browser by clicking and dragging the right edge of the Browser to the *right*.

When the Hot-Swap button on the device is activated, the current preset in the list is highlighted in the Browser.

If you don't have the Hot-Swap button turned on when you double-click a preset, the preset will be loaded as a brand-new effect at the end of the currently selected track.

Saving Audio Units and Live's Device Presets. The other icon at the far right of the device's title bar, a tiny picture of a floppy disk, is the Save Preset button. When you've set the device the way you like, click this button, and a new preset will appear in the Browser (see Figure 7.13). Type in the name that you want and press Enter. If you make further edits to the preset and press the

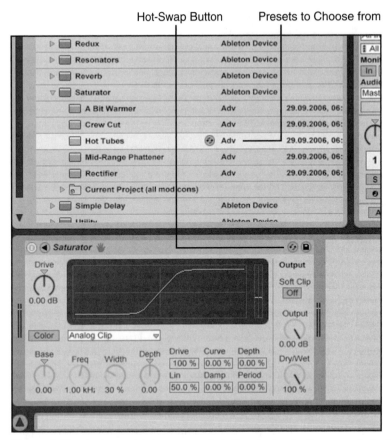

Figure 7.12 Activate this button to link the device to the presets in the Browser.

Save Preset button again, you can just press Enter without typing a new name to overwrite the preset with your new settings.

Organizing AU and Device Presets. You can probably see that the Device Browser is enhanced with the capability to sort the presets into folders within each device. When you explored the Impulse presets, you saw an Acoustic folder and an Electronic folder. If you right-click (Ctrl-click) in the Device Browser, you can choose to create a new folder from the options in the context menu. You can name the folder anything you like, and you can even drag it into another folder after it has been made, thus creating further subdivisions to your preset categories. You can drag and drop presets between the folders or copy them from one to another. These commands, plus deleting and renaming, are all accessible through the right-click context menu. This same organizational method is also implemented for Audio Units devices within the Plug-in Browser.

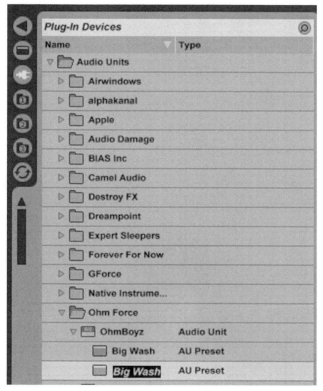

Figure 7.13 Saving a preset in the Browser. Type in a new name, or just press Enter if you want to overwrite the preset "Big Wash."

Signal Path

While all signals pass through the Track View from right to left, there are still a few ways you can vary the flow of signals through Live's mixer. Effects can be used as *inserts*, or they may be used as part of a *send and return*. This routing is determined by whether you're placing the effect directly onto one of your audio tracks or into a Return track.

Using an Effect as an Insert

When you use an effect as an insert, you are literally inserting your device into the normal signal flow of your track. In Figure 7.14, an EQ Eight has been inserted on Track 1. All of the audio coming from the clips on that track must first pass through the EQ Eight before it reaches the Volume and Pan controls in the Session Mixer.

While all of the signals on Track 1 are forced to go through the EQ Eight, some plug-ins allow you to set the balance of the original (dry) signal to the affected (wet) signal (see Figure 7.15).

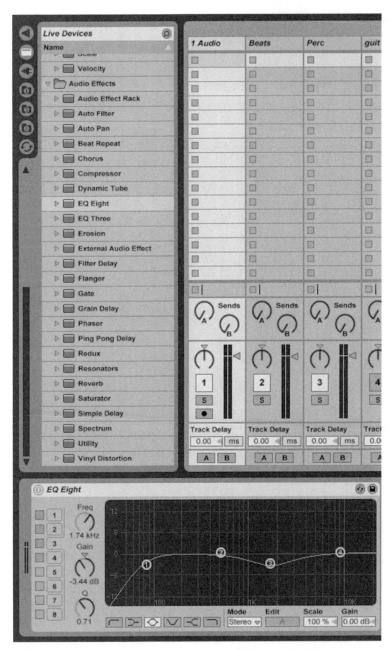

Figure 7.14 Placing an effect on the Track View of an audio, MIDI, or Master track creates an insert.

Effects best suited for insert use are EQs, compressors, gates, and filters. When you EQ a signal, for example, you want to modify the frequency content of the whole signal, not just a fraction of it. Using an effect as an insert forces the entire audio stream to pass through the effect, giving you full control of the sound.

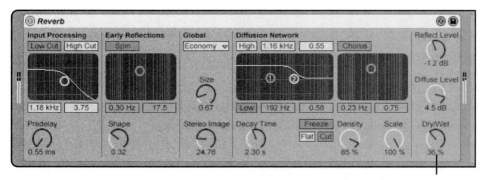

Use this knob to adjust the balance between
the effect and the original sound.

Figure 7.15 The Reverb device allows you to add only a small amount of effect to your sound, thanks
to the Dry/Wet knob. When the knob is fully clockwise (100% wet), you will hear only the reverb signal
generated from the original input. Setting the knob at 25%, as shown, will allow 75% of the original
signal to still pass through.

Using a Send Effect

Send effects are used when you want to *add* or *blend in* an effect to your sound, as opposed to
replacing it like an insert. This is achieved by sending a signal to an effect processor and then
blending its output with the Master track. In Live, you pull this off by using a Return track
(choose Insert Return Track from Live's Insert menu). A Return track is a track that cannot
house audio clips; it can only receive input from other tracks in Live. When a Return track is
created, a Send knob appears on each track. When this Send knob is turned up, audio is sent to
the Return track. By placing effects on the Return track, you can add this effect to any track in
your Set by turning up the Send knobs. In Figure 7.16, you'll see a session with one Return track,
as well as a row of Send knobs labeled A.

You use the Send knobs to dial in the amount of signal you want sent to the input of the associated
Return track. You can add effects to the Track View of the Return track (double-click the Return
track name) just as you would when adding them to a regular audio track. The portion of the
signal being sent from the Send knob will be processed by the effects and output to the Master
track via the Return track's Volume and Pan controls. You'll see that the Return track itself also
has a Send knob. This allows you to output a portion of the returned effect to another Return
track for layering. The Return track can also send back into itself, allowing you to create feedback
loops (watch your volume!). Because of the feedback risk, the Sends on Return tracks are disabled
by default. If you right-click on a send, you can enable it from the context menu.

Pre or Post? On the right side of the Session Mixer, there is a button labeled Post for each
Send knob (see Figure 7.16). These buttons determine whether the Send knobs take their
signals *pre-fader* or *post-fader*. Post-fader is the default setting for each track, which
causes the amount of signal sent from the Send knob to vary based on the track's volume

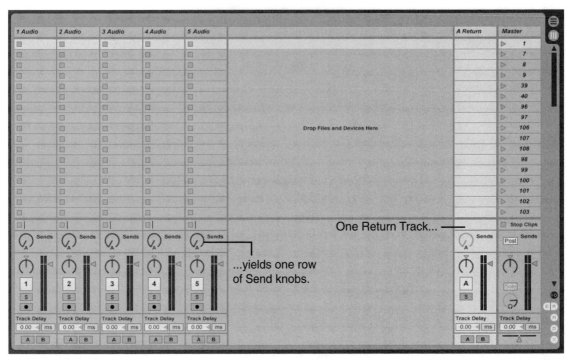

Figure 7.16 When the Return track was added to this Set, it automatically created a row of Send knobs.

slider. If you're fading down a vocal part that is sending to a Reverb, the amount being sent to the Reverb will also diminish, causing it to fade out as well.

The Pre-fader position (click the Post button to turn it to Pre) causes the Send level to remain the same, even if the track's volume is adjusted. This means, in the case of the previous example, you would still hear the vocal reverb even after you had faded the track volume fully down. That could make for an interesting way to end a song.

Keep in mind that the Send knob does not divert signals to the Return track—it copies the signal to the Return track. This means that the output volume of the source track will stay the same, regardless of the Send knob position.

So why would you want to use a Send/Return? There are a couple of reasons. First, some plug-ins, such as Reverbs and Delays, are meant to be blended with their original signals. For example, in order to add reverb to a vocal track, you would place a Reverb device on a Return track with its Dry/Wet knob set to 100% wet (every effect on a Return track should be fully wet). While the vocal is playing, you start to turn up the Send knob. This will start sending a copy of the vocal to the Return track armed with the Reverb plug-in. The reverb will generate the proper ambience, based on the incoming vocal, and the result is mixed in with the final mix. By adding reverb in this fashion, your original vocal track remains unchanged; you've simply added some reverb to your mix.

Another reason for using a Send effect is that it allows you to use the same plug-in to add effects to multiple tracks. If you have a lead vocal with three harmony parts, you can send all four vocals to the same reverb. The incoming vocal tracks from the sends will be mixed together as they enter the Return track. The group vocals will then yield a group reverb, which gets blended into the final mix; therefore, it takes only one reverb to affect four independent tracks, which is great news for your CPU usage.

Keep 'Em Going or Cut 'Em Off Many modern productions, especially in the electronica-influenced genres, employ effect-muting techniques to add emphasis to particular moments in songs. Normally, if you add a reverb effect to a hand-clap track, your ears expect to hear the full decay of the reverb, even if you suddenly mute the hand-clap track. This is accomplished by placing the reverb on a Return track and turning up the hand-clap's Send knob. When the hand-clap is muted, the signal stops being sent to the reverb as well; however, the reverb output remains unmuted, so you still hear the full decay of the reverb.

If you place the reverb effect directly onto the hand-clap track as an insert, you can use the Dry/Wet knob to attain a similar balance of hand clap and reverb. Now when the hand-clap track is muted, the reverb will be muted, too, since you're actually listening to the output of the reverb device on the track (that's why you have to use the Dry/Wet knob to hear the original signal). This can be extremely effective at the end of a build that stops abruptly. Also give this technique a try with Delay effects.

Using Sends Only

There may come a time when you want to combine the CPU-saving method of Send effects with the complete sound-replacement function of an insert. Perhaps you want to run a bunch of vocal tracks through one Auto Filter. If you were to place the filter on a Return track and then turn up the sends on your vocal tracks, you'd be combining only the original, unfiltered vocals with the filtered version being output from the Return track, which will not allow you to completely filter out the vocals. What you need to do is silence the original tracks while still sending to the Auto Filter on the Return track. You accomplish this by setting the output of the vocal tracks to Sends Only, as shown in Figure 7.17.

While the original tracks are no longer routed to the Master track, the sends still remain active, so you can funnel your sound over to the filter on the Return track. You will then use the volume slider on the Return track to adjust the level of the vocals in the mix.

Mix Trick Here's a common mixing technique employed by engineers that takes advantage of the routing explained above: Place a couple of drum parts on some tracks, preferably acoustic drums or percussion. Switch the track outputs to Sends Only and use

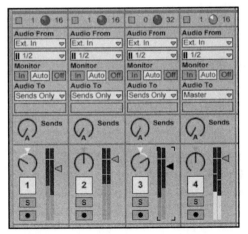

Figure 7.17   Here we have silenced the outputs of the vocal tracks by changing their output routings from Master to Sends Only. This keeps all the track functions intact, such as the insert effects (if any) and automation, but disconnects their outputs from the Master track.

the Send knobs to create a mix of the drums you can monitor through the Return track. Once you have achieved a nice blend, load a compressor onto the Return track and dial up some heavy compression, say a ratio of 10-1, attack fully counterclockwise, and a moderate release time of 25ms. Stop the clips from playing, and switch the original track outputs back to Master. Turn the volume all the way down on the Return track and start playing the drums again. While the original tracks are playing, begin to slowly raise the volume of the Return track. The compressed drum parts will start to blend in, with the originals adding beef to the drums.

The reason this is so effective is that right when a transient occurs in the original drum tracks, the compressor on the Return track kicks in and cuts off the transient (due to the short attack time), leaving only the original waveform in the mix. As the original waveform fades out, the compressor opens up again, thus filling in the space between the transients. This keeps the drums sounding natural, while adding the thickness characteristic of compression. Try this technique with other instruments that may need the assistance of compression while maintaining their original tone.

Control and Automation

As you've probably discovered by toying with a few effects so far, it's fun to tweak the knobs and parameters while audio is playing. You'll discover many new layers of musicality by carefully manipulating effects during a performance. Live gives you a number of different ways to control plug-in parameters, either with real-time MIDI control or by automatic or preprogrammed automation. MIDI control is by far the most interactive way to control device parameters and offers an excellent way to program automation, too.

Controlling Live's Devices with MIDI

Controlling Live's devices with MIDI is as easy as assigning MIDI control to the Session Mixer and clip grid (see "MIDI and Computer Keyboard Control" in Chapter 4, "Making Music in Live," if you missed this). If the device is on-screen, press the MIDI Assign button in the upper-right corner of the Live window. A bunch of colored boxes will appear over the device's controls just like they do for the Session Mixer. Click the control you want to assign; then move the control on your MIDI device. Live will instantly assign the moved control to that effect parameter, and a small box will appear on the control stating the MIDI channel and controller assigned; you will also see the MIDI Mappings window appear at the left side of the screen showing you all of the MIDI controls currently assigned. After you turn off the MIDI Assign button (click it again), the device parameter will now respond to the MIDI control. Piece of cake!

Common things to control with MIDI are the Sample Start and Loop Length in Simpler. You can create a morphing sound by moving through different areas of a long audio file with these knobs. For the Impulse, assigning a control to the global tune knob will allow you to tweak the pitch of the entire drum kit on the fly. You can also assign MIDI to the individual drum sounds—try adjusting the decay of the open hi-hat during a song.

Controlling Plug-In Devices with MIDI

Controlling the parameters of a plug-in device, such as a VST audio effect, is a little more difficult, due to the fact that each plug-in has its own unique graphical interface. Because of this, Live cannot superimpose the little squares over the plug-in controls while in MIDI Assign mode. To solve this problem, Ableton has included a small triangle located at the upper-right corner of a plug-in title bar. Press this triangle, and the plug-in window will expand to the right and show a number of horizontal sliders (see Figure 7.18).

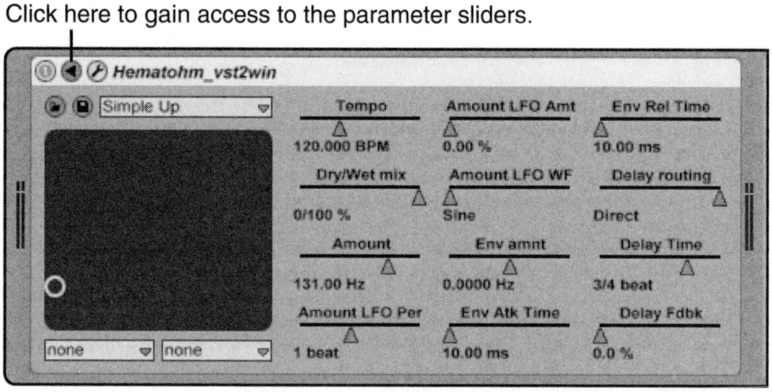

Click here to gain access to the parameter sliders.

Figure 7.18 Pressing the small triangle in the corner of the plug-in window unfolds a collection of sliders, which you can assign MIDI controls to.

Each slider corresponds to one of the plug-in parameters. Open the plug-in graphical window and move a control. You'll see one of the controls in the Track View move as well. When you press the MIDI Assign button, you will see a box superimposed over the horizontal slider in the Track View. This is where you will make the MIDI assignment. After you have clicked the slider and moved your MIDI control, disable the MIDI Assign mode, and you'll see that the plug-in parameter, including the control in its graphical window, is now under MIDI control.

Switch and Slide You may find that a parameter you want to control in your plug-in is actually a button, as opposed to a slider or dial; however, you will not find a button graphic in the small plug-in window of the Track View. This is because the plug-in's button is being represented by a horizontal slider, too. You'll see that after you drag the slider a certain distance, the plug-in's button will change state. When you move the slider back, the button will also change back to its previous state. This allows you to assign a MIDI control to the slider to control the button.

Control Surface Lockdown

Another great way to control your devices via MIDI is to use Live's control surface support. You can use this feature to easily change between and work with different devices in turn without having to individually reassign all of the controls. Here's how it works.

First, you need to designate your control surface in the table at the top of the MIDI/Sync tab of Live's Preferences. Make sure your MIDI controller is connected; then click on the drop-down menu in the Control Surface column to see a list of devices supported as control surfaces natively in Live. If your device is listed here, this means that Live already has information about it built into the program. In this case, you can simply select it here by name, and Live will know all about it. After you select it here, then designate the same device as input and output for the control surface in the next two columns (see Figure 7.19).

(Note that if your controller does not appear in the drop-down list, this does not mean that you cannot use it in Live; however, only the listed devices will support these new control surface functions.)

In some cases, with certain controllers, Live may need to send a preset dump to the external device to set it up properly before you can use it. If your controller is one of these, you will see the Dump button enabled, shown to the right of your control surface's listing in the MIDI/Sync Preferences. Make sure that your device is ready to receive a preset dump and then press this button to send the data from Live to the device. You may need to check the manual that came with your controller to do this properly.

Having chosen and set the input and output of your controller and sent the preset dump if necessary, you can now close the Preferences and start using your designated control surface to work with devices in Live. To assign your control surface to work with a particular device, simply click on the device's title bar to select it (see Figure 7.20). You will see a small hand

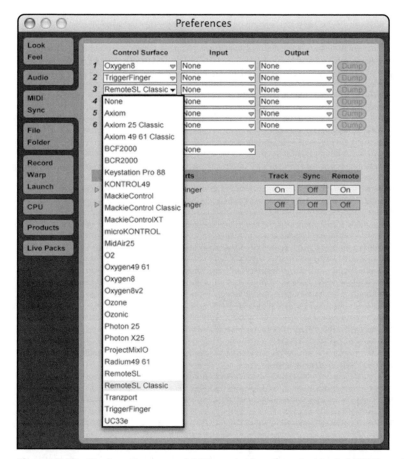

Figure 7.19   Designating your MIDI control surface in Live's MIDI/Sync Preferences.

Figure 7.20   The blue hand indicates that the Auto Filter has been instantly mapped to your control surface.

icon appear, indicating that you are currently controlling it. Click on another device, and your control will instantly shift to that device instead. Try it!

If you right-click (Ctrl-click) on the title bar, you will see a context menu including the option Lock to Control Surface for each of the designated control surfaces you have connected. This allows you to lock a particular control surface to this device, enabling you to always control a specific device no matter where your immediate focus is in Live.

If you want to see the details of how Ableton has mapped the controls of your particular control surface into Live, there is a Control Surface Reference in Live's built-in lessons containing a list of all currently supported hardware devices and the details of their instant mappings. This lesson also contains a guide to what parameters are controlled by which knobs of your MIDI controller. You can get to the lessons at any time by selecting the Lessons option from the View menu.

Modulating Devices with Clip Envelopes

While tweaking effects on the fly is a blast, creating patterns and predefined movements for the effects can add a new layer of musicality to your songs. Perhaps you want the cutoff of an Auto Filter to follow a sequence of movements that repeats every bar. Or how about a resonator that retunes itself over four bars? Both of these and more are available to you by using Clip Envelopes.

When we discussed Clip Envelopes back in Chapter 5, "The Audio Clip," you learned that they provide a way to modulate the current settings of their destinations. The same is true for modulating plug-in devices. You will set the controls for the device to one position and then use the Clip Envelopes to add or subtract values from those positions.

The process of creating a Clip Envelope for plug-ins is the same as modulating any other parameter, such as Volume and Pan. Once you've loaded a plug-in into the Track View, it will become available in the Envelopes section of the Clip View.

Automating Devices Within the Arrangement View

Just like the Volume, Pan, and Mute automation explained in Chapter 5, you can define the exact values for your device's parameters by creating envelopes in the Arrangement View. Every envelope shape you create in the Arrangement View will override the current value of the associated parameter. If you have a sweet effect dialed in, you may want to save it as a preset before drawing in automation so you can retrieve the original settings if you need them.

Just like the process in Chapter 5, effect automation can be created either by entering Record mode in the Transport bar and performing the desired movements manually or by drawing them into a track. Just like their Mixer counterparts, any plug-in control with recorded automation will have a small red box in its upper-left corner. If you manually move a control, either with the mouse or by MIDI control, the automation for that control will stop until you press the Return to Arrangement button.

Racks

One of the most exciting features of Live is Instrument and Effects Racks. These allow you to group together numerous Live devices to create a flexible "superdevice" that you can treat as a single device. Not only that, but Racks also enable you to work with effects and instruments in parallel as well as serial chains, blending together the output at the end. This makes it possible to create an infinite variety of new sounds by mixing and matching instruments and effects from your collection.

For example, you may make a bass sound with the Operator synth and double this with a different bass sample loaded in Simpler (see Figure 7.21). You can save this pair of instruments as one single device that you can recall at any time, by using a Rack. You can also create Racks containing multiple audio effects, MIDI effects, or any combination of instruments and effects that you can think of!

Figure 7.21   A simple example of an Instrument Rack featuring Operator and Simpler together.

Racks replace Device Groups, which were introduced in Live 5. Live 7 will automatically convert any Device Groups from the previous edition's Live Sets into Racks. Racks can be used like the old Device Groups, allowing you to save a chain of effects as a unit, but can also do far more.

Creating Racks

There are two different ways to create Racks. Start a new, empty Rack by dragging one of the generic Rack devices from the Live Device Browser into a track. You can then add your choice of devices to the Rack by dropping them directly into the Rack's Chain List or Devices View (see below). If you have already set up a chain of devices on a given track and you want to make them into a single Rack, simply select the title bars (Shift-click to select multiple devices) in the Track View and use the Group command from the Edit menu. Alternatively, you can right-click (Ctrl-click) in one of the title bars and use the Group command from the context menu that opens there. To break up a Rack into its component devices, repeat this operation and select the Ungroup command in the Edit menu or the context menu.

Rack Basics

The Rack window has three parts (see Figure 7.22), which you can reveal or hide as necessary. Use the buttons at the left edge of the Rack to hide or show the different sections. From top to bottom, the buttons are: Show/Hide Macros, Show/Hide Chain List, and Show/Hide Devices.

Let's look at each of these three parts, and then we'll introduce some creative ideas for using Racks in your Live Sets.

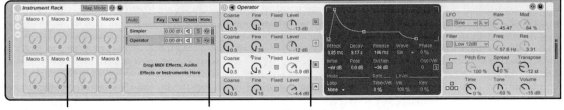

The Macro Controls   The Chain List   The devices

Figure 7.22 The three parts of the Rack window.

Chain List

Audio and MIDI input signals come into the Rack from the left-hand side, and they will first flow through the Chain List (see Figure 7.23).

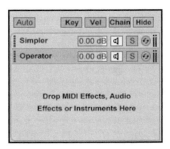

Figure 7.23 The Chain List for a basic Instrument Rack.

Here you can see a separate line for each of the parallel device chains in your Rack. We refer to them as being parallel because they process the incoming data simultaneously, rather than one after another. You can name each of these chains here so you can remember what they are. Here you can see separate volume and pan controls, activation switches, and solo buttons for each chain; use these to experiment with different ways of blending different chains in various combinations. There is also a Hot-Swap button for each chain; you can use this to load a pre-existing chain (or even an entire pre-existing Rack!) into your Rack as a new chain.

The chains for an Instrument Rack can also be viewed directly within the Session View. The title bar of a track containing an Instrument Rack will have an Unfold button next to the track name. Clicking on this reveals a mini-track for each chain in the Rack (see Figure 7.24). This provides a convenient way to make adjustments to volume and panning, and it also makes it somewhat easier to manage complicated Racks.

At the top of the Chain List, you will see buttons marked Key, Vel, Chain, and Hide. These are used to view and work with zones. These are filters that enable you to separate and/or mix the MIDI data going to multiple instruments and effects in a Rack (see Figure 7.25).

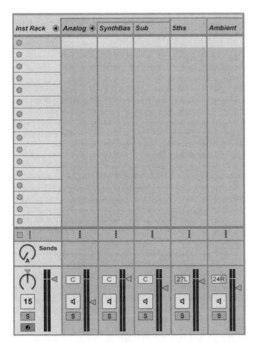

Figure 7.24   An unfolded Instrument Rack track. This rack contains chains named Analog, 5ths, and Ambient. The chain called Analog contains another Rack (!), so it can be unfolded to show.

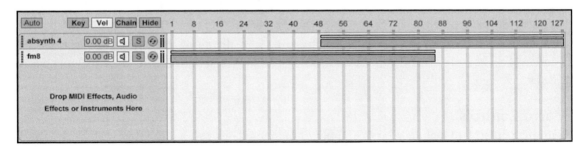

Figure 7.25   Using Velocity Zones.

(Note that if you are working with a Rack made up of only audio effects, you will not see the Key or Vel Zone types as these deal with MIDI data only.)

In Figure 7.25, we are using Velocity Zones to filter the MIDI data coming into the Rack and determine which instrument it will trigger. In this image, the lowest velocity notes will trigger the FM8 instrument, and the highest velocities will trigger Absynth 4. Notes within a middle range of velocities will trigger both instruments simultaneously.

You can also set up zones based on Key Range (click the Key button) or the Chain Select parameter. Key Range allows you to designate zones across a certain range of your MIDI keyboard.

The Chain Select parameter is an independent control that can be automated or mapped to an external MIDI knob or fader. You can use this to change between two different chains/sounds as you turn a MIDI knob, for example.

The Hide button here will hide the various zone-mapping windows, allowing you to see more of the actual devices in your chains.

Rack Devices

The devices in your Rack will appear farthest to the right, after the Chain List (see Figure 7.26). You can see only one chain at a time, selected by clicking its name in the Chain List. The devices will appear in the Rack in their usual order: MIDI effects first (if any), then instruments, then audio effects.

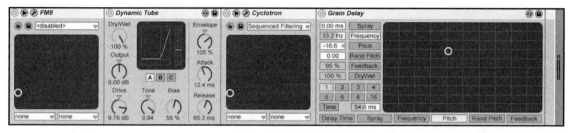

Figure 7.26 Devices in one chain of a Rack. These effects will only process the output of the FM8. Other chains in the Rack can have a completely independent set of effects.

You can add additional devices here by dragging and dropping from the Device Browser. You can also rearrange or delete devices here, just as you would if you weren't working in a Rack.

Macro Controls

With the potential to include a large number of individual devices, a large Rack can become very difficult to control, particularly in performance. The Macro Controls (see Figure 7.27) address this issue by giving you a set of eight freely mappable controls. You can view or hide the Macro

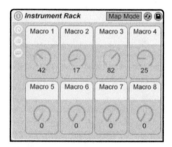

Figure 7.27 The Macro Controls.

Controls by using the Show/Hide Macro Controls button on the left-hand edge of the Rack, just below the Rack power button at top left.

Assign each of these eight knobs to control a crucial parameter of one of the devices in your Rack; this will make shaping the sound of the Rack much easier. You can use the Map Mode button at the top of the Rack to do this. Clicking this button highlights every controllable parameter of every device in the Rack, and a list of Macro Mappings will appear in the Browser at left, showing all mappings made in the entire Rack.

Click on a parameter and then on the Map or Unmap button under one of the Macro Controls to assign or unassign it. Once made, each assignment will be added to the Macro Mappings at left. Just like MIDI controllers, a Macro knob can be mapped to control many parameters simultaneously. So it would be easy, for example, to control the filter cutoff of all of the synths in an Instrument Rack with a single knob.

Then, after making your Macro assignments, click the Map Mode button again to exit Macro Mapping mode. Once you've set these up to your liking, click the MIDI button at the top right of Live to enter MIDI Mapping mode and assign knobs on your external MIDI controller to the Macro Controls. Or, if you're using control surface support, the eight Macro knobs will automatically be controlled by your MIDI controller.

Managing Rack Presets

You'll see that there are Save Preset and Hot-Swap icons available for the Rack as a whole, in addition to those of its component instruments and effects. Click the Save Preset button, and you'll see a new preset appear in the Device Browser. You can name it as usual and press Enter. The thing to notice, however, is the icon shown for this new preset. Instead of being a single box, it will be an icon showing the edges of two boxes meeting together. This is the icon for a Rack. If you look at the Acoustic presets for Impulse, you'll see that about half of them are actually Racks.

To load a Rack preset, double-click it or drag it into a track as usual. If the Rack contains a Live instrument, it will replace any other instrument currently on the track. The audio device groups (groups consisting *only* of audio devices) can be added to the end of a track (or wherever you drag them) as if they were single effects.

Racks are one of my favorite tools in Live because they allow you to create and save amazing multi-effects combinations you can recall at the drop of a hat. You can create simple effects like a Ping Pong Delay with a touch of Phaser. You can create a Simpler instrument with a MIDI Chord effect in front of it and a Reverb tacked on at the end. Just make sure to save them with meaningful names so you can remember what they all are!

Creative Ideas for Using Racks

Racks open up a wealth of new creative possibilities. Here are a few ideas to get you started creating your own Racks for recording and performance.

Layering Sounds in the Studio

The most obvious use of Racks is to layer together several individual sounds to create new sonic combinations. You can use Live's built-in instruments together with those of other companies to create exciting new hybrid sounds. A familiar sound that you've been using for a while may take on entirely new overtones when you blend it with a new instrument you're trying out.

To experiment with new instrumental combinations, simply place an empty Instrument Rack onto a MIDI channel and load two or three instruments into it. Use the Volume controls in the Chain List to mix the individual sounds into an interesting blend.

You will probably find it easier to blend your sounds together using an external MIDI controller. Assign a few knobs or faders to control the volume level of the separate chains using the Macro or MIDI Mapping mode.

Saving Favorite Effect Chains

After working with Live for some time, you will probably come up with particular combinations of audio effects that you like to use time and again. Using Racks, you can save these combinations as presets and recall them whenever you want in different Live projects.

Of course, you can also use this technique to save your favorite combinations of MIDI effects and instruments as well.

Keyboard Range Splits for Live Use

If you are using Live to host MIDI instruments and play them in live performances using a MIDI keyboard or other controller, you can use Key Range Zones to set up keyboard splits and have multiple independent sounds available to you simultaneously. In Figure 7.28, I have used these zones to set up four distinct sections of the keyboard, each with its own MIDI instrument assigned to it. In this case, I wanted to keep them separate and have designated no overlap between the individual sounds.

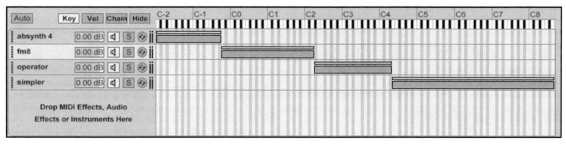

Figure 7.28 Setting Key Range Zones for multiple sounds.

Morphing Patches with the Macro Controls

You can use Macro Controls to make complex morphing effects. Try setting them up this way for some way-out effects:

First, select an Instrument Rack and add at least two different MIDI instruments. Three is better.

Using the Macro Mapping mode, assign a Macro Control to the Volume parameter of each chain in the Chain List. In addition, assign each of these Macro Controls to one or more parameters in the instruments themselves, such as a filter cutoff or a modulation control. You can also try making assignments with the rest of the Macro Controls. For more interesting results, make sure to assign two or three different parameters to each of the Macro Controls.

Then try playing a part on the keyboard and using the Macro Controls to adjust the sound. The more assignments you make to each Macro Control, the more complex the multidimensional sound changes will be.

Now that you know how to manage and control your effects and Racks, it's time to start sorting through the myriad plug-ins already available in Live. The next three chapters are a reference section to get you up to hyperspeed with Live's devices.

8 Live's Instruments

In addition to a plethora of MIDI capabilities, Live features seven software-based virtual instruments: Impulse, Simpler, Operator, and Sampler are familiar from earlier versions of Live, while Analog, Electric, and Tension have been introduced in Live 7. Impulse and Simpler come free for all Live users, while the others are included in the Live Suite or must be purchased separately.

These instruments have been designed with careful attention to the working process and creative flow in Live. As such, you'll find they permit many techniques and tricks not possible with third-party tools. These instruments are not merely demo software—they are full-fledged, high-quality instruments that will have a place in the most professional of productions. They are also great launching pads for musical ideas.

Impulse

What loop-based production system would be complete without a drum machine? Live's Impulse instrument is a unique take on drum machine design due to its sparse controls but instant usability. Open up the Live Set titled Impulse Demo 1 on the CD-ROM (Resources → Examples → Chapter 08) so you can follow along as I describe this instrument (see Figure 8.1).

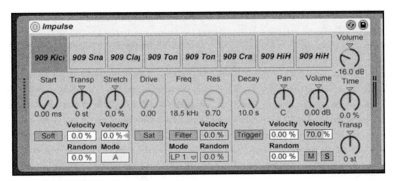

Figure 8.1 The clean and crisp Impulse interface sports eight cells for samples. Clicking the cell displays its editable parameters.

Overview of the Interface

The upper portion of Impulse is made of eight squares, or *cells*. Each can contain one sample, triggered individually—either by MIDI or with the mouse—and edited for customizing the sounds. The editing parameters are divided into five sections below the cells: Sample Source, Saturation, Filter, Amplifier, and Global Settings.

The Impulse Demo 1 Set has eight sounds already loaded into Impulse. You can play these live with a connected MIDI controller or your computer's keyboard. Try tapping the *A* key on your computer's keyboard. You should hear a kick drum every time you press the key. Now tap the *S* key. You should hear the snare drum loaded into the second Impulse cell. As you tap this key, you'll see a small green triangle appear momentarily above one of the sample cells in the Impulse interface. This symbol shows you which cell is playing at the moment. You can click with the mouse in the same area to trigger the sample. You can also play Impulse from a MIDI controller. Impulse already has MIDI note assignments for each cell. MIDI note C3 will play the first cell, D3 will play the second cell, E3 the third cell, and so on. In essence, you use the eight white keys on a keyboard controller from octave 3 to octave 4 to play Impulse. Obviously, since Impulse uses MIDI notes to trigger its sounds, you can play it with a MIDI clip, too. Go ahead and launch the clip titled Simple 1 at the top of the MIDI track to hear an example of this.

Sample Source

Now that you know how to trigger the samples, let's look at how to change the sound using the playback parameters offered in Impulse. The first section of controls (the Sample Source controls) determines the playback nature of the selected cell. The sample in a cell may be retuned, time-stretched/shortened, and have its front end cut off. Pitch can be randomized or modulated by input velocity. The Soft button performs a fade at the beginning of the sample to soften its attack.

Click on the cell named 909 Kick. This selects the cell for editing. While the MIDI clip is playing, click and drag up and down on the Transp dial. You'll hear the pitch of the kick drum change as you tweak this dial. Unlike the Transpose parameter found in an audio clip, the Transp control in Impulse does not use Live's Warp Engine. You'll hear the sample play for a shorter amount of time as the pitch increases and a longer time as the pitch decreases. If you do want to stretch or compress the length of the sample after you have transposed it, use the Stretch knob. As you increase this value, you'll hear the kick drum stretching in length. (Turning the Stretch knob down, of course, will shorten the drum clip.) The Mode button, below the Stretch knob, changes the stretching method. In Mode A, the default, Impulse waits a brief moment before stretching to ensure that the Warp Engine doesn't distort the attack of the sound. For punchy drum sounds, this is especially important. Mode B, on the other hand, begins stretching the instant the sample starts to play. Albeton recommends Mode A for sounds that are lower in pitch such as kick drums, and Mode B for higher-pitched sounds like hi-hats.

Turning up the Start dial will cause the sample to start from a position later in the file. In the case of this kick drum, increasing the Start value removes the drum's attack, because Impulse starts playing the kick drum sample *after* the attack sound of the drum. This can be used as an effect but also has one other important use: Some of the samples you may want to use in Impulse start with a momentary silence, so they start late every time you play them. (Impulse plays the silence before playing the actual sound.) The Start dial can advance the start position so that Impulse plays right at the attack of the drum, thus bringing it back into time. This saves you the hassle of having to manually remove the silence using an external wave editor.

The Soft button is somewhat related to the Start dial in that it affects how Impulse plays the beginning of the sample. When Soft is off, Impulse simply plays the sample the instant it is triggered. When Soft is turned on, Impulse will perform a short fade-in. The result is that the attack of the sample is softened without changing the length of the sound. If you try this with the kick drum, you'll hear that the "snap" at the beginning of the sound is softened, while the beefy punch of the drum remains.

The value boxes below the Transp and Stretch dials do not affect the sound of the sample directly. These are used to modulate the Transp and Stretch settings based on velocity and randomness, and the boxes fall below the dial they modulate. To hear how velocity affects these parameters, you'll need to play Impulse with a velocity-sensitive MIDI pad or keyboard. If you're using the computer keyboard, you can change its velocity using the Z and X keys, but you'll get the best results from MIDI devices. For simplicity, I've also included a clip titled HiHat Only, which has a lot of velocity changes. Click on cell seven (909 HiHat) to select it and turn up the value box below Transp. You'll hear the hi-hat begin to change pitch as it follows the velocity. Used in moderation, at about 15 percent, it adds a subtle touch of additional expressiveness to the hi-hat.

Saturation

The Saturation section is the simplest to use of the five controls in Impulse. Engage the Sat button and turn up the Drive to achieve overdriven percussion sounds. If you apply saturation to the kick drum, you'll get a distorted "gabber-house"-style kick. Give it a try!

Filter

The Filter section offers a way to perform some additional sound design on a sample after it's already loaded into a cell. Click the Filter button to engage the section. The menu below the Filter button chooses the Filter mode. You'll find the usual suspects here: Low-Pass, High-Pass, Band-Pass, and Notch filters. The Freq knob sets the cutoff frequency of the filter, and the Res knob determines the filter resonance. The last two parameters, Velocity and Random, allow you to use incoming velocity or random values to modulate the filter cutoff.

The reason this section follows the Saturation stage is that distorting a sound can yield some unwieldy high-harmonics and noise. If it's too much, you can apply a Low-Pass filter to the sound to calm it down. Try it with the distorted kick drum and a Freq setting of 745Hz.

Amplifier

The Amplifier section sets the output volume and pan position for each individual cell. The Pan knob can be used to move the hi-hat to one side of the mix while the volume control pulls it down to a quieter level. The Decay knob shapes the tail end of a sample. If the button below the Decay knob is in Trigger mode, the Decay knob will dictate the fade-out time from the moment the sample is triggered. In Gate mode, the fade-out won't begin until a MIDI Note Off message is received (when you lift your finger off a key). The Gate mode is fun, as it allows you to control the length of your sounds as you play them, such as a long snare sound on beats 1.2 and 1.4 and a short snare on beat 1.3.2. Switch the snare cell to Gate and set the Decay to 147 milliseconds (ms) to hear what this sounds like. The two Vel values determine how much the incoming MIDI velocity affects the output volume and pan position.

Global Settings

The Global section contains a master Volume knob, plus master Time and Transp (transpose) knobs. These knobs are begging for MIDI control since they are wonderful performance parameters. The Time knob can be used to shorten or stretch out all the samples at the same time. The Transp knob will transpose all the samples together as a group. Try tweaking these values during a drum fill for extra expression.

Importing Sounds

It's easy to get sounds into the Impulse cells with a couple different methods. The easiest way is to click the Hot-Swap button in Impulse, in the upper-right corner of the device interface just to the left of the Save button; it's the one with two tiny arrows going around in a circle. You will see all the presets for Impulse open in the browser. Double-click a preset to load it into Impulse.

You can also drag individual samples from your browsers straight into the cells in Impulse. Loading up eight drum sounds is super simple since you can pre-listen to the sounds in the Browser and then drag them directly into the cells. This is a great reason to create a folder on your hard drive full of one-shot drum samples.

You don't have to use premade one-shot samples to make beats, though. A popular source for drum sounds, pioneered by hip-hop producers, is to grab them right out of full drum loops. You begin by loading a drum loop into a clip slot, isolating the portion of the sound you want to use from the Clip View (see Figure 8.2a), and then dragging the clip into any one of the Impulse cells (see Figure 8.2b). I've already placed a drum loop on Track 2 for this purpose.

Cutting up drum loops for reprogramming has never been easier. If you load a warped drum loop into the Session View, it is a painless process of isolating portions of the beat since the sample region Start and End Markers snap to the beats. Isolate the first sound you want (a kick drum) by placing the region markers around it. I've already done this for you in the Kick Only clip. Drag it to the first cell of Impulse to replace the 909 Kick sample. Then isolate the next sound (a snare perhaps) in the same clip and drag it to another Impulse cell. Again, you can just use the Snare Only clip if you like. Even though you modified the clip that was used for

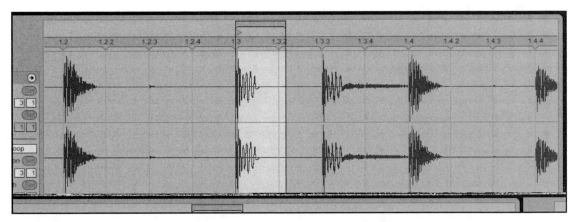

Figure 8.2a   Isolating a section of the audio clip to be loaded into an Impulse cell.

the first cell, the cell's sample will not change after you've added it to Impulse. So you can repeat the process again and again using the same clip until you populate the Impulse cells with all the parts of the loop that you want. Now, when you play the MIDI clip, your new samples will play the kick and snare parts.

MIDI Control

The MIDI notes assigned to trigger the eight cells are fixed to the white keys between C3 (middle-C) and C4 (one octave above middle-C). However, when you're editing the MIDI data of a clip driving Impulse, the normal piano keyboard will be replaced with the names of the samples assigned to each line of the MIDI data. This is the kind of helpful integration that is possible with Impulse because it is one of Ableton's built-in devices.

Has Anybody Seen My Keys? If you're using a small MIDI controller, such as the M-Audio O2 or the computer keyboard keys, you may find yourself bashing away on the notes but hearing nothing from Impulse. This frequently occurs when the keyboard has been transposed to another octave. Try adjusting the octave/transposition of your MIDI controller so it sends notes to Impulse in the proper octave. If you're using the computer keyboard for MIDI input, the Z and X keys will transpose the keys. When transposing the keyboard, you'll see the current key range listed at the bottom of the screen. You'll want to choose the C3 to D4 range to properly play Impulse. You can also use C and V to change the velocity output of the computer keyboard. As you press the keys, Live will display the new velocity at the bottom of the window.

The best form of MIDI control for Impulse comes from the use of drum pad controllers. Drum pads are starting to pop up everywhere—you can even find them on some controller keyboards

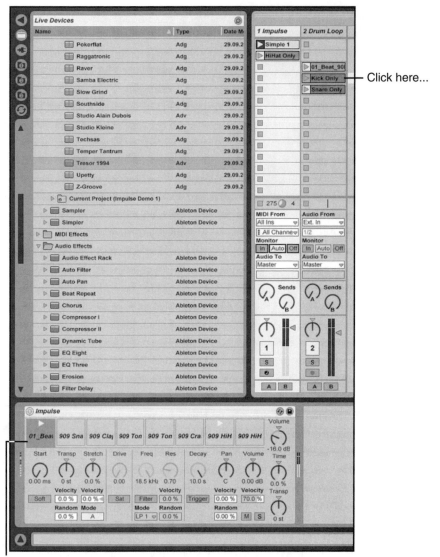

Click here...

...and drag to a cell to load a sound.

Figure 8.2b Switch back to Impulse in Track View and then drag the clip into a cell.

such as the Korg MicroKontrol. The M-Audio Trigger Finger (mentioned in Chapter 2, "Getting Live Up and Running") is especially suited for Impulse. Preset 10 is specially designed for use with Impulse—two of them, actually. Since the Trigger Finger has 16 pads, you can control two complete Impulse drum machines. Create two MIDI tracks, place Impulse instruments on both of them, set both of their inputs to the Trigger Finger, and then set the left track to listen to MIDI Input Channel 10 and the right track to listen to MIDI Input Channel 11. When you arm both tracks, the lower eight pads of the Trigger Finger will control the left Impulse, and the top eight pads will control the right Impulse. Assigning MIDI Remote Control to the parameters in Impulse follows the same method as any other control in Live. And, of course, you can also use a supported control surface to control the Impulse's parameters (see Chapter 7, "Using Effects and Instruments").

MIDI Routing

Drum parts are a collection of multiple parts, generally a kick drum part, a snare drum part, and a hi-hat part, all playing together at the same time. Because the beat comprises these smaller parts, it may make more sense to you to build the drum parts out of multiple clips, such as a clip for the kick drum and a clip for the snare. Live allows you to do this by routing the output of other MIDI tracks to the input of Impulse.

Let's try adding a hand-clap part to the Simple 1 beat in the example Set. First, create a new MIDI track and set the top MIDI To box to the 1-Impulse track. Next, set the bottom MIDI To box to 1-Impulse, as opposed to Track In. Set this way, the MIDI on the new track will be fed directly to the Impulse instrument on Track 1. If the lower box is set to Track In, the MIDI data will be routed to Track 1 itself—you will have to switch the track's monitor to In, in order to hear the new part. (This would end up muting the Simple 1 clip, which you don't want to do!)

Now, double-click in a clip slot in the new MIDI track to create an empty MIDI clip. Place notes on beats 1.2 and 1.4 of the hand-clap lane (see Figure 8.3). When you play this new clip along with the Simple 1 clip, you'll hear an additional hand clap on beats 2 and 4.

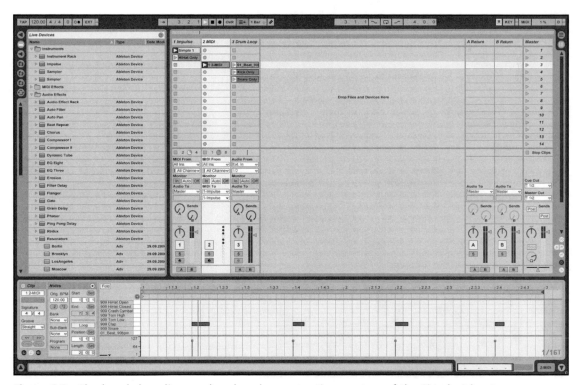

Figure 8.3 The hand-clap clips can be played one at a time on top of the Simple 1 beat.

Set this way, you can make additional variations of the hand-clap part, adding extra claps here and there throughout the clip. Then you can switch between these clips in order to change the hand-clap part while the Simple 1 beat plays unchanged.

Audio Routing

From time to time, you may want to place an effect on one or more of the drum sounds in Impulse, but you don't want to affect all of the drum sounds at once. Separating the drum sounds like this can be very important in getting the clearest overall mix, one in which each drum instrument remains distinct. To solve this, each cell of Impulse has its own dedicated output you can use as a source for another audio track and load with any effect you choose.

To see this in action, make another audio track and set its Audio From to the MIDI track containing Impulse. In the channel selector below that, you'll see a list of not only the Track Output, but also the individual drum sounds (see Figure 8.4).

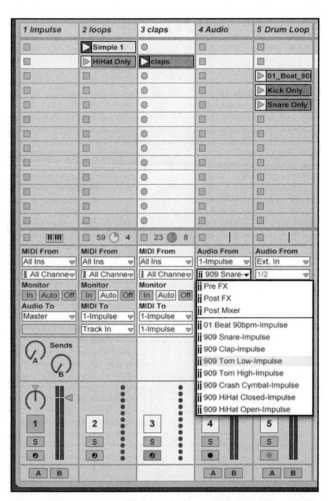

Figure 8.4 Route individual drum sounds to other tracks in the Input/Output Routing section.

After you choose one of these channels as the input for another track, that sound will cease its normal output on the Impulse track (this keeps the sound from being doubled). For this example, select the snare drum from the channel list and enable monitoring on the audio track. Nothing will sound different, but you'll see that the snare drum is now sounding out of this new audio track. Drag the Reverb preset Forest Floor from the Device Browser onto this audio track, and you'll hear a nice reverb on the snare hits only.

No Static One factor that can make your drum parts sound dull is static loops: that is, loops that are exactly the same every time they're played. To create some motion or subtle change in your drum parts, try dropping a Velocity device on Impulse and have it introduce random variations in velocity. The result will be a more human-sounding part in which each of the drums is played with a slightly different volume. See Chapter 11, "ReWire," for the lowdown on how to use the Velocity device.

After creating separate tracks to process the individual sounds of Impulse, it is often helpful to group them back together so they can be treated as a single drum part. Do this by adding another audio track to the Set and enabling its monitor. (For clarification, name this new track Drum Mix.) Once the new track is in place, set the Audio To for both the Impulse track and Snare track to Drum Mix. The outputs of these tracks will now be mixed together and used as the input for Drum Mix. You can now use the volume fader of this track to change the volume of the whole drum part at once. Of course, you could also add additional effects (compression comes to mind) to process the drum part as a whole.

After this is done, you'll have four tracks in Live representing one drum part. You can then adjust the track widths (by dragging the edge of the title bar) to collapse the Snare and Drum Mix tracks and buy yourself some space on the screen (see Figure 8.5).

As a final note, open up the Live Set titled Impulse Demo 2 on the *Live 7 Power!* CD. Here, you'll find a Set utilizing nearly every technique described above to create a house beat. Can you figure out everything we did?

Simpler

When it comes to quick and imaginative sample playback and manipulation, nothing is simpler than Simpler. What is Simpler? A simple sampler, of course. However, don't be fooled: Simpler offers a wealth of creative possibilities within its humble interface, such as independent Pitch, Filter, and Amp Envelopes, as well as portamento and other effects.

Overview of the Interface

The Simpler interface looks quite similar to Impulse, but it has one large sample window instead of eight sample cells (see Figure 8.6). Simpler works with only one sample at a time, and its contents are displayed in this main window. You can zoom in and out on the waveform by

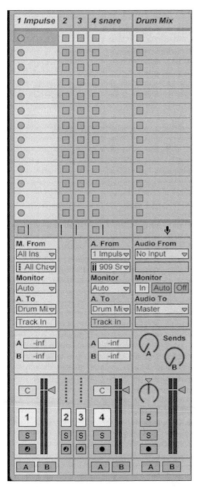

Figure 8.5 Collapsing tracks can help organize the precious real estate of the Session View.

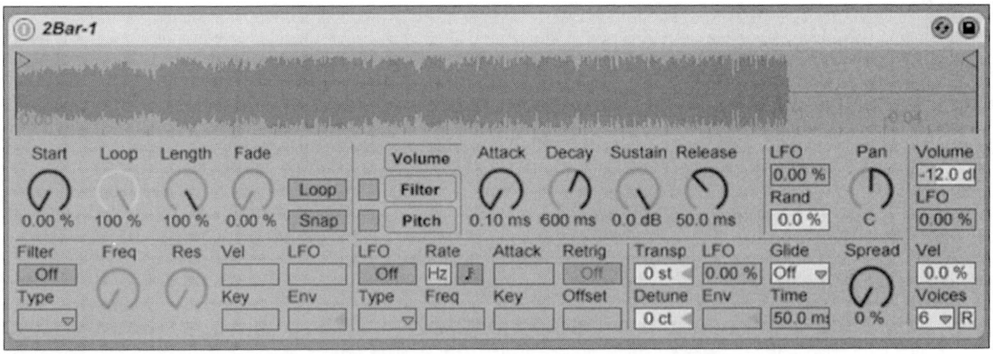

Figure 8.6 Ableton does it again with another deceptively simple interface.

clicking on it when you see the magnifying glass cursor appear and dragging up and down with the mouse.

Simpler can be loaded with a new sound either by dragging a sample from the browser or by taking an audio clip from the Session or Arrangement View. Just like Impulse, Simpler will play the portion of the sound that is between the region Start and End Markers of the imported clip. Since Simpler only holds usually one sample, any new sound dragged into the instrument will replace the previous one. Or just click the Hot-Swap button to see all the presets in Simpler's Browser and choose from these.

Note that Ableton has also given Simpler the additional ability to play multisampled instruments based on a larger set of samples. Multisampling improves the sound of many sampled instruments, particularly those based on samples of actual acoustic instruments such as those in the SONiVOX Essential Instrument Collection (EIC), included with all boxed copies of Live 7. If you are playing a multisampled instrument in Simpler, you will see the message "Multi-sample Mode" displayed at the top of Simpler instead of a sample waveform. Some controls in Simpler (the Sample Start/Loop knobs and associated parameters) will be inactive (and appear grayed-out in the interface) in Multi-sample mode. To edit these parameters further, you need to use Ableton's new Sampler instrument, sold separately: Right-click (Ctrl-click) on Simpler's title bar and choose the Simpler → Sampler command to open the multisampled instrument in Sampler for further editing. We'll learn a lot more about Sampler later in this chapter, but for now let's get back to seeing what Simpler can do.

Sample Source

There are seven sections in the Simpler interface: Sample Source, Filter, Envelopes, Pan, LFO (*low-frequency oscillator*), Tuning, and Volume. The Sample Source section is where you'll set all the parameters for the sample playback. The effect of the four knobs can be seen and heard immediately, as the changes you make will be shown graphically in the Sample Display window. The Sample Play area is shown in dark green, while the Loop area (when the Loop button is active) is shown in light green (see Figure 8.7). As you adjust the knobs, you'll see the green areas

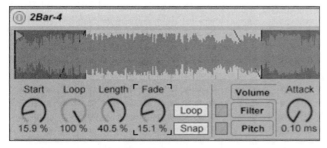

Figure 8.7 Simpler will play only the sound located in the medium green-colored area of the Sample Display window. Playback begins at the far-left edge of this section and plays all the way through to the end of it. If the Loop function is activated, Simpler will then repeat the section in bright green until it receives a MIDI Note Off message.

change. The first three knobs change the start position, loop length, and end position of the sample. The loop length is based on a percentage from the end of the sample, which allows you to loop the tail end of a sound to extend its length. The Fade knob applies a crossfade to the loop's connection points to smooth out any pops you may encounter when the sample starts over. The Snap button helps prevent these pops by forcing the start and end points of the loop area to snap to a zero crossing.

Envelopes

The Envelope section (just to the right of the Sample Source section) is where you will shape the sound as it's played. There are three envelopes in the new version of Simpler: Vol, Filter, and Pitch, which can be edited individually by pressing one of the three tabs in the Envelope section. Each of these envelopes is hard-wired to the Output Volume, Filter Cutoff, and Sample Pitch, respectively.

Every time a MIDI Note On message enters Simpler, it triggers the envelope generators. As soon as the MIDI note is received, the envelopes enter their attack phase. This is where the output rises from zero to full level. The amount of time it takes for this increase in level to happen is set with the Attack knob, which displays its value in milliseconds. After the attack time has passed and the envelope has reached full level, the envelope drops to the sustain level. The amount of time it takes to drop is set by the Decay knob. The target level is set with the Sustain knob, which shows a percentage of the full level. The envelope will stay at the sustain level until Simpler receives a MIDI Note Off message (i.e., lifting your finger off of the keyboard). Once the MIDI Note Off is received, the envelope will drop off to zero in the amount of time specified by the Release knob.

Filter

The Filter section (which is engaged with the Filter button) is used to remove certain frequencies in the sample. As usual, you've got your choice of Low-Pass, High-Pass, Band-Pass, and Notch filters. The Freq and Res knobs are used to adjust the base cutoff frequency and the resonance for the filter. The remaining controls are used to modulate the filter cutoff with the envelope, velocity, key position, and LFO. All of these modulation sources can be used at the same time for complex filter motions. The Env knob scales the amount of Filter Envelope signal used to change the filter cutoff. As the envelope value rises, the cutoff will also rise. The Vel value will scale the cutoff based on the incoming MIDI note velocity. If the value is 0 percent, the velocity will have no effect on the cutoff. The Key value is used to change the cutoff value of the filter based on the pitch of the incoming MIDI note. The higher the pitch, the higher the filter cutoff will be. This helps emulate real sounds, which get brighter as their pitch increases. The LFO knob determines the amount of LFO signal used to modulate the cutoff.

LFO

The LFO (engaged with the LFO button) can be used to modulate the Filter Cutoff, Sample Pitch, and Output Pan. An LFO can be thought of as an automatic envelope that has a repeating pattern. The shape of the LFO is selected from the small drop-down menu right below the Filter button. The Rate section changes the speed of the LFO. There are two modes here: Select Hz for a free-running, unsynched LFO set in Hertz, or select the small musical note here for an LFO synced with the project tempo and further adjusted into beat length below the LFO option. The LFO speed can be further modified with the key value. Playing higher notes will speed up the LFO when the key value increases. You can also use the Attack value to have the LFO gradually fade in instead of starting immediately when a key is pressed. This is great for lead sounds where you'd like to introduce vibrato after you've held a note for a moment.

Set the Retrig function to on, and a new LFO cycle will start every time you press a MIDI key.

Pitch

Looking now at the Pitch section of controls, the Transpose value transposes the pitch of Simpler up and down. Detune adjusts the pitch in cents, like the Detune in an audio clip. The LFO box sets the amount of LFO modulation to apply to the pitch of the sample, also known as *vibrato*. Similarly, the Envelope box sets the amount of pitch modulation applied by the Pitch envelope. The Spread knob will perform an automatic detuning of the left and right channels to create a wider sound from your sample.

Our favorite, however, is the Glide feature. When this is active, Simpler bends up or down to each consecutive note that is played. For best results, set the Voices value to 1, which will make Simpler monophonic. The Time value sets how long it takes Simpler to bend from one note to another. Used properly, you can get Simpler to react like a classic mono-synth.

Pan

Another new section in Simpler, the Pan controls specify the output location of the sound (done with the Pan knob) and modulate the pan with the LFO and randomness.

Volume

The Volume box obviously sets the output volume of Simpler, while the Vel value determines the effect of velocity—the force with which a particular note is played—on the output volume. If the value is set to 0 percent, the sample will ignore velocity information and use the same volume no matter how hard you hit a key. There is also an LFO box, which applies LFO modulation to the sound, creating a tremolo effect. The Voices box determines the *polyphony* of Simpler. Polyphony is the maximum number of simultaneous notes Simpler can produce. If the value is set to 1, Simpler will be *monophonic,* playing only one note at a time. Any time you exceed the polyphony limit, earlier notes will be cut off in favor of new ones. When this happens, the indicator next to the polyphony value will blink. Finally, the *R* button (short for *retrigger*) is used to set whether the envelopes retrigger when played polyphonically. When this option is on, the envelopes will restart with every new note played, even if you're currently holding other notes. When it's off, the envelopes will restart only after all the keys have been released.

Analog Presets Ableton has provided a number of presets in Live's Library to get you started. Most are based on small samples that act similarly to the waveforms found in analog synthesizers. Indeed, using a saw wave in Simpler is quite similar to using a saw wave in an analog synth. These tones are great for beefy basses and gnarly leads.

MIDI Control

Simpler will respond to any incoming MIDI note to create sound. Just like the other devices in Live, the Simpler dials and buttons can be assigned to MIDI controls, as described in Chapter 4, "Making Music in Live." Assigning the Sample Source controls to MIDI controllers is an extremely expressive performance technique. Altering the loop length and start positions on the fly can change the timbre and tone of the sample in wild ways as well.

Under Control When using a control surface to control the parameters of a device with a large number of parameters, such as Impulse or Simpler, you'll have to get familiar with navigating banks of controls. The implementation for every MIDI controller is slightly different, but in general there are eight knobs dedicated to controlling parameters of the currently selected device, along with a button or switch for changing banks (a different group of eight parameters). In the case of the Simpler, bank one controls the Volume Envelope and loop settings, bank two controls the filter, bank three the LFO, and so on. Every time you select a new bank from your controller, Live's status bar will display a message telling you which parameters are controlled by this bank.

I've found that the Simpler presets provided by Ableton demonstrate best what Simpler is capable of. I suggest that you inspect each of the presets and experiment with the various parameters to learn how they affect the overall sound.

Operator

Introduced in Live 4.1, Operator is Ableton's first add-on instrument, an FM synthesizer instrument. Operator is included in all Live versions after 4.1, but only as a demo. You will need to purchase an unlock code from Ableton (available separately or as part of the Live Suite) to use this instrument to its full potential. And believe me, Operator is full of potential.

Operator is basically three synthesizers in one. You can employ three different types of synthesis to craft your sounds: subtractive, additive, and FM. Unless you are already a synthesis wiz, you may want to check out the online chapter on these various synthesis types before looking at the details of this synth.

Overview of the Interface

Operator represents a slight departure from the user interface scheme set forth by Live. While Operator still conveniently sits within the Track View (see Figure 8.8), it does not display all information and parameters at once. Operator is a deep and complex synth, so many of the parameters have been consolidated into the center window of the interface.

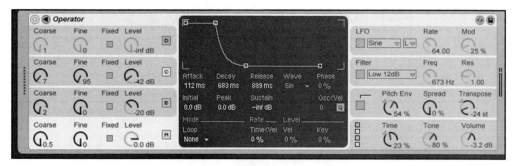

Figure 8.8 The Operator interface has two sections: the center window and the eight sections surrounding it—the shell.

Looking at the interface, you'll see a large center window, called the *display,* surrounded by eight sections, collectively referred to as the *shell.* The shell sections are (clockwise from the lower-left corner): Operator A, Operator B, Operator C, Operator D, LFO, Filter, Pitch, and Global. If you click on one of these sections, the display will change to show its associated parameters. Try it—click anywhere within the Operator A section. The display will show a graphic envelope, as well as a myriad of values below it. If you click on the Pitch section, a different set of information will be shown in the display.

Ableton has placed the most tweakable parameters of Operator into the shell so that you can access them at all times. The more intricate details—parameters that you normally "set and forget"—are neatly tucked away within the display. If you'd like, you can even hide the display, leaving only the shell exposed, by clicking the little triangle in the upper-left corner of the interface (see Figure 8.9). Also along the top title bar are the standard controls for recalling and saving presets.

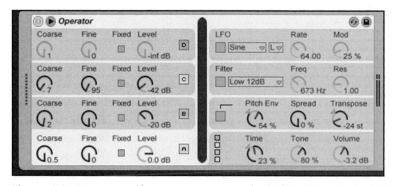

Figure 8.9 Buy yourself some screen space by hiding Operator's display.

Creating and Shaping Sounds

So how do you operate Operator? It depends on what type of synthesis you're trying to achieve. As you're about to see, Operator can pull off both subtractive and FM synthesis, and it has some additive synthesis features as well. It would therefore make sense to set up Operator to perform your desired synthesis before going any deeper.

The Algorithm

Click on the Global section in the lower-right corner of the shell. The global parameters will now be shown in the display (see Figure 8.10). If you've been clicking around through the other sections in Operator, you'll notice that this display is different from the others. Gone are the graphic envelopes, and in their place is a collection of colored squares.

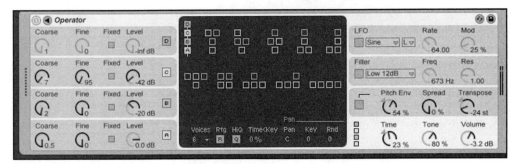

Figure 8.10 The global parameters of Operator.

While the term *algorithm* may conjure up images of mind-bending calculus formulas, you'll be pleased to know that Operator provides a simple way to visualize an algorithm using the assortment of colored squares in the display. By default, the upper-left algorithm will be active (its squares are solid colors, as opposed to outlines). If you look at the operators to the left of the display, you'll see that they have the same colors as the squares in the display. The colored squares are therefore a map, or flowchart, of how the operators interact with each other.

You can read an algorithm from the top down, but I also like to look at it from the bottom up from time to time. If you look at this first algorithm starting at the bottom, you'll see that the bottom square is a yellow A. This is Operator A. You'll also see that there is a little yellow line extending downward from this square. This line shows that Operator A will be outputting a signal that you can hear.

If you look at the next block above A, you'll see a green square with a B inside. This block has a line extending downward from it, too, but it connects to Operator A instead of being an output. This means that the waveform created by Operator B will be used to change the frequency of Operator A, which is output to your speakers. In this arrangement, Operator B is a modulator, and Operator A is a carrier.

Knowing the above, you can now see what parts Operator C and Operator D play in this algorithm: They are additional modulators. Operator D will modulate Operator C, which modulates Operator B, which modulates Operator A—the carrier. Wow! This algorithm sure offers a lot of modulation!

Click the algorithm below the current algorithm. This new algorithm has the shape of a T. Can you tell what will happen when you use this algorithm? Let's read it and see: Operator A is again at the bottom and has a line extending downward. This means you will hear this operator, just like the previous algorithm. Where this algorithm differs, however, is in the arrangement of the three modulators. Instead of being stacked such that D feeds C, which feeds B, which feeds A, each of the three modulators will work directly on Operator A.

Just to the right of the T algorithm is one shaped like a box. When you select this algorithm, you will see the familiar arrangement of Operator B modulating Operator A. The difference this time is that Operator C is now a carrier—you will hear the waveform it generates, as well as hearing the waveform generated by Operator A. You can think of this as a dual-FM synth where you can create two unique waveforms simultaneously, which can be used in layers to thicken your sound, or to create two independent sounds that interplay with each other.

You should now be able to tell how each algorithm will make the operators interact. One algorithm of special note is the horizontal arrangement found in the lower right. When using this algorithm, you will no longer be using any of the operators as modulators—they'll all be carriers. This arrangement is one that you would use in Operator for subtractive synthesis. Each operator will output its own unique waveform, which can be mixed together and filtered, very much like in a Minimoog synth.

The Operators

Leave the algorithm set to the horizontal arrangement and click on Operator A in the shell. The algorithms in the display will now be replaced with an envelope and additional parameters. These are all of the control parameters for Operator A. By default, each operator is set to produce a sine wave with instantaneous attack and release. Try playing a few notes to hear this for yourself.

Tucked away in the display is a parameter named *Wave*. The option below it is currently set to Sin—a sine wave. Click on Sin to open a menu with all of the operator's waveshapes. Try out a few of them to hear how they sound.

Normally, FM synthesis uses only sine waves. The additional waveforms here, such as the saw and square, can be used as sources for subtractive synthesis. Of course, you can also use them for FM synthesis, which will allow Operator to create sounds unlike other FM synths that have only sine waves. Additionally, the saw and square waves have multiple shapes, denoted by a number after the name. Remember our discussion of how periodic waveforms are composed of multiple harmonics? Well, the number in the waveform name tells you how many harmonics were used to create the waveshape. In the case of Sw3, only three harmonics were used: the fundamental, the second harmonic, and the third harmonic. As a result, the Sw3 waveform still resembles a sine wave more than a sawtooth wave. As you go further down the menu of waveforms, you'll see saws with greater numbers of harmonics. Sw64 uses 64 harmonics to generate the sawtooth wave and therefore sounds like the kind of sawtooth wave you're used to hearing. This same numbering scheme is true for the square waves as well.

A sine wave has no harmonics, so what are the other sine wave variations about? First, notice that the sine wave variations are lettered, not numbered. This helps alleviate confusion regarding harmonics. The sine variations are just that—slight tweaks to a sine wave that emulates the kind of waveforms generated by analog oscillators. You may not be able to hear much of a difference while listening to each of the sine waves directly, but they may cause more obvious changes to your sound when used as modulators.

Along with selecting the waveform for the operator, you can also set its tuning and volume. Tuning and volume have a tremendous impact on the sounds resulting from FM synthesis, so these controls have been placed directly onto the shell so you can access them at all times. Furthermore, it is the tuning and volume relationships between the various operators that will define your sound. As such, you can see all of the tuning and volume information for all four operators simultaneously on the shell.

Tuning has two modes: Variable and Fixed. The Variable setting (the default) causes the operator to change frequency based on the notes you play. The Fixed setting (enabled by clicking the Fixed box of an operator) causes it to ignore incoming note information and will instead sound at a specific frequency that you set in the shell. When in Fixed mode, the two tuning options will be Freq and Multi, which stand for frequency and multiplier, respectively. The operator's frequency is therefore determined by multiplying the Freq by the Multi value. If the frequency is 100Hz and the multiplier is one, the resulting frequency will be 100Hz (100Hz × 1 = 100Hz). If the frequency is 245Hz and the multiplier is 10, the operator's frequency will be 2,450Hz.

When in Variable mode, the operator frequencies are no longer shown. Instead, you are presented with Coarse and Fine adjustments, which express the operator's frequency as a ratio of the base frequency. An operator with a Coarse setting of 2 will sound an octave higher than one with a Coarse setting of 1. An operator with a Coarse setting of 0.5 will sound an octave lower. You can use the Fine adjustment to create ratios that are fractions, such as 1.5 (Coarse 1, Fine 500) or 2.25 (Coarse 2, Fine 250). When working in subtractive synthesis (with the horizontal algorithm), this will create chords where playing one note results in multiple pitches from Operator. However, when using FM, this will create harmonic or inharmonic tones, depending on the ratio.

FM in Action

Enough talk, already. It's time to hear what all of this sounds like. Load up the preset Sine Bass from the (AL7P Presets) list in Live's Browser. Play a note, and you should hear a single sine wave. You are hearing Operator A by itself. While holding the note, turn up the level of

Operator B. You'll notice that instead of hearing a second pitch as you turn up this operator, you will hear the sound of Operator A change. This is because Operator B is modulating Operator A (which you can see if you look at the active algorithm), resulting in side bands. Operator A becomes more and more brilliant (more upper harmonics) as you increase the level of Operator B (the level control is essentially the FM modulation amount). If you turn Operator B back down again, Operator A will revert to a sine wave.

This phenomenon is the reason why FM synthesizers traditionally don't have filters. As I mentioned at the beginning of this section, when a waveform is passed through a low-pass filter, it is possible to remove all the upper harmonics, leaving only the fundamental behind—a sine wave. By turning down Operator B, you're also left with a fundamental sine wave. In this case, the level of Operator B acts in a similar fashion to the cutoff frequency of a filter. So if your sound is too bright, instead of reaching for a filter, decrease the amount of modulation so that the carrier will stay closer to its original sine waveform.

A moment ago, I mentioned that the ratios of the operators in an FM system will result in harmonic (tuned) or inharmonic (untuned) sounds. The patch you were just playing with used a modulator and carrier that were at a 1-to-1 ratio—the modulator had the same frequency as the carrier. The result, as you heard, was a constant pitch that changed timbre. For your next experiment, turn up Operator B again and then play with the Coarse knob. The result will be another constant tone, but one with a different harmonic structure. As you turn up the Coarse knob, you will be changing the ratio between Operators A and B but in whole numbers (for example, 1 to 2, 1 to 3, 1 to 8, and so on).

Things start to get strange, however, when you begin to change the Fine adjustment. Hold a note and slowly increase the Fine setting. Almost immediately, the sound will go "out of tune," or more precisely, will become "without tune." This is because the frequencies of the modulator and carrier are no longer at a whole number ratio. If Operator A is at Coarse 1, Fine 0, and Operator B is at Coarse 2, Fine 20, then the ratio between the two operators is now 1:2.02, which is not a whole-number ratio.

But why does this sound so weird? When performing subtractive synthesis, slightly detuning an oscillator is a great way to fatten up a sound. Why doesn't this same principle work in FM?

The answer lies with the squished/stretched waveform and our ears' ability to detect repetitions. In the examples so far, the modulator completes a cycle at the same point the carrier does. While a modulator might cycle twice for every cycle of the carrier, they will still repeat at the same time.

If you've ever heard two records playing together but out of time, this is analogous to the relationship between a carrier and a modulator. When the modulator has a frequency that is not double (or some other whole-number multiplier of) the carrier's frequency, it will cycle around at a different point each time the carrier cycles. The result is that the squish/stretch pattern your ears were hearing is now happening at a different point in each of the carrier's cycles. Thus, your ears can no longer determine the pitch of the waveform.

This phenomenon can be exploited in the FM world by offsetting the *phase* of an operator such that its waveform begins at a different point in its cycle. You'll still get pleasing harmonic tones, but the timbre will change slightly as you adjust the phase. While the difference is subtle, it may introduce a tonal quality that you prefer.

A Hidden Modulator While the Operator algorithms select which operators will be modulators for others, there is another hidden modulation you can perform with Operator D. Click its section to show its parameters in the display. You'll notice that there is an extra parameter here, Feedback, which will change the waveform of the operator. This uses the output of the operator as a modulation input for itself. If you turn the Feedback parameter up to 50 percent, the result will be nearly identical to a sawtooth wave. Of course, if you have a waveform other than sine selected, the result will be extremely strange. Try it out!

The Envelopes

So far, the experiments with FM have concentrated only on designing a waveform using a modulator and carrier. All of our examples have been fairly static sounds—press a key and hear the sound; release the key to stop the sound. The envelopes in Operator will help bring the synthesizer to life by offering ways to automate and animate the waveforms over time.

Each operator has its own volume envelope. The LFO also has its own envelope. The Filter and Pitch sections also have their own envelopes. That's seven envelopes for a single voice! That's quite a lot compared with Simpler, which has only three envelopes per voice.

You heard in the experiments above how the volume of a modulator would affect the timbre of the carrier. Therefore, using an envelope to change the volume of a modulator will allow you to change the harmonic content of a sound as it plays, like using a filter envelope in subtractive synthesis.

Load the Operator preset titled Techno Bass, and play some notes. This sound now has some motion to it—it has an aggressive attack that quickly decays into the fundamental sine wave. Played in low octaves, this is a great bass sound similar to a subtractive bass synth. Click on Operator B and look at its envelope. It has a quick attack with a fairly fast decay and a long sustain. This makes Operator B play at full volume when you strike a note, but it quickly fades out after the initial attack. This is what creates the harmonic complexity at the beginning of every note.

This is a pretty simple implementation of the envelope—just attack and decay. However, the Operator envelopes are much more powerful than this, even more powerful than the envelopes in Simpler. Most synthesizers, including Simpler, use ADSR envelopes, which stands for Attack, Decay, Sustain, and Release. The Operator envelopes, on the other hand, are composed of six parameters: Initial level, Attack time, Peak level, Decay time, Sustain level, and Release time

(IAPDSR). This offers much more flexibility when designing your sounds because you can break many of the constraints set forth by an ADSR envelope. For example, it is possible for the Sustain level to be higher than the Attack level. In an ADSR envelope, the Attack always reaches maximum level, and the Sustain can be set only to this same level or lower.

Furthermore, the Operator envelopes can be looped, either based on time or based on the tempo of the current Live Set. This means that you can use the envelopes as pseudo-LFO sources as well, since you can create a modulation that can repeat again and again. The ability to synchronize the repeats to the tempo of the song allows you to create interesting rhythmic patterns with ease.

How easy? Click on the Operator B section and switch the Loop parameter to Beat. Now hold a note. You'll hear your bass sound retriggering every 1/16 note! You can change the loop rate, of course, by changing the Repeat value. Furthermore, the looping will follow Song Tempo if you change it in real time. If you really want these repeated notes to be locked in with your composition, select Sync as the loop mode. When it's active, you can play notes at any time you'd like, but the envelope will repeat only in sync with the beats in your song. (This works only while Live is playing.) This ensures that the triggered bass sound plays in time whether you're early or late.

The remaining parameters in the display for an operator govern how velocity and key-follow will affect the operator's pitch and level. For starters, the Vel parameter will modulate the operator's volume based on velocity—positive values will cause the operator to increase in volume as you play harder, while negative values will attenuate the operator the harder you play. If you use this setting on a modulator, it will have a similar effect to applying velocity scaling to a Filter Envelope in subtractive synthesis. The harder you play, the more FM modulation will result, thus causing a brighter sound. The Key parameter will cause the operator to play louder or softer (depending on the value you use) as you move into the higher registers of your keyboard. This is similar to the key-follow found in the filter sections of many subtractive synths.

The Osc → Vel parameter determines the impact of velocity on the tuning of the operator. Playing harder will cause the operator to increase in pitch, provided you use a positive value. Of special interest is the Q button next to this value. When active, the incoming velocity will affect only the Coarse tuning of the operator. This is handy because it will ensure that you have a harmonic interval (a whole-number ratio between the modulator and carrier), no matter what velocity you play. If you turn this button off, your velocity will affect the Coarse tuning *and* the Fine tuning, resulting in tunings that can have inharmonic results.

The final parameter, Time → Vel, is really great for adding expressiveness to your sounds. When set to a positive number, it will cause the envelope to run faster as you play with more velocity, with a heavier style. Set to a negative value, the envelope will run slower as your velocity increases. This can be used to mimic the performance of acoustic instruments whose envelopes change naturally as a result of dynamic changes.

We've covered quite a lot so far, so much that you actually have enough knowledge to create some killer FM tones, even though we haven't even touched on the sections on the right side of the shell (save for the algorithm setting). For a quick sampling of what can be done with just operators and their envelopes, take a look at the presets provided with the CD-ROM.

The LFO

Moving on to the right side of the Operator interface, we find the LFO section right at the top. On a synthesizer, an LFO is used to create repetitive automations for other parameters of the synth. On a subtractive synthesizer, LFOs will often be used to modulate the filter cutoff or the volume. The LFO of Operator can do this and much more.

For starters, the LFO is not relegated to low-frequency operation in Operator. You can actually goose this one up into the audio range, thus making it available as another audio oscillator for your FM experiments. This is done with the tiny drop-down menu next to the waveshape. The options are *L* for low-frequency mode, *H* for high-frequency mode, and *S* for sync. After that, select your Rate and Mod amount with the dials in the shell.

In order for the LFO to work at all, you'll need to turn it on with the little box to the left of its Waveform menu in the shell. Once active, you'll see all the parameters light up in its display. The display looks like the other operators, except that it has Destination boxes in place of the waveform and phase parameters. By default, the four operators will all have their pitches modulated by the LFO. You can turn these off individually, and you can also use the LFO to modulate the Filter Cutoff.

If you're using the LFO at audio rates to modulate the operators, you'll probably want to turn up the Rate → Key value to 100 percent. This will make the LFO track the keyboard so that you will get consistent harmonic results with every key you play.

Other than those parameters, the remaining settings for the LFO function like the settings for an operator. The envelope will control the modulation amount of the LFO (whose upper limit is set with the Mod dial in the shell), and the Loop parameter can be used to retrigger the LFO envelope. With this arrangement, you can create an envelope loop that will modulate the LFO while it runs at audio rates—the looping envelope essentially becomes another LFO!

The Filter

So here we are: an FM synth with a filter. With all the tonal control possible by adjusting the modulation amounts of the operators, why would Ableton put this here? The best explanation I can offer is that it offers something familiar to those new to FM synthesis. Coaxing your desired tone from an FM synth is not easy, especially for beginners. However, generating a complex waveform with FM is easy. The filter therefore allows you to treat this complex FM waveform as the starting waveform for subtractive synthesis. Thanks to Operator's FM capabilities, your subtractive experiments won't be based merely on simple waveforms like sawtooth and square. Your arsenal of waveforms is nearly limitless. Once you get a complex wave you like, you can then run it through the standard rigmarole of filters and envelopes you're used to using.

Another reason for the filter has to do with bandwidth—digital audio has a limited frequency range determined by the sampling rate. According to the Nyquist Theorem, the highest frequency recordable by a digital system is equal to half the sampling rate. If the sample rate is 44,100Hz (which is the CD standard), the highest recordable frequency is 22,050Hz. In practice, however, this top frequency is usually limited to roughly 20,000Hz (which is the upper limit of human hearing). FM synthesis is capable of producing hundreds of side bands, some of which could exist above the 20,000Hz limit. If these frequencies are left unchecked, they will create foldback frequencies that will distort the sound. The filter, therefore, allows you to remove these high frequencies so that they will not interfere with the limits of digital sampling.

Like the LFO, the filter must be turned on before it will have any effect. Do this by clicking the box just to the left of the Filter-Type menu. You'll see the center display spring to life with color, indicating that the filter is active. The filter contains the same six-parameter envelope as the operators and LFO that will modulate the Filter Cutoff frequency. The amount of envelope modulation is set with the Envelope parameter. The other parameters in the display determine how key position and velocity will affect the filter.

Operator has a total of eight standard filters types: low-pass, band-pass, high-pass, and notch, in both 12 dB/octave and 24 dB/octave flavors. The Ableton manual notes that the notch filter is not really a true notch filter, but rather a single-band parametric EQ with negative gain. The Res dial will adjust the width, or Q, of the EQ where higher values result in a narrower bandwidth.

The Pitch Settings

Below the Filter section is the Pitch section, which contains an envelope, as well as some other unique pitch-related controls. Not only will you have to switch on the pitch section to make the envelope work, but you'll also have to turn up the Pitch Env dial in the shell. You can use both positive and negative values here, so it's possible to reverse the effects of the envelope.

As with the LFO, you can choose which operators will be modulated with the Pitch envelope. Often, it's not necessary to modulate all the operators. Of course, if you don't modulate them all, you might get inharmonic results. However, this can be desirable on the attack of a sound, such as when making drum sounds.

The Spread dial in the shell will instantly turn your synth creations into stereo patches by using two voices instead of one, each panned to either side of the stereo field and detuned slightly. This is similar to the fattening technique on analog synths where multiple matching oscillators are all slightly detuned from each other. The result is a full, lush sound similar to a large group of singers, which is why this effect is sometimes referred to as *chorus*. Since Operator must create two slightly detuned tones when using Spread, your CPU load will be much higher as a result, nearly double. Use this control wisely.

All Things Being Relative Many people have asked us how we create such a wide stereo field in our recordings. They assume that everything they're hearing must be in stereo, or that we've done some sort of phase trick. This is not the case. In order for your ears to perceive a sound as being stereo, it helps to play the sound against sounds that are mono. This makes the difference between what is mono and stereo much more apparent to your ears. If there is no mono material in your recording, there will be no point of reference for your ears to say, "Wow, that sound is really wide." Don't hesitate to record or mix certain parts as mono. Their contrast against the stereo parts will not only make the stereo material sound wider, but it will also help clean up your mix because you won't have every sound filling up the same stereo space.

Next to the Spread knob is the Transpose knob, which will shift the pitch of Operator up or down by the specified number of semitones. This is a real-time control, so you can tweak it while a sound is playing.

There are two important pitch parameters in the display that we haven't discussed yet. The first is PB (Pitch Bend) Range, which determines the amount of modulation resulting from using the pitch wheel on your MIDI controller. By default, this is set to +5 semitones. This means that a pitch of C will be bent up to F if you turn the pitch wheel all the way up. The same C will bend down to G if you move the pitch wheel downward.

The last group of settings is the Glide parameters, found in the lower-right corner of the display. These work only when used in conjunction with the Voices parameter on the Global Settings display, explained in the next section, so we'll get back to Glide parameters in just a moment.

The Global Settings

The last section of Operator contains Global Settings for the instrument. You're already familiar with the algorithms contained there, but there are still a few more things you should know.

First, the Time control. This knob adjusts the speed of all of the envelopes in Operator simultaneously. You can slow them down dramatically or speed them up to a point where you hardly notice them. I've found that after you dial in a tone, you can get a sound that you like a little more by adjusting this parameter. Also, if you make a sound whose envelopes are timed to the tempo of the song, you can adjust their timing as a whole should you change the tempo of the song. Other than that, this can be a great dial to tweak while Operator is playing a programmed synth pattern—it can add expressiveness beyond tweaking the oscillators and filters.

To the right of the Time knob is the Tone knob. This knob behaves like a low-pass filter, even though it's not. This knob can be used to reduce the number of high-frequency overtones generated in FM. Often, a sound will sound okay at one pitch but may sound strange when played an octave or two higher. This is because at the higher pitches, the harmonics of the sound cross the theoretical limit imposed by the Nyquist Theorem. Those high overtones then fold back into the regular audio spectrum, which can sound unpleasant. The Tone knob can be used to keep those high harmonics in check.

The last control in the shell is the Volume knob. If we have to explain what this does, then you should probably put down this book and step away from your computer (or any piece of technology for that matter).

Within the display for the Global Settings, below the algorithms, are seven more parameters. The three parameters on the right are merely used to set the pan position of Operator's output. The Pan value lets you position the sound in a specific location of the stereo spectrum. The Key value makes the key position influence the pan. When you use it, your sound will pan to the right as you play higher notes, as if you were sitting in front of an acoustic piano. The last value, Rnd, will cause the pan position to change randomly with the specified depth.

To the left of the Pan parameters is Time ← Key. This parameter is also helpful in mimicking acoustic instruments in that the envelopes can be set to run faster (or slower if you use a negative value) as you play higher notes. If you think about a piano, you'll know that the low notes can sustain much longer than the higher notes. This setting lets Operator behave in the same way.

Continuing left, we come across the Hi-Q parameter. This is the same as the Hi-Q found in the Audio Clip View and determines the quality of interpolation used when Operator renders its sounds. Turning this on will result in a more polished sound, but at the price of CPU load.

The RTG button sets the Retrigger mode for the envelopes. If this is on, the envelopes will reset to their initial values every time a note is played. So, if you play a note that has a long release phase, playing the note again before the release has completed will cut it off abruptly as the envelope jumps back to its initial value. If this button is off, retriggering the same note will cause the envelope to enter its attack phase but start from the current level of the release phase. This is most useful for pad sounds where there should be no abrupt changes in volume as notes are played.

The last parameter at the far left of the display is Voices. This setting determines the maximum number of notes that Operator can play at once. When it's set to 2, you'll be able to play only two notes at the same time. If you play a third note while still holding the other two, the oldest note will be replaced by the new note, a technique referred to as *voice stealing*. By default, this value is 6, which is usually sufficient. However, if you are using a sound that has a long release time, it becomes quite easy to have more than six sounds playing at once, even if you aren't holding any notes. The voice stealing will cause the oldest note to stop immediately in favor of the newest note. This will ensure that you hear every note you want to play, but it can sound strange if you keep hearing these beautifully sustained notes being cut off. In this case, you'll want to increase the number of voices. Be careful, though, as each simultaneous voice requires additional CPU processing.

The other way to use the Voice parameter is to set it to 1, which turns Operator into a monophonic synth, able to play only one note at a time. If you play one note followed by another, the first note will be stopped in order to play the second. While this may not sound like such a hot feature, it definitely heats up when paired with the Glide parameters mentioned in the previous section. If you engage the Glide function (click on the G in the Pitch section), notes will now automatically bend to each new note as they are played. This works only when you're playing in a legato fashion, where each note is started before the previous one ends. If you're playing in a staccato fashion, Glide will have no effect, since there will be no overlapping notes. The Glide Time, also found in the Pitch section display, sets the time it takes for Operator to bend to the new note after it has been triggered. This effect is also known as *portamento*, and it is quite useful for synth leads and basslines.

If you're feeling ready to get into programming your own sounds with Operator, you may want to read the additional online content that gives guidelines on how to create different all types of sounds, from pads to snare drums here: http://www.courseptr.com/downloads.

Sampler

When Live 7 was released, Ableton also introduced a new Sampler instrument, available for purchase as an add-on (see Figure 8.11).

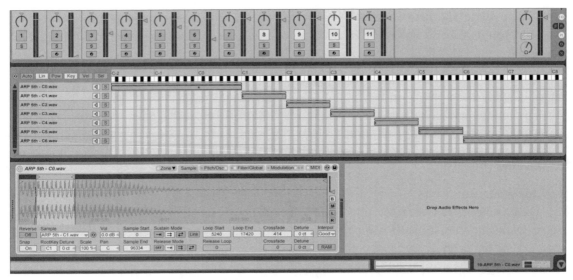

Figure 8.11 Ableton's new Sampler—this will cost you extra.

Although Live has had basic sampling functions since the introduction of Simpler, Sampler, as we saw earlier in this chapter, vastly expands Live's sampling capabilities by introducing support for multisampling, as well as a wide range of sound-design and modulation options. What does this mean? Put simply, with multisampling you can use multiple samples to define the sound of a single instrument. Instead of simply transposing a single sample up or down the keyboard, multi-sampling uses many samples to capture the sound of an instrument at multiple points in its frequency and dynamic range. In the case of acoustic instruments, Live takes samples at many different pitches and dynamic levels. A multisampled instrument includes a sample map that defines at what pitch and velocity each of these samples is played and how they are blended together. In combination with various filters and modulation sources, this allows for a much more realistic simulation of "real" instruments.

Sampler gives you the ability to load and edit patches from Ableton's Essential Instrument Collection 2 (shipping with each boxed version of Live 7) as well as import instruments from a wide range of common sample formats, including AKAI, GigaStudio, EXS (Logic), SoundFont, and Native Instruments' Kontakt. Of course, you can also create your own multi-sampled instruments incorporating any number of sample zones and modulate the sounds with Sampler's built-in LFOs and filters. You'll find that Sampler has many of the features of other popular sampling applications; it is also well integrated with the rest of Live and has a classic Ableton-style interface.

The theory and practice of multisampling could fill an entire large book on its own. Setting up the intricate sample mapping required to accurately re-create the sound and feel of a complex acoustic instrument like a violin is an advanced topic that we can't really cover here in any depth. If you are interested in manipulating and creating your own sampled instruments, consider getting a more general book on the topic. In this section, we'll try to give you a brief intro to Ableton's Sampler and the specific functions that set it apart. We'll also try to give you some creative ideas for how you might want to use Sampler in your own Live Sets and productions.

Looking at the Sampler interface, you'll see that its functions are organized into a number of different tabs, including Zone, Sample, Pitch/Osc, Filter/Global, Modulation, and MIDI. Let's have a look at each of these and see how it works. Open up the Live Set titled Sampler Demo 1 in the Resources → Examples → Chapter 08 folder on the included CD so you can follow along as I describe this instrument.

Just a quick word of credit here before we go on: The samples used to demonstrate Sampler in this section (included on the CD) were made by my friend and fellow author Matt Piper at M-Audio. Matt sampled the sounds of the pots and pans in his kitchen one night, and I liked the sounds so much that I have used them here (with Matt's permission, of course!).

The Zone Tab

Clicking on the Zone tab brings up Sampler's Zone Editor, used to map samples across key and velocity ranges. The Zone Editor opens in its own special window, directly above the Track View (see Figure 8.12).

Figure 8.12   The Zone Editor showing key mapping.

On the left side of the Zone Editor is the sample layer list. All of the individual samples belonging to a given instrument will appear here, referred to as *layers*. For very large multisampled instruments, this list might be hundreds of layers long. (Note that selecting any layer by clicking on it will load its sample into the Sample tab for examination.)

The rest of this window shows either the Key Zone Editor or the Velocity Zone Editor, depending on whether you have selected the Key or Vel button above the list. In Figure 8.12, I have created a custom instrument by importing four "kitchen bowl" samples from my private library; you can see here in the Zone Editor how the different samples are mapped across the keyboard. Samples are triggered only when incoming MIDI notes lie within their key zone. By default, the key zones of newly imported samples cover the full MIDI note range. Zones can be moved or resized by clicking and dragging in the middle or from their right or left. Zones can also be faded in or out over a number of semitones at either end by clicking and dragging the narrower small line above (see Figure 8.13). This makes it easy to set up smooth crossfades from zone to zone.

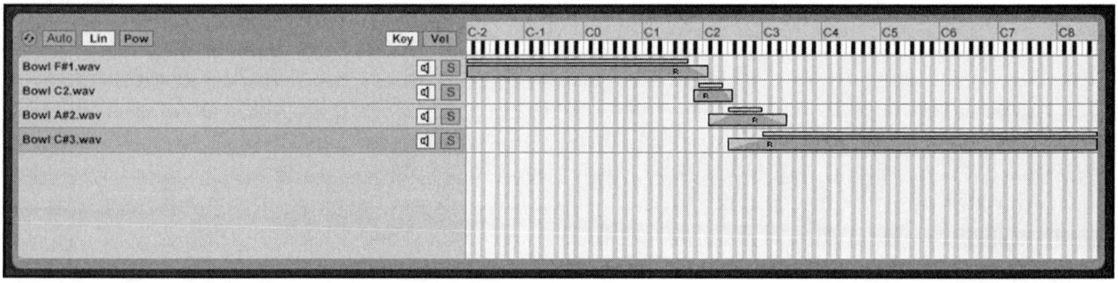

Figure 8.13 Setting up crossfades between key zones.

The Zone Editor can be used both for mapping sample zones across keys, as we see here, as well as for mapping samples to be triggered by specified velocity ranges. In Figure 8.14, we have a pad sound composed of three long samples, overlapped by velocity. The combination of samples we will actually hear when a note is played depends on the velocity of the triggering MIDI notes.

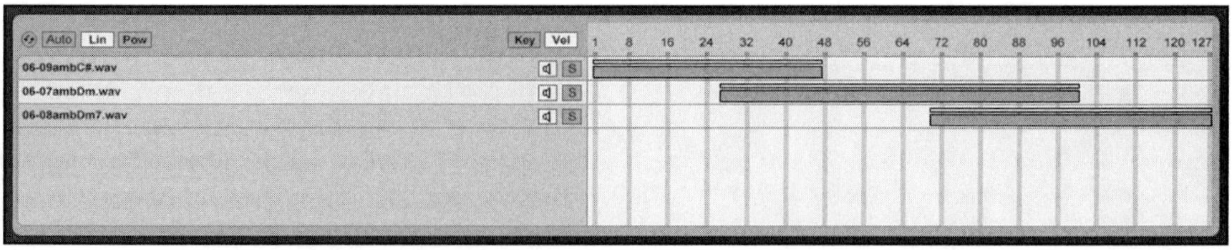

Figure 8.14 Velocity mapping in the Zone Editor.

The Sample Tab

The Sample tab is where you can set the playback characteristics of individual samples. A large part of this tab is devoted to displaying the waveform of the sample you currently have selected (see Figure 8.15). The name of the sample is displayed below in the Sample drop-down chooser box. You can select a particular sample to edit by clicking on it in the Zone Editor window, by using this chooser, or by clicking the Hot-Swap button next to the chooser, which will take you to the Browser and show you a list of samples used in the current instrument.

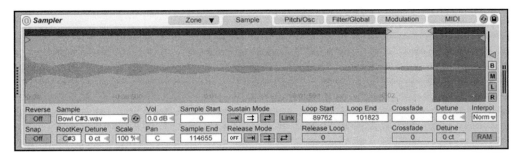

Figure 8.15 The Sample tab.

At first glance, the Sample tab appears similar to the display of Simpler, and it serves a similar function. However, Sampler gives you more power to control how each of your samples plays back and loops. Note that the settings in the Sample tab will affect one particular sample only, the one you currently have selected.

- RootKey sets the reference pitch for the current sample. When a given sample is triggered by an incoming MIDI note matching the RootKey, it will be played back at its original pitch. MIDI notes higher or lower than the RootKey will transpose the sample accordingly.

- Detune allows you to make fine adjustments to the sample tuning, +/−50 cents.

- Volume allows you to adjust sample volumes individually.

- Pan adjusts the left-right position of individual samples.

- The Reverse button causes the entire multisample to play backwards when triggered. In this case, sample playback begins from the sample end point and proceeds backwards to the sample start point.

- When the Snap button is engaged, the start and end points of your sample will snap to the waveform zero-crossing points in order to avoid clicks or pops in playback.

To the right, the rest of the controls in the Sample tab work together with the Global Volume envelope in the Filter/Global tab to determine how your samples should be played back.

The Sample Start setting determines where the playback of the sample will begin when triggered, while the Sample End setting determines where playback will end.

Sustain and Release

The various Sustain and Release modes, selected by clicking one of the buttons shown in Figure 8.16, allow you to specify a loop in playback to sustain your sound longer in a wide variety of interesting ways.

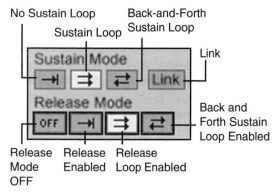

Figure 8.16 The Sustain and Release mode buttons.

These buttons allow you to toggle between any of the Sustain and Release modes.

When the No Sustain Loop button is selected, the sample will play from beginning to end, until either it reaches the sample end or the Volume Envelope (on the Filter/Global page) comes to the end of its release stage, whichever comes first.

With the second button, Sustain Loop, enabled, the sample will play from the beginning until the loop end, at which point it will revert to the loop start and begin looping.

The Back-and-Forth Sustain Loop button, the third button, plays the sample from the beginning until reaching the loop end point, and then it will start playing backwards until it reaches the loop start, continually "looping" back and forth.

Toggling the Link button will automatically set the sample start to the same point as the loop start. If you have already entered a different sample start point, you won't lose it when you click Link; it simply becomes inactive while the loop start is in use.

Activating Sustain Loop also allows you to enable Release Loop with one of the Release mode buttons. Like the Sustain Loop, the Release Loop has several different modes. If the Release mode is off, the default, then the Master Volume Envelope's release stage will affect the sound during the Sustain Loop, and the sample will stop playing at the end of the loop. When you toggle the

Release Enabled button, the sample will play through to the end once the Master Volume Envelope reaches the release stage.

Changing to the next button, Release Loop Enabled, means that the sample will play straight through to the end and then jump back to the beginning of the Release Loop; it will keep looping until the Master Volume Envelope reaches the end of its release.

Alternatively, with the next mode, Back-and-Forth Release Loop, enabled, the sample will play until reaching the end of the Release Loop, and then it will start playing backward until it reaches the Release Loop's start and keep looping back and forth like this until the Master Volume Envelope reaches the end of its release.

In addition to these looping functions, there are also a few more helpful controls on the Sample tab.

The Sustain- and Release-Loop Crossfade (labeled *Crossfade*) settings allow you to set loop crossfades in order to help remove pops and clicks in your audio you may hear when you play back the sample loops. Experiment with different settings here to find the best results for a particular sample.

You can also use the Sustain- and Release-Loop Detune (labeled *Detune*) parameters here to make small adjustments in pitch as desired.

The Interpol (interpolation) control lets you decide which algorithm you want Sampler to use when transposing samples. You can choose from No, Normal (the default), Good, Better, or Best Interpolation. Your choice here can have a significant impact on the overall quality of sound coming out of Sampler, but you also need to remember that selecting Better or Best here will increase the hit on your CPU.

You can engage the RAM mode switch if you want to load the entire multisampled instrument into your computer's RAM memory instead of streaming it from disk in real time (the default mode). This will give you better performance when manipulating a sound in Sampler, but if you have many samples loaded into RAM, this will eat up your available memory quickly and adversely affect the performance of your computer/software. (By default, Sampler will load only the beginning of each sound into memory at first and then stream the rest of the sound from your hard drive as it plays.)

The next tabs include a number of controls that allow you to shape and modify the sound of your samples. Let's look at what you can do with them.

The Pitch/Osc Tab

The Pitch/Osc tab (see Figure 8.17) contains a range of controls for Sampler's Modulation Oscillator and Pitch Envelope, used to modulate the audio output from the playback in the Sample tab.

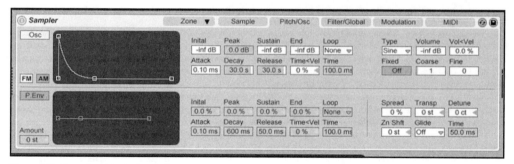

Figure 8.17 The Pitch/Osc tab.

The Modulation Oscillator

The upper part of the Pitch/Osc tab is occupied by the controls for Sampler's Modulation Oscillator. This oscillator makes no sound of its own but is used instead to modify your samples via frequency or amplitude (FM or AM) modulation; you can toggle between these two modes using the FM and AM buttons on the left side of the interface. If you use the Modulation Oscillator for amplitude modulation, you are affecting the volume; you can use this to create interesting tremolo effects or other more radical changes in volume. Used for frequency modulation, the Modulation Oscillator can transform your samples by creating FM-style effects reminiscent of Ableton's FM-based synth Operator, described in the previous section.

The Modulation Oscillator's control interface features an image of an envelope at left, showing the ADSR Envelope stages for the oscillator. If you select a long attack time here, then the effect of the oscillator will fade in slowly. You could use this with AM oscillation to create a tremolo effect that slowly fades in after a note is struck, for example. You can change the envelope settings by moving the breakpoints of the envelope itself or by adjusting the values in the readouts.

There are a range of waveforms to choose from for the Modulation Oscillator, including a selection of basic sine, sawtooth, and square waves. You can choose these in the drop-down chooser labeled Type. You can also adjust a number of parameters here to affect the speed and synchronization properties of the waveform, whether or not it is synced with the tempo of your project.

The Pitch Envelope

The lower part of the Pitch/Osc tab contains an additional set of controls for a separate Pitch Envelope. There is a Breakpoint Envelope here, as well as numerical controls. This envelope can be used to create pitch changes in your samples. The setting just to the left of the envelope, labeled Amount, will adjust the total amount of pitch-shifting effect, in semitones.

The Filter/Global Tab

The Filter/Global tab (see Figure 8.18) contains the controls for Sampler's powerful morphing filter, as well as a Global Volume Envelope. Both of these affect the master output of Sampler.

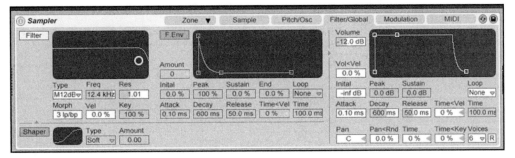

Figure 8.18 The Filter/Global tab.

The Filter

The filter in Sampler has a number of different modes available, including a Morphing filter (M) with 12 dB and 24 dB varieties, as well as standard low-pass, band-pass, and high-pass types. The Morphing filter is interesting in that it can smoothly morph from one filter type to another, for example from low-pass to high-pass, sweeping across the frequency spectrum. Try routing the Morph control to an external MIDI controller and automating it for some very interesting filter effects.

The Volume Envelope

The Volume Envelope is a global envelope; it will affect how the final output of Sampler is heard. You have standard Attack, Decay, Sustain and Release controls here, as well as Master Volume and Pan controls. Use this to control the articulation of your entire multisampled instrument.

The Modulation Tab

The Modulation tab (see Figure 8.19) gives you four different modulation sources you can use to continuously modulate and change nearly any parameter in Sampler. There is a Modulation Envelope here, as well as three separate LFOs and a familiar range of controls.

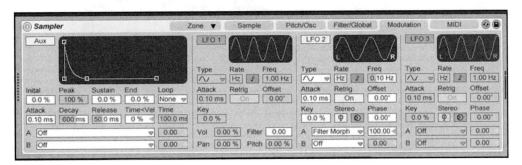

Figure 8.19 The Modulation tab.

Modulation Envelope

The leftmost section of this tab is the interface for the Modulation Envelope. It can be switched on by using the Aux button on the left edge of the interface. If you click the drop-down choosers labeled A and B at the bottom of this part, you will see a long list of other parameters in Sampler. Any of these can be selected as a destination to be modulated by the envelope. The A and B choosers enable you to select two simultaneous modulation targets to be affected.

LFOs

There are three LFOs here you can also use to modulate a wide variety of parameters in Sampler. The first one, labeled LFO1, has four particular global parameters: Volume, Filter, Pan, and Pitch. The other two, LFO2 and LFO3, can be freely assigned to a list of parameters in Sampler; just as with the Modulation Envelope, the A and B choosers here enable you to select two simultaneous modulation targets to be affected by each LFO.

Each of these LFOs can be set up to run freely or to sync to the tempo of your Live Set. You can choose which of these behaviors you want from each LFO by clicking on the Hz (Hertz) button or on the small button with a picture of a musical note just to the right of it. Then use the control to the right of this (labeled Freq or Beats, depending on which mode you have selected) to set the exact frequency of the oscillator. You can select from a variety of standard waveforms for each LFO, such as square, sawtooth, and sine waves.

The MIDI Tab

I'm sure you won't be surprised when I tell you that the MIDI tab (see Figure 8.20) is the place where you set up MIDI modulation routings for Sampler. This tab allows you to use various MIDI parameters as modulation inputs and use them to affect various parameters in Sampler. Let's look at how to do this.

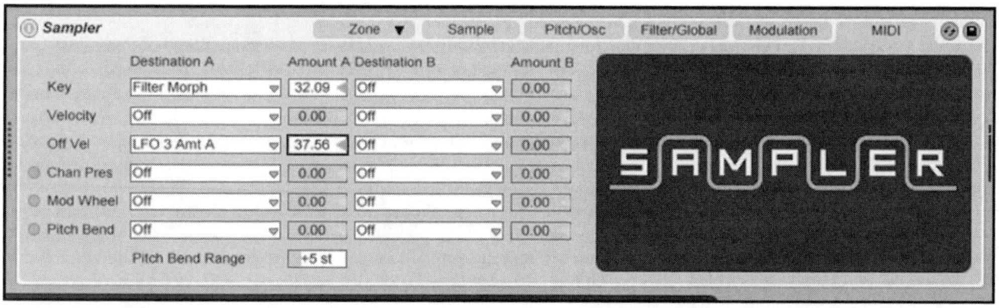

Figure 8.20   The MIDI tab.

The interface here allows you to take the MIDI input from a number of specific parameters. The MIDI parameters available as sources for modulations are listed along the left-hand edge of the tab, including Key (pitch), Velocity, Off Vel (release velocity), Chan Pres (aftertouch), Mod Wheel, and Pitch Bend. Any of these input sources can be mapped to two different modulation destinations simultaneously, using the Destination A and Destination B drop-down choosers. You can set the amount of modulation with the Amount A and Amount B controls. By routing the Velocity parameter to control volume, for example, you can make your samples play back more loudly or softly when those channels receive higher or lower MIDI velocity messages, for example, when you play harder or software on your MIDI controller keyboard. (Note that you can also do this with the Vol ← Vel control on the Filter/Global page.)

These assignments can make a big difference in how responsive the sampled instrument is to your touch. Have a look at the MIDI assignments in some of the SONiVOX instruments or quality instruments from third-party companies to get some ideas about how these assignments can be best used to imitate the behavior of acoustic instruments or allow you more control over purely electronic sounds.

Importing Third-Party Instruments

As mentioned previously, if you already own any collections of multisampled instruments in AKAI, GigaStudio, EXS (Logic), SoundFont, or Kontakt format, you can import these into Sampler for easy access in Live. To import a third-party instrument into Sampler, find the file in Live's Browser and double-click it to import it. The third-party instrument will be converted to a Sampler preset. You can see all of your imported instruments in the Device Browser under Sampler → Imported (see Figure 8.21).

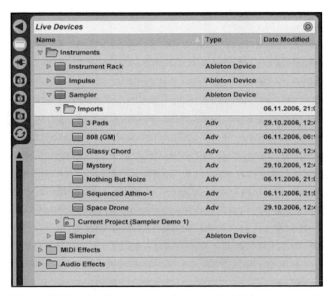

Figure 8.21 Looking at your imported third-party sample instruments in the Browser.

Some more complex multisampled instruments will be converted to Instrument Rack presets using multiple instances of Sampler in order to better translate the sound of the original. For most multisample formats, Live will import the audio samples into the Library, where they will appear as new samples under Samples → Imported. However, note that in the case of Apple EXS24/GarageBand and Kontakt multisample formats, Live will create new Sampler presets that reference the original WAV or AIF sample files. This means that they will not work if you remove the original WAV or AIF samples. (However, Live's File Manager also offers the option to collect and save these external samples into the Library if desired.)

New to Live 7

Live 7 has been a big release for Live instruments. Ableton has partnered with Applied Acoustic Systems to deliver three new synthesizers based on physical modeling technology. Physical modeling concerns itself with creating mathematical equations that imitate or "model" the behavior of real-world acoustical events. Two of the new synthesizers, Electric and Tension, are based on familiar physical processes: hammers hitting tone bars and guitar picks plucking strings, for example. Analog, on the other hand, models behavior that goes on under the hood of an analog synthesizer, so from a synthesis standpoint, it's going to be a bit more familiar.

While this may sound fairly pedestrian, get ready for a major paradigm shift if you've never worked with a modeling synth before. Because you'll be working with controls that model physical events, you'll need to be aware that many of the parameters dramatically affect each other. Especially in the case of Tension, it's possible to create patches that don't create any sound at all! You'll need to think more in terms of inventing and playing an instrument, rather than twiddling knobs. (Will a very smooth bow moved very quickly across a violin string with very little force produce any sound? What if you move it slowly?)

With Live now sporting so many instruments, we could spend an entire book on them alone. By necessity, we'll focus on getting at the essential concepts to each instrument and give you some ideas about how to dig in and create your own sounds.

Global Parameters

All three of Live's new instruments have a Global section that gives you control over the overall characteristics of the device. The parameters offered here are ones such as polyphony and pitch bend range that aren't particular to the type of modeling that the instrument does. So instead of covering them with each instrument, we'll start out with this handy reference that can be applied to all of them. Just bear in mind that each synth does not have every single one of these parameters.

- **Voices:** Controls how many notes can sound at once. Reducing the number of voices will save CPU power.

- **Semi:** Transposes the entire range of this instrument in semitones.

- **Detune:** Makes fine pitch adjustments to the entire range, to a maximum of 50 cents (one half of a semitone).

- **Stretch:** Allows the adjustment of the instrument's *temperament*. Increasing this value will change the tuning such that higher notes are slightly sharper and lower notes are slightly flatter, which for pianos can result in a more natural and brilliant overall sound.

- **Pitch Bend:** Controls how much the instrument will respond to pitch bend messages. Adjustable from 0 for no response at all to 12 for a full octave of pitch bend.

- **Error:** Introduces a random amount of tuning variation to each note (as might happen with an unfretted string instrument like a cello).

- **Priority:** Determines how the instrument handles the maximum number of voices (set by the Voices parameter) being exceeded. When more notes are sounded than Voices permits, Priority will tell the instrument which notes to prioritize (and which to cut off): High (cut off the lowest notes first), Low (cut off the highest notes first), or Last (cut off the oldest notes first).

- **Unison:** The Unison switch copies the final output of your instrument, creating a stack of either two or four voices. Unless used in conjunction with the Detune and Delay parameters, all this does is make the signal louder. Slight detuning will create a chorusing effect, while larger values can be used to create strange, out-of-tune harmonies. Increasing the Delay amount will make each of the additional layers to be delayed up to 100ms.

- **Portamento:** Causes each note to slide into the next at a rate determined by the Time parameter. With Legato enabled, only notes that overlap will slide together. The Proportional setting will automatically adjust the portamento time so that larger intervals slide longer than shorter ones.

Electric

Electric, the simplest of the new Live instruments, is an electric-piano modeling synth (see Figure 8.22). Instead of reproducing actual electric pianos through sampling, physical modeling

Figure 8.22 Ableton's new Electric gives you the power to design a wide array of electric pianos.

is used instead. This means that sound is produced via mathematical equations representing the various physical aspects of the instrument itself.

Electric's interface is divided into four sections dedicated to different aspects of how an electric piano produces sound: the mallet, the metal fork that gets struck by the mallet, the damper that controls the tine's resonance and the magnetic pickup that converts the sound into electricity. The fifth section, Global, deals with overall instrument settings that aren't electric piano specific.

Mallet

This section controls the characteristics of the mallet, or hammer, that causes the metal fork to vibrate. Stiffness represents how hard the surface of the mallet is, so lower values will produce a gentler attack, while higher values will tend to make the sound more percussive and less full bodied. Force is the speed at which the mallet hits the fork, with higher values tending to produce more overdrive and "growl." Since both of these controls affect how much the fork is made to vibrate, they interact with each other closely. For example, both values affect the overall volume of the sound, but in different ways. A very hard mallet hitting the fork with a small amount of force will tend to produce a hard attack, but a relatively weak overall sound. A soft mallet hitting a fork very hard will produce a much fuller sound at a similar volume to the first setting, but with a much weaker attack. Both of these parameters can be modulated by both the velocity and the pitch of incoming MIDI notes. This is where physical modeling gets interesting. It's fairly intuitive to see that modulating the force with velocity will create a real-world situation whereby more force is applied as you strike the key harder. However, we are also given the option of making our electric piano's hammers get harder as we play louder (or softer if you want).

The Noise subsection models the noise of the hammer hitting the fork, so it also affects the attack of the piano sound. Noise, however, is independent of the tone that the fork produces. Think of it as an additional percussive attack that you can blend in using the Level control to give the sound more definition. To get a better understanding of how Noise affects the sound, turn both of the Level controls in the Fork section down to 0% and play with the noise Pitch and Decay.

Fork

Some electric pianos, such as those made by Yamaha, use actual strings to produce sound—just like an acoustic piano. The most familiar electric piano sound, however, is the sound of a hammer striking a metal tuning fork—the design of the famous Rhodes piano. The tuning fork consists of two distinct parts: a stiff metal wire (the "tine") and a tuned metal resonator (the "tone bar"). The tine is struck by the hammer, and it in turn causes the resonator to vibrate, creating a distinct pitch.

To understand how the Tine and Tone subsections of the fork work, start by turning the Level control for Tone to 0% and the Level and Decay for the Tine to 100%. This will allow you to hear clearly only the Tine portion of the sound. It sounds very much like you might imagine a hammer hitting a stiff wire—a high frequency "ping" with very little body to the sound. Increasing the Color control will bring out more of the high frequencies, while reducing it will make the sound darker. The Decay control can be used to make the sound range from a short percussive hit to a drawn-out ring.

Once you have a handle on the Tine part of the sound, the Tone section is fairly self-explanatory. This is obviously the sound of the tuned resonator that produces the lion's share of the piano's tone. Again, you can get familiar with this aspect of the piano's sound by turning down the Level control in the other sections and listening to it by itself. The Decay control adjusts how long the note rings out while the key is held down, while the Release determines how long the note rings after the key is released. Don't expect to hear long release times like you would with a synth, however. Because we're modeling the behavior of a vibrating piece of metal in contact with a damper (see below), the release time is necessarily fairly short.

Damper

In a real electric piano, the dampers are what control the sustain feature of a note. When a key is struck, the same mechanism that moves the mallet also moves the damper away from the fork so it can resonate. When the key is released, the damper moves back into place, causing the tone bar to stop ringing. In the Damper section, you can control both the hardness of the damper surface and the noise made by the dampers moving back and forth.

As the Tone value is increased, harder dampers are modeled, and the damper noise becomes brighter and more pronounced. The Att/Rel knob controls whether damper noise is heard on the attack or the release of the note, with −100% being attack only, 100% being release only, and 0% being both. To hear what the Damper section is doing, it's easiest if you crank the Att/Rel knob to 0% or greater so it sounds when the note is released. The damper noise on the attack is much harder to hear since it's masked by the attack of the piano. Also, it's important to note that the amount of damper noise heard can be greatly affected by the Pickup settings.

Pickup

Much like an electric guitar, the vibrations produced by a mallet-striking fork are converted into an electrical signal through the use of a pickup, so they can be amplified. The Pickup section allows you to customize the design and position of the pickup, which has a huge impact on the final sound. Before looking at the knobs, you'll want to turn your attention to the pickup type (the R and W buttons in the lower left-hand corner of the Pickup section). When set to W, the pickups have the high-end bite typical of the electrostatic pickups in a Wurlitzer piano. The R setting has the pronounced mids and full low end associated with a Rhodes piano's magnetic pickups.

To get familiar with the Symm and Distance controls, start out with Distance at 100% and Symm at 0%. Symm controls the pickup's symmetry in relation to the fork. At 50%, the pickup is centered directly in front of the tine. Moving the knob to the left moves the pickup increasingly above the tine, emphasizing the higher harmonics, while moving it to the right shifts the pickup position lower, emphasizing lower harmonics. Note the dramatic change as you sweep symmetry from 0 to 100%.

Distance controls how far from the fork the pickup is. The further away the pickup is from the fork, the more spectrally balanced the sound will be, while moving it closer will emphasize the frequencies produced by the part of the fork it is closest to, and produce more overdrive. Adjusting the distance has a different effect, depending on what type of pickup you are using. In the case of the W pickup, decreasing the distance will increase the high-end bite and decrease the amount of bass overall. The R pickup works a little differently. First, watch your speakers and your ears because decreasing the distance of the R pickup increases the volume of the sound. As the R pickup is moved closer, there is an overall increase in drive and intensity in the highs and mids without much low-end attenuation.

Global

The Global section gives you control over the overall characteristics of Electric. For information on this section, see the "Global Parameters" section, earlier in this chapter.

Tension

Tension is the most interesting and unusual beast of the new Ableton instruments (see Figure 8.23). As a "string-modeling" synth, it takes the modeling concepts that we saw in Electric to a whole different level. Where Electric models a specific type of instrument, Tension applies modeling generically to the entire range of stringed instruments, ranging from cellos to pianos. The many parameters offered by this instrument also give us the opportunity to create some bizarre sounding instruments that could never exist in the real world.

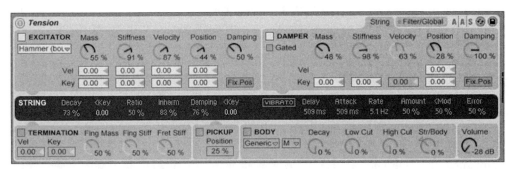

Figure 8.23 Tension allows you to create stringed instruments of many different types, including oddities such as a violin played with piano hammers.

The Tension interface is broken into several sections modeling different aspects of a stringed instrument: the Excitator that causes the string to vibrate; the Damper that reduces the string's vibrations; and the Termination, which emulates the effects of fingers and frets, the type and size of the instrument's body, the pickup for emulating electric instruments, and finally the string itself. Tension also features a second page of parameters for the filter and other aspects of the instrument not related to string modeling.

Note that each section has an on/off switch next to the section name, allowing you to bypass a set of parameters completely. While learning how to use Tension, it's going to be helpful to turn off other sections while learning a new one. It's a necessary evil (or benefit) of modeling that many parameters closely interact with each other. For example, a bow that is applied to a string with very little force will only produce sound if the bow is moved very slowly. There are many such interactions in this instrument.

Excitator

This first section deals with one of the most fundamental aspects of any stringed instrument: the physical relationship between the string and the object that "excites" it into motion. Here we can choose to use a bow, a piano hammer, or a plectrum (pick) to get our sound going. Depending on the Excitator you choose from the menu, you'll be presented with different parameters for defining the object you've chosen and the way that it's used. With this section turned off, you'll probably get no sound at all out of Tension, although it is possible to create sounds that consist of damper noise and the string's decay.

For a bow, you'll first see the parameters for Force (how hard the bow is pushed against the string) and for Friction (the amount that the bow material naturally resists the string). Velocity determines the speed at which the bow is moving, while position moves the bow all the way from the string's end (0%) to its midpoint (50%).

Hammers have a totally different set of parameters. Here you adjust the mass and stiffness of the hammer, followed by the speed at which it hits the string (Velocity), and the hammer's location (Position). The final control, Damping, controls the stiffness of the mechanism that brings the hammer into contact with the string. At higher values, the action is very "springy," so the hammer bounces right off the string, allowing it to vibrate loudly. At lower values, the hammer action is very stiff, muting the string somewhat as it lands firmly upon it.

Hammer (bouncing) simulates a hammer that is dropped onto the string and allowed to bounce multiple times. Again, here you see a complex interaction of forces. Generally speaking, the velocity is going to have the largest effect on how much the hammer bounces, with low values producing little volume and a series of rapid bounces that can become as subtle as a slight buzz and the highest values emulating the behavior of a hammer dropped from a very great height, producing a long trail of bounces with several seconds between the initial attack and the first bounce.

A plectrum is a fancy name for a guitar pick. It has the same set of parameters as a hammer, with the exception of protrusion, which replaces mass. Protrusion specifies the amount of the surface of the pick that comes in contact with the string. Lower values mean just the tip of the pick is being used to pluck the string, while higher values use more of the pick and result in a louder sound.

Damper

The Damper section controls how the string is made to stop vibrating. In the case of a piano, it emulates the behavior of the felt dampers coming into contact with the strings when the key is released (and the sustain pedal is off). In the case of a guitar, the damper could be the guitarist reducing the pressure on the string with the fingering hand or using the palm of the strumming hand to mute the strings.

Looking at the Damper's controls, you'll see that they are the same as those of the Hammer in the Excitator section. This makes sense, because the sound produced by the damper is affected by all of the same qualities—the overall mass, the stiffness of the damper's surface, the velocity with which it comes into contact with the string, as well as its position along the length of the string. The final control, Damping, determines how stiff the damper mechanism is.

String

Here is where we set the properties of the string itself. The Decay and Ratio work closely with one another. The Decay setting controls both the string's initial decay time (right after the attack) and the release time (after the key is released). With Ratio set to 0, the string's decay will begin after the note is struck and continue to decay naturally regardless of how quickly the key is released. At 100, the note will decay naturally as long as the key is held down but will cut off abruptly as soon as the key is released. To get a better sense of this, set Decay to a high value and then experiment with different Ratio values, making sure to test each value with both a long key press and a short one.

The Key value can also be used to control how much note pitch will modulate the decay time. The trick here is that since we're modeling real-world strings, lower notes will always decay longer than higher ones. (Just imagine what happens when you hit the lowest note and the highest note on a piano with the sustain pedal on.) The Key control modulates this natural behavior. So by raising this value you can make the higher notes ring longer and the lower notes shorter than they usually would. Lowering the Key value will exaggerate the instrument's natural decay behavior.

The Inharmonic and Damper controls both affect the tone of the instrument in dramatic ways. Inharmonic controls how much the upper partials of the string are out of tune with the harmonic series. As opposed to a theoretical perfect string that produces a perfectly pure tone, strings in the real world have inharmonic qualities. Depending on the Excitator you are using, you'll notice different effects from increasing this value. With a bow, the upper frequencies of the sound will become more like noise, whereas a hammered string will simply begin to sound more out of tune with itself as the higher harmonics are detuned.

Termination and Pickup

Termination applies to stringed instruments that are fingered. In other words, an individual string is "terminated" or ended on one of its ends by a finger, and possibly a fret, as opposed to a piano or a dulcimer where the strings are fixed between two pegs and tuned to the desired pitch.

The Finger Mass refers to the force that is being applied with the finger. At lower values, the pitch becomes less distinct as the string is terminated in a less stable fashion. If Fret Stiffness is increased with a low Finger Mass setting, you will hear the string buzzing against the fret, much like it did during your first guitar lesson! With a low Fret Stiffness, you'll generally get a less distinct pitch from the string—unless, that is, you increase the Finger Stiffness to compensate for the lack of clear frets on the neck.

Switching on the Pickup section changes the sound from that of an acoustic instrument to the output of a magnetic pickup. The Position control changes the location of the pickup. At 0, the pickup is placed at the string's termination point, much like the bridge pickup on an electric guitar. As the value is increased to 50, the pickup is moved closer to the midpoint of the string, more like an electric guitar's neck pickup.

Body

The Body serves two purposes in the creation of our modeled string instruments. First, the instrument body acts as an amplifier of the strings' vibrations, which can add additional fullness and a longer decay to the sound. The Body also filters the frequencies that it radiates, further coloring the final sound.

To get an understanding of the different body types, try experimenting with different ones, first setting High and Low Cut to 0 and setting the Str/Body ratio to 100 (all body sound, no direct string sound). Turning up the Decay as well will tend to exaggerate the effect of the body and make its effects even clearer. As you might expect, a piano body offers the smoothest response across the frequency spectrum, while the violin body tends to bring out the higher frequencies more. Next to the Body Type menu, there is a menu to select the size, ranging from extra small to extra large. Larger body sizes tend to make the instrument sound more diffuse and further away, while small sizes make the instrument sound closer and more present.

Filter/Global

The Filter section (see Figure 8.24) is located on Tension's second page of parameters and consists of a multimode filter that can be modulated with both an envelope and an LFO. In addition to the

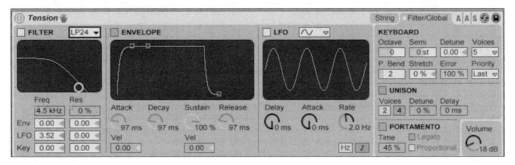

Figure 8.24 The Filter section can be used to give some additional flavor to your modeled string instruments.

common filter types, you'll also find a formant filter (F6 and F12 in the Filter menu), which is a filter modeled on the resonance of the human vocal tract. Adjusting the resonance of this filter sweeps through the vowel sounds A, E, I, O, U and is capable of producing some very powerful resonant frequencies, so be prepared to lower the output volume, or you may find yourself running into some nasty distortion. Below the Frequency and Resonance controls, you'll find additional controls to specify how much you want these values to be modulated by the envelope and the LFO.

For the Global parameters, see the "Global Parameters," earlier in this chapter.

Analog

Analog is Ableton's take on a classic subtractive synthesizer (see Figure 8.25). Two oscillators and a noise generator feed two filters and two output amplifiers. There are two independent LFOs that can be used to modulate nearly any aspect of the sound, and each module has its own Envelope section as well. So much has been written about the principles of subtractive syntheses that instead of covering all of this ground for the millionth time, we're going to focus most of our energy in this section on what makes this little synth unique.

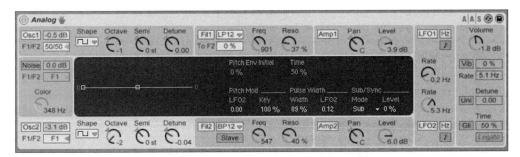

Figure 8.25   Analog is a powerful analog-style subtractive synthesizer.

Analog's interface is similar to Operator in that it is divided into a series of modules that surround a center window that will be updated to provide additional parameters for whichever module is currently selected. Again, here we will use the terminology *shell* to refer to the basic controls in the outer ring of the interface and *display* to refer to the center window.

The modules for Analog are as follows: two oscillators, a noise generator, two filters and amplifiers, the LFOs, and finally the Master. Clicking anywhere in any of these modules will change Analog's display to show its envelopes, LFO routing, or any other parameters that may apply. Finally, also note that the name of each section (for example, "Osc1") is also a switch that can be used to turn the module on or off.

Oscillators and Noise

The oscillators are where the sound begins. In the Osc modules, you can select the shape of the waveform, adjust its volume and tuning, and set whether it gets routed to Filter 1, Filter 2, or both. The default value for filter routing is 50/50, meaning the signal is split equally to both filters. Dragging up or down in this control will show the ratio of how much signal is distributed to each filter, until the display reads F1 (Filter 1 only) or F2 (Filter 2 only), at which point the signal is no longer split between the two filters.

With the Osc1 or Osc2 module selected, the display contains controls for adjusting the oscillator's pitch, pulse width, and optional sub or sync oscillator. A graphical display on the left can be used to make the oscillator's pitch rise or fall into its target pitch. This display corresponds to the Pitch Env Initial (the starting pitch) and Time (how long it takes to reach the final pitch) controls, seen to the right. Below, you can determine if the pitch is to be modulated by the LFO. The LFO's are "hard wired" to their corresponding oscillators—Osc1 can only be modulated by LFO1, and Osc2 can only be modulated by LFO2.

The Pulse Width section is only enabled when a square wave is selected as the waveform shape. Try sweeping this from 0 to 100, and you'll hear the tone go from being narrow and pinched to big and fat. Modulating the Pulse Width with the LFO is a great way to add some subtle movement to your sound. Note that unless the LFO is actually switched on, the LFO modulation amount will be disabled.

Hidden within each Oscillator module is a second oscillator that can be controlled via the Sub/Sync section. When Mode is set to Sub, an additional note will sound one octave below the pitch of the main oscillator. The volume of the Sub tone is set by the Level control. If you want some real nastiness, however, try setting Mode to Sync. When set to Sync, the additional oscillator is not heard directly. Rather, it is used to control the main oscillator by forcing it to restart from the beginning of the waveform for each cycle of the sync oscillator. This changes the harmonic content of the main oscillator, with the pitch and intensity increasing as you increase the Ratio (the frequency of the sync oscillator).

Finally, in between the two oscillators is the Noise module, a sound generator that produces white noise. Noise has many uses—not only in producing percussion sounds, but also for adding a bit of extra attack or texture to an otherwise dark sound. All of the controls for Noise are located in the shell. The filter routing works just like it does for the oscillators, and the Color control is a simple low-pass filter that can be used to reduce the high-frequency content of the noise.

Filters and Amplifiers

Once the sound wave leaves the Oscillator module, it proceeds on to the filters. While filters are an essential part of most sounds, strictly speaking they do not need to be used. Both Filter modules can be turned off, and Analog will work just fine. Which filter(s) will be used to shape your sound is determined by the filter routing in the Oscillator modules.

While the two filters are essentially identical, they do have a few subtle differences. Both have menus for selecting a filter type and the usual frequency and resonance controls. The first difference between the two is that Filter 1 has a control called "To F2," which can be used to send the output of Filter 1 to Filter 2. This gives you the option of running the two filters in series (one after another) instead of in parallel. To fully understand what is possible here, however, it's also important to understand that the filters and the amps are hard-wired to each other—in other words, Filter 1 automatically is passed to Amp 1, while the same holds true for Filter 2 and Amp 2.

Let's look at an example. For starters, we'll assume that we have both filters and both amps turned on, and that both of our oscillators are routed to Filter 1 only. Filter 1 is set to send 100% of its signal to Filter 2. This causes the output of Filter 1 to be sent both to Amp 1 *and* Filter 2, because the "To F2" control is a send—it taps the signal and passes it to the second filter without interrupting the signal flow to Amp 1. This means that if you want to truly hear the filters operate in series, you need to turn Amp 1 off completely. Now the signal will flow from Filter 1 to Filter 2 to Amp 2 and then on to the master output. If you leave Amp 1 turned on, you'll hear a combination of the output of Filter 1 along with the output of Filter 1 and Filter 2 running in series.

Filter 2 features a Slave switch, which allows its cutoff frequency to be controlled from Filter 1. With Slave enabled, the Frequency control of Filter 2 controls the difference between the two cutoff frequencies. This could be used to create a dual filter with two peaks that are always the same distance apart. Then, whenever Filter 1 is modulated, whether manually or by an LFO, Filter 2 will follow it.

With either of the filters selected, Analog's display will display options for the envelope (see below), as well as a few other options. Selecting a drive mode will cause the filter to overdrive, with the Asymmetrical modes tending to create a more harmonically rich sounding distortion and the Symmetrical modes being a bit on the nastier side. The Frequency Mode and Resonance Mode sections allow you to specify how much the filters are modulated by the LFOs, the pitch (Key), and the envelope. The display looks nearly identical when the Amp modules are selected, the only difference being there is no Drive control, and the Modulation section applies to Volume and Pan.

Filters and Amp Envelopes

Since the Envelope sections for the filters and the amplifiers are identical in design, we'll discuss them both together. The envelope is an ASDR (Attack, Decay, Sustain, Release) envelope that can be adjusted either by dragging the breakpoints in the graphical display or by changing the values in the numerical display to the right. In the numerical part of the envelope display, you'll see one special value in additional to the usual ASDR values: Sustain Time. The standard Sustain value is a decibel level—the volume that the note sustains at while you hold the key down. By default, Sustain Time is set to "inf," meaning that the note will sustain indefinitely as long as the key is held. Sustain Time allows you to specify a length of time that the note will decay over, even if the note is held down.

At the far right of the envelope display, you'll see the Loop menu, which allows for some very interesting variations to your sound. By selecting one of the loop modes, you'll be telling Analog to repeat a part of the envelope instead of playing it through start to finish. AD-R will repeat the Attack and Decay portions of the envelope until the key is released, while ADR-R will repeat the Release portion as well. This makes it possible to use the envelope as more of an LFO, cycling through a series of values. When ADS-AR is selected, the envelope works normally until they key is released, at which point the Attack portion repeats before the Release, which could be used to create an additional swelling or short attack at the end of each note.

Looking to the left, there are a few switches above the graphical display that are worth mentioning. First, the Linear and Exponential switches are used to control the type of slope that occurs between the envelope's breakpoints. Linear slopes are increments or decrements in value that change at a constant rate over the time of the envelope segments (which is a fancy way of saying they are straight lines!). Exponential slopes start out as straight lines but curve more dramatically towards their destination point as they get closer. Because exponential curves tend to approach their target value very quickly before curving, they sound shorter than linear envelopes.

The Legato switch can be used to make your envelopes sound more, you guessed it … legato! In practice, this means that instead of the envelope starting over every time a new note sounds, the envelope will continue if the two notes overlap. In other words, if a new note is played while another is held down, the new note's envelope will start at the existing note's envelope position instead of beginning from the attack phase. Finally, the Free switch can be used to bypass the Sustain portion of the envelope. Since the envelope will now jump from the Decay to the Release phase, it will always be the same, regardless of how long the note is held. The most common example of a Free envelope is a percussion sound—a short attack and decay phase immediately followed by a release.

Making Filter Envelopes Work If you're finding that adjusting your filter envelopes isn't doing anything, it's probably because you haven't entered a value in either of the envelope (Env) fields for the filter. Unlike the Volume Envelope (which works automatically), you have to specify how much the Filter Envelope should be modulating the filter's frequency or resonance, or it won't do anything at all! In the display, enter an envelope amount under Freq Mod or Res Mod to specify how much the filter should be modulated by the envelope. Bear in mind that the frequency or resonance value shown in the shell is the starting value for the filter. The Env field can then be set to a positive or negative value to indicate whether the envelope should be increasing or decreasing that value as the envelope plays.

LFO

The two LFOs are completely independent of each other and can be used to control a variety of other parameters, as discussed in the previous sections. The only control here is the Rate, since the LFO amount is controlled within the module that it is being used to modulate. The rest of the controls for the LFO are located in the center window.

Use the Wave and Width selectors to control the shape of the LFO. When the Triangle wave is selected, the Width control can be used to change the wave shape to a ramp up or ramp down. With Rectified selected and Width at 50%, the LFO is a square wave, while modulating Width in either direction changes the pulse width. Retrig (the R switch) controls whether or not the LFO starts over (is "retriggered") with each key press.

Offset is used to adjust the phase of the wave. With a tempo-synced LFO, this could be used to move the peaks of the wave that occur before or after the beat. Delay will wait a specified length of time after a keypress to begin the LFO, while Attack will cause the amplitude of the wave to fade in over the amount of time specified.

Global

Most of Analog's Global parameters are covered in the "Global Parameters" section, earlier in this chapter, but a few things warrant special attention. The first switch in this section turns Vibrato on or off. Vibrato is a simple LFO that modulates the pitch of the oscillators. Only two controls are available here: the Amount, which controls the depth of the modulation, and the Rate, which controls the speed. The last switch in this section is marked "Gli" for Glide. For information on Glide, refer to the "Portamento" section, earlier in this chapter.

At the left-hand side of the display, you'll see some colored boxes. These are Quick Routing schemes, which can help speed the process of setting up a new patch. Unlike the similar-looking algorithms in Operator, these shortcuts are just timesavers—all they do is set the filter routing and turn the amplifiers on and off. For example, clicking on Quick Routing 4 (in the lower right-hand corner) sends both oscillators into Filter 1, the output of Filter 1 into Filter 2, and turns off Amp 1 so that only the output of Filter 2 is heard.

Drum Racks

Drum Racks may be the single most exciting addition to Live 7. A Drum Rack is an Instrument Rack that is customized for, drum roll please … programming drums. While Drum Racks have much in common with standard Instrument Racks, they have a number of unique features. We'll focus on those features in this section.

What's particularly interesting about Drum Racks is that they have no built-in synthesis or sample playback capabilities. As opposed to powerful, complex plug-ins like Battery 3 and Stylus RMX, a basic Drum Rack is incredibly simple. The beauty of the Drum Rack is that it can be incredibly powerful and complicated, but it doesn't have to be. Instead of having to deal with piles of features from day one, you get to decide how involved your Drum Racks are. When you're learning, you can keep them simple. As you get more comfortable, you can turn them into programming monsters using macros, nested Racks, effects, and MIDI devices.

Pads and Chains

When an empty Drum Rack is dropped onto a track, it appears as 16 pads, each one displaying the name of the MIDI note it is mapped to (see Figure 8.26). While only 16 pads can be displayed at a time, there are actually 128 pads available—one for each possible MIDI note. The grid to the right of the pads shows an overview of all 127, while the black square highlights which 16 are in view. Drag the square to show a different group of pads.

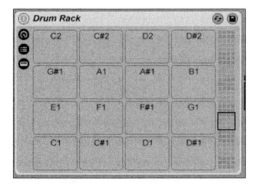

Figure 8.26   An empty Drum Rack.

Pad Control If you use a pad controller that's listed as one of Live's supported control surfaces (such as the Akai MPD32 or the M-Audio Trigger Finger), you're in for a treat. Set up your controller as a control surface in the MIDI tab of the Preferences dialog. Then record-arm your Drum Rack track, click in the title bar, and Live will hand over control to your control surface.

If your control surface is set up properly, the 16 pads on your controller will always stay mapped to the 16 pads that are in view for the Drum Rack. If it's not working, make sure that you are on the default preset for your controller (try preset #1). If it still doesn't work, you may need to do a preset dump. Check the documentation to determine how your device receives dumps; then click the Dump button next to your controller in the MIDI Preferences tab. Live will transmit the data to configure your controller properly.

Creating a basic drum kit with a Drum Rack is easy. Just drop a drum sample from the Browser onto any pad. Once you've dropped the sample, the pad will be updated to display the sample name instead of the note name. A play button for previewing the sample will appear, as will mute and solo switches. To see what's going on under the hood, you'll need to look at the Chain List and the devices of the Rack. The buttons for showing these are to the left side of the pads and look and function identically to those on a standard Instrument Rack. After you've clicked the Show Chains button, a few buttons that are unique to Drum Racks appear in the lower left-hand corner (see Figure 8.27).

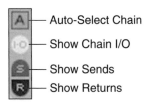

— Auto-Select Chain

— Show Chain I/O

— Show Sends

— Show Returns

Figure 8.27 These buttons give you access to the custom features of Drum Rack chains. They are only visible when the Show Chains button is highlighted.

The first button, Auto Select, makes it easy to find and view the chain you want by automatically showing the chain for the last pad that was triggered. The next shows additional input and output options for the chains. With this turned on, you can view the MIDI routing options and choke groups for each chain (see Figure 8.28). The Audio To setting is only used for Return Chains, which we'll discuss later. The bottom two buttons, marked S and R, are for viewing the sends and returns. Yes, Drum Racks have their own send/return bussing system!

Figure 8.28 Our new Drum Rack with the chains, devices, and I/O shown.

First, notice the far right-hand side of the rack. As I mentioned a moment ago, Drum Racks have no built in sample playback capability, so here you'll see that Ableton's solution to this is to automatically create a Simpler when a sample is dropped onto a pad. The Simpler offers loads of options for tweaking the playback of the sample, so this is an excellent solution. There's no reason, however, that you need to use the Simpler to play back your samples, nor is there any reason that your Drum Racks need to be based on sample playback. You can just as easily drop a synth onto a pad and use synthesis to create your drum sounds.

Once you've picked out some samples or synths and gotten a basic drum kit together, you can start customizing your sounds with effects. Drop a Saturator into your snare chain to add some extra bite or a Velocity device into your hi-hat chain to generate some random velocity variations. See where this is going? Your Drum Racks can become completely customized beasts with features that can rival any drum program out there. Your imagination is really the only limit.

It's also important to note here that a pad isn't limited to triggering only one sampler or synth. Want to create a sound that consists of several layers of samples, or synths, or both? No problem. You can create a layered sound out of several samples in one step, if you want. Simply select a group of samples in the Browser and hold down Ctrl/Cmd while dropping the samples on to the pad. Live will automatically create a nested Rack with one chain for each sample (see Figure 8.29). Triggering the pad will play all of the samples simultaneously.

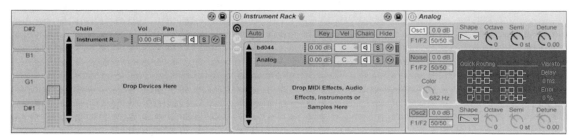

Figure 8.29   Here's a chain in a Drum Rack that triggers both a kick drum sample and an Analog instrument, for some low-end madness.

If you want to create layered sounds manually, just navigate to the device you want to add additional layers to and use Ctrl/Cmd+G to insert the device into an Instrument Rack. Now you can create layers by adding chains to the new Rack. Of course, if you own Sampler, or you want to design your drum sounds in a plug-in like Native Instrument's Kontakt, you can add additional layers directly within the sampler without adding additional chains.

MIDI Routing

When the I/O section of the Chain List is in view (refer to Figure 8.28), it's possible to adjust the MIDI routing of the chain. The Receive menu specifies what MIDI note triggers the chain. This is determined automatically when you drop a sound source onto a pad. If you change this value, you'll see the change reflected in the pad display. In other words, if you've dropped a sample called Kick1 onto pad C1 and then change the MIDI Receive for this chain to D1, you'll see Kick1 jump to that pad. Each pad is hard-wired to its note and location.

The Send setting is much more flexible. Here you can choose what note is sent to your sound source. By default, it's set to C3, which is the Simpler's default root note. So, a C3 will play back the sample at its original pitch. Modifying this setting could be particularly useful if you want to use a pitched sine wave as a kick sound. Change the Send note so the pitch matches the key of your song.

Choke Groups

Occasionally, it's necessary to configure some of the sounds in your kit so that playing one stops or "chokes" the other. The classic use for this is hi-hat. With a real world drum kit, you can have an open and closed hi-hat sound happening at the same time. Whenever the closed hi-hat plays, the open one should stop immediately, and vice versa.

If you've used the Impulse drum machine, you may already know that it has one choke group hard-wired to cells 7 and 8. Just hit the Link switch on pad 8, and the two pads automatically choke each other when played. Drum Racks offer the flexibility of 16 different choke groups, which can be assigned to any group of pads. To set up the choke group, choose a choke group number from the Choke menu (refer to Figure 8.28) and assign it to all of the sounds you want included in the group. It doesn't matter which number you use—just make sure to use the same number for each sound. Now triggering any of the sounds in the group will automatically cut off any of the others.

Sends and Returns

To use the built-in sends and returns of a Drum Rack, you first have to create a Return Chain (just like in Live's Mixer where you created a Return track, and the Send knobs were automatically created). First, show the Return Chains by clicking the button marked R at the lower left-hand corner of the Drum Rack. Now, you can drag an effect in to create a new chain, or you can right-click in the drop area and select Create Chain to create an empty Return Chain. More on why you would want an empty Return Chain in a minute. Just like Live's main mixer, you can create as many Return Chains as you want.

Once you've created a Return Chain, you can view the sends (see Figure 8.30). Now you can dial in as much effect as you want for each drum individually. By default, the output of your returns will be mixed in with the output of the Drum Rack. This, however, can be changed so that the output of the returns is routed to a Return track in Live's Mixer. This could simply be for convenience, or this routing could be used to send your drums to an effect in one of the Mixer's Return tracks.

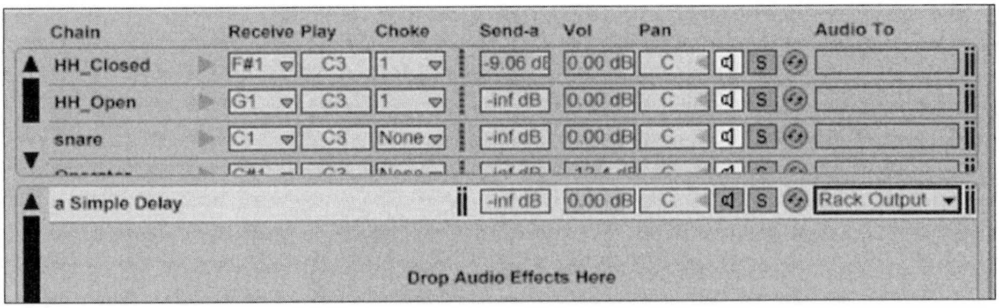

Figure 8.30 In this example, the closed hi-hat is being sent to the Simple Delay.

For example, let's say you have a reverb on Return track A in Live's Mixer. You have a Drum Rack to which you want to add a bit of this reverb to just the hand claps and nothing else. To do this, just create an empty Return Chain and send the hand claps to it. Then, in the Audio To menu of the Return Chain, set the output to Return track A, where your reverb is located.

As things get more complicated with your Drum Racks, you may want to start working with them using the Chain Mixer (as seen in Figure 8.31), rather than the Drum Rack interface. Here you can access everything we've discussed so far from a much less cluttered interface. Double-clicking on the title bar of any of these mini-tracks will display the devices of that drum's chain as if it were a regular track.

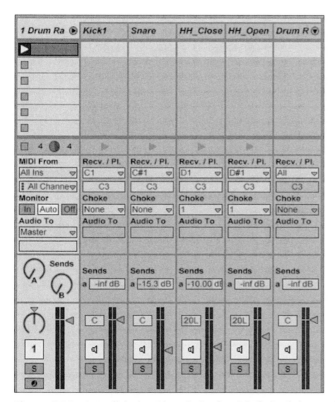

Figure 8.31   Just click the triangle in the title bar of the track, and all of the Drum Rack's chains become mini-tracks in the Mixer.

Extraction Team   Once you're done programming your drums, you may want to split each drum out to its own individual track. To do this, just right-click in the title bar of a drum in the Chain Mixer or the Chain List and select Extract Chains. Now you've got a new track with just that one drum and a new MIDI clip containing just the part for that drum. This technique is particularly useful if you need to render each drum to an individual audio track for mixing in another program.

9 Live's Audio Effects

Ideally, when you mix down a song you are creating a sonic picture, a three-dimensional landscape of sound in which every instrument, voice, and noise has an individual place yet blends with the others in a cohesive fashion. This is not a simple task, as there are many obstacles to overcome in the process. Instruments may have similar timbres and occupy the same area of the frequency spectrum, making them hard to differentiate from one another. Some parts may vary in volume so greatly that they are inaudible at times while overpowering at others. You may be suffering the consequences of poor gear—cheap mics, audio interfaces, cables, and more—all could be contributing to the degradation of your recorded sound. Audio engineers have devised a number of tools over the years to overcome these problems and help you achieve the ultimate mix.

Effects first manifested themselves as hardware boxes that could be connected to a mixing console. Normally, when dealing with hardware effects, you get to use each box only once. If you use an effect processor to generate a reverb, you will need to find another hardware box to generate a chorus. This can become quite costly if you need to use a large palette of effects in your mix. In fact, you've probably seen pictures of large recording studios with walls of rack-mounted devices for this very reason. Thanks to the increasing power of computer processors, it is now possible to re-create these effects using software. Software effects, commonly referred to as *plug-ins,* are extremely useful, since one effect program may be used multiple times in a project.

On a computer, you can use multiple instances of effects with ease. This means if you use a reverb plug-in to add some space to a voice, you can use another instance of the plug-in to create a different reverb for a snare drum. In fact, you can use as many instances of the plug-in as you want, as long as your computer's CPU can handle the work.

The number of effects available to those with even a modest computer system can be staggering. There are truly hundreds, perhaps thousands, of effects programs available from a myriad of developers and hobbyists. The quality of these plug-ins can be astounding; many software emulations rival their hardware counterparts. For convenience and power, Ableton has included a suite of effects integrated into Live to help bring your projects to life.

As you go through these explanations, please don't just look at the pretty pictures and take my word for it—drop these effects on a track and listen to how they alter your sounds. You will learn by doing.

We now present you with the ultimate guide to Live's built-in audio effects—all 23 of them.

EQ and Filters

The first batch of effects we'll dive into are the filters and equalizers (EQ for short). These types of signal processors are used to attenuate (reduce in volume) and amplify (increase in volume) only specific frequency ranges within an audio signal. Engineers will use filters and EQs to finely craft the frequency distribution of their mixes, resulting in beautiful, rich, and detailed masters (final mixes). Of course, these tools can also be used to radically distort sound, creating unique effects in their own right.

EQ Eight

A parametric EQ is a powerful frequency-filtering and timbre-shaping tool (see Figure 9.1). While many hardware and some software mixers have some type of equalization available on every channel, you will need to add an EQ plug-in manually to a track anytime it's needed in your Live project.

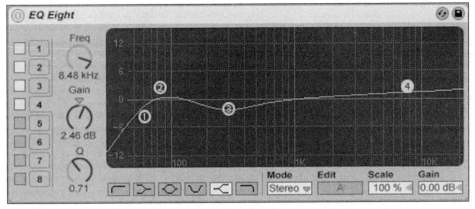

Figure 9.1   Live's powerful EQ Eight. In this example, only bands 1-4 are in use. If you turn off the bands you're not using, it saves CPU power.

The goal when using an EQ is to either boost or diminish certain audio frequencies in order to overcome problems arising from poor recordings, reduce muddiness from overlapping frequencies in other sounds, or emphasize certain characteristics of the sound to make it cut through the mix. The frequencies are often referred to as lows, mids, and highs or other subdivisions such as low-mids or high-mids. High frequencies are found in the register called *treble*, while low frequencies are referred to as *bass*. Low-mids, mids, or high-mids make up the middle section (from left to right) of the sonic spectrum. Live's EQ Eight features up to eight adjustable bands, or filters, each of which can be individually enabled or disabled.

Each filter can be used to cut or boost frequencies ranging from 30Hz to 22kHz, using one of a variety of different filter types, also known as *curves*. Each filter can be turned on or off using the eight switches running vertically across the left side of the interface. Next to each on/off switch is a tab, which, when clicked, will cause the freqency, gain, and Q (resonance or bandwidth) for that band to be shown on the knobs to the right. Adjustments to these values can be made either by using these knobs or by moving the numbered circles in the graphical display. The Q can be adjusted by dragging vertically while holding down the Alt key.

The filter type for each band is specified by first selecting a band and then using the switches along the bottom to specify the filter type. For example, to make band 3 a notch filter, first click on tab number 3; then click on the notch filter switch. Then you can move on and select other bands to specify their filter types.

The filter types, from left to right, are as follows:

- **Low-cut:** Also known as a high-pass filter. Removes almost all frequencies below the specified frequency. For this filter type, Q adjusts the resonance (how much the cutoff frequency is emphasized or reduced). Gain has no effect for this filter type. Using these to remove unnecessary low frequencies from as many tracks as possible can really clean up your mixes.

- **Low-shelf:** Reduces or boosts all frequencies below the specified frequency. With a low Q setting, the gain change will be a gentle linear slope. At high Q values, the change becomes more drastic, and you get an additional emphasis around the filter frequency (for example, if you're cutting with a high Q, you get a boost right above the filter frequency and the greatest gain reduction directly below it). This is the style of EQ that you'll find behind most home stereos' bass and treble knobs.

- **Bell:** A parabolic-shaped boost or cut of a given range of frequencies. For this filter type, the Q adjusts the bandwidth of the filter—how much the adjacent frequencies are affected. This is where the most surgical adjustments in a mix occur. Cut a little here, boost a little there....

- **Notch:** Like a bell curve with extremely high Q and extremely low gain. Gain has no effect for this filter type. It's especially useful for removing problems such as resonant room frequencies.

- **High-shelf:** Same as low-shelf, but acts on high frequencies.

- **High-cut:** Also known as a low-pass filter. Same as low-cut, but cuts low frequencies.

Perhaps the most misunderstood power that EQ holds is its ability to preserve headroom in a mix. By reducing less important frequencies in a sound or cutting frequencies that conflict with other instruments, you end up with mixes that sound louder and clearer. For instance, if the meat of a sound is in the bass, such as a bass guitar or synth, you may want to reduce the high-frequency content of this sound to make space for your singer's voice and your drummer's hi-hat. In this case, you'd use the EQ to reduce the highs and possibly to boost the lows in the bass track.

Conversely, you can often benefit by using a high-pass filter on vocals and other instruments that don't have a lot of low frequency content. Especially when working with voices and real instruments, there are often low frequencies, such as rumble from air conditioners and the like, doing nothing but consuming headroom and muddying up your mix. In addition to solving problems, EQs can also do a lot to sweeten certain sounds. Using a high shelf to boost 10k can help acoustic guitars sparkle, and a bell to boost 60Hz can give electronic kicks the extra power you're looking for.

Double Stack For more drastic cuts, boosts, and effects, try stacking EQs by assigning the same parameters to two or more bands. For example, two low-cut bands both set to 150Hz and a Q of .75 will cut low frequencies more steeply than one band will.

EQ eight can be run in a variety of modes, selectable from the Mode menu. Stereo is the standard mode for all stereo and mono signals. L/R differs from Stereo in that it allows you to equalize the left and right channels of a source separately (see Figure 9.2). Select L in the Edit switch to EQ the left side; then hit Edit again to switch over and EQ the right side. Bear in mind that L/R mode can be used to create stereo effects on mono sources by EQing left and right differently. M/S

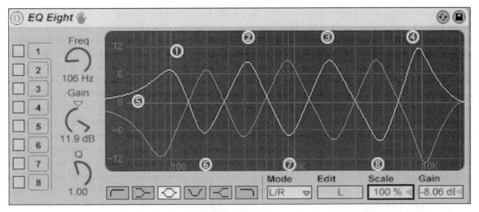

Figure 9.2 In L/R mode you can EQ left and right channels separately. While you can see both EQ curves simultaneously, you can only edit whichever band is shown in the Edit switch.

mode is for sources recorded using the Mid-Side microphone technique. (You can read all about M/S miking at http://www.wikirecording.org/Mid-Side_Microphone_Technique.)

The Scale control is an ingenious bonus that allows you to change the gain of all EQ bands simultaneously. So, if you've created the perfect EQ curve but decide that you've laid it on a bit thick, you can scale it back a bit and apply less EQ overall (see Figure 9.3). The Scale control goes all the way up to 200%, so you can use it to increase gain as well. Finally, the Gain control should not be overlooked. Remember that boosting and cutting frequencies changes the overall gain of your signal. If you're doing a lot of boosting, then you'll probably need to bring down the gain to avoid clipping.

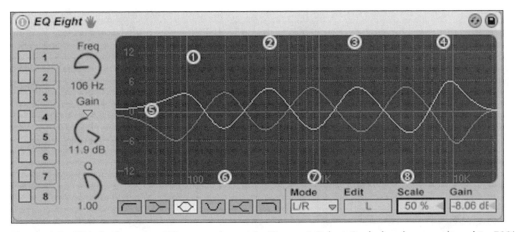

Figure 9.3   This is the same EQ curve shown in Figure 9.2, but Scale has been reduced to 50%, halving the gain of every band.

Kick Me! (Part 1) Sometimes cutting frequencies is more effective at getting something to stand out in a mix than boosting. Take acoustic kick drums, for example.

Many people will try to add bass with an EQ to get it to cut through the mix—it is the "bass" drum after all. The end result is that you end up feeling the kick more (your subwoofer will really be bumpin'), but not really hearing it cut through any better. The reason the drum is muddy in the mix is because it is occupying the same frequency bands as other instruments in the mix.

To get that deep yet punchy tone that will slice through the mix, try using a bell filter with a high Q setting to cut frequencies in the 150 to 200Hz range. What you're looking to cut here is the drum's resonant frequency. Once you've pulled it out, you'll be left with a sound that's punchy without overwhelming the low end. The resonant tone may not be very strong on your kick, so experiment with how much gain to cut it by—a little may do the trick. By cutting this tone, the bass now occupies its own space (the low frequencies where you feel it and the high frequencies where you hear it) and cleans up the sonic image. (The range from 150Hz to 250Hz can be extremely problematic in many mixes.) Apply some compression (see below), and you've got your kick tone.

EQ Three

While EQ Eight specializes in precision frequency crafting, the EQ Three is designed for more drastic EQ effects. Modeled after the EQ banks found on many DJ mixers, the EQ Three allows you to "cut holes" in the frequency spectrum and make broad adjustments to the overall sound of a track.

The EQ Three is concerned only with three frequency bands: lows, mids, and highs. As you can see in Figure 9.4, the EQ Three has three main dials: GainLow, GainMid, and GainHi. The frequency range of these dials is determined by the FreqLow and FreqHi knobs at the bottom of the effect. The GainMid knob will boost or cut all frequencies between FreqLow and FreqHi. The GainLow will adjust all frequencies below FreqLow, and the GainHi knob will handle everything above FreqHi.

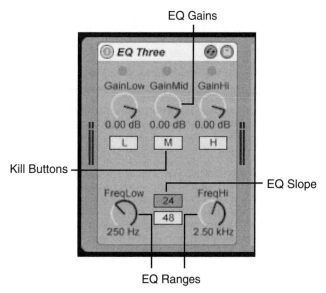

Figure 9.4 Lows, mids, and highs are under your complete control with EQ Three.

What makes the EQ Three uniquely different from other EQ plug-ins, including the EQ Eight, is its ability to completely remove, or *kill,* entire frequency ranges from your audio. You'll see that, as you turn the Gain knobs down, they'll eventually reach infinity, meaning the frequencies are completely cut. If you want, you can use the green kill buttons (labeled L, M, and H) located below each Gain knob to toggle that frequency range on and off with ease.

The 24 and 48 buttons determine the slope, either 24 dB/octave or 48 dB/octave, at the edges of the frequency bands. This setting will be most apparent when using the Kill feature of the EQ Three on a full song. For example, drag a whole song (an MP3 with lots of bass) into a clip slot and place an EQ Three on the track. Click the 48 button, place the FreqLow control at 200Hz, and kill the low band—you'll hear the bass disappear from the song. Now try clicking the 24 button. You may notice that you can hear a little more bass.

When set to 48, the EQ Three reduces the volumes of all the frequencies below 200Hz at a rate of 48 dB per octave. If your song has two tones in it with matching volumes at 100Hz and 200Hz, the 100Hz tone will sound 48 dB quieter with the EQ Three settings above. Reducing a sound by 6 dB results in the sound being half as loud as it was originally, so cutting a sound by 48 dB nearly removes it entirely. When you switch the EQ Three to 24, it now reduces the 100Hz tone by only 24 dB, thus making it slightly more audible than before.

Using the kills of the EQ Three when set to 24 will result in a smoother sounding cut, while the 48 setting will sound a little more abrupt and synthetic. You can use whichever setting suits your taste.

The EQ Three is especially useful on the Master track in Live. Go ahead and assign MIDI controllers to the EQ Three's controls and have fun sucking the bass out of the mix right before a huge drop, or slowly remove the upper elements of the music until only the gut-shaking bass is left.

Sonic Jigsaw Puzzles Try placing three different drum loops on three different tracks, each armed with an EQ Three. Then isolate the bass in one track, the mids in another, and the highs in the remaining track. You'll now have one hybrid beat consisting of kicks, snares, and hi-hats from different loops. Try swapping or automating the kills for other rhythm combinations.

Auto Filter

One of Live's greatest live performance effects, Auto Filter (seen in Figure 9.5), is a virtual, analog-style filter with four selectable classic filter types (high-pass, low-pass, band-pass, and band-reject). Each of these can be controlled via the effect's X-Y controller and modulated by an envelope and any of seven different low frequency oscillator (LFO) shapes. As you may have gleaned from the EQ Eight explanation, suppressing certain frequencies allows you to carve out specific problems or overcooked frequencies. The Auto Filter can do this as well, but it shines as a creative effect capable of a wide variety of sounds.

Filter Frenzy Low-pass, high-pass, band-pass, band-reject … what does it all mean? Low-pass simply means that the low frequencies pass through the filter, but nothing else does. For instance, your bass guitar and kick drums will be audible, though a little

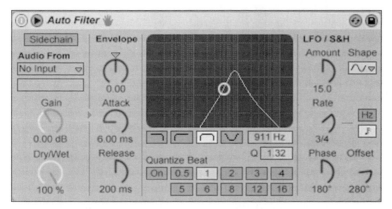

Figure 9.5 Live's Auto Filter device. If you've just been reading so far, you really need to get up and try this one. No, really.

dull-sounding due to the lack of highs. Some sounds may disappear completely, such as hi-hats. Conversely, a high-pass filter will allow shimmering cymbals and sparkly guitars and synths to pass but will suppress basses and any other instruments in the lower frequency range. How low is up to you. Band-pass filters are basically high-pass and low-pass filters put together; thus, only frequencies falling between the two filters will pass, sounding similar to a telephone at times. Band-reject filters work opposite of band-pass—only audio lying outside of the cutoff frequency can pass.

Frequency and Resonance

To get going with Live's Auto Filter, you will want to select a filter type—Low-Pass is a good starter—then use the X-Y controller to dial in Frequency (X-axis) and Q (Y-axis). The frequency range for the Auto Filter is adjustable between 46.2Hz and 12.5kHz. Increasing the Q (resonance) control will increase the intensity of the filter by adding a resonant peak to the curve, while lowering it will cause the filter to roll off more smoothly. If you really crank up the Q, you can get some very intense effects as you move the filter frequency. This can be lots of fun, but be sure to watch your volume!

LFO

To the right of the X-Y controller is the LFO, which can be used to modulate the filter frequency. The Amount knob controls the amplitude of the modulation, while the Rate controls its speed. Next to the Rate knob is the Shape menu. These waveshapes are fairly self-explanatory—the sine wave at the top creates smooth changes, while the square wave creates choppy ones. (The "Auto Pan" section, later in this chapter, contains a more thorough discussion of wave shapes.) The best way to get a feel for the different waveshapes is to crank up the Amount, add a bit of resonance, and listen. The bottom two waveshapes are random (sample and hold), the first one being mono, while the second generates separate random values for the left and right channels.

When the Phase control is set to 180 degrees, the LFO will generate opposite modulations for the left and right channels, creating a stereo effect. In other words, as the frequency of the left channel is increased, the frequency of the right channel is decreased. Increasing or decreasing the Phase will bring the phase relationship of the left and right LFOs closer together until eventually they become identical.

The Rate control can be adjusted in Hertz by clicking the Hz switch or synchronized to the tempo by clicking the switch with the note icon. Depending on which you select, there are different options available for the Phase control. When Rate is set to Hertz, two switches appear near the Phase knob. When the lower switch is clicked, the Spin knob appears. Spin changes the speed of the left and right LFOs relative to each other, creating a swirling effect. When Rate is set to tempo sync, the Offset knob appears. This can be used to create some interesting rhythmic effects. As you increase the Offset, you shift peaks and troughs of the LFO off the beat instead of right on it.

Envelope

The Envelope knob determines how much the input signal's volume will modulate the filter frequency. This type of modulator is commonly known as an *envelope follower* because it creates an envelope that "follows" the signal's amplitude. Positive values cause the filter frequency to be turned up, while negative values turn the frequency down as the volume increases.

The effect can be fine-tuned by using the Attack and Release controls. Attack determines how long it takes for the frequency to reach its maximum value, while Release determines how long it takes for it to return to its original value. Crank the Envelope knob to get familiar with these controls. Short Attack and Release times will tend to give you a funky, clucking effect since you'll get more of the filter sweep for each note. Longer times will tend to make the effect more subtle because it takes longer for the filter to open up, and it tends not to release all the way back to its original value before opening again.

DJ Magic A common DJ trick is to mix two beat-matched songs, one with a low-pass filter and the second with a high-pass filter. Whether you decide to do this with an Auto Filter or one of the EQs is up to you. The result is more than simply mixing two songs—the creation of an entirely new song is made from the combined frequencies (highs from one, lows from the other) of the two tracks. Without cutting some of the frequencies, the two songs could sound like a jumbled mush when played simultaneously. Keeping the best frequencies does require some practice and will vary according to the musical content. If you are new to this concept, it can be a huge ear opener.

Sidechain

In the figure at the beginning of this section, you may have noticed the Sidechain section of the Auto Filter to the left of the Envelope section. This section is only displayed if you click on the small triangle in the title bar. Sidechaining is new to Live 7 and opens up a whole new world of possibilities for the effects to which it has been added. (The Gate and Compressor have Sidechain sections as well.)

Sidechaining refers to having an audio source other than the one you are currently processing trigger the envelope for an effect. In other words, in the case of the Auto Filter, you can have the envelope follow the dynamics of any track in Live, instead of following the dynamics of the signal that you are processing with the Auto Filter. Let's take a look at how this works.

If you tried out the Beat Quantize example earlier, you'll want to keep working with the same sustained pad for this example as well. You'll also need another track to serve as the sidechain source. This can be an audio or a MIDI track, but it should output something percussive with strong transients. Now, in the Sidechain section, set the Source to the percussion track, as seen in Figure 9.6. Also, make sure the LFO Amount is set to 0. There's no reason you can't use the LFO at the same time, but for learning purposes, it's best to keep it simple.

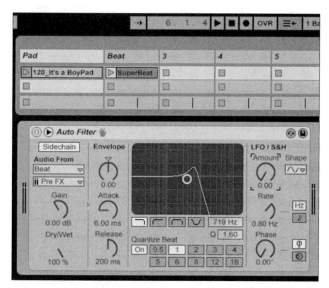

Figure 9.6 Specify a Sidechain input to have the envelope of your Auto Filter follow a different audio source.

Now, play back both clips and slowly raise the Envelope control. As you do this. you'll hear the filter on the pad begin to rise and fall with the hits in the drum loop. If you're not getting enough of an effect even with the envelope cranked, you can increase the gain to feed more signal to the sidechain. The Wet/Dry knob controls how much the sidechain signal is mixed with the direct signal before it is sent to the envelope. In the current example, a setting of 50% would mean that the envelope would follow the dynamics of a 50/50 blend of the drum loop and the pad. At 0%, the sidechain is bypassed completely.

Quantize Beat

The Quantize Beat parameter affects filter modulation (generated by either the LFO or the envelope) by forcing the filter frequency to change in tempo-synchronized steps. The steps are specified in 16ths ranging from .5 (32nd notes) to 16 (1 bar). To get a feel for what this Quantize Beat does, load it on a track with a sustained pad and configure the Auto Filter, as shown in Figure 9.7. You may have to adjust the frequency so you hear a nice up-and-down sweep. Now, try clicking the On switch a few times. As it goes on and off, you'll hear the modulation go from a smooth sweep to a choppier sound. This is the sound of the filter frequency jumping to a new value once every 16th note. Now you can experiment with other Beat values and play with the Phase as well.

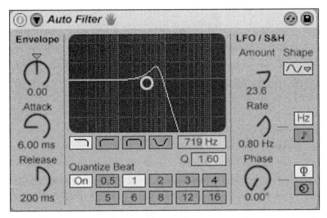

Figure 9.7 Quantize Beat can chop up and tempo-synchronize an otherwise smooth filter sweep.

Pre or Post? In the sidechain example above, you may have noticed that the Sidechain Source is set to Pre FX (refer to Figure 9.6). This is because we want to tap the signal before it gets to the mixer. By using either the Pre or Post FX setting, we can mute the Sidechain track in Live's Mixer and still have it reach the Sidechain input. This way, you can get the rhythmic envelope without having to hear the drum loop! Pre FX is especially useful if you have some heavy effects on a track, but you want to use that sound unaffected to control an envelope.

Dynamic Processing

What are dynamics again? *Dynamics* in audio refers to the volume or amplitude of a sound. More specifically, it refers to the *change* in volume of a sound. The sound of a drum kit can range from quiet ghost notes on a snare drum up to the thundering sound of the kick drum and toms, and it is therefore considered to have more dynamic range than a distorted guitar, which usually plays at a more consistent volume.

It therefore makes sense that dynamic processors would alter the volume of signals passing through them. But why would you want to do this? Like EQing above, dynamic processing can be used to compensate for problems arising in the recording process. It can also be used to help parts stick out from a mix or to create dramatic, volume-based effects.

Auto Pan

The simplest dynamic processing effect to understand is the Auto Pan. It will automatically pan the position of the track from left to right in cycles. It does this by alternately turning down the volumes of the left and right sides of the channel. When the left side is turned down, the sound will be heard from the right, thus making it sound as if the track were panned to the left. The mixer's Pan control is not affected at all.

The Auto Pan interface is split into two sections. The top section contains a graphical representation of the volume pattern being applied—for display purposes only. The Auto Pan is adjusted by using the knobs and buttons on the lower half of the interface.

When the device is first loaded, it will have a flat line through the middle of its display, and you will hear no effect. The reason you hear nothing is because the Amount knob is set to 0%. As you turn this knob up, you'll hear the sound begin moving left and right. The higher you set the Amount knob, the "wider" the left-to-right movement will be.

As you increase the Amount knob, you'll also see the graphic begin to change on the Auto Pan interface. When the Amount reaches 100%, you'll see two sine curves on the screen in different colors. The blue curve represents the left channel, and the orange curve represents the right channel. What these curves tell you is that when the left channel is at full volume (the highest point of the blue curve), the right channel will be at its lowest volume (see Figure 9.8). As the left channel drops in volume, the right channel will rise, and vice versa. The button below the Amount knob will switch the left and right pan assignments when it is activated; in this case, you'll see the colors of the two sine curves change.

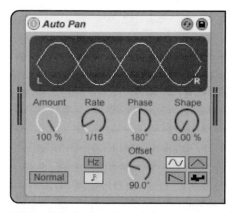

Figure 9.8   By looking at the picture in the Auto Pan window, you can see the relationship of the left and right channels over time.

The Rate knob next to the Amount knob will change the speed of the left-right motion created by the Auto Pan. You'll see that as you turn up this knob, not only does the left-right speed increase, but you'll also see the graphic waveform change in kind.

Below the Rate knob are two selection buttons. By default Hz is shown, meaning that you will define the rate of the Auto Pan in terms of cycles per second. So, if you set the Rate knob to 1Hz, the Auto Pan will complete one left-right cycle in one second. If you increase the value to 2Hz, the left-right pattern will happen twice every second, and so on. If you click on the button that looks like a 1/16 note, you will be able to define the Auto Pan cycle time in terms of beats. For example, when set to 1/4, the left-right pattern will repeat every quarter note. If you change the tempo of the Live Set, the Auto Pan will also change to maintain the cycle-per-beat relationship.

Next on the list of Auto Pan controls is the Phase knob. If you move this knob while watching the waveform graphic, you should get a pretty good idea of what it does. The knob adjusts the phase relationship of the left and right curves, or the position where the waveforms start. When set to 180 degrees, the two curves are out of phase, meaning one channel is at full volume while the other is silent. If you twist this knob down to 0 degrees, the two curves will now be in sync (you'll see only one curve), resulting in the left and right channels' changing volume in sync. The Auto Pan will no longer pan the signal from left to right—it will simply turn the volume of the whole signal up and down! This is where the Auto Pan device begins to function beyond what its name implies. We'll show you how to take advantage of this in a couple of ways.

There is a pair of buttons below the Phase knob. When you click the bottom one, the Phase knob turns into a Spin control. What this does is alter the rates of the left and right waveforms. With Spin at 0%, the left and right run at the same speed. As you increase Spin, you'll see that the right channel begins to increase in rate compared with the left channel. With this feature enabled, the sound will no longer appear to pan back and forth between the left and right. Instead, a strange wobbly pattern will result.

Before we get into the tricks, though, let's finish looking at all of the Auto Pan's controls. Below the Phase knob is the Offset knob. This is essentially a global phase knob, as it changes the phase of both curves in relation to the song. This is extremely helpful when the Rate is synced to the song tempo. When you start the song and the offset is at 0, the Auto Pan will output only the left signal. At the beginning of the song, however, you may want the pan to start in the middle. To do this, turn the Offset knob until the graphic display shows the two waveforms crossing each other at 90% at the left edge of the window, as shown in Figure 9.8.

The last knob on the Auto Pan is the Shape knob. As this knob is turned clockwise, the waveform will slowly morph into a square wave. When set to 100%, this will cause the Auto Pan to flip-flop the audio between the left and right channels—there will be no motion through the center. Of course, setting this knob at an amount less than 100% will allow you to hear some of the left-right transition.

In real terms, we use this knob to make the pan "stall" at the left and right extremes. Sometimes, even though the Amount knob is set to 100%, it doesn't sound like the sound is fully panning from left to right, especially when being mixed in with the other parts of the song. This is because the sound is panned fully left and right for only an instant before the Auto Pan begins to pan it back again. Turning up the Shape knob results in flat lines at the top and bottom of the waveform, therefore causing the pan motion to sit at these extremes for a moment before panning back to the other side. The result is a more pronounced panning motion that can be heard better over an entire mix.

The final controls of the Auto Pan are the Waveform Selection buttons. You've been using the sine waveform thus far, so try clicking on some of the others to see what they look like. The button in the upper-right is for the triangle waveform. As the name suggests, the waveform looks like a triangle at the top and bottom. When using this waveform, the left-right pan motion is linear—the left-to-right speed remains constant. This is different from the sine waveform, where the pan motion would slow down as it reached the left and right extremes. The button in the lower-left is for the sawtooth, or ramp, waveform. This is a unique waveform in that it does not create a smooth side-to-side panning motion. Instead, it will pan a sound in one direction (determined by the Normal/Invert button) and then immediately reset before panning again. This means that the motion goes from left to right and then immediately to left before panning to the right again. The last button in the lower-right is for a random waveform where the volumes of the left and right channels are changed at random. You'll notice that when this waveform is selected, the Phase knob changes to Width. This knob will adjust the left-right deviation of the randomness. When set to 0%, the random pattern will influence the left and right volumes identically, resulting in random changes to the sound's volume. When set to 100%, the difference between the left and right volumes will increase, resulting in random panning patterns.

So what were all those secrets and tricks I was alluding to earlier in this section? The secrets involve using the Auto Pan for something other than panning. This stems from the use of the Phase knob. When Phase is set to 0 degrees, the Auto Pan will simply turn the volume of the sound up and down. Try this out: Load a song onto a track and use Auto Pan. Set its Rate to 1/8, Shape to 100%, Phase to 0 degrees, Offset to 270 degrees, and Waveform to sine. As you increase the Amount knob, you'll begin to hear the track volume jump up and down in 1/8-note steps in sync with the song. Turn up Amount to 100%, and you'll have chopped the song into tiny slices!

Now that you've got the strobe effect going, start playing with the Rate knob to change the speed of the strobe. Turning the Shape knob below 100% will also reduce the abruptness of the strobing. For a really crazy effect, try slightly altering the Phase knob. When the two waveforms are just slightly out of phase, you'll hear each strobe zip across your speakers as one side is turned on just slightly before the other.

This strobe effect is great to use during a DJ set, especially when mixing between two tracks. You can use it to remove all of the sound between the beats (set the Rate to 1/4, and you'll only hear the 1/4-note beats) making the transitional mix smoother. This can also be a great effect to use on vocals from time to time.

Compressor

Compression can add clarity and power to your mixes if done properly. Done wrong, it can suck all life from what once was a brilliant track. For audio engineers, compression is one of the hardest things to learn to use properly and is one element that separates the big fish from the little guppies. Live used to have two compressors: Compressor I and Compressor II. In Live 7, both of these models have been wrapped into a new device simply called *Compressor*, which contains not only the functionality of both of its predecessors, but many new features as well. But before we get into the details of this device, let's spend some time discussing the basics of compression.

Compression Basics

In brief, a compressor is a device that will automatically turn down the volume of sound passing through it. For example, have you ever noticed how the commercials on TV are louder than the show you're trying to watch? This isn't your imagination—it's true. They play the commercials louder as a way to get your attention. For most of us, it just makes us reach for the remote or run from the room. Wouldn't it be great if you could buy something that would turn down the TV whenever something loud came on? It would keep the commercials at the same volume as the TV show, and it would also keep loud things like car explosions from blasting your neighbors awake in the middle of the night. Well, that something you'd buy would be a compressor.

So you go out and you buy this compressor for your TV. You hook it up, but there are a few settings you have to choose before it will work. The first one is called Volume Trigger. You set this one to the volume where the box should start killing the volume. You set this to a point just slightly louder than the TV show you're watching. This guarantees that the compressor doesn't turn down your show at all. However, when a commercial comes on, it will be louder than the Volume Trigger, and the compressor will engage.

The next control you're supposed to set on this thing is the Kill Amount. The deal is that, when the compressor engages as a result of the Volume Trigger being exceeded, the volume will be turned down by the Kill Amount. Setting this to infinity makes the compressor turn down the volume to match the Volume Trigger. Thus, the commercial is turned down to the volume of the TV show.

The third setting is the Cutout Time. This setting sets the time the compressor takes to turn down the volume once the commercials start. If this value is set to a long time, like five seconds, the compressor will take five seconds to turn down the volume when the commercial comes on. The point here is to cut the volume on the commercial the moment it comes on, so you set the time to 10ms. Now, the commercial is turned down within 10ms of coming on.

The last value is Back-in Time. This is the opposite of the Cutout Time where you now specify how long it should take for the compressor to turn the volume back up again after the commercials are over. You don't want to miss any of the dialogue when the show starts, so you set this to one second.

So that's it; you've now mastered the compressor. It turns down commercials that exceed the volume of your TV show within 10ms and then returns the volume to normal one second after the commercials are over. Nice.

If you've looked at a compressor at all, hardware or software, you know that we replaced the real names of the controls with fake, yet more descriptive, names in the television commercial examples above. Here's the decoder: The Volume Trigger is really the Threshold control. The Kill Amount refers to the Ratio. Cutout Time and Back-in Time refer to Attack and Release, respectively. You will see all of these controls on Live's Compressor, shown in Figure 9.9.

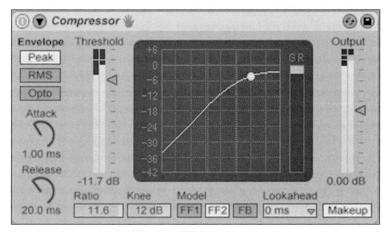

Figure 9.9   Here is Live's Compressor.

Many people believe that a compressor makes sounds louder. But, as you can see in the illustration above, a compressor makes loud sounds quieter. Still, engineers do employ compressors as part of a technique for making sounds louder. Compressors make the dynamic range of audio smaller, so the overall level can be higher. Imagine that you have some audio that ranges from −30 dB to 0 dB. If we compress the audio such that every peak over −10 dB is reduced to be no greater than −10 dB, we can then raise the level of the whole signal by 10 dB. Now we have audio that ranges from −20 dB to 0 dB, resulting in a much greater perceived loudness.

It's not too hard to understand what a compressor does or what the various controls are supposed to do. What is difficult is to determine whether you need compression and how to set the compressor when you do. You may have a hard time hearing a part in the mix, but sometimes the fix is simple, like a little boost of an EQ band, or simply turning up the part. Other times, compression is just what is called for. When learning, it's best to work with dramatic settings on your compressor (low Threshold, high Ratio) because it makes the compression easier to hear. In your final mixes, however, its best to err to the side of less compression until you really know what you're doing.

Threshold, Ratio, Attack, and Release

Compression is useful in two main situations: keeping wily transients under control and smoothing out the overall dynamic content of a part over a length of time. Examples of parts with lots of transients are drums and vocals. The "crack" created when a drumstick hits a drum can be extraordinarily loud in comparison to the lingering tone of the drum. Vocals also tend to have all sorts of sudden transients as singers change their volume or position or occasionally overemphasize consonants in the lyrics.

How do you properly compress a sound with a lot of transients? The technique involved is nearly identical to the process used to set the compressor for the TV in the example above. You need to identify the volume at which you want to start compressing, how much to compress once the volume reaches that point, and how quickly the Compressor should respond. In order to set the Threshold to the proper level, you'll need to be able to see the point where the Compressor starts to work on your sound. To do this, set the Ratio (the Kill Amount) to the maximum, reduce the Attack (Cutout Time) to its minimum, and set the Release (Back-in Time) to 500ms. Place the Threshold (Volume Trigger) at its highest setting and start playing the sound. With the Threshold at maximum, the sound will not exceed this level, and the Compressor will never engage. As you start to move the Threshold downward, there will be a point where you notice that the Gain Reduction meter starts to respond. This means you've found the Threshold at which some of the transients are loud enough to trigger the Compressor. As you keep moving the Threshold slider downward, the Gain Reduction meter will begin to respond more often and will also show a greater amount of attenuation.

If you keep reducing the Threshold, there will come a point where nearly every element of the sound you're compressing, the transients and the quieter tones, will all be beyond the Threshold, thus causing the Compressor to work nonstop—always in some state of gain reduction. This is a sign that you are probably using too much compression, as nearly every element of the sound is being attenuated. Back off the Threshold to a point where only the heavy transients are triggering the Gain Reduction meter.

The compressor's Ratio control determines the amount of compression expressed as a ratio of the input volume to the output volume. For instance, 2-to-1 compression means that when a sound goes over the threshold by 2 dB, you will hear only a 1 dB increase at the output. And 4 to 1 would mean that for a 2 dB increase, only a 1/2 dB change would be audible at the output. You may also notice that for larger Ratio settings, the sound may become muffled or muted as a result of the volume squashing what is going on. As you dial in your compression for a given track, you will want to watch the downward-spiking indicator on the Gain Reduction meter. Extreme gain reduction, such as −12 dB and below, will often cut the life out of your sound, although you may occasionally want to overcompress an instrument as a special effect.

Compressor's other two controls, Attack and Release, determine how soon after a sound crosses the threshold the compression will begin to work and how long the compression remains active after the sound has dropped below the threshold. Typically, a small amount of attack time

(5 to 10ms) is best for retaining some sense of dynamics (varying degrees of loud and soft in the music). Short attacks are great for instruments like drums and percussion, as well as vocals. Longer attacks are most often used with horns, bass, and longer sorts of sounds where the volume increase (crescendo) is also slower.

A compressor's release settings are often less noticeable when long. A long release time means that the compression continues to work for a given length of time (in milliseconds) after it has been engaged and the signal level has dipped back below the threshold. Typically, a short release time will force the compressor to repeatedly engage and disengage (start and stop), and a listener will be more apt to hear the repeated contrasts (sometimes referred to as *pumping* or *breathing*), as well as low-frequency distortion. Short release times can still be a cool-sounding effect for drums and diced-up pieces of audio (where the signal repeatedly crosses the threshold).

If you've been experimenting with the Compressor, at this point you've probably noticed that even though we've been applying all sorts of "gain reduction," the signal isn't getting softer—in fact, it's been getting louder. This is due to the Makeup switch (in the lower-left corner) being activated. It's automatically compensating for the amount of gain reduction being applied to the peaks and bringing up the overall level of the signal. While this works nicely, there might be times where you just want to turn down errant peaks without bringing up the overall level. To do this, just turn off Makeup. Whether or not it's turned on, you can always tweak the output level using the Level control.

Knee

The Knee control is called that because it adjusts the point in the compression graph where the line bends, i.e., the "knee." As the knee is increased, the bend in the line rounds out. What this represents is the Ratio and the Threshold becoming more dynamic and gradually applying gain reduction as the signal approaches the Threshold.

Especially with high ratios, the sound produced by compressors can be harsh and unnatural. This is partly caused by a compressor leaving a signal completely unprocessed and then slamming on the gain reduction every time the threshold is passed—a behavior known as "hard-knee" compression. By increasing the knee, we can specify a range of decibels below the threshold over which gain reduction should be applied. In other words, with a Threshold of −10 dB, a Ratio of 10:1, and a Knee of 10 dB, a small amount of gain reduction will occur to signals hitting −20 dB (the Threshold minus the Knee value). For signals between −20 dB and −10 dB an increasing amount of gain reduction will be applied until the full Ratio of 10:1 is reached for signals exceeding −10 dB. The result of this "soft-knee" compression is that the dynamic structure of the Compressor's output is closer to the original signal, and a more natural sound is produced.

Kick Me! (Part 2) After you've used the EQ Eight to dial in a nice kick drum tone, place a Compressor on the track. You'll use the Compressor to shape the amplitude of the kick sound just like using an ADSR envelope on a synth.

The setting for the Ratio dial depends on the amount of attack already present in the kick sound. If there's already a decent amount of punch, a ratio of 4 to 1 may be all that's necessary. If the kick is flat and has no life, a 10-to-1 ratio may be in order.

You'll need a fairly short attack time, somewhere in the neighborhood of 5 to 20ms. If the attack is too short, the drum will sound short, snappy, and clipped.

Use a slightly longer setting for the release, 25 to 50ms, depending on the bass drum's acoustics. If the drum has a long tone (perhaps there was no padding inside), a longer release will keep the tail end of the tone from popping up in volume after the loud transient of the drum has passed. If, on the other hand, the drum has a short tone or if the drum is played quickly, a short release time will allow the Compressor to fully open before the next drum hit. If the release time is too long, only the first kick drum hit will sound right, while the others that follow shortly after will not sound right because the Compressor is still attenuating the signal.

The threshold should be at a point where every kick played at normal volume will trigger the Compressor. But if the threshold is too low, the Compressor will squash the volume and never let go!

Compression Models

Along the bottom of the Compressor, you'll see three different compression models. FF1 and FF2 are the old Compressor I and II models, while FB is a new model that has been introduced in Live 7. FB stands for feed back—the type of circuit design in the classic compressors upon which this model was based. FF stands for feed forward, a more contemporary type of compressor design. In brief, feed back compressors have their level detection circuit at the output of the compressor—after the gain reduction circuit. While this may sound awfully strange, it resulted in a very pleasing sound that is still much sought after today. The Teletronix LA-2A, the UA 1176LN, and the API 525 are all feed back compressors. Feed forward compressors offer more accurate attack and release times, so they can be very useful in shaping transients (think kick and snare).

FF1 is an effect-oriented compressor. Use it when you want something to sound compressed. It's great at getting a squashed, over-compressed sound and can really make a drum loop pop out. It should, however, be used sparingly and deliberately. Too much of this sort of compression will probably make your mixes sound lifeless and somewhat harsh. FF2 is a more refined compressor and can be used to shape transients with a much greater degree of transparency. FB is the most subtle of the bunch. Try this one out on vocals, and you'll be surprised at how much gain reduction you can apply before it starts to sound squashed. The FB model is great for thickening and adding some additional heft to your sounds.

Envelope Modes

This is where you control the behavior of the Compressor's level detector. In Peak mode, the Compressor will respond to any signal that goes over the threshold, whereas RMS responds more slowly and will have less effect on transients. The advantage to RMS is that when applying compression to complex sources, such as an entire mix, you may not always want an overall gain reduction in response to an individual transient. However, since RMS will allow transients greater than the threshold to pass straight through, it's not well suited to anything where you need very accurate control, such as drums.

Opto is a different beast entirely. This emulates the behavior of compressors that use a light source and a photo-sensitive element to detect gain. Again, this tends to create smoother, more natural sounding compression at the expense of accuracy. In conjunction with FB mode, you can get some really wonderful, natural sounding compression. Try comparing Opto to Peak with the FF2 model and a low threshold/high ratio combination. You'll hear some pronounced differences, with Peak mode likely being a bit evener, but Opto a bit more lively—even to the point of breathing, or pumping, often in a musical way.

Towards the lower left-hand corner, you'll also see a menu called *Lookahead*. Because compressors are responding to audio in real time, they typically suffer from the attack responding a bit too late. By increasing the Lookahead amount, you can increase the Compressor's accuracy in responding to fast transients. Lookahead is disabled for the Feed Back Compressor model because looking ahead just isn't possible when you're detecting gain changes from the Compressor's output. Anyway, this isn't the type of compressor you want to be using for ultra-fast and accurate compression.

Sidechain

Expanding the Sidechain section (see Figure 9.10) reveals a more complex set of controls compared to the Gate and Auto Filter. To the left, you'll see the familiar Sidechain controls, which work

Figure 9.10 The Sidechain section features an EQ so you can trigger compression using only certain frequencies of the sidechain source. The settings here show how you might trigger bass compression using the kick drum in a drum loop.

exactly as described in the "Auto Filter" section of this chapter. To the right is the Sidechain EQ section, which allows you to equalize the sidechain source before it triggers the Compressor. Please note that the sidechain determines only what the Compressor hears—EQ will not process the output signal. A classic use of sidechain compression is to use the kick drum to trigger gain reduction in the bass track. This helps solve the problem of competing frequencies in the low end of a mix.

But what if your kick drum is already mixed into a drum loop? No problem. Once you've set the sidechain input to the track that your drum loop is on, enable the EQ section. Now, solo the bass track and click the headphones icon (Sidechain Listen) directly to the left of the EQ switch. Now you're hearing the sidechain source (the drum loop) instead of the bass track. Select the low-pass filter and bring the frequency down until most of the other drums disappear. Now you can turn off Sidechain Listen and tweak the Compressor controls until you're getting the desired amount of gain reduction. You can even adjust the Wet/Dry mix and boost the Sidechain Gain control so you're getting compression triggered both by the kick and the bass.

The Sidechain EQ can also be used without an external sidechain source. In this case, a copy of the audio that you are compressing is used to feed the sidechain. This technique is frequently used for *de-essing,* which is the process of softening the sharp "sss" sound that can occur in vocal parts. By filtering out all the lower frequencies or boosting the sibilant frequencies (often 8kHz and higher), you can force the Compressor to respond only when a strong "sss" escapes the vocalist's lips. Typically, this will require some careful tweaking of the threshold and a very fast attack.

Gate

Gates can be thought of as backward compressors, and therefore the two are often discussed (and used) together. Where compressors focus on reducing volume spikes above a certain threshold, gates help weed out low-level noise beneath a certain threshold. The result of using a gate is usually a cleaner, less cluttered, and overall more pleasing audio signal. Gates are a tool for reducing quiet hums, microphone bleed, and background. That said, Live's Gate device is an excellent utility for this kind of work.

A gate effect operates just like it sounds. Certain audio can make it through the gate while other audio cannot. The threshold, or minimum requirement, to get through an audio gating effect is set by the Threshold slider. Any incoming sound quieter than the threshold will cause the gate to close, thus attenuating the signal. Gating can be an excellent effect to apply when attempting to eliminate excess noise, hiss, hum, or undesirable reverb decay. You may find that a slight gate effect can really clean up your drum loops. Many producers use gates on drums like toms or snares so that they can capture the essence of the instrument at its highest volume point and eliminate all weaker background sounds. Figure 9.11 shows Live's Gate effect.

The small triangle next to the Threshold bar can be dragged with the mouse to set the minimum level of output required to pass through the gate. The lower the threshold, the more sound gets through the gate. As sound passes through the gate, you will see the small circular LED light flicker.

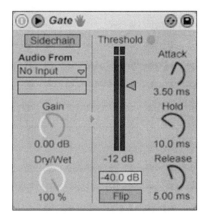

Figure 9.11 Live's Gate effect.

All or Nothing? So far, we've discussed a gate as a tool only for completely removing quiet audio signals from your tracks. From time to time, you may desire a milder effect where some sound still gets through even while the gate is closed. This is commonly used for toms so that part of the decay and tone from the toms still sits quietly in the mix even after the initial attack has passed. If the gate closes completely, it may sound like the toms are overdubbed or pasted into the composition as they pop in and out of the mix. To remedy this, the Gate effect has a numerical value right below the Threshold slider. The default setting is −40 dB, which means the gate will reduce the incoming sound by 40 dB when it's closed. Try raising this value while the gate is closed, and you'll hear more of the input signal bleed through. Of course, if you're looking for a brick wall gate effect, reduce the range to −inf.

The Attack, Hold, and Release settings determine how the gate effect is applied. For instance, a sharp/short attack will make the gate open quickly when the threshold is exceeded, sometimes resulting in harsh, audible clicks. A longer attack will sound more relaxed as the gate takes longer to close on sound crossing the volume threshold. Be aware that having a long attack time may cause the gate to open after the initial attack of the sound has already passed. Use this setting judiciously.

Similarly, the Hold and Release functions affect how long the gate remains open after the signal has fallen below the threshold. Think of Attack as how quickly the gate will open, and Release and Hold as relating to how quickly the gate will close. The Flip switch turns the gate upside down—only signals *below* the threshold will get passed. While not often the most practical thing, the Flip switch can be used to generate some interesting glitchy effects on your beats.

The sidechain opens up loads of creative possibilities for the gate. Its settings are identical to those described in detail in the "Auto Filter" section. Try the Auto Filter example (involving a sustained pad and a drum loop) with the Gate. By opening and closing the Gate using a beat, you can turn the pad into a chopped-up rhythm part.

Delay Effects

Ableton's Delay effects group may just be the company's most creative effects ever. Each effect features solid tools for assembling new rhythmic variations and creating innovative textures with repeated long sounds. While many of the Delays have some similar controls, each Delay is also somewhat specialized and has some unique features. As you explore them one by one, don't be afraid to do lots of experimenting and get lost in your own creativity.

Simple Delay

While you may think we are starting simple, Live's Simple Delay (seen in Figure 9.12) is still a formidable stereo, tempo-syncable delay, with a rhythmic beat-division chooser.

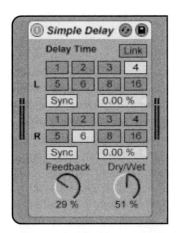

Figure 9.12   Live's Simple Delay plug-in.

Looking at the device, you can see two separate beat-division choosers—one for the left channel and one for the right. If you are in Sync mode—where the small sync box is illuminated in green—each boxed number represents a multiple of the 1/16-note delay time. For instance, choosing a 4 would mean a four-1/16-note delay, or a full 1/4-note hold before you would hear the delayed note sound. An 8 would be two beats, and 16 would be four beats—typically an entire measure. In either of the beat-division choosers, you can select 1, 2, 3, 4, 5, 6, 8, or 16 for your delay multiple.

As mentioned, this beat dividing works only if the green Sync button is depressed for that channel (right or left). *Sync* means that the delay is set to synchronize with the song tempo (beats per minute). If you disengage the Sync, you can manually set delay time with precision of up to 1/100 of a second by click-dragging (up or down) on the time field box. Note: With Sync engaged, this same box allows adjustment of the delay time by a percentage. This means that you are slowing or speeding up the delay below or above the current project tempo. In other words, you can add a little slop, or even approximate a triplet, if your delays are sounding too strict.

Delay Relay By setting extremely short delay times (less than 30ms with the Sync off), you can create some wild thickening, phasing, and metallic-sounding effects. To hear what I'm talking about, try setting both delay times to 1, 10, and then 30ms, with the Dry/Wet set to 30% and Feedback set to 70%. Although these effects may not result in a lingering discernible delay, these flaming, buzzing, and biting sounds can be a creative playground.

The Dry/Wet knob determines how much of the effect versus original sound you hear. *Dry* is the term audio engineers use to refer to the original sound, while *wet* is the delayed or affected sound. A setting of 12 o'clock, or 50%, for Dry/Wet will create a delay signal that is at the same volume as the original. A 100% Wet setting means that you will no longer hear the original sound, only the delay effect.

Feedback controls the duration and intensity of the effect. By increasing the percentage of Feedback, you raise the effect's signal output to its own input. The circular signal created by Feedback will radically shape the delay, from slapback echo (short delay time, low feedback) to a wild echo chamber potentially spiraling out of control (with large amounts of feedback).

All Wet When effects plug-ins are located in one of the Return tracks, it is generally best to set the Wet/Dry setting to 100% wet. Since the original source sound is likely still audible through Live's Mixer, there is no need to route this signal again through the effect.

Ping Pong Delay

Like a game of Ping-Pong, Ableton's Ping Pong Delay (pictured in Figure 9.13) plays a game of stereo tennis with your sound by serving it up from left to right. In looking at this device, you may notice that many of the controls are similar to the Simple Delay covered earlier. Like Simple Delay, Ping Pong Delay is a stereo delay with built-in tempo synchronizing ability and sports the same delay-time beat-division chooser boxes, as well as the same Dry/Wet and Feedback controls; however, Ping Pong Delay is a little more creative in terms of what frequencies actually get delayed (repeated). You will find a band-pass filter, complete with an adjustable X-Y controller axis to adjust both the cutoff frequency and the width of the frequency band (the Q). You can select between 50Hz and 18kHz and a Q from .5 to 9 dB.

Notice that the same Sync and delay time boxes are also present in Ping Pong Delay. When Sync is activated, Ping Pong Delay will rhythmically synchronize your audio delays—from left to

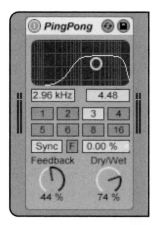

Figure 9.13   Live's Ping Pong Delay bounces a signal from left to right.

right—according to your beat-division chooser. Once you deactivate the Sync, you can set the delay time manually from 1 to 999ms.

For those of you who have used Live for a while, you may have missed the update to the Ping Pong Delay—a tiny little button labeled *F*. This is the Freeze button. When activated, it will cause the Ping Pong Delay to repeat indefinitely without fading away and without adding new audio into the loop. Therefore, you can "freeze" what is repeating by activating this button. When you deactivate it, the delay will continue to decay and repeat as normal.

Rub-a-Dub Thanks to the Band-Pass filter in the Ping Pong Delay, it's possible to simulate old tape-style delays. Every time a sound feeds back through the Ping Pong Delay, it passes through the filter and has part of its sonic character changed.

Set the filter frequency to about 200Hz; then set the Q to somewhere around 5. Crank the feedback up all the way and send a single sound, a snare for example, through the effect and listen to it bounce back and forth. As the sound is repeatedly delayed, you'll notice that it gets darker and darker. This is because the filter is removing the high-frequency character of the sound as it repeats. Try automating the Band-Pass filter as it repeats for more dub-style goodness.

Filter Delay

Next in Live's group of delay effects is the powerful Filter Delay. This effect is actually three delays in one: one stereo delay and two mono delays—one on each stereo channel. Individual delays can be toggled on and off via the L, L + R, and R boxes on the far left, seen in Figure 9.14. Similarly, each high- and low-pass filter can also be switched on and off via the green box labeled *On* (default setting) in the upper left-hand corner next to the X-Y controllers.

EQ/Delay Band   Filter Dots   EQ Output
(on/off)   (click and drag)   Pan & Volume

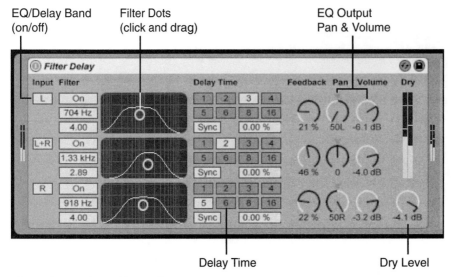

Delay Time   Dry Level

Figure 9.14   Live's Filter Delay.

The Filter Delay device is made up of three individual delays, each with its own filter. The X-Y controllers work in the same way as the Ping Pong Delay. The Y-axis determines the bandwidth (Q), while the X-axis shifts the frequency. Each delay also features its own beat-division chooser with tempo-syncable delay times.

On the right-hand side of the plug-in, you will see Feedback, Pan, and Volume controls specific to each delay. Each feedback control will reroute the delayed signal back though that delay's input (just like all Live delays). Each delay's Pan knob can be used to override its default setting. For instance, if you pan the L delay (top delay) to the right side (with the top Pan knob), you will hear it on the right. Volume controls the wet signal or delayed signal for each delay. Finally, a lone Dry control knob is located in the upper right-hand corner. For a 100% wet signal, turn the Dry setting to 0.

Super-Spacey Echo To achieve truly cosmic delay dispersion, set the filter on the L delay channel to approximately 7kHz, the L + R channel to 1kHz, and the R channel to 140Hz. Set all Qs to 2.0. Pan the L channel hard-left, the R channel hard-right, and the L + R channel in the center. Choose the same delay value for all three channels, but offset the L channel by −1% and the R channel by +1%. Leave the feedback at 0 for all channels at this point.

Now, when a sound is fed into the Filter Delay, the resulting slapback will happen in stereo. The L channel, which is only high-frequency content, will sound first from the left speaker. The L + R channel will happen next, providing the mid-range component from both speakers. The R channel will follow all of this by giving us the low-frequency content on the right. This makes the delay image in stereo, plus the image moves from left to right as it happens.

Try experimenting with different time offsets to intensify the panning effect. Increasing the feedback on the channels will cause the delay to trail off in three different directions.

Grain Delay

Grain Delay is among Live's more complex and creative effects. The Grain Delay is the same as Live's other delays in that it has many of the same controls—Delay Time, Feedback, Dry/Wet mix, and Beat Quantize settings. While the other delays we've seen so far had a filter at the input stage, the Grain Delay has a granular resynthesizer instead. The basic concept is that Grain Delay dissects audio into tiny grains, staggers the delay timing of these grains, and then opens up a toolbox full of pitch, randomized pitch, and spray controls for some far-out sound design results. While all the common delay controls exist in this device, the lion's share of the Grain Delay interface (seen in Figure 9.15) is taken up by a large parameter-assignable X-Y controller.

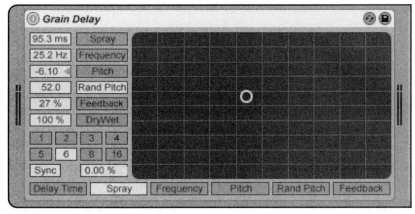

Figure 9.15   Live's Grain Delay takes audio apart and randomly reassigns the pitch before replaying the sound.

With Grain Delay's X-Y interface, you can quickly control two parameters of your choosing (one for X and one for Y) to allow for some wild interaction. Make sure you choose two different modifiers to achieve the maximum tweak factor. Hint: Try using Feedback on one axis and then choose either Random P(itch), Pitch, or Frequency on the other.

Frequency

This is the second parameter in the delay interface, but its setting affects all the others, so I'll explain it first. In the Grain Delay, small grains of sound are quickly dispersed. The Frequency setting determines the size and duration of each grain that will be subsequently delayed and can range from 1 to 150Hz. The default setting of 60Hz means that each second of incoming audio is divided into 60 grains. This means that a low setting creates a large grain, while higher settings create smaller grains. High Frequency settings (lots of small grains) will help keep sounds with rhythmical timing, such as drum loops, intact through the resynthesis process. Low-frequency settings will sound more natural for long sounds, such as textures and pads. If you are having trouble getting a desirable setting out of the Grain Delay, set the Frequency to 150 and work backwards from there.

Spray

The Spray parameter roughs up the sound, adding noise and garble to the delayed signal. This setting will allow the Grain Delay to choose a random delay offset amount for each grain. If the Frequency setting above is a high value, the effect of Spray will be more pronounced, as there are more grains to randomize every second. The delay time for Spray can range from 0 to 500ms. Small values tend to create a fuzzy-sounding delay effect, while a larger Spray setting will completely take apart the original signal.

Pitch versus Random Pitch

Like the Spray parameter, Random Pitch tends to throw sound around. The amount of randomness can range from 0 to 161 in terms of intensity (0 being the lowest intensity). The plain old Pitch parameter ranges from 12 to −36 half steps, while allowing for two-decimal-point interim values. In other words, fine-tuning a delayed signal's pitch to an actual, discernible tone would be best suited for the Pitch control; trying to eliminate, destroy, or add movement to a pitched signal is the strength of high Random Pitch values. You can use Pitch and Random Pitch in tandem for some robotic and wild pitch modifications. As with the Spray control above, the higher the Frequency setting, the more pronounced the Random Pitch effect will be as there are more grains to be resynthesized.

Putting Grain Delay to Use

Now that you have some idea of just what kind of mischief the Grain Delay is up to, it's time to get familiar with using Grain Delay's X-Y interface.

Along the X (horizontal) interface, lining the bottom portion of the effect, you will see the boxes for Delay Time, Spray, Frequency, Pitch, Random Pitch, and Feedback. The vertical Y-axis can be set to control Spray, Frequency, Pitch, Random Pitch, Feedback, and Dry/Wet controls. Each parameter's current value will be displayed in the respective boxes on the left-hand side of the device, regardless of which axis is set to adjust them.

Any parameters set to correspond to X or Y can be controlled by moving the yellow circle. Vertical moves affect the Y-axis, while horizontal moves alter the X-axis. Exactly which parameters you control are up to you. To set feedback to be controlled by the Y-axis, simply click on the vertically aligned box labeled *Feedback* just above the Dry/Wet setting. To enable the X-axis to control the delay time (in terms of beat division), click on the Delay Time box while Sync is activated. To control actual delay time, disengage the Sync button by clicking on it, and you can set the delay from 1 to 128ms.

Shift My Pitch Up One of the more straightforward applications for the Grain Delay is to provide an echo at a pitch different from the original track. Leave the Spray and Random Pitch values at 0 and choose your delay time normally. If the Pitch value is at 0, the Grain Delay will work like the Simple Delay in that it delays only the incoming signal. Change the Pitch setting to transpose the echo to a new note. For example, choosing a Pitch setting of 12 will cause the delayed signal to come back an octave higher than the original. This can be fun on vocal parts.

Chaos Is Good Another way to use the Grain Delay is to mangle a sound beyond comprehension. This is best achieved when using an impulse sound—something short like a drum or cymbal hit, the last word of a vocal, or a horn stab. Place a bunch of random values into the Grain Delay; then feed it your impulse sound. The Grain Delay will spit out a rearrangement of all the little grains in the impulse sound. Increasing the Frequency setting will add even more randomness to the mix. Try automating some parameters for more movement as the Grain Delay runs its course.

Chorus

When you listen to a group of people singing a chorus, each member of the group has slightly different timing and intonation, even if they're singing the same words with the same melody. The result is a large and lush vocal sound achieved by the variations in all of the voices.

The Chorus effect attempts to re-create this phenomenon by taking the input signal, delaying it by varying amounts, detuning it, and then blending the results with the original. In other words, Chorus effects assume that two sounds are better than one. It is common to run synthesizers, guitars, vocals, and strings through a chorus. The doubling, or even tripling, effect of a chorus makes solo voices sound more powerful, takes up more space in a mix, and therefore sounds more "present."

Live's Chorus (see Figure 9.16) features two parallel delays that can be set for .01 to 20ms or linked by activating a tiny equals sign (=).

Delay 1

The effect's first delay will always be active when the Chorus is on. To adjust the delay's timing, slide the fader. The adjustable HighPass filter knob allows you to bypass chorusing low frequencies, which can often become muddier and less defined when doubled. The definable range is 20Hz to 15kHz. Delay 1 can be used on its own or in parallel with Delay 2.

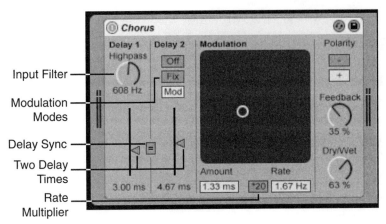

Input Filter

Modulation
Modes

Delay Sync

Two Delay
Times

Rate
Multiplier

Figure 9.16 Live's Chorus effect. Note the tiny equals sign (=) sign between the delays. This button syncs the two.

Delay 2

Chorus's Delay 2 can add even more thickness and intensity to your sounds. Delay 2 can run in two separate modes, Fix and Mod, and can be bypassed by selecting the top visible button labeled Off. Fix mode will force Delay 2 to the timing specified by its slider. Mod mode will allow the delay time to be modulated by the effect's Mod source.

Modulation

The Chorus's Modulation section is where the effect gets its movement. This section controls a sine wave oscillator (an LFO), which can be used to change the timing of the two delays. Whether you are going for completely unrecognizable new sounds or just looking for a little more stereo spread, you will want to spend some time fiddling (click-dragging) with the Modulation X-Y controller. Horizontal moves change the modulation rate from .03 to 10Hz, while the vertical axis increases the amount of modulation from 0 to 6.5ms. So, if Delay 1 is set to 1ms and you have a modulation amount of 1ms, the LFO will continually change the delay time between 0 and 2ms. The modulation rate changes the speed of the LFO from subtle movements to bubbly vibrations. You also have the option of typing in values by simply clicking on the box, typing a number within the allotted range, and pressing the Enter key.

The LFO will modulate both delays in stereo. This means that the delay times used for the right and left channels will be different, which increases the stereo intensity of the effect. This also means that if both delays are being modulated, there will be four different delay times at any given moment. How's that for fattening up a sound?

If you are looking for radical sonic redesign, the *20 button multiplies the Chorus' LFO rate by 20. While this may not sound great all of the time, the *20 multiplier will push the envelope of the dullest of sounds.

Feedback, Polarity, and Dry/Wet

For increased intensity, the Feedback control will send part of the output signal back through the delays. The more feedback you elect to add, the more robotic and metallic your sounds will become. The positive and negative polarity switch determines whether the signal being fed back to the delays is added to or subtracted from the new input signal. To hear the greatest contrast between the two polarities, you should use short delay times and increase the Chorus Feedback. The results are often frequency and pitch related: A low-frequency sound becomes a high-frequency sound, a pitch may shift by as much as an octave, and so forth. Finally, the Dry/Wet control determines the amount of original versus chorused signal going to output.

Phaser

The Phaser (see Figure 9.17) introduces phase shifts in the frequencies of a sound. When this effect is in motion, it has a sort of whooshing sound that can give your sounds a smooth sense of warmth and motion. It can also cut into your sounds if cranked up too far, thanks to some unorthodox controls.

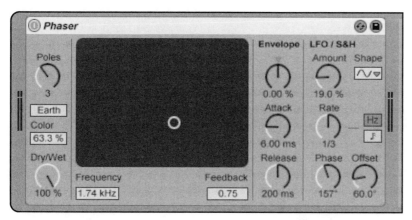

Figure 9.17   Star Fleet requires that you be equipped with a Phaser at all times.

Poles

The Phaser uses a series of filters to create the phase shifts you hear in the sound. The Poles control sets the number of filters, or notches, that are used in the Phaser. If you use a low number of poles, the Phaser effect will not be as pronounced as when you use a larger number of poles.

Color and Mode

The button below the Poles knob sets the mode for the Phaser. The button toggles between Earth and Space. Live's manual is pretty ambiguous about what differentiates these modes, except to say that they adjust the spacing of the notch filters. The Color control will further change the relationships of the filters when Earth mode is active.

Dry/Wet

You should know what this knob does by now—it changes the mix between the original dry signal and the phased signal. Blending the two together can soften the effect of the Phaser.

Frequency and Feedback

The large X-Y area in the middle of the Phaser is for adjusting the center frequency and the feedback amount. Move the dot on the screen left and right to adjust frequency (or use the number box in the lower-left corner). Vertical movement will adjust the feedback (whose number box is in the lower-right corner). You normally won't find a feedback control on a typical Phaser, but it's a control that Ableton added to its Phaser to help emphasize the Phase effect.

Envelope

This section is identical to the envelope follower you'll find in the Auto Filter device. It works by using the volume of the incoming signal as a means to modulate the frequency of the Phaser. The speed at which the envelope follower responds to changes in input volume is governed by the Attack and Release knobs. Use the top knob to increase the envelope's influence on the Phaser frequency.

LFO

Again, this control is a duplicate of the LFO control found in the Auto Filter. You'll use the Speed controls to set the LFO rate either in relation to the current tempo or freely in Hertz. The relation of the left and right LFOs is set with the Phase/Spin controls. Finally, the LFO's overall influence on the Phaser frequency is set with the Amount knob.

Open the Phaser example in the Chapter 9 folder and launch the first scene. You'll hear two loops playing simultaneously: a drum loop and a hi-hat from Operator. Both of the sounds are being run through Phaser devices in their Track Views. The hi-hat track is using the LFO to slowly modulate the phase over two bars. The Drum Loop track has its Phaser controlled by a Clip Envelope. Listen to each track individually and toggle the Phaser devices on and off to compare with the original sounds. Also, try adjusting the Feedback and Poles of each Phaser—the results can be fairly pronounced as these parameters are increased.

Flanger

The Flanger (see Figure 9.18) bears an extremely close resemblance to the Phaser, both in design and use. A Flanger works by taking a sound, delaying it by a slight amount, and then modulating the delay time while blending it back with the original sound. This introduces constructive and destructive interference between various frequencies in the sound, producing a characteristic comb filter effect. The Flanger has a much more metallic edge than the Phaser. Its sound can become quite abrasive with high-feedback settings, as you'll see in a moment.

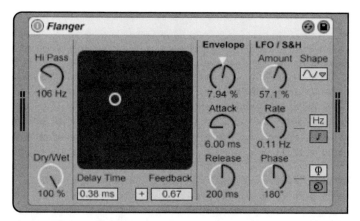

Figure 9.18 In the old days, flanging involved playing two identical recordings on tape machines, then touching the flanges of one of the tape reels to subtly shift the timing of the two recordings. Live's Flanger makes the same effect easier and cheaper to achieve.

Hi Pass Filter

As mentioned previously, the Flanger will make a copy of the input signal and mix it back in with the original after a briefly delay. This will result in flanging throughout the entire frequency spectrum. Often, this can product inharmonic (unpitched) results, which can make melodic parts "muddy." To alleviate this effect, you can pass the input signal through a hi pass filter. When the delayed signal is mixed back in with the original, the flanging will take effect only on the higher frequencies, leaving the low frequencies intact.

Dry/Wet

You know this one already.

Delay and Feedback

This looks quite similar to the X-Y control in the Phaser, doesn't it? Functionally, it's the same—horizontal movements adjust the delay time, while vertical movements increase the feedback. Because the Flanger uses a delay, there will be a pitch to the effect, which is related to the Delay Time parameter. As the delay time is shortened, the pitch will seem to rise. When you crank up the Feedback, the pitch will become even more pronounced.

Envelope and LFO

These two sections are identical to the Phaser and Auto Filter above except they modulate the delay time of the Flanger. To hear the Flanger in action, open the Flanger example in the Chapter 9 folder. This is the same Set as the Phaser example above, except that Flangers have replaced the Phasers. I think you'll agree that this sound is a little more metallic and aggressive. To push things to the max, switch the Feedback polarity of the Flangers by clicking the small + button next to the Feedback number box in the bottom-right corner of the X-Y control.

Reverb

Reverberation occurs when sound bounces off a surface, usually many surfaces, several times. In the process of reflecting, the original sound dissipates, becoming diffuse and muddy and eventually disappearing altogether. Depending upon the shape and reflective qualities of the room, certain frequencies will be more pronounced than others in the reverberated sound, or tail.

While Ableton's Reverb device, added in version 1.5, may not be a full-fledged delay, it is certainly from the same echo-related family. The number of controls may seem daunting, but as we step carefully through the signal path, you will see that each knob and X-Y controller is there only for your benefit. Before we get carried away, take a quick look at Figure 9.19.

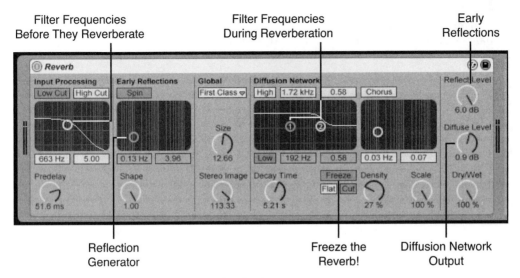

Figure 9.19   Live's feature-laden Reverb plug-in.

Input Processing

The first link in Reverb's signal chain is the Input Processing section. Here you have on/off selectable Low- and High-Cut filtering, as well as a Predelay control. The Low-Cut and High-Cut X-Y interface allows you to trim your input's frequencies before they are reverberated. Similar to Live's other delays, the X-axis shifts the frequency of the cut (50Hz to 18kHz), while the Y-axis changes the bandwidth (.50 to 9.0). You can also turn each filter off by deselecting its green illuminated box. I recommend spending some time playing with this filter each time you use this effect. Think of these filters as altering the acoustic characteristics of a room. For instance, a concrete room may not reproduce low frequencies as well as an acoustically engineered studio room. Each room will favor completely different frequencies.

Also, check out the Predelay control for adding milliseconds of time before you hear the first early reflections, or delayed sound, of the forthcoming reverberation. While the Predelay can range from .50 to 250ms, to simulate a normal-sounding room, the Predelay works best below 25ms. For large cannons, go long, baby.

Early Reflections

Early reflections are the first reverberations heard after the initial sound bounces off the walls, floor, or ceiling of the room—yet they arrive ahead of the full reflection, or tail. At times, they sound like slapback delays, or mushy portions of the whole reverberated (diffused) sound. The Reverb houses two early reflection controls: Shape and Spin. Spin's X-Y interface controls, Depth (Y-axis) and Frequency (X-axis), apply a subtle modulation to early reflections. Results may range from shimmering highs to whirligig panning flourishes. For quicker decay of early reflections, try increasing the Shape control gradually toward 1.00. Lower values will blend more smoothly with the normal reverb diffusion.

Rethink Your Reverb Because Reverb is Ableton Live's most processor-intensive effect (actually, reverb is almost always the most CPU-hungry effect, Ableton's or anyone else's), it's often best to use it on a Return track instead of putting it onto individual tracks. This way you can use the same reverb (instance) for multiple tracks. The added bonus with this strategy is that by using the same reverb, it will sound as if all of the instruments were, in fact, played in the same space. Of course, this may not be the best idea for every song, so use this technique at your discretion.

Global Settings

In Reverb's Global settings section, you can select the quality level of the reverb: Eco, Mid, or High. The three settings will demand small, moderate, and large processor power, respectively. You may also determine the size of the imaginary room via the Size control, which ranges from .22 (small/quiet) to 500 (large/loud). A Stereo Image control allows you to select from 0 to 120 degrees of stereo spread in the reverberation. Higher values will be more spread out, while lower ones will approach a mono sound.

Diffusion Network

The Diffusion Network is by far the most complex-looking area of the Reverb effect. These controls help put the final touches on the actual reverberation that follows closely behind the early reflections. From here, you will be able to decorate and control the finer points of the reverberated sound. To begin with, High and Low shelving filters can further define your imaginary room's sound. By shaving off the highs, for instance, your room may sound more like a concert hall or a large auditorium, while brightening up the diffusion (raising the high shelf) will approximate a "bathroom" reverb. Similar to X-Y–interface-controlled filters, each filter's X-axis determines frequency, while the Y-axis controls bandwidth. Turning these filters off will conserve some system resources.

Beneath the High and Low shelving controls, you will find the Reverb's Decay Time settings, which range from an extremely short 200ms to a cavernous 60-second-long tail. Long reverbs are mesmerizing but can make audio sound muddy and jumbled if used profusely.

To test the coloring and sonic quality of your reverb, you can use the Freeze control. Any time you press Freeze, Reverb will indefinitely hold and reproduce the diffusion tail. This frozen reverb can be a handy diagnostic tool for shaping your overall sound or a creative trick to make new sounds from a piece of reverb. Typically, I will freeze the reverb when I am first setting it up and then stop all other loops and sounds. After analyzing the reverberated sound for a moment, I often tweak parameters to weed out extreme or obnoxious low or high frequencies, or to change the reverb's modulation.

When Flat is activated, the low- and high-pass filters will be ignored. In other words, your frozen reverb tail will contain all frequencies. An active Cut command prevents further audio from being frozen, even if it is passing through the Reverb. For instance, you may want to analyze the tonality of the reverb tail. To do this, you play your audio through the Reverb, then press Freeze, and then press Cut (to cut off future audio from snowballing into a wall of useless noise). Even if you stop playback, the frozen Reverb sample will continue to play. While Reverb is frozen, you can make adjustments to the Diffusion Network settings and more acutely decipher their impact. Try starting and stopping audio a few times to analyze the differences between your project's audio and the reverberating audio. Is the reverb tail adding unwanted mud? The second X-Y interface in the Diffusion Network, labeled Chorus, can add subtle motion or wobbly effect to the overall reverb tail diffusion. When not in use, deactivate the Chorus button to save system resources.

The final section in Diffusion Network controls the density (thickness) and scale (coarseness) of the diffusion's echo. The Density control ranges from .1% (a lighter-sounding reverb) to a 96% rich and chewy reverb, while Scale can run from 5 to 100%, gradually adding a darker and murkier quality to the diffusion. A high Density setting will diminish the amount of audible change made by Scale controls.

Output

The Output section is the final link in the Reverb signal chain. At this stage, just three knobs, Dry/Wet, Reflect Level, and Diffuse Level, put the finishing touches on your Reverb Preset masterpiece. Dry/Wet controls the ratio of original, unaffected sound to affected, reverberated sound that you hear coming from the effect's output. When using Reverb in one of Live's Return tracks, I recommend using a 100% Wet setting, as opposed to using Reverb on a regular track, where settings between 10 and 45% sound more natural.

The Reflect Level control knob adjusts the amplitude (level) of the early reflections specified in the Early Reflections box, from −30 to +6 dB. The louder you make the early reflections, the more you will hear an echo of the true sound (which will sound even more like a slapback delay as opposed to a reverb).

In similar fashion, the Diffuse Level controls the amount of Diffusion Network level in the final Reverb output. A low diffusion level will diminish the tail of the reverb, while a high amplitude of Diffusion Network will increase the presence of reverb in your mix.

Resonators

Here's a fun device for techno-heads and sound designers: Resonators (see Figure 9.20). When sound is fed through the resonators, it causes the virtual resonators to start vibrating, creating a tone at their set pitches and volumes.

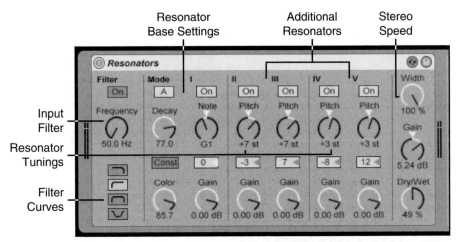

Figure 9.20 The Resonators device will start generating pitches based on an input signal.

To begin, crank the Dry/Wet mix knob fully clockwise to isolate the sound of the resonators. Turn off the Input Filter so a full-range sound is feeding the device. Adjust the settings for Resonator I first, since the other four resonators base their tones and pitches on the first. You'll see that you have control of the decay of the resonators (best heard on sparse percussion tracks), as well as the color and pitch. Once the first resonator is set, engage the other resonators and use the Pitch knobs to set their frequencies relative to the first. This makes it simple to create chords using multiple resonators; then transpose them all using the first resonator's Pitch knob.

Resonators II and III and Resonators IV and V can be panned apart from each other by increasing the Width knob. This can help create a lush tonal pad that blends well with a mix. You can also use the input filter to remove frequencies that may be overpowering or saturating the resonator banks. The Gain knobs are used to achieve a blend between the various resonators, allowing you to emphasize certain pitches over others.

Tuned Reverb Try adding a Resonator effect right after a Reverb effect on your vocalist's Return track. Build a chord with the dials on the effect and set it fully wet. Now the Reverb effect will cause the resonators to ring in tune with the song, adding an ethereal sound to the voice.

Distortions

This brings us to the third group of Ableton's devices: the Distortion effects. While each of these effects can quickly and drastically alter your audio content, taking time to learn the ins and outs of these babies can take your mixes to a whole new level. In Live 7, a High Quality mode has been added to the Saturator and the Dynamic Tube to reduce aliasing artifacts in high frequency sounds. This mode is turned on by right-clicking in the device's title bar and selecting Hi Quality from the context menu. There's only a small CPU hit for using this feature, so it's generally recommended to turn it on.

Saturator

We'll start with the Saturator device (see Figure 9.21) as this is the most straightforward type of distortion. This is a distortion based on overdriving the input signal, which is a common effect to apply to guitars, drums, and even vocals. Use it to make your sounds fatter, dirtier, warmer, or edgier. The Saturator effect has been changed and upgraded substantially in Live 7, with a wave-shaping function that can create really extreme distortion sounds.

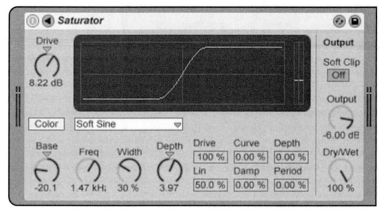

Figure 9.21   The Saturator: instant fatness or gateway to destruction?

Waveform Display

The top of the Saturator interface is dominated by the large waveform display. Manipulating the controls below the display will give you insight into how the effect modifies your signal by looking at the resulting curve.

You can choose six different modes of signal shaping using the drop-down menu below the display: Analog Clip, Soft Sine, Medium Curve, Hard Curve, Sinoid Fold, and Digital Clip, each with its own distinct characteristics. The Waveshaper mode allows flexible control of the waveform through the six adjustable parameters listed just below the drop-down menu:

- **Drive:** Not to be confused with the Drive knob (see below), determines the amount of influence of the waveshaping effect.

- **Curve:** Adds harmonics to the signal.

- **Depth:** Controls the amplitude of a sine wave superimposed over the distortion curve.

- **Lin:** Alters the linear portion of the shaping curve.

- **Damp:** Flattens the signal, acting as a sort of super-fast noise gate.

- **Period:** Determines the density of the ripples in the sine wave.

These controls are specific to the Waveshaper and are not available in other modes.

Drive

On a dynamic distortion unit such as this, the Drive knob is where you'll demolish your sound; you'll find this to the left of the waveform display. The higher the Drive amount, the more the input signal is amplified. This forces more of the signal into the distortion range, slaughtering the sound at high levels. Of course, if you're getting too much distortion, you can reduce the Drive into negative amounts so that only a slight portion of the signal is distorted.

Below the Drive, you'll see the DC offset switch. This removes extremely low frequencies that can't be heard, but consume headroom in your mix—especially when processed with an effect that increases gain, such as the Saturator.

Color

When the Color toggle switch is on, the four controls below it also become active. These controls are similar to the tone controls on a guitar amp. The Base knob will increase or decrease the amount of bass distorted by the effect. The last three knobs allow you to set a high-frequency EQ with specs for Frequency, Width, and Depth (gain).

Output

As you increase the Drive amount, you will increase the volume of the distortion, often to the point of overpowering other instruments in your mix. Pull the Output down a bit to bring the sound back where it should be. A Dry/Wet control here allows you to set the amount of effect being heard. When the Soft Clip button is activated, an additional instance of the Analog Clip curve will be applied to the final output.

Open the Saturator example to hear how the Saturator demolishes both a drum loop and a bass sound. Try the other shapes while the loop is running to become familiar with their sounds, and don't forget to check out the sounds with the Saturators turned off.

Quality, by Default Here's a trick to make sure that you always use the Saturator and Dynamic Tube effects in High Quality mode. After turning High Quality mode on (by right-clicking in the title bar and selecting it from the context menu), right-click in the title bar again and select Save as Default Preset. Now, every time you insert the device, High Quality mode will be enabled. This same technique can be used on any device to create any default values you want.

Dynamic Tube

The Dynamic Tube effect models the distinct effect that vacuum tubes can have on audio (see Figure 9.22). It doesn't really sound like most distortion effects. It can provide some extremely subtle effects, somewhere between compression and distortion, while its more aggressive settings sound like equipment malfunctioning!

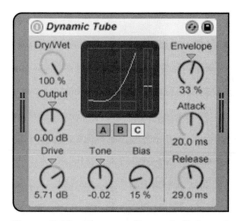

Figure 9.22   The new Dynamic Tube saturation effect.

This effect allows you to choose between three different tube models: A, B, and C, with C being the most distortion-prone tube and A being the cleanest of the bunch. With Bias set at 0, tube A won't produce any distortion at all. It can, however, produce some very "hot" sounding compression.

Open up the Dynamic Tube example set and listen to the drum loop with and without the effect. Try sweeping the Tone knob to both of its extremes and then listen to what happens when you bring Envelope down to −300%. With a negative Envelope value, less distortion is produced for louder sounds, bringing back more of the loop's original punch.

Tone

The Tone control allows you to determine what frequencies (higher or lower) are most affected by the tube-distortion effect.

Drive

The Drive control sets how much of the incoming signal is routed through the tube. Setting the Drive control higher will result in a dirtier output.

Bias

The Bias control works in conjunction with the Drive control. It determines how much distortion the tube is capable of producing. As you turn this up to the top, the signal will really start to break apart into dirty, fuzzed-out noise. You can modulate the Bias control with the Envelope controls at right. The higher the setting of the Envelope knob, the more the Bias setting will be influenced by the level of the input signal. You can use the Attack and Release knobs to adjust how quickly the envelope reacts to the input.

Erosion

As anyone who's done any subtractive-synthesis or frequency filtering knows, deconstructing a sound can be a creative endeavor. Erosion uses an unusual method for sonic degradation. By rapidly modulating a very short delay time, strange distortion artifacts are created. The modulator can be Noise, Wide Noise, or Sine, as seen beneath the X-Y interface (pictured in Figure 9.23).

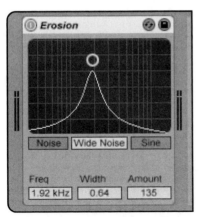

Figure 9.23   Live's Erosion device window, primarily taken up by its unusual X-Y field.

Depending upon which mode you currently have active, Erosion will use either a sine wave or a noise generator to modulate a very short delay. The only difference between the two noise modes is that Wide Noise uses a separate noise generator for each channel, resulting in a stereo effect.

To control the degree of Erosion's effect on a sound, move along the Y-axis to change the level of the modulation signal and the X-axis to control the frequency. For Wide Noise, the Width can be adjusted by holding Alt (Option), while dragging vertically.

Redux

While you're digging into tools for sonic decimation, you will definitely want to check out Live's Redux device. Redux (see Figure 9.24) is a bit-depth and sample-rate reducer that can make even

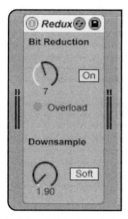

Figure 9.24   Live's Redux is a talented bit-depth and sample-rate reducer.

the prettiest of guitars, or anything else for that matter, saw your head off. Of course, results need not be this drastic if you are capable of restraint. In fact, reducing the fidelity of a sample is like a tip of the hat to old Roland, Emu, and Akai 8- and 12-bit samplers—or even old 2- and 4-bit computer-based samples (Commodore 64, anyone?).

The controls for Redux are split into two tidy sections, with a Bit Reduction knob and On/Off switch on top, and a Downsample knob and Hard/Soft switch on the bottom. The default position for Bit Reduction is 16-bit (off). As you reduce the bits, you will hear an increasing amount of noisy grit infect the sample. Anything below 4 bits causes a dramatic increase in gain, so use caution. The numerical setting will indicate the bit depth (e.g., 8 = 8 bit, 4 = 4 bit). Extremists can try trimming it down to 1 bit—ouch, that hurts!

When it comes to sample-rate reduction, the settings are a little more inexact. In Hard mode, downsampling will stick with whole integers such as 1, 2, and 3 (up to 200) for dividing the sample rate, while in Soft mode you can adjust from 1 to 20 to the nearest hundredth of a point (1.00 or 19.99). A setting of 1 means you are not hearing any sample-rate reduction—oddly, the higher the number, the lower the resulting sample rate.

For a quick course, spend a minute perusing the Ableton factory presets, such as Old Sampler and Mirage. This will give you a basic template to work from. Also, while you are in Playback mode, try toggling between Hard and Soft Downsampling with different settings for a cool effect.

Vinyl Distortion

The imperfections of vinyl have actually become quite lovable these days. Whether you are missing the dust pops and crackles of an old record or the warped vinyl sound of a record left out in the sun, vinyl has a certain retro charm. Though CDs and digital recordings are great, they are hopelessly clean and free of these impurities. Of course, Ableton thought about this, too, and as a result, we have Vinyl Distortion (Figure 9.25).

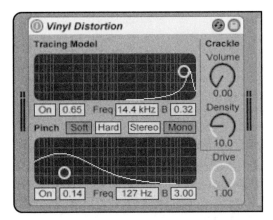

Figure 9.25   Live's Vinyl Distortion effect hopes to make you miss your turntable just a little bit less.

Vinyl Distortion is divided into three separate sections: Tracing Model, Crackle, and Pinch. While the controls for Tracing Model and Pinch look identical, each section generates a totally different sound. Also note that the Soft/Hard and Stereo/Mono switches are also a part of the Pinch effect. If Pinch is off, these controls will remain grayed out (inactive).

Tracing Model adds a subtle amount of harmonic distortion to your audio as a means of simulating wear and tear on vinyl or an old stylus. To adjust the intensity of the distortion, increase the Drive by moving the yellow circle along the Y-axis (which ranges from 0.00 to 1.00). Adjust the frequency of the harmonic on the X-axis (which ranges from 50Hz to 18kHz), or input a value manually by typing in the box. To adjust the size of the bandwidth you are affecting, hold down Alt (Option) and click-drag forward or backward on the yellow circle.

The Pinch section of Vinyl Distortion is a more drastic and wild-sounding distortion at the input level. The resulting richer stereo image is from Pinch's 180 degrees out-of-phase harmonic distortions. Like the Tracing Model, you can increase the intensity of the distortion through the Y-axis. The X-axis will configure the frequency range. You will want to pay special attention to the Soft/Hard boxes to the right of the X-Y interface in the Pinch section. Soft mode is engineered to sound like an actual dub plate (acetate), while Hard mode will sound more like a standard vinyl record. Also, the Stereo/Mono switch applies to the Pinch effect only.

No vinyl simulator would be complete without a vinyl pop and crackle effect. Crackle provides two simple controls: Volume and Density. Volume is obviously the level of the hiss and crackle in the mix. Density adds a thicker amount of noise to the output. Note that you will hear the crackle and hiss whether Live is in Playback mode or not, because effects are always running. If you forget this, you might just take a screwdriver to your audio interface trying to figure out where all the noise is coming from!

Miscellaneous Tools

This last section of devices covers two of Live's more esoteric plug-ins: the Beat Repeat and Utility. These devices aren't necessarily effects since they don't really change the sound that passes through them. The Beat Repeat repeats certain segments of the sound as it passes through, while the Utility device offers some basic gain and phase adjustments.

Beat Repeat

Techno-heads, rejoice! Ableton brings you the Beat Repeat device (see Figure 9.26). Now you can produce the stereotypical beat-stutter with just a few simple gestures—you can even program repeats to happen automatically.

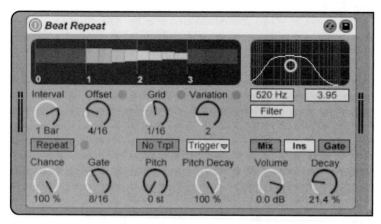

Figure 9.26   Th-Th-Th-This dev-v-v-v-ice is sw-ee-ee-ee-ee-t!

Repeat

Open up the Beat Repeat example Set and launch the first scene, titled Manual. This will start a drum loop running. The beat will play without being repeated. Go ahead and click the Repeat button in the Beat Repeat interface. Woo-hoo! There it goes, repeating away. Click the Repeat button again to turn it off, and the regular beat will resume. Obviously, the Repeat button is named well.

Grid and Variation

You set the size, or length, of the repeated segment with the Grid knob. Turn on Repeat and try tweaking this knob. You'll hear the Repeat size change in real time—an awesome effect for remixing. The No Trpl button will remove the triplet values when scrolling through the grid sizes, which is handy if you want to keep all the rhythmic repeats in sync.

The Variation knob just to the right of the Grid knob introduces randomness to the grid size. When set to 0%, the grid will always be what you've set with the Grid knob. As this value increases, Live automatically changes the grid, based on the mode selected in the pop-up menu below the knob. When you select Trigger in that menu, Live gives you a new grid size anytime you start the Repeat function. It will hold the grid size until you stop or retrigger the Repeat. The 1/4, 1/8, and 1/16 settings will change the Grid setting at the specified time interval. The Auto setting will change the grid size after every repeat. This can get really hairy, as you can have a single repeat of 1/64 followed by a repeat of 1/6, followed by 1/16, followed by 1/2, etc. The results are truly unpredictable!

Mix, Insert, and Gate

These three buttons control the output mode of the Beat Repeat. So far, you've been using the Insert mode. In Insert mode the original drumbeat is silent while Repeat is on. Click on the Mix button and try using the Repeat button. In Mix mode, you'll hear the original drumbeat while the Repeat is occurring—the two are being mixed together. The final mode, Gate, will allow sound to pass only when Repeat is on. When Repeat is off, the output of the device will be silent. This mode is useful when you've placed the Beat Repeat on a Return track, especially if you've chained additional effects after the Beat Repeat.

Volume and Decay

The Volume knob sets the volume of the repeated sounds. Note that the first repeat is always at the original volume. I like to decrease the volume a little bit so that the music comes back in heavier after the repeat. It's almost necessary to turn this down when you're using small grid sizes, as the repeats become so fast that they start to make a tone of their own.

The Decay knob will cause the volume of each consecutive repeat to be quieter than the first. This means that your repeats will slowly (or quickly) fade away to silence each time you trigger Repeat.

Pitch

The Pitch controls can be used to introduce pitch shifts into your repeats. The Pitch knob will simply transpose the repeated sound down by the specified number of semitones. The Pitch Decay knob works similarly to the Volume Decay knob above, except that it makes the pitch drop farther and farther with each consecutive repeat. It's possible to make the repeated sound drop so low in pitch that it becomes inaudible. This is a neat tool to use in conjunction with the volume decay because you can make your repeats drop in pitch and fade away at the same time.

Filter

This filter functions in the same way as the filter in the Ping Pong Delay, except that the repeated sounds are not fed back through this filter. When Repeat is on, you can engage the filter and choose a specific frequency range for the repeats. This can give your repeats a lo-fi sound in comparison to the normal part. You can even change the filter frequency and width while Repeat is running for even more animation.

Chance and Interval

So far, I've been showing you how to use Beat Repeat in a completely hands-on fashion, which is how you might use Beat Repeat in a live situation. However, as I alluded to earlier, you can set Beat Repeat to perform repeats automatically. This is the purpose of the Chance and Interval knobs.

In your experiments so far, the Chance knob has been set to 0%. This means there is no chance that the Beat Repeat will automatically trigger itself. If you turn this value up to 100%, Beat Repeat will automatically trigger at the rate specified with the Interval knob. If Interval is set to 1 Bar, Beat Repeat will activate itself every bar. If you set Chance to 50%, there will only be a 1-in-2 chance that the Beat Repeat will trigger.

Offset and Gate

These last two knobs determine when an automatic repeat will start and how long it will last. When Offset is set to 0, the repeat will start the instant it is called by the Interval and Chance knobs. If you turn this knob clockwise, you'll see it count up in 1/16 notes—with the knob turned up halfway, the value will be 8/16. This means that the Beat Repeat won't start until the third beat of the bar. You'll also see the Repeat markers move in the display as a visual aid.

The Gate knob sets how long the repeats will last once triggered. If set to 4/16, the repeat will last for a quarter note. If set to 8/16, the repeats will last for half a bar. Therefore, using Offset and Grid, you can specify any location in the audio to repeat, as well as how long to do it.

To hear all these properties at work, launch the Automatic scene. This will play the same drumbeat, but through a Beat Repeat on another channel.

Utility

The Utility device (see Figure 9.27) gets a section all its own. This device isn't so much an effect that will make your audio sound weird. Instead, it can provide a number of different subtle changes to the audio for adding the right touch to a mix.

Figure 9.27 The Utility interface provides easy access to simple tools.

The first two options are self-explanatory: Mute and Gain. Although you have similar controls elsewhere in Live, Ableton provides these on the Utility device for use as insert effects.

The DC switch can be used to filter out DC offset, as well as extremely low frequencies that are below the range of human hearing but still consume headroom in your mix. Use the Stereo/Left/Right/Swap drop-down menu to hear just part of your mix or swap the stereo channels. Selecting Left or Right will mirror one channel to both sides, so this can be useful with stereo audio files from which you want to use only one channel.

The Panorama control can be used to play back a stereo track in mono (at 0%) or to remove all of the mono information (at 200%). Intermediate adjustments can be made to make a source sound narrower or wider.

When doing a mix, it is a good idea to check for mono compatibility. When the sound of the left channel of your mix is blended with the right channel, certain frequencies may start to interfere with one another, or you may discover phase cancellation problems. In some cases, guitars may not sound as full when heard in mono. Sometimes, the vocals will sound too loud. In extreme cases of phase cancellation, some of the parts may completely disappear from the mix!

If you do run into phase-cancellation that completely removes a part from the song when in mono, Utility can be used to correct it. If you've determined that a stereo track is out of phase, you can use the Phz-L or Phz-R button to invert the phase of either the left or right channel. If you're not worried about mono compatibility, you'll find that kicking one side of a track out of phase from the other will make the resulting audio sound amazingly wide, almost as if the sound were coming from behind your head.

External Devices

The two devices we'll discuss next don't process or produce audio. Instead, they are special utilities for interfacing with external hardware and ReWire instruments.

External Effect

Using external effect boxes in your Live productions has never been easier. Insert an external effect device in a track and select the inputs and outputs your processor is connected to, as seen in Figure 9.28. Audio from the track will now be routed through your external device. Then you can use the Gain knobs to adjust levels to and from the device. What's really cool, though, is that there is a Wet/Dry knob for blending the send and return signals. This means that you don't have to mess with the Mix control on an external effect. You can just leave your effects set up with direct signal at 0% and make fully recallable adjustments of the wet/dry balance from within Live.

The remainder of the controls in the External Audio Effect device deal with timing issues. The Phase switch lets you invert the phase of the returned signal to correct phase cancellation

Figure 9.28 The External Audio Effect shown above will route audio through whatever hardware is connected to input and output #4 on your audio interface.

problems that could occur when blending dry and processed signals. The Latency control lets you compensate for delay incurred by routing the audio to and from the hardware device.

The benefits here become obvious quickly. If you have enough I/O on your audio interface, you can keep external processors connected and create presets for them. Not only can you quickly access your hardware in this fashion, you can also insert your hardware devices anywhere in a device chain or a Rack.

External Instruments

External Instruments allows you to control an external synth from a MIDI track but make it behave like a virtual instrument track. What you once had to do with two tracks—a MIDI track to control the synth and an audio track for returning the audio from the synth—can now be done with a single track.

Setting up an external instrument is easy. Just choose the MIDI port and channel your synth is connected to, and then select the audio input(s) the synth is plugged into, as seen in Figure 9.29. Once you've got your connections made, the synth's audio will return directly to the MIDI track.

The big difference with External Instruments is that the I/O section can access ReWire instruments as well (see Figure 9.30). This means that you could set up a session in Reason with your favorite synths or Combinator patches, and access them using External Instruments devices. Not only does this save you tracks by combining the MIDI out and the ReWire synth's audio into a single track, but it also makes it easy to include ReWire synths in Instrument Racks as well.

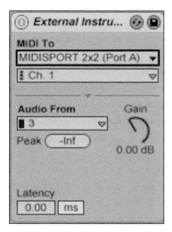

Figure 9.29   The External Instrument shown above is sending MIDI to the synth connected to MIDISport port A. The synth is connected to input 3 and will return its audio directly to the device.

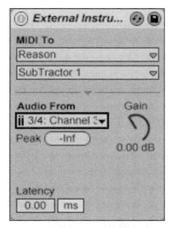

Figure 9.30   This External Instrument is sending MIDI to a Subtractor synth in Reason and receiving audio on ReWire bus3/4.

Multitimbrality Even if you don't use external synths or ReWire, External Instruments may still have a trick up its sleeve for you. If you've got any multitimbral synths (such as Stylus RMX or Kontakt 3) in your Live Set, these will show up in the I/O options for your External Instruments.

WHO'S USING LIVE? Shawn Pelton *Chances are, even if you don't know his name, you've already been rocked by the rhythms of super session drummer Shawn Pelton. If you've seen* Saturday Night Live *within the last 13 years, you've heard him play—he's been with the band longer than any other member. On top of this steady gig, you'll also find him backing up artists such as Bob Dylan, Rod Stewart, Bruce Springsteen, Sheryl Crow, Edie Brickell, The Brecker Brothers, Buddy Guy, Joan Osborne, Hall & Oates, Celine Dion, Billy Joel, Luciano Pavarotti, Spice Girls (another guilty pleasure—sorry...), Loudon Wainwright, Peter Frampton, Robert Palmer, Bruce Hornsby, Adam Sandler, and Vanessa Williams.*

We were fortunate enough to speak with Shawn while prepping this book, and he gave us the inside scoop on what he's doing with his current project, House of Diablo (www.houseofdiablo.com), which is an eclectic three-piece composed of Brian Mitchell on vocals, keyboards, and electronic voodoo; Edward Potokar playing homemade analog tone generators and jewel-encrusted gizmotrons; and Shawn on his drums and "electrified swamp water."

"House of Diablo has been described as deep-fried swamp music mixed with abstract noise and groove electronics," Shawn says. "Imagine if Booker T. and the MGs crashed into Dr. John's backyard in 1968 with King Tubby at the grill, then they woke up in the year 2013 with DJ Shadow's cousin in the band and subtonic transmissions from Saturn."

To achieve the ultra-dubby sound for the group, Shawn uses Live to create layered beats, which he can feed through sets of delays all controlled from three foot pedals and an Evolution UC-33e fader controller. An image of his Live Set is shown in the following figure.

"The first seven faders on the UC-33 correspond to the first seven tracks in Live, which all contain various rhythmic elements and loops. The three knobs above each fader are used to control the effect sends on each track, which are tied to three delays with different rhythmic settings—1/16 note, 1/8-note triplet, and dotted-1/8 note. The three knobs above the eighth fader control the feedbacks of the three delays, while the fader itself is assigned to Live's crossfader.

"I also have three pedals set up near my hi-hat that are assigned to Live's Start, Stop, and Tap Tempo. This allows me to start and stop the backing rhythms and also change their tempo at will. The resulting tempo is then transmitted via MIDI to any of the other cats in the band who need it."

10 Live's MIDI Effects

MIDI effects, like audio effects, allow you to alter data as it is passed from a clip to the track output. A MIDI effect can be used by itself on a MIDI track whose output is some external MIDI sound device, or one or more can be used before a virtual instrument in the Track View.

It's important to understand the place of the MIDI effect in the chain of events that occurs on a track. MIDI data in a clip is played through the MIDI effect, which alters the data in some way. The altered MIDI data is then sent to the MIDI destination, which is either an external MIDI device or a virtual one loaded in Live, which reacts accordingly. Note that MIDI effects do not change the sound that is produced by an instrument the way audio effects do. MIDI effects change the notes playing those instruments, resulting in an entirely new part. This is why, for example, the Pitch MIDI effect won't change the pitch of the drums coming from Impulse. If this doesn't make sense right off the bat, don't worry—if you're like us, you learn by doing. So pop open the Chapter 10 folder in the Library and check out the Live Sets in there as we reveal the wiring behind the six MIDI effects in Live.

Arpeggiator

Since we are discussing the MIDI effects in alphabetical order, we get to start with the coolest MIDI device of them all, the Arpeggiator. Arpeggiators came into existence in the early days of monophonic synthesizers. *Monophonic* means "only able to play one note at a time." When synthesizer technology was in its infancy, that's all you could hope to get out of a synth—just one note at a time. This isn't much of a problem if you're playing a lead or melody part. The trouble arises when you try to play a chord (two or more notes at once), which a monophonic synth is incapable of. The solution devised was an arpeggiator that would quickly play all the notes you held on the keyboard in series or other repetitive patterns. As a result, even though the notes don't play simultaneously, you can "hear" the chord being played because the notes are played in such quick succession. You *really* have to play this one to understand it, so go ahead and open the Arpeggiator set from the Chapter 10 examples provided with this book.

After the Set loads, press a key on your MIDI keyboard, or just use the computer keyboard to play a note. What is this? You hold down a note and a steady stream of eighth notes comes out? Now try holding down two notes. Instead of hearing both notes playing eighth notes, Live will play each of the notes alternately. Now try holding three notes. Live will now play each of the three notes in series and repeat. That's the Arpeggiator at work (see Figure 10.1), intercepting your played notes and turning them into a sequence of notes before handing them over to the Simpler loaded in the track.

Figure 10.1　The Arpeggiator on this track is creating instant sequences from the MIDI notes it receives.

There are many ways to tweak the performance of the Arpeggiator. You can change the note order employed by the Arpeggiator, the speed at which the notes are played, the length of each note, and the quantization in relation to the grid of the current Set.

Style

The Style drop-down menu is used to select the note-order pattern employed by the Arpeggiator. The default setting is Up, which means that the Arpeggiator plays each of the held notes in sequence starting from the lowest note and working up to the highest before repeating. The Down option is the exact opposite—the Arpeggiator starts with the highest note and works down before repeating. The UpDown and DownUp patterns are simply hybrid patterns made from the individual Up and Down patterns. The UpDown style will make the Arpeggiator play up the note sequence and then back down again before repeating. The DownUp style does the opposite. The Up & Down and Down & Up modes are the same as the UpDown and DownUp modes, except that the top and bottom notes of the scale are repeated as the Arpeggiator changes direction.

The Converge style works by playing the lowest note followed by the highest note. It will then play the second lowest note followed by the second highest. The pattern will continue by playing the third lowest note followed by the third highest note, and so on, until all the notes in the scale are exhausted. The pattern will then repeat. The Diverge style is the opposite of Converge, and Con & Diverge places the two patterns end to end.

The Pinky and Thumb styles are interesting in that they alternate the note order with the highest and lowest note played, respectively. For example, when using the PinkyUp mode, the

Arpeggiator will play the lowest note followed by the highest note (the "pinky note"). It will then play the second lowest note followed by the highest note again. The Arpeggiator will continue to work up the scale of held notes, alternating each with the high "pinky note" until the pattern repeats. The ThumbUp mode works in the same way, except that the lowest held note (the "thumb note") gets inserted between each step of the scale.

The Play Order style is nice in that the Arpeggiator works through the scale of held notes in the exact order as you played them. For example, if you play the notes C, E, G, and A, the resulting pattern will be "C E G A C E G A C E G A …." If you play the notes in a different order, like E, C, G, then A, the pattern will be "E C G A E C G A E C G A …."

The Chord Trigger style breaks away from the traditional arpeggiator methodology in that it plays more than one note at a time. In fact, it repeatedly triggers every one of the notes you held down. The result is a stuttered chord.

The final style options are random modes that will generate unpredictable patterns from your held notes. The Random mode simply chooses a note at random from your held notes for each step it plays. In this mode, it's possible for Live to choose the same note repeatedly—it's truly random. The Random Other pattern is a little more controlled. It will create a random pattern from your held notes, play it, and then create another random pattern and play it. The result is that you have fewer repeated notes, because Live will play all the notes at least once before it creates a new pattern. The Random Once pattern is like Random Other, except that it builds only one random pattern. After the Arpeggiator plays the random pattern once, it will play it again identically. The result is a new random pattern every time you play new notes, but a pattern that repeats while you hold the notes. Pretty cool, huh?

Groove

The Groove menu is identical in function to the Groove setting found in the Clip View. Choosing a groove here will cause the Arpeggiator to offset its notes as the Groove Amount is increased. This will allow you to create swinging arpeggiations on the fly!

Hold

The Hold button will automatically latch, or sustain, the notes you play so that you don't have to continually hold notes while a pattern plays. Switch this on and try playing a chord. When you release the notes on your keyboard, the Arpeggiator will continue to play. Now, play another chord. The Arpeggiator will stop the old pattern and will start the new one when it receives your new notes.

Offset

This dial is used to offset the start point of the Arpeggiator pattern by the specified number of steps. For example, if the style is set to Up and you play a C-major triad, the resulting pattern from the Arpeggiator will be "C E G C E G …." If you set Offset to 1, the pattern will be "E G C

E G C...." The starting point of the pattern has been shifted to the right by one step; therefore, the pattern begins on the second note of the chord (E) as it plays.

Rate and Sync

The next two parameters, Rate and Sync, are related to one another. The Rate knob is used to set the speed at which the Arpeggiator plays each step of its pattern. The default selection is 1/8 notes. When the neighboring Sync button is on, the Rate will be constrained to note values. If you turn Sync off, the Rate will now be running free of the current project tempo and will play at the exact rate specified here in Hertz. You'll find that you can get the Arpeggiator running quite fast when you turn Sync off, even to a point where the individual notes in the scale are blurred. This is a neat special effect and is also reminiscent of SID-based synth music, like that of the Commodore 64 of yore.

Gate

This dial is used to set the length or duration of each note played by the Arpeggiator. By default, this value is 50%, which means that the notes are only half as long as the rate at which they are played. Therefore, with Rate set to 1/8, the notes are only 1/16-note long. If you set this to 25%, each note will only be 1/32-note long. This is a great parameter to tweak while the Arpeggiator is running.

Retrigger

The Retriggering parameters can be used to cause the Arpeggiator to restart its pattern when triggered with a new note or in rhythm with your song. The default Retrigger mode is Off, which means that the Arpeggiator will never restart its pattern, even if you play new notes while the Arpeggiator is running. The pattern will only restart when you stop all notes and play new ones. If you set this to Note, the pattern will restart any time a new note is played. Therefore, if you're holding three notes and play a fourth note, the Arpeggiator will immediately restart, now including the fourth note in its pattern. The last mode, Beat, will cause the Arpeggiator to automatically restart at the rate you specify with the neighboring knob. By default, this value is set to one bar. If you hold a three-note chord while this is on, you'll hear the Arpeggiator pattern start over on every downbeat of a bar.

Repeats

By default, Live will arpeggiate the notes you play for as long as you hold them. This is because the Repeats amount is set to Infinity by default. If you change this knob to a numerical value, the Arpeggiator will only run its pattern the specified number of times before stopping. Setting this to a low value, such as one or two repeats, and choosing a quick setting for the Rate will cause the Arpeggiator to "strum" the notes of your chord. That is, they'll play quickly and then stop. This little burst of arpeggiation is reminiscent of old video game soundtracks.

Transposition Controls

Grouped together into a column near the center of the Arpeggiator are the Transpose controls. These parameters will allow the Arpeggiator to shift the pattern in pitch as it repeats. Start by turning the Steps knob to 1. Now play a single note. You'll no longer hear a single note being repeated. Instead, you'll hear two notes: the note you're holding plus a note one octave higher. This is because the Distance knob is set to +12 semitones, which is an octave. By turning Steps to 1, you've instructed the Arpeggiator to shift its pitch by the Distance amount once for each repetition of the pattern. Turn Steps up to 2 and listen to what happens. Now the Arpeggiator plays three notes for each key you press. This also works when holding multiple notes—the Arpeggiator will play the pattern once and then play it again for each step indicated, transposing by the Distance amount each time.

Now try this: Set Steps to 8 and Distance to +1 semitones. Now when you hold a single note, the Arpeggiator plays nine notes chromatically. If you hold C, the Arpeggiator will play C C# D D# E F F# G G# and then repeat. This is because the Arpeggiator is shifting the pattern (which is only the one note you're holding) eight times after it has played the original pitch, transposing it one semitone each time. Change the Distance amount to +2 and listen to what happens.

Obviously, you can create some transposition patterns that will fall outside of the key you're working in. To remedy this, there are two menus that can be used to constrain the notes to those of a selected key and mode. With the top Transpose menu, choose Major or Minor. After you make your selection, you can choose a root note with the Key menu below it. For example, set the Transpose menu to Minor and change the Key menu to D. Now press and hold D. All the notes in the resulting pattern will be transposed to the nearest note within a D-minor scale.

Velocity

The final controls in the Arpeggiator are for modifying the velocity of notes as they play. Normally, these functions are off, which makes each note of the arpeggiation pattern sound at its played velocity. That is, if you press C lightly while striking G hard, the resulting pattern will have quiet C notes and loud G notes.

The purpose of the Velocity controls here is to create a pseudo-envelope for the volume of the arpeggiation. Of course, this will only work with sounds that are velocity sensitive. When you turn Velocity on with the top button, the Arpeggiator will modify the velocities of the notes as they repeat. The bottom dial sets the Target velocity, and the Decay knob above it determines how long the Arpeggiator takes to modulate from the original velocities to the Target. For example, if you set Target to 10 and Decay to 1,000ms and play a note with full velocity, the Arpeggiator will reduce the velocity of each consecutive note it plays to 10 over one second. You can invert this, of course, by setting a high Target velocity and playing quiet notes—the velocity will increase to the Target over the specified Decay time.

The Retrigger button will cause the velocity scaling to restart with each new note that is added to the chord. Otherwise, new notes will be constrained to the current values of the decaying velocities.

Chord

The Chord device (see Figure 10.2) will generate new MIDI notes at pitch intervals relative to an incoming MIDI note. This will allow one MIDI note to trigger a chord on the receiving instrument.

Figure 10.2 The Chord device allows you to build a multinote (up to six notes) MIDI chord from one input note.

When the Chord device is first loaded, it will have no effect on incoming MIDI notes—they will pass straight through. If you move the first Shift knob, it will become active. The knob sets the interval in semitones for the new MIDI note. Setting the Shift 1 knob to +4 and playing a C will cause both a C and E note to be sent from the plug-in. Setting Shift 2 to +7 will create a C-major chord when you play just the C note. Playing G will result in a G-major chord (G, B, and D). You can define up to six notes to be added to the incoming note using the dials. Just below each dial is a value that determines the velocity of the new note relative to the velocity of the incoming note. You can use this if you don't want all of the notes in the chord to be the same volume. If Shift 1 is set to .50 (50%), the E in the resulting chord will only have a velocity of 64 when the incoming C has a velocity of 127. Try slowly changing this value while playing repeated notes to hear how the additional note fades in and out of the chord.

Dance Chords Chord stabs and pads are a staple of electronic music. Originally, these fixed chords were created by detuning some of the oscillators in a synthesizer so that they sounded at musical intervals (usually +7—a perfect fifth) against the base oscillators.

The Chord effect can create the same sound on instruments that don't have individual tunings for their oscillators. There are a number of chords already built for your use in the presets.

Note Length

The Note Length MIDI effect (see Figure 10.3) can be used to change the duration of incoming MIDI note messages. This can be used in some cases to tighten up a drum part, for example, or make a MIDI part sound more rhythmically consistent. It can also be used to trigger your MIDI instruments with Note Off messages instead of Note On messages.

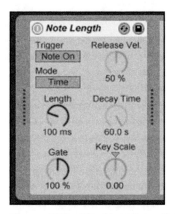

Figure 10.3 The Note Length MIDI device.

The Note Length MIDI effect has two trigger modes, which you can toggle to Note On or Note Off. In Note On mode, only the timing controls are active: Mode, Length, and Gate. You can use the Mode toggle button to sync the durations to the song Master Tempo, or not, as you like. The Length knob selects the base length of the MIDI notes that the effect will output, and the Gate modifies this base by the percentage you select. For example, as in Figure 10.3 above, if Mode is set to Sync, Length set to 1/4, and Gate set to 50%, the Note Length effect will output eighth notes (half a quarter note).

In Note Off mode, this MIDI device will output MIDI note messages when you *release* your fingers from your MIDI keyboard. This will cause the notes to play through your MIDI instruments, and the length of the notes produced can be set using the timing controls below. You can also use three other controls in Note Off mode: The Release Velocity control determines the velocity of the output note (relative to the velocities of the notes you played on your controller), and Decay Time sets the length of time it will take for an incoming note's velocity to decay to zero. The Key Scale control can be used to alter the length of the output MIDI note messages, according to the pitch of the notes you play on your controller, from low to high. Set positive or negative values here to invert the relationship of pitch to note length.

Pitch

The Pitch device transposes the MIDI notes sent to an instrument, resulting in a higher or lower part (see Figure 10.4). This can be very handy in a variety of situations, such as finding the best key for a singer. Let's say you have a MIDI track playing a piano accompaniment. Just drop a Pitch effect on to the track and dial in the new key.

Figure 10.4   Twist the Pitch knob to transpose the MIDI data passing through the effect. Easy, huh?

There is a situation in which the Pitch effect will have unusual results—when transposing MIDI used to play drum parts. It is a standard convention to assign drum sounds to individual notes of a scale. By transposing the MIDI notes going to a drum instrument, you are assigning MIDI notes to new instruments. For example, if a kick drum sound is loaded into the first cell of the Impulse instrument and a snare is loaded into the second pad, MIDI note C3 will trigger the kick, and D3 will trigger the snare (see the Impulse section in the next chapter). So if MIDI data is programmed into a MIDI clip for the kick drum, the clip will contain a pattern of MIDI notes, all C3. If we run this through the Pitch effect with the Pitch knob set to +2, the MIDI notes will be transposed up to D3, and the kick program will trigger the snare. So instead of pitching up the kick drum, the Pitch effect transposed the kick information up to the snare key range.

This situation may also arise when using patches on synthesizers that have splits. If you try to transpose the MIDI information out of the appropriate key zone, the synth will start playing the notes with the patch assigned to the other zone.

Midi Range The two values at the bottom of the Pitch device set the range of notes that can be used with the effect. If the bottom value, labeled Lowest, is set to C3, only MIDI notes C3 and higher will be allowed to enter the effect. The Range value determines, by interval, the highest note that can enter the effect. So, if the range is set to +12, notes C3 through C4 will enter the effect. Only after the incoming notes have passed the range test will they be transposed up or down.

Random

As the name suggests, the Random device will randomize the incoming MIDI notes. We can determine how liberal Live is with its randomization using the controls shown in Figure 10.5.

Figure 10.5 The Random MIDI device will shift the pitch of incoming notes a different amount every time.

The first control in the effect is the Chance value. This knob sets the odds that an incoming MIDI note will be transposed. At 0%, the effect is essentially bypassed because there is no chance a note will be transposed. At 100%, every MIDI note will be subject to randomization. At 50%, roughly every other note will be randomized. Once a note is chosen by the effect to be transposed, it will be shifted using the rules set up with the three remaining controls. The three parameters make up part of a sort of formula that determines the transposition.

The Choices parameter determines the number of random values that can occur. If the value is set to 3, a random number with a value of 1, 2, or 3 will be generated. This value is then passed on to the Scale knob. The value of this knob is multiplied by the random value from the Choices knob. The resulting number is the semitones to shift the MIDI note. So, if the Scale knob is set to 2, the resulting random transpositions will be 2, 4, or 6 semitones. The final variables in the formula are the Sign buttons. If Add is selected, the resulting random value will be added to the MIDI note, causing it to move up in pitch. Sub will subtract the random value from the current note. The Bi setting will randomly choose between adding or subtracting the value. The indicator lights on the plug-in panel will show when the note is being transposed up or down.

Let's run some quick examples to make sure we understand the math behind the plug-in.

1.   If the Choices knob is set to 1 and the Chance knob is set to 50%, about half the time a transpose value of 1 will be generated by the Choices knob. If Scale is set to

12 and the Sign mode is set to Add, the incoming notes will be transposed up one octave half of the time.

2. If the Choices knob is set to 4 and the Chance knob is set to 100%, a transpose value of 1 to 4 will be generated for every MIDI note. We then set the Scale knob to 3 and leave the Sign mode on Add. In this situation, every note will be transposed (Chance at 100%) by one of the following semitone amounts: 3, 6, 9, or 12 (1[Choices] × 3[Scale] = 3, 2 × 3 = 6, 3 × 3 = 9, and 4 × 3 = 12).

3. If the Choices knob is set to 2, the Scale knob is set to 12, and the Sign mode is set to Sub, the resulting transposition will be either 1 or 2 octaves down (1 × 12 = 12 and 2 × 12 = 24).

Above the direction switches is an additional switch for selecting Alternate mode instead of Random mode. In Alternate mode, the effect will cycle through all of the possible values in order. So, in example 2 above, the output will be transpositions of 3, 6, 9, 12 in order, repeatedly.

Scale

The first time we played with this effect, our first thought was how much fun it would be to sneak this in on an unsuspecting keyboard player. Scale allows an incoming MIDI note to be mapped to another one. You can tell the plug-in that you want every incoming D# transposed up to E. You can also tell it that you want incoming Es to be taken down to Cs. Remapping pitches like this would leave a keyboard player scratching his head wondering what had happened to his keyboard.

While Scale is perfect for practical jokes, it has practical uses as well. Don't play keyboards well? Don't know your scales? The Scale device will transpose all the wrong notes you play to the proper pitches for the appropriate key. This mapping is achieved with a 12 × 13 grid of gray squares. The columns in the grid refer to the input notes, while the rows refer to output notes. The Base knob determines the note in the bottom-left corner of the grid. If the Base note is C, then the first column on the left is the input for C notes. The next column over is the input column for C# notes, and so on. The row on the very bottom of the grid is the output row for C notes. The next row up from it is the output row for C# notes.

If you look at Figure 10.6, you'll see that the bottom-left grid square is on. This means that when a C note enters the far left column, it runs into the orange indicator in the last row, which is the C output row. So, in this case, all entering C notes will still exit as C notes. The next column over is the input column for C# notes. As you look down the column, you run into the indicator light on the third row from the bottom. If the bottom row is the output row for C notes, then this third row is the output for D notes. This means that when a C# note enters the Scale effect, it leaves as a D note.

Incoming MIDI notes are fed into the columns...

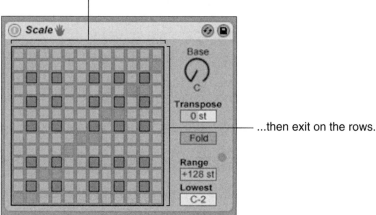

...then exit on the rows.

Figure 10.6   The Scale effect lets you remap MIDI notes using a unique grid interface.

The Scale effect can be a bit confusing and takes a while to get used to. Here's another way to get familiar with how it works. In the Chapter 10 example set, select the Scale track and record arm it. Play the note C, and notice the lower left-hand corner light up. Now, click a different box in the leftmost column and play the note C again. What note is being output now? Just count up in semitones from the bottommost box (or turn your head sideways and imagine that you are looking at the grid as a vertical piano keyboard!). If you've clicked four boxes up from the bottom, you'll now be hearing the note Eb.

You can use the grid to create musical scales. The pattern of indicators on the grid in Figure 10.6 is that of a major scale. C is chosen as the Base, so you are working with a C-major scale. Any attempt to play a black key on the keyboard will result in the MIDI note being transposed up to its nearest neighbor in the scale. Changing the Base control to G will change the scale to a G major. Every key played on the keyboard will now be forced to one of the pitches in the G-major scale.

No Scale? So you're just starting out and don't know all your musical scales? No problem. Ableton included the patterns of common scales in the Presets menu of the Scale effect. You can load one of the patterns and then use the Base knob to adapt it to your working key.

The Transpose box does what the Pitch effect does, allowing you to transpose any incoming MIDI data by a fixed value. The Range and Lowest controls can be used together to define the pitch range within which the Scale effect will be applied. (The effective range starts at the Lowest setting and reaches upward over the area of the keyboard set in the Range box.)

In Scale The Scale effect can keep you in key, and it can also keep the results of a Random effect in key, too. If the Random plug-in is generating too many notes that are out of key, load up a Scale effect and set it to the appropriate scale. Any stray note from the Random effect will be knocked into key by the Scale plug-in.

By combining a Random and a Scale plug-in, you can make a random arpeggiator that arpeggiates the pattern of notes entering the chain.

The Fold switch will prevent Scale from outputting any notes more than six semitones higher than the input note. However, it doesn't just make these notes disappear. Instead, it drops these notes down an octave. In other words, if you've mapped an incoming D3 such that that a B3 would be output, enabling the Fold switch would cause B2 to be output instead.

Velocity

The previous four MIDI effects in Live are concerned with controlling MIDI pitch information. Velocity, on the other hand, deals with (can you guess?) velocity data. It's very much like a Compressor or Scale plug-in for velocities. The grid display is like the display used in the Scale device (see Figure 10.7). Input velocities are mapped across the X-axis (the bottom of the grid), while output velocities are on the Y-axis (the right edge of the grid).

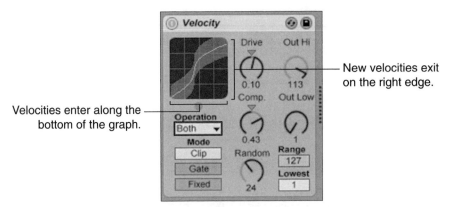

Velocities enter along the bottom of the graph.

New velocities exit on the right edge.

Figure 10.7 The grid of the Velocity effect shows the effect of adjusting the various parameters in real time.

In its default setting, there is a straight line from the bottom-left corner of the grid to the upper-right corner of the grid. This means that every input velocity maps to the same output velocity.

Increasing the Drive knob will cause the line in the grid to begin to curve. This new shape shows that low input velocities (near the left edge of the grid) are mapped to higher output velocities.

This will raise the volume of notes played quietly while leaving the loud notes basically unchanged. Decreasing the Drive knob below zero has the opposite effect, causing loud input velocities to be mapped to lower output velocities. Only the loudest input notes will still leave the plug-in with high velocities.

The Comp ("Compand"—meaning Compression/Expansion) knob is like the Drive knob, except that it creates two curves instead of one. Turning this knob up past zero exaggerates the velocity curve by making quiet notes quieter and loud ones louder. Lowering the Comp knob below zero has the opposite effect, forcing more of the values to the middle of the range. Be aware that, like the Pitch effect, the Velocity effect is changing the notes fed into an instrument. Because of this, increasing the Comp knob will not make the part sound compressed as it would if you placed a Compressor after the instrument. It will merely limit the velocities sent to the instrument while the instrument continues to output an uncompressed sound.

The Random knob defines a range of randomness that can be applied to the incoming velocities. As this knob is increased, a gray area will form on the grid showing all the possible velocities that may result from the random factor.

The Out Hi and Out Low knobs determine the highest and lowest velocities that will be output from the effect. The Range and Lowest values work like their counterparts in the Pitch and Scale effects. The Clip, Gate, and Fixed buttons determine the action taken when an input velocity is outside of the operation range set by the Range and Lowest values. In Clip mode, any velocity outside of the range will be bumped into range. The Gate mode will only allow notes with velocities within range to pass. Fixed mode will force every incoming velocity to be set to the value determined by the Out Hi knob. Finally, the Operation menu can be used to specify whether the effect should process the incoming note's velocity, release velocity, or both.

Breath of Life Velocity randomization can add a human breath of life to a programmed drum part. Humans can't play with the consistency of a machine, so randomizing the velocities of the drum parts can make the beat sound less repetitive. This is especially effective on hi-hats and shakers.

---

11 ReWire

W hile Live is an amazing audio production environment, you still may want to generate sounds using other software tools. Virtual instruments and plug-in effects give you access to a plethora of third-party programs. But what do you do if the program you want to use is "bigger" than just a plug-in or an effect? What if you want to harness the power of another computer program? Well, you just ReWire it together with Live!

What Is ReWire?

Power users have been synchronizing sequencers and computers for years, as it was the only way they could produce the all the various sounds they needed. The limited hardware solutions of yesteryear required that many be used simultaneously to achieve a fully orchestrated sound. Most of the first synthesizers were monophonic (they could only play one note at a time), so multiple units were necessary for achieving chords and other simultaneous sounds.

Synchronizing multiple computer systems is common as well. One computer can be playing back audio files through effects while another computer is running virtual instruments. One could be a Mac and the other could be a PC if you wished. The point is that each system doesn't provide the entire solution on its own and has to be augmented by another.

With the wide variety of music-making software, there are bound to be some applications that have their own unique features, workflow, and sound—Live is no exception. But do you have to run Live on one computer and the other program on another? With the advent of ReWire, the answer is no. ReWire will allow you to run both programs on the same machine simultaneously. But ReWire does much more for you than just allow multiple applications to run. It will keep the applications in sync with each other and allow audio and MIDI to pass from one to the other.

Masters

In a ReWire setup, there's actually no wiring that you have to be concerned with. ReWire functions transparently between compatible applications, allowing operation to be as seamless as possible. In any ReWire setup, there is always one program designated as the *ReWire Master*. The ReWire Master is the program that will be communicating with the computer's audio hardware and will accept audio streams from other ReWire applications. You must open the ReWire Master application before any of the other programs you want to use.

Slaves

Only one application can be the ReWire Master, so all the other programs running will be *ReWire Slaves*. Slaves don't actually communicate with the computer's audio hardware at all. Instead, their audio outputs are routed to the ReWire Master application. This rerouting of audio happens automatically inside the computer after a program is launched as a ReWire Slave. Since the audio is being passed through the Master application, you will not hear the Slave application unless the Master program is set to pass the Slave's audio to the computer's audio hardware.

Using ReWire with Live

Live can act as both a ReWire Master and a ReWire Slave. Not all programs have the capability to function in both modes. For example, Steinberg's Cubase SX sequencer can only function as a ReWire Master. Propellerhead's Reason can only be used in Slave mode. So if you wanted to use Live and Cubase together, Cubase would be the Master and Live would be the Slave. If you wanted to use Reason, Live would be the Master and Reason would be the Slave. How does the operation of Live differ when running as Master or Slave? Since ReWire was designed to be transparent for the user, little will change in Live's operability either way. There are a few differences, of course, and we'll explain these next.

Using Live as a ReWire Master

When Live is used as a ReWire Master, it will operate exactly the same as when it's used by itself. When Live is the only ReWire application running, it will be in Master mode. This is true of any ReWire application that is capable of Master mode. The way a ReWire application knows it's the Master is that it has been launched without any other ReWire Masters running. So, to run Live as a ReWire Master, launch it first and then launch any applications you want to use as Slaves. The way an application knows that it's a Slave is that it has been launched with a Master application already running. This means that even a Slave-only application like Reason must be launched after the Master application.

When Live is hosting a ReWire Slave application, the Slave's audio outputs will be available as inputs into the Session Mixer (see Figure 11.1). In the Input/Output Routing section, you'll be able to choose the ReWire application in the first box and the desired channel(s) from that program in the second box.

Once you have selected the ReWire source for a channel, it will behave exactly like any other audio channel with an input selected. You can hear the audio from the ReWire source by switching the channel's monitoring to On or by arming the track for recording with monitoring set to Auto. You can record the audio from the external application as a new clip in the track, either by recording a clip in the Session View or by pressing Record in the Control Bar and recording directly to the Arrangement. This is the same process for recording any other audio source on an audio track, as explained in previous chapters.

Figure 11.1 Here outputs 1 and 2 from Reason are inputs for Track 1 in the Session Mixer. We can hear the audio output from Reason by switching Monitor to On.

If you don't want to record the ReWire Slave as audio, you can still incorporate its audio streams in a Live mixdown when you select Render to Disk from the File menu. If the ReWire Slave applications are running, and their channels in the Session Mixer are being monitored, their audio will be mixed in with the rest of your Live Set when rendered. Laptop owners who have fast CPUs often prefer to run the ReWire applications in real time. Since laptops generally have slower hard drives, it's sometimes easier for the computer to run the ReWire applications, as opposed to streaming more audio from disk.

While audio can only flow from the ReWire Slaves to the ReWire Master, it is possible for MIDI to flow in the opposite direction. This allows you to control compatible ReWire Slave applications the way you would control a virtual instrument in Live. Just as you can select a ReWire Slave application as an input to an audio track, you can select a slave at the output of a MIDI track (see Figure 11.2). You can select the Slave application with the upper box and the destination channel/device in the lower box.

A destination channel will only be listed if there are devices or elements in the Slave application that are active and able to receive MIDI messages. For example, if you load an empty rack into

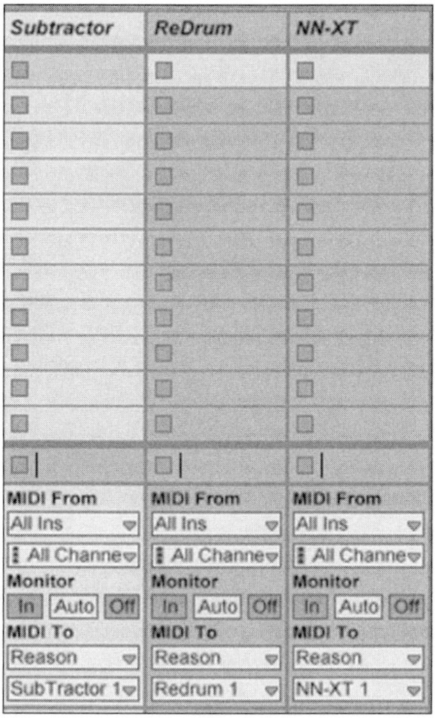

Subtractor	ReDrum	NN-XT
▣	▢	▢
▢	▢	▢
▢	▢	▢
▢	▢	▢
▢	▢	▢
▢	▢	▢
▢	▢	▢
▢	▢	▢
▢	▢	▢
▢	▢	▢
▢	▢	▢
▢ │	▢ │	▢ │
MIDI From	**MIDI From**	**MIDI From**
All Ins ▽	All Ins ▽	All Ins ▽
⋮ All Channe▽	⋮ All Channe▽	⋮ All Channe▽
Monitor	**Monitor**	**Monitor**
In Auto Off	In Auto Off	In Auto Off
MIDI To	**MIDI To**	**MIDI To**
Reason ▽	Reason ▽	Reason ▽
SubTractor 1▽	Redrum 1 ▽	NN-XT 1 ▽

Figure 11.2 These three MIDI tracks are being routed to the Subtractor, ReDrum, and NN-XT modules in Reason. They can now be programmed and automated using the power and convenience of Live's clips.

Reason, there will be no output devices listed in the lower box. If you make a few devices, like a Subtractor, ReDrum, and NN-XT sampler, these devices will be individually selectable in the lower box of the MIDI track's Input/Output section.

Not all ReWire Slave applications are capable of receiving MIDI input from the Master application. If a program is not able to receive MIDI, it will not be listed as an available output destination in the MIDI track.

Remember, in order to hear the results of your MIDI messages sent to the ReWire Slave, you'll need to have an audio track set up to monitor the return signal from the Slave. So instead of the MIDI track outputting the audio (as would happen when a virtual instrument is loaded onto a MIDI track), you'll need another audio track to hear the results. This means that the MIDI info leaves on one track, and the audio returns on another.

External Instruments-Internally The External Instrument device, introduced in Live 7, allows you to handle sending MIDI to a ReWire application and receive the audio back from that application in the same track. It's as easy as dropping an external device into a

MIDI track and configuring it using the same settings you would for a ReWire track. For a complete explanation of External Instruments, see Chapter 9.

Using Live as a ReWire Slave

The exact steps for opening Live as a ReWire Slave depend partly on the ReWire Master application you use. In some cases, you may need to enable ReWire channels in the Master application before Live is launched as a ReWire Slave; otherwise Live may be confused and try to configure itself as the Master as well (which means it will not do what you want). Be sure to check the ReWire Master application's manual for recommendations on how you should do this. The only hard and fast rule, though, is that the ReWire Master must be launched before Live. When launching Live, it will detect the presence of the Master application and therefore automatically load itself in Slave mode. (You'll see a little message about this on the Live splash screen during bootup.)

When using Live as a ReWire Slave application, you'll notice many subtle differences in available options throughout the program. The first thing to be aware of is that like all ReWire Slave applications, Live will be communicating with the ReWire Master program instead of the computer's audio hardware. Because of this, Live's Audio Preferences will not be available and will instead be replaced with a screen stating that audio is being handled by the Master application.

Also missing from Live in Slave mode are settings for MIDI output, MIDI Sync, and Remote Control Surfaces. Only the MIDI input settings will be available as usual for Remote Control and playing virtual instruments.

Another difference will be the available output routings for audio in the Session Mixer. When looking at the Master track output assignment, you'll find that the list is populated with Mix and Bus names instead of the outputs of your audio interface. These buses are the pathways that lead from Live into the ReWire Master. The ReWire Master will receive the buses individually, allowing you to route one Live track to one channel of the Master's mixer while routing a different Live track to another. You can then process the channels separately in the Master application however you want.

Note that ReWire also gives you the ability to access your Ableton plug-in instruments in Live when it is running in ReWire Slave mode. This means that you can program MIDI parts in your ReWire Master and then send the MIDI data to Live to control Live's built-in instruments (Impulse, Simpler, Operator, and Sampler). However, please note that this will not work with any third-party VST or AU instruments, which will not load if you are in ReWire Slave mode. This can still be very useful, though, in cases when you want to use the MIDI programming facilities in another sequencer to control the instruments in Live.

Let's look at how to set this up with Digidesign Pro Tools. (The procedure for setting up ReWire varies from host to host, so consult your sequencer's documentation if you're working with a program other than Pro Tools.) First, start Pro Tools and open a new session. Then make sure that you have at least one audio track, instrument track, or aux input; ReWire input can be received on any of these track types. Then, insert the Ableton Live ReWire plug-in on the track (see Figure 11.3a). When the plug-in window opens, select Ableton Live: Mix L-Mix R, as seen in Figure 11.3b.

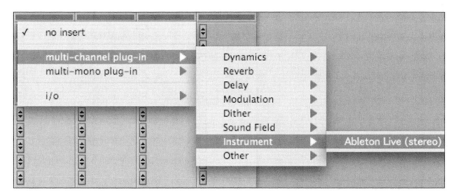

Figure 11.3a   Configuring a track in Pro Tools to receive ReWire input from Live.

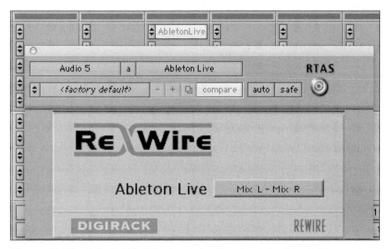

Figure 11.3b   Mix L–Mix R is the default output for Live's Master track when running as a ReWire Slave.

Now you are ready to work with Live. Go ahead and open the application now; you should see the message "Running as ReWire Slave" in Live's splash screen as it starts up. (If you get an error about having two ReWire Master applications open at the same time, you missed something when setting up Pro Tools, so quit Live and check the steps above again before relaunching it.) Looking over at the Master track in your Live Set, you'll see that the Master output is set to Mix L/R, the same input we selected in Pro Tools (see Figure 11.4).

Figure 11.4   Live's Master Out is being sent to the same ReWire bus that our Pro Tools track is receiving on.

Even before there is sound coming out, you'll be able to see ReWire at work. Notice that pressing Play in either Live or Pro Tools causes both sequencers to start running, and that changing the tempo in Pro Tools causes Live's tempo to change as well. Now you can drop some clips into Live or open an existing Set in Live, and you'll hear Live's Master output through Pro Tools.

If you want to control Live's instruments from Pro Tools, there are a few additional steps. First, create a MIDI track and place one of Ableton's instruments on it—for this example, we'll use an Impulse. Next, create a MIDI track in Pro Tools (if you haven't already—the order of the steps isn't important here). Set the output of your MIDI track in Pro Tools to the Live track, as seen in Figure 11.5. That's it! Now you can program your Impulse from the MIDI track in Pro Tools. Interestingly, you can simultaneously play a MIDI clip on the Impulse track in Live while also sending MIDI data from Pro Tools—the setting of the Monitor switch is irrelevant.

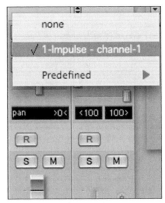

Figure 11.5   Setting up a MIDI track to control the Impulse on Track 1 in Live.

In the previous example, all of Live's tracks are sent via the Master track to a stereo track in the host. It's also possible to route tracks from Live directly into individual tracks in the host. To do this, just select a ReWire bus for a track's output in Live (instead of the Master), and create a track in your host to receive audio via this bus. Figures 11.6a and 11.6b show how to do this in Pro Tools.

Figure 11.6a   Choosing a ReWire bus as the output for a track in Live.

Figure 11.6b   Receiving audio from the same ReWire bus on a track Pro Tools.

ReWire Power

Using ReWire Slave applications with Live gives you an expanded list of sound sources to create with. Frequently, you may just want to create some audio loops in a ReWire Slave application, record them in Live, and then close the Slave program. The real-time nature of Live lets it load ReWire Slaves, use them, and then close them, all while Live continues playing—without glitches. This makes ReWire a viable live-performance tool since Live's ReWire hosting is rock solid. Of course, as with all other procedures in Live, be sure to try this out a few times before a show to confirm that your computer can handle running multiple audio applications at once without causing audio problems. You'll also want to make sure that any ReWire Slaves you're using are stable enough for live use as well.

Many users flock to Live because of its ability to operate as a ReWire Slave. The unique loop-based and time-compression tools of Live can be used in concert with standard production programs like Digidesign Pro Tools. While Live is feeding into Pro Tools, you can use Live to audition loops at the Pro Tools tempo. You can quickly add drum loops or MIDI parts that remain under user control. You can add Warp Markers to takes done with Pro Tools to fix timing problems. Once all the correct parts are made, the results can be rendered as audio into Pro Tools.

In this chapter, we have looked at the most common ways to use ReWire with Live and other ReWire Slave and Master applications. ReWire is an incredibly exciting, creative, and fun aspect of Live. Many musicians and producers we have met come to Live because of its ability to ReWire. Rest assured, once you begin linking software applications, you will be hooked. Take time to explore your favorite ways of linking Live. In the next chapter, we will explore some of our favorite power tips for working with Live.

Groove by Yourself While the tempo control in Live will have an effect on all ReWire applications, the Groove setting is solely for the use of Live. Increasing the Groove will cause Live to start swinging while the other applications keep to a straight-time feel.

WHO'S USING LIVE? Dykehouse *Michael Dykehouse blends guitar-based rock with swirling atmospheres and lush electronic production (www.ghostly.com/1.0/artists/dykehouse/). He has released two albums,* Dynamic Obsolescence *(Planet Mu, 2001) and* Midrange *(Ghostly International, 2004), both to critical acclaim.*

"My musical interests began with garage bands and four-track based bedroom production," explains Dykehouse. "As my tastes began turning away from more traditional rock leanings, I began using hardware electronics to flesh out my ideas. Over the last five years, I began the gradual implementation of software."

Dykehouse now uses Live for both composition and performance. "As a Mac user, I have used most of the DAWs available over the years, and none holds a candle to Live's ease of use, power, and flexibility. The fact that Live 4 (which was the first version I became familiar with) seemed infinitely more stable and intuitive than either Pro Tools or Logic was the impetus of my switch. There aren't endless windows cluttering up the screen, on-the-fly arrangements are a dream, and the program seems much more efficiently coded (meaning less of a pull on my CPU) than its competitors."

Dykehouse frequently makes use of Live's ReWire capabilities during production and performance. "I use Live with Propellerhead's Reason, as both are rock solid in their compatibility. Furthermore, I can't live without the Warp functions (and now Auto-Warp!) of Live. No other OS X program performs this function with the ease and flexibility that Live does. Live is a permanent fixture in my studio. Thank you, Ableton!"

12 Playing Live...Live

Most books written about music-production software would not include a chapter like the one you're about to read. It's not because the writers of this book are deranged or just trying to be different. It's because Live can actually live up to its name in a live performance. As you will discover, it's a true treat to use the same software to create your music *and* perform it. You won't have to worry about converting songs from media your composing software uses into something Live can use. You won't have to worry about transferring effect and instrument settings. The same tools you use to write can be used to play—just like any other instrument. After all, should the two processes really be that different?

Because of its flexible control methods and instant response to user input, Live is the perfect companion for a gigging musician. Live performs wonders in all types of scenarios, ranging from DJ gigs to improvisational music and theater. Regardless of what type of musician you consider yourself to be, I recommend reading all the information presented in this chapter. Any technique relating to the use of Live is pertinent—innovations can come from taking ideas from one musician's style and applying them to your own style.

DJ

DJ or not, every one of you reading this book should study this section. Using Live to DJ exploits some of the unique (and potentially confusing) features of the program and extends them to the *n*th degree. You already know that Live can sync loops together using its Warp Engine. DJs use this powerful mechanism to sync *entire songs* together. They also use an array of clips to manufacture new arrangements of the songs, literally creating their own remixes right in front of the dancing masses. By learning the techniques employed here, you'll achieve a firmer grasp on Warp Marking and real-time control.

Assembling Your Audio Files

The process of DJing with Live is twofold: First comes the work of ripping and Warp Marking your songs (prepping the files), followed by the joy of putting it all together (performing). A great feature for DJs is Live's support for multiple compressed and uncompressed file formats: You can use WAV, AIFF, SD2, MP3, AAC, Ogg Vorbis, Ogg FLAC, and regular FLAC, which provides a wide range of compatibility with other software programs.

Ripping

If the song you want to use is on a CD, you will need to copy the music from the CD to your computer using a process known as *ripping*. There are many programs that do this, quite a few of which are free. While you can find a deluge of programs to try by typing "CD ripper" into Google, I recommend Apple's iTunes (www.itunes.com). It's available for both Mac and PC, it's free, and it has a number of features that will prove helpful when building your DJ music collection. I'm going to use iTunes in my instructions here, but you can use your favorite ripping program instead with the same results.

Take It with You Before we get too far, we need to mention external hard drives. If you're a DJ compiling a collection of audio files for your performances, a big hard drive is a good thing to have. It will keep all of your music in one place. And if you have multiple computer systems that you use (a desktop at home and a laptop for gigs), you won't have to store the collection on both systems. The hard drive will become your virtual record case.

Before you start ripping CDs, consider a few setup options for the ripping software. First, you should check the ripping format. Many programs these days default to MP3 or a similar compressed format for ripping so you can transfer the results to a portable player such as an iPod. If you decide to rip to a compressed format, make sure to take into account that Live plays compressed files by uncompressing them into WAV files in the background and storing these uncompressed files in the Decoding Cache (see Chapter 2, "Getting Live Up and Running"). With disk space being as cheap as it is, ripping to uncompressed WAV files will make your life simpler in the long run. However, if you are tight on disk space or need to work with MP3s for some other reason, here are a few recommendations.

Drag and Drop On a Mac, there's no need to use a ripping program as long as you don't need to compress your audio files and you don't mind having your music collection in AIFF format. Pop a CD into your Mac, and open it in the Finder. You'll see all of the CD tracks as AIFF files, and as long as you're connected to the Internet, all of the track names will be downloaded as well. Just drag the files to your hard drive, and you're done.

The only concern with using AIFFs is that they are not natively supported by some Windows applications. However, most pro audio applications can use or import them, and utilities for conversion, such as AWave (www.fmjsoft.com), are readily available.

First, MP3 compression has different quality settings. Since MP3 is compressing your audio, it's throwing away bits that it thinks you can't hear. The lower the quality settings on the MP3 converter, the more info will be thrown away, eventually becoming noticeable to your ears. The most important quality factor for making MP3s is the *bit rate*. I recommend converting your songs to MP3 with a bit rate of at least 256 kilobits per second (kbps) or higher. When setting the bit rate, you normally have an option for specifying *constant bit rate* (CBR) or *variable bit rate* (VBR) compression. CBR is a little bit safer than VBR as nearly every MP3 player (software or hardware) will read CBR files. Some programs and hardware have difficulty with VBR. VBR compression also takes longer to perform because the encoder must analyze the entire song before compressing. CBR, on the other hand, begins compressing immediately.

In iTunes, you'll find the compression options under the Importing tab of the Preferences (see Figure 12.1). iTunes provides a number of preset compression settings—I recommend choosing Custom from the Setting menu to gain access to all of the compression options, including VBR. For programs other than iTunes, you should be able to access these settings from their Preferences or Options menus. Check the program's documentation if you can't quickly locate these parameters.

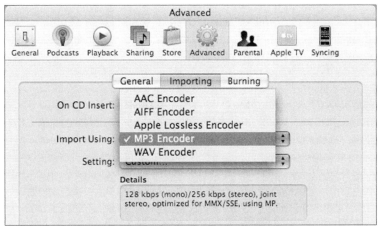

Figure 12.1   The iTunes Importing options allow you to specify MP3 or WAV as your preferred file type. You can also select the compression quality with the Setting menu.

Now that you've specified the format for ripping your files, you still need to tell your ripping program where to put them. Some programs will ask you for a location to save the files each time a song is ripped. Others will have you select a destination directory for the audio files. Regardless of the method employed by your software, I do recommend making some sort of logical arrangement of your songs in your collection. For example, you could make a folder called *Breaks* and store all your breakbeat tracks there. You could make another folder called *DnB* and store all your drum-and-bass cuts there. Whatever method you choose, it should be easy for you to navigate during a show. You don't want to be left searching for a song when the current song ends!

iTunes Note iTunes can organize your music in folders for you automatically. Click the Advanced tab/button in iTunes Preferences. The first window shows the location where iTunes will maintain your library. You can use the Change button to specify a new location, such as your external hard drive. Next, make sure the first two checkboxes are checked. This will cause iTunes to maintain the library and also move any imported songs into this location (in case the songs already exist elsewhere on your hard drives).

When you examine your iTunes music folder, you won't see any music files. Instead, you'll find a list of folders with artist names. Inside each of these artist folders are additional folders for albums. Open the album folder, and you'll find all the songs you ripped from that album. When accessed through Live's Browser, iTunes makes locating a song a snap.

Now that your audio programs are properly configured, it's time to start ripping. When you insert a CD, the program will identify it and usually allow you to select specific tracks in case you don't want to import the entire CD. After you've selected your tracks, you can start the ripping process. For iTunes, you'll right-click (Ctrl-click) on your selection to expose the context menu and choose Convert Selection To. Now sit back and wait.

iTunes Note 2 When you're connected to the Internet, iTunes will automatically search for the information on the CD you've inserted. It can find almost any CD and load the artist's name, album name, and all of the track names for the CD and fill them in for you. iTunes is not the only program that can do this, but you may have to enable the feature manually in other applications. If you don't have an Internet connection, you'll have to type in the names yourself.

Converting

With the rise in popularity of online music stores, such as Apple's iTunes or Bleep (www.bleep.com), you may already have the song you want to play as a digital music file on your computer. Perhaps the song is so hard to find that you're able to buy it only as a download. While these purchased downloads are in a compressed format that Live can play, many of them are protected with DRM (Digital Rights Management). This ensures that you, the buyer of the file, are the only person who can play them. In order to play these files, you'll need to use a program that can deal with protected files. Unfortunately, Live does not have provisions for these protected files, so you will not be able to play them natively. The solution for this is to burn the files to a CD (which iTunes will allow you to do, even with protected files) and then rip the CD back into iTunes. If you want to maintain the audio quality of the CD-burned song, rip the CD back into your computer using an uncompressed format, such as WAV or AIFF; otherwise you'll be recompressing the audio and further degrading the sound quality.

The best thing, though, is to purchase music from an outlet such as Beatport (www.beatport
.com), Emusic (www.emusic.com), or iTunes Plus that sells unprotected files; this makes the
whole process much easier.

Recording

If you don't have your song on CD or as a digital music file, you'll have to import it the hard
way. If the track you want is on vinyl, you'll need to connect your turntable to your computer's
audio interface. This will probably require that you go through a DJ mixer or home preamp,
since most audio interfaces do not allow for a direct connection of turntables. Once you've got
your signal entering a channel on Live's Session Mixer, you can record the song as a new audio
clip (see Chapter 5, "The Audio Clip." if you forgot how to do this).

Warp on the Fly Did you know you can add Warp Markers to an audio clip that is recording? Simply press the Tap button along with the song, and Live will insert Warp Markers
with your tapped beats. This is great when recording tracks that have a varying tempo,
such as a song that was recorded without the assistance of computers or metronomes.

Warp Marking Your Songs

Now that you have your songs in AIFF or WAV format, you're ready to begin the second step of
prepping a file for DJing. In order for Live to keep the song in time with any others that you may
be playing, you'll need to place Warp Markers in the file to indicate the location of beats in the
track. Warp Marking an entire song sounds like quite an undertaking, but you'll quickly gain a
rhythm that will let you complete a song in only a minute or two—maybe less.

Auto-Warping

Live features an Auto-Warping algorithm that can analyze any long file you import into your
Set. While we sometimes wish that the Auto-Warping algorithm were the ultimate solution for
prepping files, there are many instances in which it won't work properly. To be fair, Live usually
screws up only the *phase* of the song. That is, it will get the overall tempo of the song right but
will not put Warp Marker 1 on the first downbeat of the song. In this case, your song will play in
sync, but offset from the proper downbeat. It will then be up to you to manually shift all the
Warp Markers into the proper location. This can normally be done by clicking on a Warp
Marker (to select it) and then pressing Ctrl (Cmd)+A, which is the key command for Select
All. This will select all the Warp Markers, allowing you to drag them right and left as a
group. If you don't shift all the Warp Markers, you'll correct the timing only from the first
Warp Marker to the second. From that point on, the song will still be out of sync because
you haven't shifted any of the other markers.

The Nudge If you don't have time to correct a phase error as described above, you can offset the clip using the Nudge buttons found in the bottom-left corner of the Clip View. Each time you click one of these buttons, the current play position will be offset by the current Global Quantize amount. That is, if Global Quantize is set to 1/4, each click of the Nudge buttons will offset the clip by one-quarter of a bar (one beat).

If you need to make an extremely minute adjustment, set the Global Quantize to None. Now each click of the Nudge buttons will result in a slight shifting of the clip.

Manual Warping

Even with Live's Auto-Warp technology, it still often works best to Warp Mark your tracks by hand to get the tightest synchronization possible. By warping the songs manually, we can place as many markers as are required to get the tempo correct, and we can place the markers perfectly in line with the transients in the song (something the Auto-Warping technology doesn't do too well).

The best way to begin Warp Marking a song is by determining its original tempo. Start by turning off the Warp button in the Clip View. This will make the clip play at its original speed, regardless of the tempo of your Live Set. Launch the clip and begin tapping along with the song using the Tap Tempo button. It's best to use a key assignment for this instead of clicking with the mouse. After you've tapped some beats, Live's tempo will start to settle around the song's tempo. Since Live's Tempo display is accurate to two decimal places, you'll probably get tempos like 125.82 BPM or 98.14 BPM instead of round numbers like 110 BPM or 85 BPM. Chances are, however, that the tempo is actually a round number if the song was created by a computer or sequencer. So, if Live says the tapped tempo is 102.15 BPM, it's probably just 102.00 BPM. Go ahead and double-click the Tempo display and type in the rounded tempo; then activate the Warp button in the Clip View. Live will place the tempo of the project in the clip's Seg BPM box. (On the rare occasion that this doesn't happen, you can type the tempo into this box by hand.)

Now that you have the right tempo, you need to align the grid with the first beat of the song. Zoom in to the waveform display and move Warp Marker 1 into position with the first beat of the file. Don't worry if you don't find the first downbeat until later in the song (perhaps the song has an ambient intro that drops into the beat further in), since the grid also has negative values (grid lines to the left of Marker 1). You can still place the Start Marker before Marker 1, so starting on bar −6 is starting 16 bars before the beat drops (see Figure 12.2). This is especially cool because you can play a song with a completely nebulous, rhythmless intro yet drop on the beat perfectly 16 bars later. Try that with a record!

After you've determined the tempo and placed Marker 1 at the first recognizable downbeat of the song, the remaining grid markers to the right should be pretty close to, if not dead on, the beats. Turn on Live's Metronome and listen to the track against the click. The song should start

You can place the Start Marker at a location before Warp Marker 1.

Figure 12.2 Even though you don't hear the first drumbeat until bar 17 of this song, you can place Warp Marker 1 at this location and start the song from bar −6.

out perfectly aligned with the click. If the track stays in time all the way through, then the clip is ready to go; however, chances are that the song will start to drift ahead or behind the click as it plays. This is due to slight differences in BPMs between Live and the song. Perhaps the song is actually running at 101.98 BPM (even computers can be a little off). After a few minutes, the discrepancy will add up to a complete misalignment with the beat, shown in the figures below.

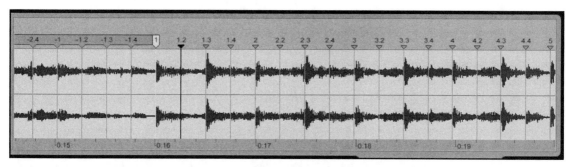

Figure 12.3a The beginning of the song looks like it's aligned properly...

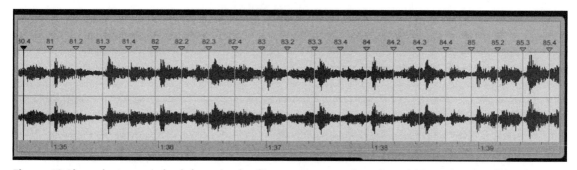

Figure 12.3b ...but as you look later in the file, you can see that the grid is no longer aligned.

To compensate for the "drift" you may encounter, you can place additional Warp Markers to keep the clip synchronized to Live. Placing a Warp Marker every 32 bars is usually sufficient. To make the process as easy as possible, turn on Loop in the Clip View and use the Region/Loop Markers to inspect small sections of the song one at a time. For example, create a two-bar loop and place it at the beginning of the clip. Launch the clip and listen to the two bars against the click. If the beats are aligned with the click, move the loop region to the right to bar 32. Listen to the loop around these two bars. Here, you may notice that the clip doesn't line up exactly with the click anymore. Create a Warp Marker in the middle of the loop area (bar 33) and move this marker to properly align it with the beats in the clip (see Figure 12.4). You should now hear bars 32 and 33 looping in time with the click. Furthermore, everything between bar 1 and bar 33 should be perfectly aligned as well. Repeat the process by moving the loop region to the right another 32 bars (bar 64). Check this new loop area and adjust if necessary. Repeat the process to the end of the clip.

I added a Warp Marker and adjusted it to line it up with the beat.

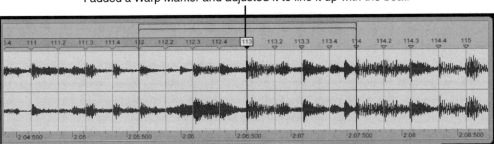

Figure 12.4 I was inspecting various sections of the song two bars at a time. When listening to this section, I had to create a Warp Marker to align the song to the beat.

After you've placed your Warp Markers to ensure proper timing, press the Save button in the clip. This will save the location of the Warp Markers so they'll be recalled the next time you import the clip from the Browser. You can also check the Warp Mode to make sure that you're using the most effective method for time stretching. Complex mode is usually the best, but you may want to use Beats or Tones mode if your CPU is overburdened.

Now that you know the process for Warp Marking long files, sit back, grab a frosty beverage of your choice, and start clicking away. You'll want to have every file in your collection saved with the correct Warp Markers so that the songs will play in time every time you use them in a set.

Slop into Solid Gold With the ability to time-align audio files, many DJs are incorporating songs into their sets that weren't recorded to a steady tempo. Old songs from the Grateful Dead or Led Zeppelin can be Warp Marked to the point where they will play back perfectly to a rigid dance beat.

The process is the same as described above, except that you'll be making many more Warp Markers for these types of songs. Instead of placing a Warp Marker every 32 bars through the track, you'll probably want one every *two* bars. If the band was moving wildly in and out of time, you may need to be even more meticulous.

The payoff is worth the extra work. You can really mess with your audience by introducing this old music into your set. Furthermore, traditional DJs will be trying to figure out what you're doing since this is beyond the capabilities of their turntables.

Organization

Live's Browser offers a world of convenience for DJs. One thing you can do is create multiple clips for a single song. After you've Warp Marked a song, duplicate this clip a couple of times and set the Start and Loop points of the clips to useful areas of the song. For example, the first clip in the track can be the whole song. The clips below it can be the first verse, first chorus, second verse, breakdown, or any other sections you want. You can then grab all these clips at once and drag them to the Browser. At this point, you'll have made a new Live Set, and you can give it the name of the song you're editing.

While performing your DJ set, you can import this Live Set instead of just the single MP3 file. What will happen is that you'll end up loading all of the clips you made, so you'll have instant access to various sections of the song. You can jump directly to a chorus, loop the breakdown for an intro, or extend verses. If you make additional variations during your performance, you can drag the clips back to the Browser as a Live Set so you can use them again at your next show.

It can sometimes be beneficial to spend some time with the EQ 8 to shape the frequency content of the track. Often, when recording a song from vinyl, the bass is not as prominent as in a song that is ripped from CD. Therefore, we use the EQ Eight to boost the bass and make any other appropriate adjustments so that the song will sonically match any others that we might be spinning at the time. If the song is really old, you can add Compressor to beef up the song—the "brick wall limiting" used in today's CD mastering makes old tracks sound weak by comparison.

Resample or Save? Once you've added effects to a track, such as EQ and compression, you can decide either to resample the track and print the effects to a new file or drag the clip to the Browser and save it as a Live Clip. Both have advantages.

If you save your track as a new Live Clip, the effects get saved along with the clip. The next time you drop the Live Clip into a set, the effects will get placed on the track, with one condition: There can't already be any effects in the Track View. You have to either drop them into the Drop Area (to create new tracks) or drop them into tracks with no devices on them. Otherwise, only the clips will get imported.

The advantage of resampling is that you create a new audio file with the effects recorded into it. Now, when you use the new file, you get the sound of the effects no matter what track you drop it into, and you also save CPU power.

How much you end up using the Browser during your set, as opposed to creating a Set with the clips you plan on using in advance, has a lot to do with the speed of the computer and hard drive you are using. The most likely time for Live's audio output to hiccup is during tasks such as instantiating plug-ins and importing Live Sets. So, if you're using the technique described above for importing clips during a performance, make sure to practice and make sure that Live can manage everything you plan on doing without interruption. For many, the best technique ends up being able to create a Set with every track you may use already in a clip slot.

Performance Techniques

Now that you've got your Warp-Marked files ready, we are going to discuss the techniques used for cueing and mixing songs. We'll start by looking at traditional DJs, their equipment, and their performance methods. You'll see how Live can do the same things, plus a few never possible before.

Beat Matching

The whole concept of DJing revolves around blending one great song into another great song, without interrupting the flow or rhythm of music. Quite often, this requires aligning the tempos of the two songs so they play in sync with each other, a technique known as *beat matching*. DJs using turntables or CD decks will use their Pitch Adjust sliders to slow down or speed up a new song to match the tempo of one that's already playing. Once the tempos are matched, the DJ will start the new song and begin to fade it in, usually with the crossfader on his mixer. Since the tempos are matched and the DJ started the track at the right moment, the beats of the two songs will be playing on top of each other. The beat will remain constant as the old song is replaced by the new one. While performing this mix, the DJ will probably have to make minute adjustments to the playback speeds of the records or CDs in case they begin to drift out of sync.

The process of beat matching two songs in Live involves nothing more than having files with proper Warp Markers. Once Warp Markers are in the right place, Live will know how to play that file at any tempo. So, any song can be matched in tempo with any other simply by loading the two clips and launching them—this is no different from importing drum loops of different tempos into the same Live Set. Using Launch Quantization, Live will start the songs in sync so you'll never have to worry about making tiny adjustments to keep the songs from drifting. Just fire and forget. Easy!

The DJ Mixer

The whole DJ setup centers around the DJ mixer, a specialized mixer with controls specific to DJs. The DJ's audio sources (turntables and CD players) are connected to the mixer, and the output is connected to the sound system. The mixer has audio channels with EQ, the ability to pre-listen to tracks (cueing), and a crossfader for mixing between audio sources. Some advanced mixers will also have effect loops, allowing external processing boxes to add beat-synced delays, whooshing flanges, and other tweaks to the mix. To emulate a DJ mixer with Live, you'll use features of the Session Mixer, which we'll discuss in a moment. But most important, you'll want a MIDI control device to offer you the same tactile control that DJs are accustomed to.

We briefly mentioned some MIDI controllers in Chapter 2, and a good portion of them can suit a Live DJ quite well. The Evolution X-Session, as well as Faderfox's various tiny MIDI controllers, for example, will give you just the right assortment of controls to get the job done. The most important things are a crossfader control (for assignment to Live's Crossfader), at least two controls to adjust the volumes of the tracks you'll be mixing (these can be faders or knobs), six knobs for EQ controls, and some keys or buttons for triggering mutes, EQ kills, and effects. Since Live allows you to assign any MIDI knob or button to a control, you could certainly use a different type of MIDI controller from the ones mentioned here for the same tasks. For example, you could use a vertical fader on your device as a crossfader, as long as you can get used to the vertical orientation (you probably won't be pulling off any flares, crab scratches, or cuts with this, but it still works for smoothly blending between tracks). Even though Live displays its volume controls as vertical faders, you could use the knobs of your controller to adjust volumes. There are some DJ mixers that actually use knobs instead of sliders for a vintage feel. If worse comes to worst, you can still achieve a great mix just by using your mouse and computer keyboard; the point is to make sure you have adequate control of your mix so you can shape it at will.

In Figure 12.5, I have set up Live's Session View like a standard two-channel DJ mixer. There are two audio tracks each assigned to different sides of the crossfader. There are EQ Threes loaded onto each of the audio tracks, plus a Compressor II on the Master track. Two Return tracks are in use for Ping Pong Delay and Reverb devices, but you can load any kind of effects you'd prefer.

In order to cue or preview tracks, you'll need an audio interface with four outputs—two outs for the main mix and two others to feed your headphones. Many audio interfaces, such as M-Audio's FireWire series or Echo Audio's Indigo cards, have built-in assignable headphone outputs, which are perfect for this application. In the Master track, choose outs 1/2 for Cue and 3/4 for Master. (You may need to enable these outputs in Live's Audio Preferences if they aren't available in the menus.) Connect outputs 3/4 to the speakers or sound system and plug a pair of headphones into the audio interface. If your interface doesn't have a built-in headphone amplifier, you can use an external amplifier, such as a home stereo or small mixer, or purchase a small headphone amp box from your local music store.

To make Live's Cue system work, click the Solo button just above the Preview Volume knob (see Figure 12.6). The button will change to Cue, and you'll see small headphone icons in the buttons where the solos used to be in the Session Mixer. This button will switch only if you've assigned the Cue and Master to different outputs, as explained above. Clicking a headphone icon will route that track to the Cue bus, thus allowing you to hear it on your headphones. Please note that enabling Cue on a track does not remove it from the Master Output. You'll need to turn off the Track Activator button so only you may hear it. Once the track is properly cued, engage the Track Activator to send the track back to the Master track and out to the dance floor.

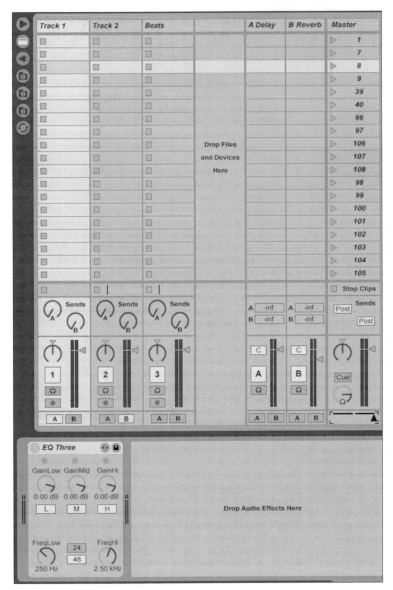

Figure 12.5   A simple Live Set ready for DJing.

To prevent the chance of mistakes caused by forgetting to deactivate the Track Activator, we've varied the session's setup by adding another audio track whose Track Activator is always off (see Figure 12.7). By leaving it off and leaving Cue on, any audio clip placed in this track will be heard in the headphones only. Once you're done cueing, drag the clip from this preview track over to one of the main audio tracks in the Set.

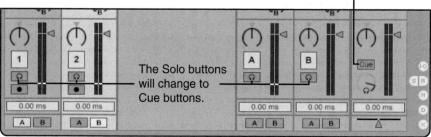

Click here to switch to Cue mode.

The Solo buttons will change to Cue buttons.

Figure 12.6 To enable Live's Cue function, click the button above the Preview Volume knob. The solo buttons in each track will change to headphone icons.

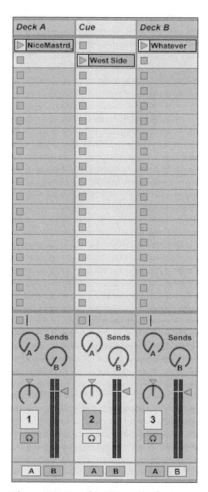

Figure 12.7 This DJ setup features an additional "cue track." You can place any audio clip you want on this track for private headphone tweaking before dragging it onto one of the "live" tracks on either side. You don't have to switch any Track Activators or Cue buttons with this method.

If you've been trying this out as you read, then you'll know that you can hear your cue track only in the headphones. What if you want to hear the main tracks in your headphones, too? You could simply click their Cue buttons, thus adding their signals to your headphones, but you have no control of their volume in relation to the cue track. Instead, make another Return track. In Figure 12.8, you'll see that the new Return track is letter C and has been labeled Cue Mix. Both of the main tracks have their Send C knobs fully clockwise, thus feeding their signals into Return track C. The trick is in the Input/Output Routing section: The Track Output is set to Ext. Out 1/2, which are the headphone outputs. As you turn up the Volume slider on this track, the main tracks will blend in with the cue track in your phones. You can even pan the main mix over to one side by panning the Cue Mix track.

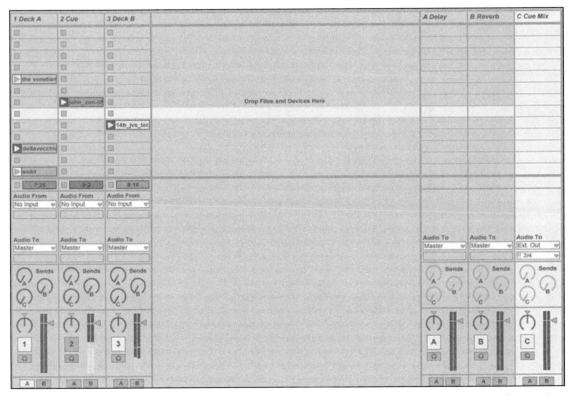

Figure 12.8 By using another Return track, you can create a mix for your headphones. Isn't the routing flexibility of Live handy?

You're probably starting to see how Live can be "made" into a DJ mixing machine with thoughtful use of tracks and signal routing. To get your hands on the fun, start assigning controls in your MIDI controller. You can set up your system any way you like, but we have a few recommendations:

- **The Crossfader:** Even if you don't have a horizontal slider on your MIDI controller to mimic the movement of a real crossfader, assign something—be it a vertical slider or a knob—to this control in Live. Even twisting a knob to perform a crossfade can feel smooth and musical, even if not true to form. Another option for Crossfader control is to select the Crossfader with your mouse and then use your computer keyboard's right and left arrow keys for smooth crossfades.

- **The Track Volumes:** While you may think that mixing two tracks should be as simple as setting their Volume sliders to the same position and just using the Crossfader, you'll find that some songs you play are just louder than others. This could be due to different mastering techniques and sonic content. Regardless of the reason, you'll want to have easy access to the volumes of each track; as you begin crossfading, you may need some extra play in the volumes to keep the mix even.

- **EQ Kills:** As mentioned above, instances of EQ Three are loaded onto each of the "live" tracks. Assign MIDI buttons (Ctrl [Cmd]+M) or keys (Ctrl [Cmd]+K) to your computer keyboard so you can "cut" frequencies on the fly. When you deactivate the low band of an EQ Three, it will remove almost all the bass and kick drums. The other two buttons, Mid and High, will have the same effect on their own frequency bands. Try taking out the low from one track while taking out the high from the other. How many three-band combinations can you make?

- **Tempo and Groove:** Assign two knobs to these controls—you'll be able to change the speed and feel of your mix at will. Your records have turned into sonic rubber bands!

Looping

Live gives you the ability to define Clip Loop points on the fly by using the Set buttons for the Loop Position and Loop Length parameters in the Clip View. While a clip is playing, you can press the Set Position button, and Live will move the Loop Start Marker to the closest downbeat. When you press the Set Length button, Live will place the Loop End Marker here and will immediately begin to loop the file. You can also assign MIDI notes or keys to these Set buttons in the Clip View, allowing you to define loops from an external controller. Furthermore, the mappings will work on whichever clip you have selected, which keeps you from having to reassign the MIDI and Key commands every time you load in a new clip.

Beats

Thanks to the fact that you Warp Marked all of your audio files and they are playing on a temporal grid, you can create MIDI drum parts to augment the beats in your DJ mix. Load a Drum Rack or an Impulse onto a MIDI track and build a kit of your favorite drum sounds. As your songs are playing, you can record MIDI clips and overdub rhythms that will be perfectly aligned with the main tracks. Even if you launch a new song, everything will stay perfectly synced together. In Figure 12.9, I've added the Impulse track and have an assortment of MIDI grooves to play stacked in the Session View.

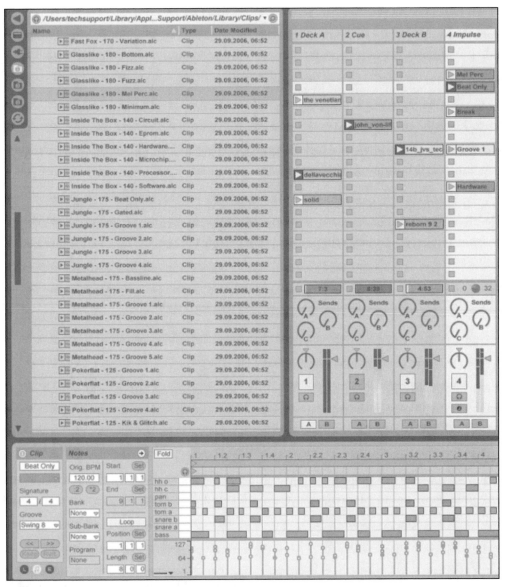

Figure 12.9 There's nothing better than a kick drum part or extra hi-hat pattern for adding emphasis to your mixes. It also helps maintain continuity when fading between tracks—your beats stay solid on top, making the transition sound surprisingly transparent.

Live Remix

Remember above when I mentioned saving clips for various sections of the song? Having these on hand will allow you to create live remixes on the fly. When you move the clips into a live track (see Figure 12.10), you'll be able to launch the clips in any order you want, literally remixing the arrangement of the song right in front of your audience. How many clip variations can you make for your remix?

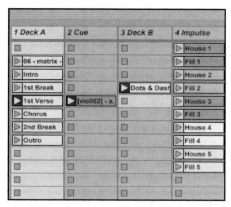

Figure 12.10 The seven clips in the track called Deck A are sections from a larger song. You can jump from the intro to the first verse to the second verse, skipping the chorus. You can then come back and play the chorus twice instead of once—whatever you feel like.

Effects

To spice up your DJ Set, don't forget to take advantage of Live's great assortment of audio devices. A few of them, such as Beat Repeat, Auto Pan, Auto Filter, and EQ Three, are perfect for augmenting rhythms, emphasizing breakdowns, or smoothing over transitions. While I like to have EQ Threes on each of the tracks in my Set, I'll usually place the Beat Repeat, Auto Pan, and Auto Filter on the Master track so they'll affect the entire mix. Don't forget that almost all of the Live devices will synchronize to the current project tempo, so you'll be able to do things that are perfectly in sync with the songs you're playing. Have fun!

Band

Many gigging bands are using some form of accompaniment, either prerecorded tracks or beat boxes, to embellish their sound. Many times, the bands feature multi-instrumentalists who write more parts for a song than can be played at once. When you have the multitracking capabilities of Live at your disposal, you can easily compile the parts you need for accompaniment and break them into scenes. As you perform, you can move through the scenes, or you can record an arrangement to play again during a gig.

Click Track

In order to stay synchronized with Live, one or more members of the band may want to listen to a *click track,* which is a metronome sound synchronized with the parts in your song. Usually, this amounts to nothing more than turning on Live's metronome and setting the Cue output to a pair of headphones (like we did in the DJ example above). The drummer will usually be the one begging for the click. He'll play along with the metronome in the headphones, and the band will play along with him. As a result, you all play together with Live.

Of course, since everything is tempo-synced in Live, you could use a regular drum loop as the click track. Instead of turning on the metronome, load a drum loop onto a track and send it to the headphones. Many musicians will find it easier to play against a drum loop, as opposed to the generic metronome sound.

If needed, don't hesitate to let other members of your band hear the click. A simple earphone run up the back of a shirt will suffice. The more members of the band who are locked in with the click, the tighter the sound.

Tap Tempo

Along with playing to Live's click track, you can make Live play to *your* click track. Assign a MIDI button or key to Live's Tap Tempo button. As your band plays, you can tap in your tempo, and Live will follow it. A drummer can assign an electronic trigger to the Tap Tempo and then tap a few beats here and there to keep Live in sync. This is exactly what Shawn Pelton does when he plays with House of Diablo.

Count Off Give Live four taps as you count off the beginning of your song. Live will start on the downbeat along with the rest of your band, and it will continue playing at the tempo you tapped.

Live Effects

Besides being a flexible backup player for your band, Live can also act as a sound engineer. To add an echo to your lead singer's vocals, run his mic into an input on your computer's audio interface and select it as an input on an audio track. Switch the track's monitoring to On and place a Simple delay on the track. Your singer's live vocals will pass through the delay, which you can control with MIDI or your mouse. You can also record automation for the effect and play it back as part of the arrangement. You can program Live to turn the delay on and off at specified times, change the feedback, and so on. This can help emphasize choruses and breakdowns. So you don't completely freak out the sound guy, you can set the output of the vocal-processing track to an independent output of your audio interface (see Figure 12.11) and run a cable to the engineer so he can still control the overall mix of the show.

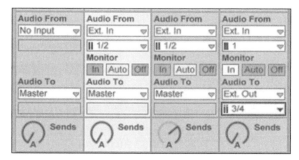

Figure 12.11 Track 4 is processing the live vocals. The effected vocals are being sent to outputs 3 and 4 of the audio interface.

Improvisation

Many improvising musicians shy away from computers, especially in live situations, because they feel they are too constricting. Many jazz pieces have a loose structure; certain sections of the song will be explicitly defined (the entrance, ending, and main musical ideas), while others will be completely nebulous (the solo sections). You can see how a traditional sequence may hamper this freeform approach.

Elastic Arrangement

You've heard us refer to the results of Live's Warp Engine as "elastic audio," allowing you to stretch and pitch audio files any way you'd like. The same thing can be said of a musical arrangement in Live—you can jump around and change the length of any section of the song on the fly. This is accomplished by arranging your clips by song section within the Session View (see Figure 12.12). You can then launch scenes as you progress through the song.

1 Piano	2 Audio	3 MIDI	4 Audio		A Return	B Return	Master	
▷ Piano Roll	▷ Frets 01	▷ Percs	☐				▷	Start
☐	▶ AcoustLoop	▶ Rock 1	▶ Blades01				▷	A
▷ Target Mon	▷ AcoustLoop	▷ Rock 2	☐				▷	B
☐	▷ AcoustLoop	▷ Percs 2	▷ Mellow Ton				▷	Josh Solo
▷ Target Mon	▷ ElectricSho	▷ Rock 2	☐				▷	John Solo
☐	▷ AcoustLoop	▷ Percs	☐				▷	Danny Solo
▷ Piano Roll	▷ ElectricSho	▷ Rock 1	▷ Mellow Ton				▷	Vamp
☐	☐ 45 ⟳	☐ 16 ⟳ 4	☐ 16 ⟳ 4				☐	Stop Clips
Ext. In ▽	Ext. In ▽	All Ins ▽	Ext. In ▽				Cue Out	
‖ 1/2 ▽	‖ 1/2 ▽	‖ All Channe▽	‖ 1/2 ▽				‖ 3/4 ▽	
In Auto Off	In Auto Off	In Auto Off	In Auto Off				Master Out	
Master ▽	Master ▽	Master ▽	Master ▽		Master ▽	Master ▽	‖ 1/2 ▽	

Figure 12.12 The sections of the song are just waiting to be launched. Launching them live, as opposed to playing to an arrangement, will let you determine the course and speed of the song as you play it.

As I've said before, it's not necessary to move through the scenes in a straight top-down order; it's just easier to visualize your song that way when writing. You can set up the scenes any way you like, but just make sure that you have the ability to launch them quickly. Instead of using the mouse to launch the scenes, use keyboard keys or assign MIDI notes on a controller. One of the most intuitive methods involves assigning the scenes to buttons on your guitarist's pedal board. He can then switch sections of the song as easily as he changes guitar tones. Or your keyboardist can take charge. It doesn't matter who controls the arrangement. Live's universal MIDI mapping allows any MIDI device to control it. You could even trigger scene changes from an EWI (Electronic Wind Instrument) or a MIDI body suit!

The important thing to realize is how easy it is to control Live during a performance. If your sax player is performing the greatest solo of his career, you can extend his solo without doing anything at all. As long as the clips in the solo section are set to loop, they will repeat indefinitely until he signals to move on to the next section. Once he gives the signal, you can trigger the next scene. There's no need to *do* anything to extend a section; it will happen naturally as you allow Live to loop. All you have to do is launch the various sections of the song when you're ready for them.

Live also gives you the ability to place Locators within the Arrangement View for quick reference. You can create a new Locator at the cursor point by choosing Add Locator from the Insert menu. You can assign MIDI notes or keys to these markers, allowing you to jump to different locations of the arrangement on the fly. This is similar to using scenes, except you're still working within a linear layout. With this feature in use, you can jump back or ahead to different sections of the song at will—the jumps will even follow the Global Quantize setting to ensure there are no rhythmic anomalies when bouncing between the various markers.

Real-Time Loop Layering

Using Live's recording functions within the Session View, you can easily record new clips and set them looping on the fly. This is excellent for creating "sound on sound" layers during a show. A guitarist can play a simple bass line and loop it, and he can layer a rhythm part on top of it. He can then improvise on top of his new loop creations, making a song right before his audience's eyes (and ears).

The method for achieving these layers is best accomplished with a MIDI pedal board, like the one explained above. You can control Live with your feet, leaving your hands free to play your instrument. The pedals will each be assigned to the relative MIDI controls in the MIDI Assignment mode. Tapping a pedal the first time will start recording a part; tapping again will begin looping what just recorded. If you have eight pedals and eight audio tracks, you can grab eight different loops and play them at the same time. For more control, you may want to use a row of MIDI knobs on an external controller to adjust the mix of your loops.

Live's relative mapping controls are visible only while in MIDI or Key Assignment mode. When these modes are active, you'll see another row of play boxes appear above the Input/Output

Routing Strip (see Figure 12.13a). When you assign a MIDI note or key to these play buttons, they will individually trigger the clips in the selected scene. In Figure 12.13b, pressing q will launch the clip Nice in scene 1, which is currently highlighted. If the Scene Highlight is moved to scene 2, pressing the q key will launch the West Side clip instead.

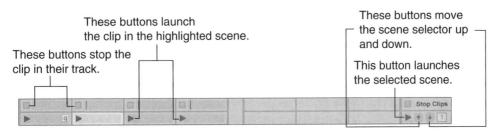

Figure 12.13a The relative play controls trigger individual clips from selected scenes. These relative controls will disappear when you exit MIDI or Key Assignment mode, but they will still be active.

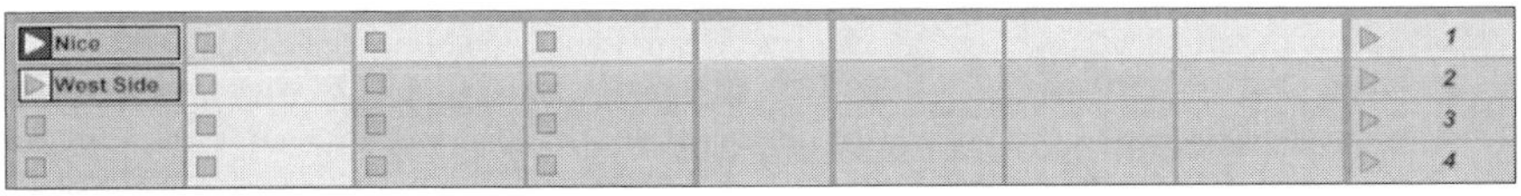

Figure 12.13b Now, you can launch any clip in Track 1 by highlighting the desired scene and pressing the q key.

This relative mapping also works for tracks that are armed for recording (see Figure 12.14). When q is pressed now, Live will begin recording a new clip in the empty slot. When you press q again, Live will stop recording and begin playing the looped clip. By assigning each pedal to one of these relative slots, you can fire off recordings with the push of a pedal. You can also assign pedals to the stop boxes located right below the relative play controls. You can then stop any playing clip in a track by pressing one of these pedals. Also, remember that Live supports multiple mappings. This means that you could assign the same MIDI message to stop recording in one track and begin recording in the next. Instant overdubbing!

Figure 12.14 Here, clips can be recorded using the same relative buttons by arming the tracks for recording. The stop boxes will stop the playing or recording of any clip on the track.

Theater

Sound cues are one of the most important elements for adding realism to a stage production. Even though an actor may drop a glass on stage, it is usually accompanied with a breaking-glass sample from the theater's sound system (this ensures everyone in the back hears the glass break). Other sound effects, such as wind, rain, thunder, city traffic, church bells, and crying babies, will also play through the house system. For small theater companies, musical scores fit the bill when there's no room (or budget) for a live orchestra. Live performs wonders in this environment, adding all of these elements instantly with just the push of a button.

Sound Effects

In order to play a sound instantly when using Live, you'll need to turn off any Launch Quantization that may be on, either in Live's Control Bar or individually in your clips. You don't want to trigger a sound and have Live wait for the quantize time before playing it. By switching these quantize settings off, Live will play the clip the instant it is triggered. Whenever possible, we also recommend that you switch off Warp so the sample will always play at its original pitch and speed.

One-shot sound effects would include things such as the breaking glass, a gunshot, doorbell, clock chime, or phone ringing. These sounds happen once and do not loop. For these types of sounds, simply turn off the clip's Loop button. The sound will then play only once every time it's triggered.

For other atmospheric effects, such as rain, traffic, and wind, you will need to loop the sound so it can play for an undetermined amount of time. With the clip's Loop button engaged, you can launch the clip and then slowly fade it in. The sound will stay there until you turn it down again, usually at the end of a scene. Remember that if you need more than one sound effect playing at a time (perhaps someone gets shot in the streets on a rainy night in Chicago), you'll need to have them all on individual tracks.

Performance Sounds Contemporary theater companies and performance artists are starting to use sensors on their actors' bodies to trigger sounds. Each movement they make can generate unique MIDI messages, which Live can use for triggering clips. A sensor could be used to trigger a gunshot sound when the actor pulls the trigger of his prop gun, thus adding more realism to the performance.

Music Cues

Along with adding sound effects, Live can also be used to play the musical score for the show. Each song, or section of a song, can be made into a clip, allowing you to trigger it at the right moment. You can vary the speed of the music by adjusting Live's tempo. You can even transpose a musical part to another key if your singer's voice is in a different range.

In essence, each musical piece is treated just like the one-shot sound effects explained above; however, to maintain tempo control, you'll want to have Warp turned on in these clips. As you fire off the clips, you can tap a new tempo to keep the music in time with the production. You can even count off the piece with four taps, just like a conductor counting off the beginning of a song. If a piece of music calls for a hold before proceeding to the next section (perhaps there's some dialogue between the verses), split the song into two clips (see Figure 12.15). The first clip will play the song up to the hold and stop. The second clip will begin right after the hold and continue through the end. You can do this for as many holds as there are in the piece.

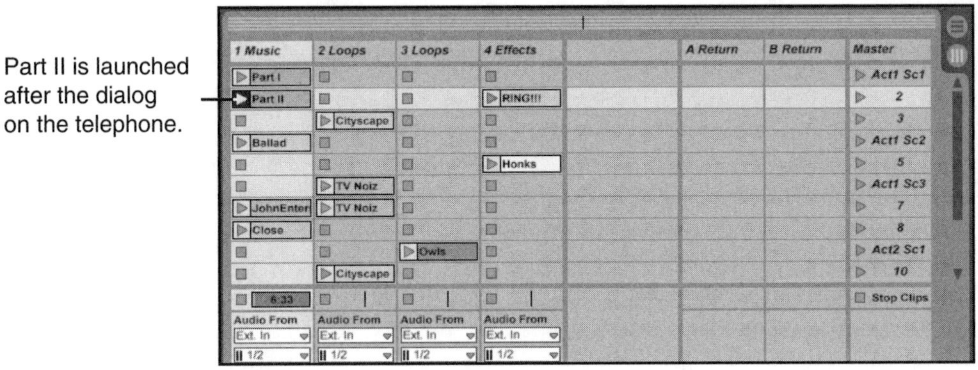

Part II is launched after the dialog on the telephone.

Figure 12.15 The clips in Track 1 are actually the same song. The first clip starts at the beginning of the song, while the second clip starts at the beginning of the second verse.

Whatever your purpose—DJing a party, playing at a bar, or performing a stage show—Live can support your endeavors in creative ways limited only by your imagination. Since Live is always responding to your input, you will be in control throughout the performance.

WHO'S USING LIVE? Gauss Control Gauss Control is Andrés Criado, a brilliant producer and DJ from Spain who also runs the Undress Records label. I first heard of this guy while listening to some DJ mixes I'd downloaded from the Internet. His mix stood out from the rest due to his excellent song choices, but also due to the fluid method in which he mixed the tracks together. After listening to the mix a few times, I wanted to find out the names of the tracks he was spinning. I surfed over to www.gauss-control.com and, to my surprise, I found Ableton Live staring right back at me! Andrés loves Live so much, he actually designed his Web site to look like Live. It was there that I found out that he actually wrote all the tracks in his mix—original productions. Things finally came into focus: Andrés is an artist who uses Live exactly the way it should be used. He uses it for everything from composition to live performance. Additionally, since he composes his songs in Live, he has intricate control over the arrangements of his tracks because he mixes them part-by-part while performing Live.

"When I saw Live for the first time, I knew immediately that this software was made to perform and work properly on the stage," Andrés says. "I prefer a simple layout and new approaches to programming, as opposed to a perfect simulation of an old machine. I love the layout of Live—made for functionality while being beautiful and useful. That's why my Web site looks like Live.

"When I started using Live, I always found solutions for my sequencing problems immediately—it is so intuitive and easy to use. I do use Live for sequencing tracks, but not only Live. Live is not a closed production environment like other applications. I use Live for sequencing loops, hosting virtual instruments, and for mastering, too. I think Live is the only one that can do all. It's great to play live sets with the same software used for sequencing the tracks because I don't have to learn a new program again and export files, effects, etc.

"Another good point about Live is that it is giving producers a place on the stage. Not too long ago, producers were closed away at the studio. Now, we have a chance to play out regularly like a DJ."

13 Live 7 Power

You've covered a lot of ground since setting Live's Preferences in Chapter 2, "Getting Live Up and Running." You've learned how to record and modify clips and how to arrange them in the Session and Arrangement Views. You're a master of quantizing and Warp Marking, and you can spiff up your mix with effects.

Everything up to this point has been left-brain oriented, so we're now switching gears and will focus on the creative, right-brained things you can do in Live. We're going to look at how a little "misuse" of some of the tools, such as Warp Markers, can allow you to morph beats into new ones. We'll also show you how Follow Actions can make your performing tasks a whole lot easier. You'll even learn how to sync two computers together, as well as learn some final optimization techniques. More than anything, you'll see how thinking outside the box can help Live continually adapt to your working style.

More Warp Markers and Envelopes

We cannot stress the importance of understanding Warp Markers enough—they are the essence of Live. The amount of groove massaging made possible by Live's Warp Markers is truly limitless. At first, you may be frustrated by how to specifically adjust a beat or loop to make it sound the way you're hearing it in your head or to get it to align properly within your audio project, but with a little practice, you will develop an intuition for how Warp Markers gradually shift a pattern's events. In the following list, we have outlined a few of our favorite techniques to get you started. After you master the examples, take time to experiment with Ableton's powerful Warp tool. There really are no rules, so go for it!

- **Feel:** The trouble and triumph of loop-based music is its repetitive nature. While repetition can be magic for keeping a dance floor moving, "feel" can become stagnant, ultimately making music monotonous and uninspired. To combat the static quality of loop-based music, it is important to add a little variety from time to time, even if the results are basically imperceptible to the untrained or unsuspecting ear. There are several methods for doing this, but the easiest I've found is to subtly (not randomly!) change the volume of some beats in a few of the repetitions. For instance, say you are working in Live's Arrangement View and you have played four measures of a loop. On bar 4, you might try attenuating (reducing) the volume of a few of the beats with a Clip Envelope (shown in Figure 13.1). Don't underestimate how much subtle volume changes can contribute to groove. It usually works best to play with the volumes of subdivisions (hi-hats and percussion), although adjustments to main beats (such as the kick and snare drums) can be effective as well.

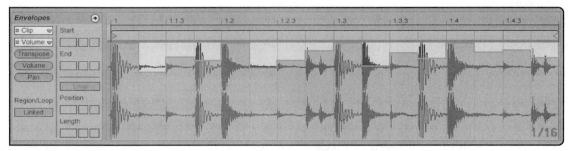

Figure 13.1   Altering the volume here and there can add realism to loops.

- **Ahead of and Behind the Beat:** Drummers and bass players have developed a unique relationship through the years. An artist's "feel" is often as important as what is being played. One musical dialogue common to the tradition of drummers and bassists (including organ and synth bass) is that of playing ahead of the beat and behind the beat. For example, the bass player may play right on the beat, while the drummer plays the 2 and 4 snare hits slightly behind. Or perhaps the drummer plays ahead of the beat, ever so slightly rushing the snare, hi-hats, and cymbals while the bass player lays back. These subtleties are often what distinguish music that is rhythmically competent from that which is inspiring. In Figure 13.2a, we have provided a simple drumbeat. Notice that the beats line up perfectly with Live's Warp Markers. In Figure 13.2b, we have pushed a few Warp Markers to the left to make the snare hits feel sluggish or behind the beat, while in Figure 13.2c, we have pushed the same Warp Markers slightly to the right of the snare for a more rushed feel—ahead of the beat.

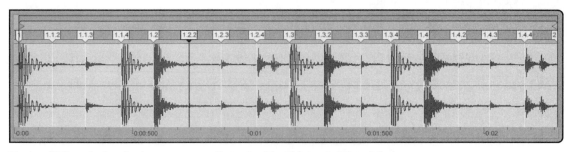

Figure 13.2a   A simple drum groove aligned with Ableton's Warp Markers.

- **Extending One–Shot-Style Loops:** Sometimes, a looping sample plays too often. Examples such as a single drum hit firing every eighth-note instead of every quarter or a horn section

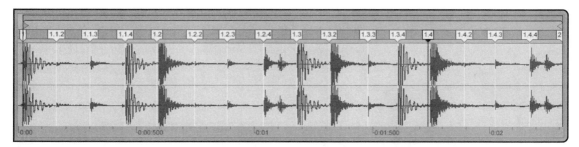

Figure 13.2b   Moving the Warp Markers to the left makes the beat feel more laid back.

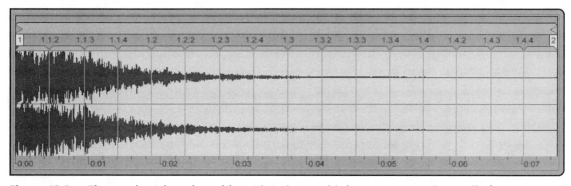

Figure 13.2c   Moving the Warp Markers to the right makes the groove feel "on top."

blast on every downbeat instead of every measure come to mind. If you want the blast (shown in Figure 13.3a) to happen once every measure, you can use a Volume Envelope. By unlinking the length of the envelope and making it one bar in length, you can mute beats 2, 3, and 4, resulting in the blast being heard only on beat 1 (see Figure 13.3b).

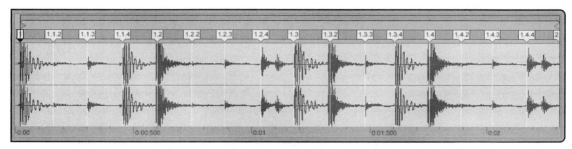

Figure 13.3a   The one-beat-long horn blast. Listening to this loop gets annoying really fast.

Beat-Wreckin' Clinic

Making breakbeats, funky drum patterns, and fills is often best done via trial and error—especially since so much of the music made on computers is programmed in this fashion and

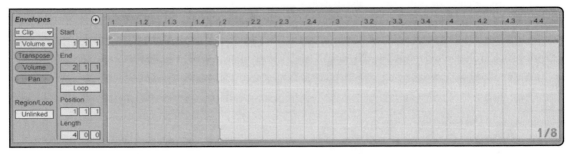

Figure 13.3b Ah, much better. We've muted the last three beats so we hear the horns only once a measure.

not played. That said, here are a few ideas for making your looped drum and percussion grooves freak the beat.

- **Slice 'n' Dice:** With the introduction of Slice to New MIDI track in Live 7, chopping up and rearranging your loops has never been easier. See Chapter 5, "The Audio Clip," if you need a refresher on how this works, but essentially this command chops up your beat and lets you play it back with MIDI. Not only does the resulting Drum Rack come tricked out with some interesting macros for glitching up your beat, but you can also remove and repeat individual hits or completely reprogram the beat using the MIDI Editor.

- **Surgical Slicing:** Even though Slice to New MIDI track may be the latest and greatest technique for beat mangling, an older technique for editing beats warrants mention as well. Take any drum loop in Arrangement View and use Live's Split command—Ctrl (Cmd)+E—at common rhythmic subdivisions (1/4-, 1/8-, and 1/16-note settings), as shown in Figure 13.4a. Then rearrange the order of the newly made clips. Doing this in the track below the original track makes it easy to refer back to the original beat (see Figure 13.4b). You can copy a slice multiple times if you want, and you can leave others out. If you just do this randomly, many a "happy accident" will occur. With practice, you can work in less random fashion and begin

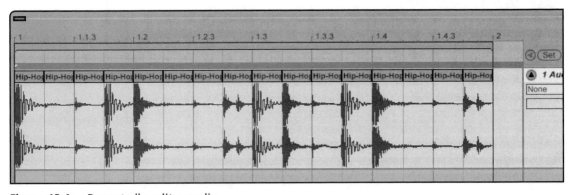

Figure 13.4a Repeatedly split any clip.

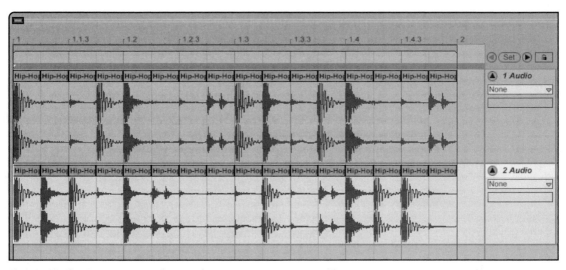

Figure 13.4b   Rearrange and copy the components as you like.

doing edits on purpose. As always, if you are pleased with your results, consolidate the parts into a new loop.

- While cutting a beat into tiny slices that you can rearrange is a great way to create microedited beats, you can also load these individual slices into the pads of an Impulse or a Drum Rack by dragging them from the Session or Arrangement View directly into these instruments. This way, you get the power of using MIDI to rearrange your beats and the flexibility of customizing each slice just the way you like it.

- **Double for Nothing:** Another quick trick for adding rhythmic variety to stale loops is to use Live's :2 and *2 buttons (shown in Figure 13.5) to double or halve the original tempo. Try sectioning off a 1/4- or 1/8-note portion of a loop by using Live's Split command and then doubling or halving the tempo of the smaller section.

Double and
Halve Buttons

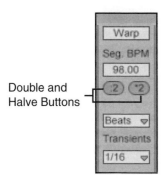

Figure 13.5   Use these buttons to halve or double a small section of a loop.

- In Figure 13.6, we have halved the last 1/4-note section of the larger loop to change the feel slightly. Experiment with other subdivisions, or try doubling the groove, for the best results.

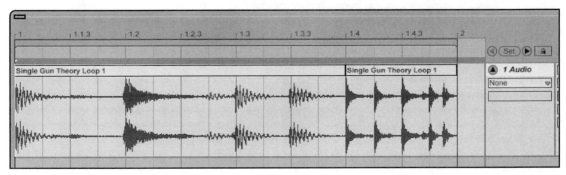

Figure 13.6 Split a loop and then halve the new segment to create a fill.

- **From the Start:** An easy effective trick is to take any of the segments created in the preceding examples and change the Sample Start for a freshly made loop segment. For example, you could take the section we halved in 13.6 and move the start time to 1.2.3. For this particular drum groove, it creates a very realistic and normal sounding drum fill or groove variation.

- **Controlling with Clip Envelope:** Another great way to scramble beats is to create a Clip Envelope to control a loop's Sample Offset. To do this most effectively, make sure that you are in Beats mode and then select Sample Offset in the Clip Envelope drop-down menu. After you see the flat red line, use Live's Pencil tool to reshape the beat as you like (see Figure 13.7). Each horizontal step represents a single 1/16-note offset. Moving the sample offset line down moves the offset back, while moving it up moves it forward. In Figure 13.7, the offset of beat 1.1.2 is being moved back 1/16, so the kick drum from beat 1 repeats.

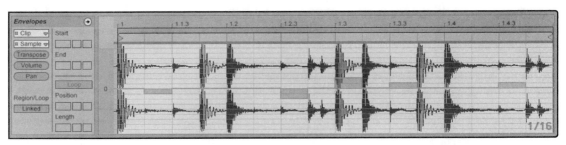

Figure 13.7 Move the clip's play position using the Sample Offset Envelope to create variety.

- **The Rhythmic Microscope:** When you're lining up a loop's feel with other loops and recordings, try working with smaller sections, one at a time. I find this trick helpful when working with varying degrees of swing or unusual syncopations. Work with the first half of the loop until it feels like it complements the feel of the song, and then move to the second half.

Harnessing Follow Actions

Can anybody say "hidden genius?" The Follow Actions section of the Clip View should be in huge, obnoxious flashing letters because this is some serious stuff. The carefully thought-out rules governing Follow Actions will allow you to do innumerable things limited only by your imagination. Not only can they be used to enhance live performances, but they are also a wonderful compositional aid, helping you to create variations you might never have thought of on your own.

- **Mini Song Structures:** If you wanted to play one clip for three bars followed by another clip for one bar, you could copy the two clips to the arrangement, extend the first to three bars, and then tack the second clip on the end (see Figure 13.8). You could then consolidate the clips into a new one and drag it back to the Session View.

- With Follow Actions, you can create the same arrangement in the Session View without rendering any new clips. By stacking the two clips on a track, you can set the Follow Actions, as shown in Figure 13.9. The top clip will play for three bars and then trigger the clip below

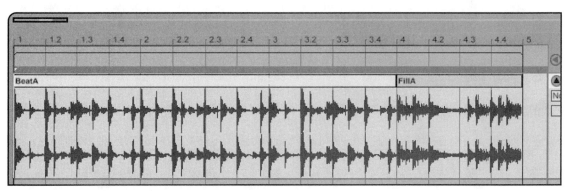

Figure 13.8   This four-bar arrangement gives us three bars of the BeatA clip followed by a bar of FillA.

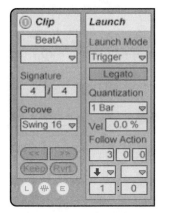

Figure 13.9   By setting the top clip in Figure 13.8 to the settings shown on the left and the bottom clip to those shown on the right, Live will play that same arrangement, but from the Session View.

it. The bottom clip will then play for a bar and trigger the top clip, starting the cycle over again.

- **Loop Variations:** Here's another technique for preventing your loops from becoming stale. This involves a collection of parts that are subtly different from one another. One example is two drum clips that are the same, but where one has an extra snare hit in it. Set the Follow Action of the first clip to randomly trigger the second one from time to time. You'll set the second clip to re-trigger the first. The result is that you get a constant beat with an additional snare hit thrown in occasionally, mimicking the way a real drummer would modify his beat on the fly. When you set up your Follow Actions, make sure one of the options triggers another clip and that the other option is set to Play Again. Play Again ensures that the Follow Action will be performed again in case Live chooses not to trigger the other clip (check out the "Follow Actions" section in Chapter 5 for a refresher).

- **Pickup Notes:** Not every musical phrase starts on the downbeat of a bar—some start just a few beats before. Take the song "Happy Birthday to You," for example. The two syllables in "hap-py" take place before the downbeat—the word "birthday" happens on the downbeat. Normally you would have to trigger this clip a bar before you wanted it to start. The clip would play silence until it reached the first word (see Figure 13.10). While this does work, it doesn't always "feel" right to trigger a clip that early before you want to hear it. The second way is to start the clip right on "happy" and change its Launch Quantize setting to 1/4 so you can launch it on the right beat. The downside is that you no longer have the comfort of Bar Quantization.

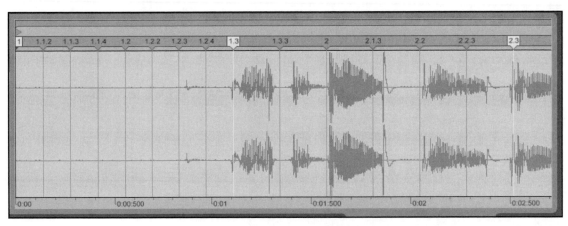

Figure 13.10 This clip needs to play all the silence at the beginning in order to come in at the right place.

With Follow Actions, you get the best of both worlds: You can Launch the clip with the accuracy of a low Quantize setting while being assured that the part will continue on the beat. To see what I mean, take a look at how "Happy Birthday" is now set up using two clips (see Figures 13.11a and 13.11b). The first clip is "happy," while the second clip is "birthday to you, happy birthday…" and so on. The second clip has a Launch Quantization of Bar. No matter what happens, this clip will start on the downbeat and play in time. The first clip, however, has a quantize setting of 1/16. Its Follow Action will trigger the next clip after only one 1/16 note. (Its Follow Action Time is set to 0.0.1.) So, 1/16 after the "happy" clip is triggered, the main clip will be triggered; however, the main clip will not start immediately because it has to wait for its Quantize setting. This means that if the pickup (the "happy" clip) is played a little early or late, the rest of the song will still play in time. This can be a neat tool if your pickup phrase is a whole bar in length. You can trigger it at a bar, half bar, one beat, or any amount and still have the rest of the phrase in time. You'll just hear more or less of the first clip, depending on when you launch it.

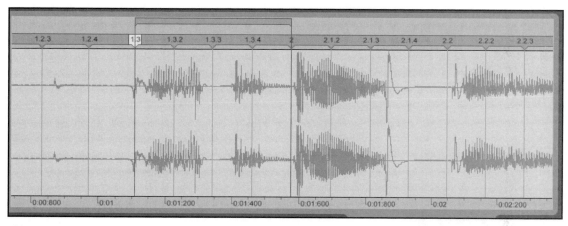

Figure 13.11a   This is the "happy" clip. It is set to trigger the next clip, the "birthday" clip, only one 1/16 note later. Since Live won't let you type a value of 0.0.1 into the boxes, click and drag down on the Time value to reduce it to 0.0.1.

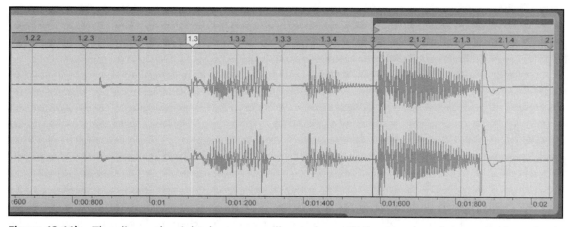

Figure 13.11b   The clip on the right, however, will not play until the downbeat because its Quantize is set to an entire bar.

■ **Drum Fills:** Triggering drum loops during a live show is always fun, but I don't like having to retrigger the main beat once the fills are done. Follow Actions can be used to make sure the main beat always comes back. Figure 13.12 shows a stack of drum parts. The top clip is the main beat. Every clip below it is a variation or drum fill. Each of these variations has Follow Actions settings matching the ones shown in the figure. By having all of the fill clips trigger the main beat right after they start, we're guaranteed that the main beat will start on the next bar (the main beat clip is set to Bar Quantization). In fact, since each of the fill clips has a Launch Quantization of only 1/16, we can launch multiple clips one after the other, literally piecing fills together in real time. You can create additional variations by setting the Launch mode for all or some of your fills to Repeat.

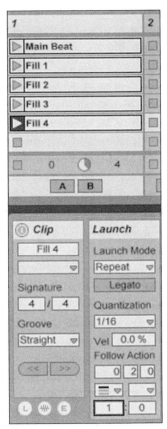

Figure 13.12 The top clip is set to Bar Quantization, while the others are set to 1/16. Each fill clip launches the first, so the beat will always kick in after the fills.

Don't just try this with beats; try it with other types of parts, too. Create multiple clips and treat them with different effects and parameter tweaks. Set them to Legato mode so that the playback position is traded off as you switch clips. It will sound like you're performing crazy processing on the part as you switch between the clips. Most important: Assign these fill clips to MIDI notes for playability!

- **Drum Wreck:** Take the concept above and make dozens (hundreds?) of variant clips. Set them all to Legato with an Any Follow Action. Set the Follow Action times to something pretty short (1/8 or 1/16) and let it rip. Live will start randomly jumping between all your variations at light speed. Render the results so you can grab a great part when it happens.

Minimizing Performance Strain

Effects guzzle plenty of valuable CPU juice. To combat the ill effects of, well, too many effects, I frequently rely on the following tips and workarounds, listed in order of preference.

- **Freeze Track:** This feature will render everything on the track into new audio files so effects and virtual instruments can be disabled. Simply right-click (Ctrl-click) on the track's name and choose Freeze Track from the Context menu. Live will calculate new clips for each clip in the track and then disable all of the devices running on the track. The result is that your used CPU percentage goes down. The beauty of freezing tracks is that you are still free to launch the frozen clips, use basic editing commands such as Copy and Paste, and adjust mixer settings such as Effects Sends, Track Volume, Track Pan, Mute, and Solo. If you need to edit anything that gets disabled by Freeze, you can unfreeze the track, make your edits, and then re-freeze it.

- This is also a neat way to transfer songs to a friend. If you're using instruments and effects that your friend doesn't have, you can freeze the tracks before saving the Live Set. Once it is saved, you can give the Live Set to your friend. He'll open it up and find the tracks still frozen. He can trigger these frozen clips any way he likes so he can still rearrange the parts you've given him.

- Using the Flatten command will turn your frozen track into a standard audio track and will permanently remove the devices. Obviously, you lose some flexibility by doing this, but you gain the ability to manipulate Warp Markers and envelopes—something you can't do with frozen tracks.

- **Streamline Effects:** Many of Live's effects contain sections or modules that can be turned off. I've mentioned that by deactivating unnecessary bands of Live's EQ Eight, you can shave a couple of points from your CPU meter (see Figure 13.13). Live's Reverb has a menu to select the quality mode (Eco, Mid, or High), which affects CPU usage as well. Some other sections of effects that can be turned off are Reverb's Filtering, Spin, Diffusion, and Chorus Activation buttons, Chorus's Delay 2 Portion, and Filter Delay's L, L + R, or R delays or filters.

- **Sends and Returns:** For effects that are typically a blend of dry and effected sounds, such as delay and reverb, you can save CPU power by using Return tracks. Simply take any effect that you have created on more than one track and instead "share" it on a Return track.

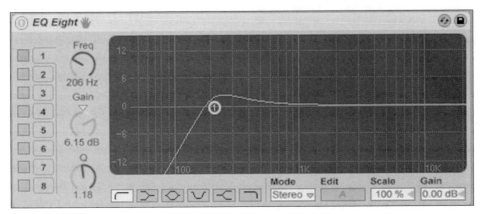

Figure 13.13   You can turn off modules of an effect plug-in to save power.

For example, if you are using several instances of Live's Reverb on several different tracks, instead place one Reverb on a Return and then turn up the Send knobs on each of the tracks to be effected. You can then delete the multiple Reverb plug-ins for each track and save a ton of processing power. It's also possible to make return effects behave like insert effects by using the Sends Only output on the channels (as seen in Figure 13.14).

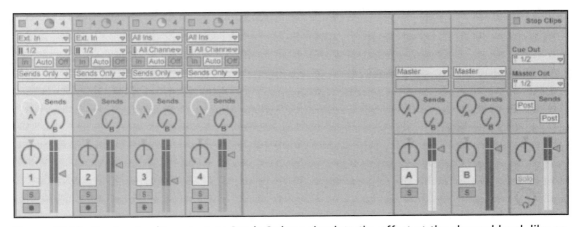

Figure 13.14   Route a track's output to Sends Only to simulate the effect at the channel level, like an insert.

- **Render Audio with Effects:** Sometimes using the Returns or streamlining the effects just doesn't do the trick. If this is the case, and you can't do without any of the effects (or instruments) you're using, it's probably time to resample. While Track Freeze is often all that is necessary to render CPU-intensive tracks, the advantage of resampling is that you can mix down several effect-laden clips into a single clip. After doing so, you can delete the original files and effects from your Set. Just make a habit of saving the new Set under a different name so you can always get back to the original if you need to tweak the levels or effects of the individual clips. In Figure 13.15a, you'll see a scene with several loops running through multiple audio effects plug-ins. In Figure 13.15b, the scene has been recorded into a single clip by creating a new track and setting its input to Resampling. Notice the dramatically improved CPU efficiency.

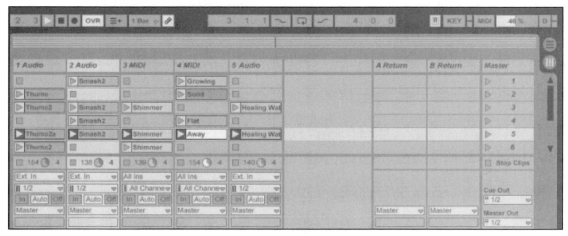

Figure 13.15a   Several heavily effected clips playing in Live.

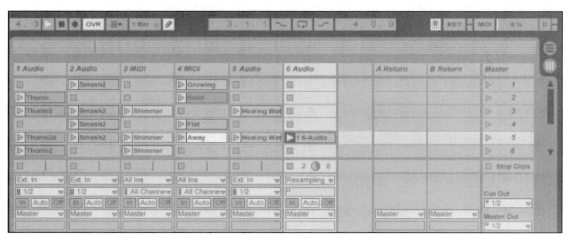

Figure 13.15b   Once rendered as a single loop, the clip no longer needs original effects and loops.

Templates

Live lets you save only one template, and it is loaded every time you launch the program; however, with all the different uses for Live, chances are that you won't be able to create a "one-size-fits-all" template to handle every situation. You can, however, create a collection of templates by saving empty Live Sets. Load up Live, set the track count, effects, instruments, tempo, MIDI and Key assignments, and so on as desired; then save the Set. When you need to use the template, load the empty Set and start working.

Examples of some templates may be Basic DJ Setup, DJ Setup with Impulse, Multitrack Recorder, or Fav MIDI Instruments. The DJ templates may resemble those shown in Chapter 12, "Playing Live . . . Live." The Multitrack template may have eight audio tracks already set to the individual inputs of your audio interface. The metronome may also be on and prerouted to the Cue output. The Fav MIDI Instruments template may load virtual instruments that you always use, such as LinPlug Albino, Native Instruments Reaktor, or the GMedia impOSCar. Anytime you start a new song, you can load the template that will get you going the fastest.

Also bear in mind that Sets can be imported into other Sets by dragging them from the Browser. Using this technique, you could keep a very minimal basic template and then add in other Sets (for example, Favorite Instruments), as needed.

Rename Me! When loading an empty Live Set as a template, immediately save it under its own name. This will prevent you from accidentally overwriting the template with your current project, as when you press Ctrl (Cmd)+S.

On a Mac, you can easily prevent editing your templates by selecting "Get Info" for your template in the Finder and checking the Stationary Pad option. Then, any time you open the template, a copy will automatically get made.

Linking Two Computers

For my last tip, I'll show you how to use MIDI clock to keep two or more computers in sync so you can jam with other Live users. First, decide whose computer will be the master, and set that computer to send MIDI clock by enabling Sync output (see Figure 13.16a). Next, you'll need to configure your slave computer(s) to receive sync from the master, as shown in Figure 13.16b. Connect the MIDI output that you're sending sync on to the MIDI input that you've configured to receive sync. Finally, for each slave computer, you'll have to click the EXT switch that appears in the left-hand corner of the Control Bar when you tell Live to receive MIDI sync (see Figure 13.16c). Once you do this, the slave computers will automatically begin playback when you start the sequencer on the master computer.

MIDI Ports		Track	Sync	Remote
▷ Input:	Kore controller (In)	Off	Off	Off
▷ Output:	Kore controller (Out)	Off	On	Off

Figure 13.16a In the MIDI/Sync tab of Preferences, configure the master computer to send MIDI sync.

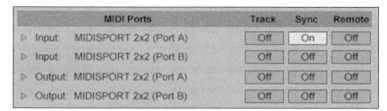

Figure 13.16b   For each of the slave computers, enable sync for a MIDI input.

Figure 13.16c   Turning on the EXT switch gives tempo and sequencer control to the master computer.

Inexpensive MIDI splitters and multiple outputs can make the number of players limitless, although you might want to consider some advance organization. You might assign one musician to cover the drum and percussion loops, another the synths, and another sound effects. Or you might have two Live musicians playing within the same band, or add a singer for a futuristic improv trio. The future of Live may just include two, three, or more musicians getting together, patching their laptops into the MIDI chain, firing up a ReWire application or two, and then jamming the night away. For added fun, try recording the output to some kind of multitrack recorder.

As you can imagine, there are many more tricks and tips still waiting for you to discover. There are as many different ways of working with Live as there are different kinds of music. The more time you spend experimenting, the more you will discover what works for you. And that's really all that matters. There's no "right" way to work with Live, just different methods, some of which you will find more efficient and inspirational.

Also, check out Ableton's user forum, which will teach you that no matter what you've learned, someone else is doing things totally differently. Sometimes, you'll pick up tricks that will greatly enhance your workflow, and sometimes you'll just be reminded that finding your own way is the most important thing of all. Either way, you're invited to share your ideas and interact with other Live users. It's a great community to be a part of.

In closing, I offer you my sincere thanks for taking the time to read this book. Should you stumble onto a tip, trick, or scrap of info that doesn't quite work as advertised, there is most likely an update waiting for you at www.ableton.com (click on downloads). My experience is that Ableton Live 7 is elegant, musical, forward thinking, dynamic, and inspirational. I hope you find it to be the same and enjoy many hours of making your own musical vision a reality.

WHO'S USING LIVE? Steve Tavaglione Steve Tavaglione is a woodwind, flute, and wind synthesizer (EWI) player, as well as a sound designer for movies, TV, and records. His movie credits include *Finding Nemo, American Beauty, Lemony Snicket's A Series of Unfortunate Events, Road to Perdition, Cinderella Man, Jarhead,* and many others. For TV, he has worked on *CSI: Las Vegas, CSI: New York, Charmed, Lois & Clark,* and *Supernatural.* His record credits and performances include work with Roger Waters, Michael Jackson, Sergio Mendes, Chaka Khan, Sly and the Family Stone, John Patitucci, Vinnie Colaiuta, Dave Weckl, Frank Gambale (a fellow Musician's Institute alumnus), Luis Miguel, and scores of others. Here's what this prolific musician has to say about Live:

"Since I started using Live, which was day one of its first release, possibilities I could have only previously imagined became realities for me. I tend to approach music from an almost childlike place in the first moments, then let the project at hand shape my sense of play into a workable scenario.

"With Thomas Newman, I create soundscapes to handshake with normal and very eclectic acoustic instruments. Since we layer sound and rhythm together, I find that Live is the perfect solution for both. For instance, I will see what key, if any, we are working in and check the tempo, and then acoustically record a flute, clarinet, or whatever, directly into Live. After recording the lick, I will copy and paste the single lick maybe three or four times into different clips and change the pitch of the licks into harmonies. I will match the tempo with picture, and I will be hearing interesting passages within minutes. If the harmony changes, so can the harmony of the clips.

"I also like to record samples to a clip dry, then reverse the sample and add reverb. I then resample it to another clip, then re-reverse the sample. What I get is a backwards reverb leading to a forward-played sample.

"Another thing I do is combine older samples with newer ambiences that I have made to create new ambiences. I then render them as new samples. In that way, my sample library continues to evolve as I treat these samples with VST effects and tempo and pitch warping. Every day is a new creative day for me with Live.

"I use Live on two laptops with an Evolution or M-Audio keyboard controller along with the full gamut of VST plug-ins, including all Native Instruments plug-ins, GigaStudio, Propellerhead Reason, and others."

Index

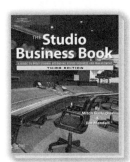